The Evolution of Electronic Dance Music

The Evolution of Electronic Dance Music

Edited by Ewa Mazierska, Tony Rigg and Les Gillon

BLOOMSBURY ACADEMIC
NEW YORK • LONDON • OXFORD • NEW DELHI • SYDNEY

BLOOMSBURY ACADEMIC
Bloomsbury Publishing Inc
1385 Broadway, New York, NY 10018, USA
50 Bedford Square, London, WC1B 3DP, UK
29 Earlsfort Terrace, Dublin 2, Ireland

BLOOMSBURY, BLOOMSBURY ACADEMIC and the Diana logo are trademarks of
Bloomsbury Publishing Plc

First published in the United States of America 2021
This paperback edition published 2023

Copyright © Ewa Mazierska, Les Gillon, Tony Rigg, 2021

Cover design: Louise Dugdale
Cover image: Photograph of Graham Massey's Studio by 808 State.

All rights reserved. No part of this publication may be reproduced or transmitted in any form or by any means, electronic or mechanical, including photocopying, recording, or any information storage or retrieval system, without prior permission in writing from the publishers.

Bloomsbury Publishing Inc does not have any control over, or responsibility for, any third-party websites referred to or in this book. All internet addresses given in this book were correct at the time of going to press. The author and publisher regret any inconvenience caused if addresses have changed or sites have ceased to exist, but can accept no responsibility for any such changes.

While every effort has been made to locate copyright holders the publishers would be grateful to hear from any person(s) not here acknowledged.

Library of Congress Cataloging-in-Publication Data

ISBN: HB: 978-1-5013-6636-9
PB: 978-1-5013-7959-8
ePDF: 978-1-5013-6638-3
eBook: 978-1-5013-6637-6

Typeset by Deanta Global Publishing Services, Chennai, India

To find out more about our authors and books visit www.bloomsbury.com and sign up for our newsletters.

Contents

List of figures — vi
List of contributors — vii
Preface: Growing up with EDM *Graham Massey* — xi

Introduction: The past and future of electronic dance music
   Ewa Mazierska, Les Gillon and Tony Rigg — 1

Part I Discursive and technological production of EDM
1. The meanings of 'electronic dance music' and 'EDM' *Anita Jóri* — 25
2. Is *électro* a French cultural exception? *Mathieu Guillien* — 41
3. UK sampling practice: Past, present and future *Justin Morey* — 63
4. EDM, meet AI: Cognitive tools and (non)biological artists in electronic dance music *Andrew Fry* — 81

Part II EDM stars and stardom
5. Avicii and mental health of EDM stars *Melanie Ptatscheck* — 105
6. Where's the drop? Identifying EDM trends through the career of Deadmau5 *Tristan Kneschke* — 124
7. Deadmau5's relationships with authenticity and fame *Jeremy W. Smith* — 145
8. Second-hand stardom: Connotations of sampling for electro swing *Chris Inglis* — 164

Part III Dance music scenes
9. The evolution of electronic dance music spaces in Leeds, UK *Stuart Moss* — 181
10. Ageism and sexism in Manchester's club culture *Kamila Rymajdo* — 211
11. Transformation of dance culture in Poland as a battle over taste in music *Ewa Mazierska* — 233

Notes — 257
Index — 266

Figures

2.1	*Télérama*	46
2.2	French Touch flyer	48
2.3	Art of France	51
2.4	Drexciya	59
5.1	Bergling in poor health condition	112
5.2	Avicii on stage	112
8.1	You're All I Want For Christmas' by Caro Emerald	170
9.1	Letter sent to arrested attendees of the Love Decade rave in Gildersome, Leeds, 1990	189
9.2	The Leeds Corn Exchange	191
9.3	Movement at Victoria Works, Leeds	199
9.4	Discarded nitrous oxide canisters on a Hyde Park doorstep, Leeds	203
10.1	DJ Paulette	216
10.2	Mix-Stress	220
10.3	Kath McDermott at the Haçienda	226
10.4	BB	229
11.1	Dancing in *Dorożkarz Nr 13* (*Cabman Nr 13*), directed by Marian Czauski	235
11.2	Early Polish DJ, Marcin Jacobson, in Musicorama (photo courtesy Marcin Jacobson)	238
11.3	First Polish DJ, Jana Kras (photo courtesy Marcin Jacobson)	239

Contributors

Andrew Fry runs *Sounds et al*, a record label and publisher exploring sound, curation and collaboration, currently based in New York, NY. The label has released work from artists including Dolphin Midwives, Kaori Suzuki and Benoît Pioulard, and has curated and promoted events, exhibitions and performances in North America, Europe and Asia. Prior to this, Fry worked in the London music industry for a decade. At present, his research is focused on the intersection of art and technology, and he is learning Spanish.

Les Gillon is a researcher and music practitioner based at the University of Central Lancashire in the School of Arts and Media. He writes about popular music and is active in practice-based music research that explores composition and improvisation, the use of non-Western music traditions and interdisciplinary collaboration. In addition to his research in the field of music, he also writes on aesthetics and the visual arts. His monograph *The Uses of Reason in the Evaluation of Artworks* (2017) uses the Turner Prize as a case study to explore fundamental questions about the nature, purpose and value of art.

Mathieu Guillien was born in Paris and discovered electronic dance music (EDM) at the age of ten. Already following a classical music training to become a pianist, various encounters encouraged him to eventually undertake academic studies and write about techno music, at a time when such a topic was unwelcome in the French academia. This led to the completion of his doctoral thesis in 2011, published three years later under the title *La Techno minimale*. He has been teaching the history of African American music between 2005 and 2015 at the Sorbonne Nouvelle University and since 2017 at the University of Evry.

Chris Inglis is a musicologist based in Cardiff, Wales, whose research explores the emergence and development of the electro swing genre. After studying at De Montfort University and the University of Sheffield, in 2019 he received his doctorate from the University of South Wales. He has previously had chapters published in *Continental Drift: 50 Years of Jazz from Europe* (2016) and *Popular Music in the Post-Digital Age: Politics, Economy, Culture and Technology* (2019).

Contributors

Anita Jóri is a research associate at the Vilém Flusser Archive, Berlin University of the Arts (Universität der Künste Berlin, UdK). She studied applied linguistics and history, and finished her PhD thesis 'The Discourse Community of Electronic Dance Music' in 2017 at Eötvös Loránd University, Budapest, Hungary. Her research interests include EDM cultures, gender and diversity issues in EDM scenes, and applied linguistic methodologies. Jóri is also a chairperson of the German Association for Music Business and Music Culture Research (GMM) and a curator of the discourse programme of Club Transmediale Festival.

Tristan Kneschke has written for a variety of publications including Tiny Mix Tapes, Pop Matters, Metal Sucks, Decoder Magazine, The Wild Honey Pie, Echoes and Dust, and Hyperallergic, among others. He was Subrewind's former managing editor and has written extensively about video for industry sites No Film School and Premium Beat. He records as Metamyther, an experimental electronic music project exploring three-movement song structures.

Graham Massey is a multi-instrument musician, accomplished on keyboards, guitar, drums and soprano saxophone, and a proponent of experimental jazz-rock. A prolific writer and producer, his rich ability to move between and blend genres creates a set of wildly free-ranging music. Graham was a founding member of the internationally successful electronic group 808 State and his collaboration, remixing and production credits feature key contemporary music artists including David Bowie, Quincy Jones, Bjork, Goldfrapp, SMD, Primal Scream, YMO and many others.

Justin Morey is Senior Lecturer in music production and the music industries at Leeds Beckett University, UK. His main research interest is in sampling as a creative practice within British dance and electronic music, which has been the focus of the majority of his published work. He has a background in sound engineering and music production, having set up and run a recording studio in London from 1995 to 2003. As a co-writer and producer of dance and electronic music, he has had records released through labels including Acid Jazz, Ministry of Sound and Sony.

Ewa Mazierska is Professor of Film Studies at the University of Central Lancashire. She published over twenty monographs and edited collections on film and popular music. They include *Popular Polish Electronic Music, 1970-*

2020: A Cultural History (2021) and *Popular Viennese Electronic Music, 1990-2015: A Cultural History* (2019). Mazierska's work was translated into many languages, including French, Italian, German, Chinese, Korean, Portuguese, Estonian and Serbian. She is the principal editor of a Routledge journal, *Studies in Eastern European Cinema*.

Stuart Moss is a senior lecturer at Leeds Beckett University, an advisory board member for Entertainment Management at the University of Central Florida and Vice President Digital Learning for the Asia Pacific Institute for Events Management. Stuart has worked in higher education for twenty years and has a range of publications, including two edited textbooks about the entertainment industries and strategic management in the entertainment industries. A former raver and passionate fan of electronic music from the 1970s onwards, Stuart has been personally and professionally connected with the club scene in Leeds since the early 1990s.

Melanie Ptatscheck is a visiting professor for popular music studies at Cologne University of Music and Lecturer at University of Paderborn and Osnabrueck University of Applied Sciences. She holds a PhD in popular music studies from Leuphana University of Lueneburg and an MA in popular music and media science from the University of Paderborn. Focusing on mental health from a social science perspective, she works at the interface between public health and popular music studies. Her research interests include careers in music and labour markets, self-concepts and narrative theory.

Tony Rigg is a music industry practitioner, consultant and educator affiliated with the University of Central Lancashire where he co-founded the Master of Arts programme in Music Industry Management and Promotion. He is also Head of Music Business Education at the School of Electronic Music, Manchester. He has occupied senior management roles in market-leading organizations, including Operations Director for Ministry of Sound, and overseen the management of more than one hundred music venues and thousands of music events. He also co-edited (with Ewa Mazierska and Les Gillon) *Popular Music in the Post-Digital Age: Politics, Economy, Culture and Technology* (2018) and *The Future of Live Music* (2020).

Kamila Rymajdo is a Manchester-based journalist and academic, predominantly writing about music, popular culture and the Polish diaspora. She is a researcher at Manchester University and a contributor to magazines including *Dazed*, *i-D*, *Vice* and *Mixmag*. Previously, she worked as a music editor at the Skinny North and ran a club night. Her academic writing has been published in edited collections including *Contemporary Cinema and Neoliberal Ideology*, *Heading North* and *Popular Music in the Post-Digital Age*.

Jeremy W. Smith is a lecturer of music theory at the University of Louisville. His research is on the theory and analysis of contemporary popular music broadly construed, with a special focus on 'continuous processes' in EDM. A secondary research interest is video-game music and music in multimedia generally. Jeremy received his PhD in music theory from the University of Minnesota in 2019. He is also a performing musician that has played euphonium and trombone with local ensembles throughout his career.

Preface

Growing up with EDM

Tracing the roots of electronic dance music is like trying to find the source of a river – is it where two tributaries meet or do you follow those back to springs in the landscape? It is now undoubtably a mighty confusing torrent that cannot know its own growth daily in the world. Truly an international language. Tower of Babel or return to one language?

From a personal point of view the seeds of electronic music grew hand in hand with progressive music in the 1970s. When first encountering robotic disco such as 'I Feel Love' by Donna Summer, the language was somewhat paved by a group like Tangerine Dream. There were always some distant German experimenters at work with sequencers. Of course, Kraftwerk made the neatest version of the futurist sound and a conversation was struck up in the 1970s with Black American club culture, particularly early hip-hop and electro. Pioneers such as Stevie Wonder, Bernie Worrell and Herbie Hancock took synthesizers into social music. Meanwhile, the technologists from different parts of the globe pushed emerging microchips towards a more affordable and attainable marketplace and over time into the hands of the musically hungry.

My clubbing life began in the early 1980s with the opening of what now is the legendary Hacienda club in Manchester, UK: a large space with dreadful acoustics and inadequate sound system, its shortcomings in its early years being well documented. The only kind of music that survived well in this environment was stripped back electronics. The only people who were DJs back then were music-sensitive obsessives who were catering for expressionistic dancers. Of course, this culture did not come directly from the Hacienda. There were clubs within a square mile that did it better. But something about the size and socially fluid mix made it a conversational/experimental platform unlike the smaller venues. Somewhere in this Venn diagram, a weekly portal to Detroit and Chicago's exciting progressive dance music opened up like a transatlantic cable. We couldn't get enough so we attempted to start to make it ourselves.

The reason I was always in that club was due to the fact I had a free pass having released some records on Factory (who owned the club) as a member of Biting Tongues. Our band emerged during the DIY post-punk era and lived off fumes for about ten years. The post-punk era had many one-off electronic-based singles, probably labelled 'industrial music' back then, groups like the Human League, the Normal, DAF, Cabaret Voltaire and Throbbing Gristle all had machines at the heart of the sound.

By the mid-1980s Biting Tongues were producing records that were long liner grooves, taking cues from a wider world view – Fela Kuti, Harmolodic Jazz and dub techniques with emerging digital manipulation. We probably had more in common with people like Bill Laswell in New York, though if only we had known that at the time. He was mixing jazz improvisers with drum machines and hip-hop to form new hybrids such as Rockit by Herbie Hancock. I loved making records but getting studio time in the 1980s was expensive and rare. I bypassed that by signing up to an audio engineering course at SSR in Manchester, one of the first courses of its kind in the country if not the world. This brought me into immediate contact with the new samplers, synths and Atari computers.

Samplers were particularly interesting as I had always worked in a sound collage kind of way. Around the same time I was getting my mixing desk skills together. I was running a cafe across the road from Eastern Bloc Records in central Manchester. It was an unofficial youth club for the DIY culture of UK hip hop and electro – demos using drum machines and cheap Casio synths were brought to the shop and a number of projects were set in motion via the shop and my access to the studio a few streets away. One of our projects was 808 State and some of our early attempts at an acid house sound gained traction in the UK via plays on Radio One's John Peel show.

808 State came about through improvisation sessions at clubs and private parties, radio sessions and in the studio, the emerging rave scene supported the loose approach to the music. A few settings were pre-prepared on the machines, but largely it was an exercise in keeping the groove and polytonal layers as abstract as possible, alienated vibes were key at first. But eventually there were known tunes and a repertoire emerged. In the early days when there was no attempt at traditional performing, we looked like we were technicians working at the back of the hall. Within a year or so we were either playing a handful of our known tunes at a big rave for say twenty minutes or expected to put in a much more polished show with guest singers/rappers/visuals for big venues like the G-Mex Centre in Manchester or Brixton Academy in London. A very

steep learning curve! By autumn 1989, we had signed to ZTT records. ZTT had a formidable legacy of high-tech production progressive pop. And within that context we were now aimed at daytime radio as well as the clubs. There was a lot to consider when entering the studio, and I must point out we were still largely writing in the studio rather than at home. The inspiration was still very strong from attending clubs and listening to what was coming through the record shop as imports from not just the United States but also domestic and European releases. It really helped me that I stuck to the formula of writing in a Long Play Album format, which for dance music was not standard practice. Many electronic musicians began to write for DJs only, very understandably and one of the strands of our thinking.

In the pre-internet age, pop culture was still the primary carrier wave for this emerging shift in the sound of music – radio, TV and the music press all still as important as the DJs and night clubs. That's a fight on many fronts. In the early 1990s we took our show to the United States for the first time. We were licensed to Tommy Boy Records – a well-established New York hip hop label. We didn't really know how the new EDM was playing out over the vast diversity of the United States. We had a lot of feedback from New York clubs, but you kind of had to spend a while there to unpick that eco system alone. L.A. was putting on some large raves, we played one at Long Beach Exhibition Hall – it became clear that the West Coast radio had taken up some of the EDM. Certain stations would result in certain demographics – a large Hispanic audience for instance. Texas was also a strong rave town with large events, again with direct links to one radio show. We expected Detroit and Chicago to have an established audience for dance music, but I guess it was felt to be just about records and clubs. Having said that Detroit artists were very welcoming on our first arrival – and the second time we attended a huge event in a rail yard organized by the Plus 8 label. The rest of our touring over the early 1990s involved the rock establishment bending a little bit more towards accommodating electronic acts – I think acts like Depeche Mode and Front 242 opened up that a lot at the time. This kind of suited 808 State to align a little more along being an alternative act rather than pure techno. We joined New Order's 1993 tour across the States which helped expose us to a wider audience.

The American experience made our albums a split in two directions – on the one hand we tried to have big stadium techno, but balanced with a more ambient sensibility, which we were always strong at but never wanted to be defined by. We were always trying to avoid being tied to a genre, to be limited. The diversity of artists we worked with as remixers or collaborators was one of the joys of the new era – it was a cultural Glasnost that reflected the optimism of the 1990s. As time went on, you could see electronic acts become defined by a laboratory approach – a second wave of UK bands was to be willfully abstract and ploughed the experimental edge of technology a little deeper, the Artificial Intelligence compilation on Warp records being a notable release (Aphex Twin, Autechre, Plaid), while others became more linear and more in line with clubbing trends (Leftfield, Underworld, Chemical Bros). Many more subgenres defined club culture by this point as the rise of the DJ and super club became prevalent.

808 State launched our first internet fan site in 1994 – we talked of directly feeding exclusive music to our listeners, giving direct communication and news. The reality was that it took a few more years before bandwidth could handle any of these intentions. Maybe it took a good ten years for the internet to loosen the grip of the music industry on how music flowed to the people.

During the mid-1990s EDM continued to mutate into other forms such as Drum & Bass and Triphop, flying the flag of UK multiculturalism from its major cities. Growing up in the UK with a love of music, I have always associated its development in relationship to countercultural movements of the day, be that progressive music to punk and beyond.

I always saw dance music from an anti-establishment position. Early rave was about the self-empowerment through taking back dead spaces, reclaiming the night-time and erasing cultural boundaries. This thread was especially reinforced after the Criminal Justice Act of 1994 whereby 'large gatherings' and 'repetitive beats' were being targeted as antisocial behaviour by the then Conservative government. EDM certainly brought a greater understanding in my home city of Manchester, it was the most social behaviour, living culture that re-energized a city's possibilities and networks beyond just music. When large gatherings do occur legitimately or not, I often find it to be a rare opportunity to read the cloaked identity of where and who we live alongside. It may not be the whole truth but it is valuable to do once in a while, to simply live outside in a crowd – that Glastonbury feeling – it feels both ancient and current. Particularly poignant as I write this during the lockdown of 2020.

808 State were the last band on at Glastonbury Festival in 1992 alongside the Orb and the Shamen in other headline slots. It felt like EDM had taken up position as the new voice of the people – like a reinstatement of the purpose of transcendent music, as common global musics strive to bond and uplift.

As we now look at thirty years or more of the murmurations of EDM, it seems like algorithms are beginning to take force – if a formula for big room techno is working well it tends to simply repeat itself, similarly in commercial radio formulas. The age of AI is coming. Data is king. At Music Tech Fest (a conference at the University of Stockholm) in 2019, I witnessed a lot of talks about possibilities of AI in music and I must say with dismissive ears until I was turned on to the idea that you could be playful with programming and that human idiot glee could be an ingredient. The neural network band Dadabots actually seemed to bring fun and irreverence back to the table. Of course, this abuse/reuse of the tools has always been fundamental in great musical development. Think Roy Rogers to Hendrix with the same instrument. Taste makers rise and fall based on sophisticated codes unreadable to the casual listener. Each branch of music has a dialect and root system that means a great deal to its connection with an audience. We need the storytellers, we need the music lovers to take us by the hand and place it on our hearts. Every city has the potential to grow its micro cultures – little basements, scruffy outposts where the communion is brought about by eccentrics with a deep knowledge of how to build a story as grand as any opera.

I'm thinking how do we grow another Andrew Weatherall? His loss last year generated a significant mourning in the electronic music community – he was not a great musician, he was not a stadium DJ more important than those roles, he was a shaman among us! Yet, EDM never stops. It is growing and changing, as this excellent collection demonstrates.

Graham Massey

Introduction

The past and future of electronic dance music

Ewa Mazierska, Les Gillon and Tony Rigg

The International Federation of the Phonographic Industry (IFPI) survey from 2019 ranked 'dance', a name which increasingly replaces the term 'electronic dance music' (henceforth EDM), as the world's third most popular genre, after pop and rock, which translated into an estimated 1.5 billion people regularly listening to it (Grogan 2019; Watson 2019). This very fact suggests that it is a phenomenon worth investigating by researchers interested in popular culture. There are additional factors why this genre deserves attention. One of them is its place in the history of popular music. We refer here to the fact that the popular music industry of the past 150 years, really indeed from the period of Romanticism, has been dominated by song with its characteristic structures and with lyrical content central to its meaning and to its commercial appeal. EDM marks moving away from this paradigm. As Simon Reynolds states in his influential essay 'Historia Electronica: The Case for Electronic Dance Music Culture', it marks a shift from song to track (Reynolds 2007: 316). This does not mean that EDM gives up on the human voice entirely, but when it is used, it is often distorted, so that it sounds like one of the instruments, de-humanized and robotic or the lyrics are reduced to repetitive catchphrases (Thornton 1995: 75; Reynolds 2007: 316; Tompkins 2011: 22).

While EDM represents a break from this continuity, it is more closely relatable to older forms of popular music – jigs, polkas, Morris tunes, mazurkas, etc.: music that is typically instrumental, consumed socially and in public places, rather than in solitary or domestic contexts and intended to lead to bodily movements rather than just listening. EDM also represents a break with the more recent past of popular music, marked by the primacy of rock, perhaps the most notable innovation in popular music for half a century or more. This is reflected in a shift in the status of the musician. While previous forms of commercial popular music, most importantly pop and rock, focused on the performer (typically singer-songwriter in the case of rock), whose individuality was of great importance to the fans and the music industry, in EDM the audience cares much less about the authors of the song, if at all; it is the experience on the dance floor which matters most (Reynolds 2007: 315). Such a turn from the artist to the consumer of music and the culture which binds them together is reflected in the title of the well-known academic journal, devoted to EDM, *Dancecult*, which alludes to the primacy of culture in EDM over the production of music, as well as to cult, understood as the consumers' devotion to their favourite genre. Focus on culture is further underscored in the editorial to the first issue of *Dancecult*, where we read:

> From dancehall to raving, club cultures to sound systems, disco to techno, breakbeat to psytrance, hip hop to dub-step, IDM to noisecore, nortec to bloghouse, global EDMCs are a shifting spectrum of scenes, genres, and aesthetics. What is the role of ethnicity, gender, sexuality, class, religion and spirituality in these formations? How have technologies, mind alterants, and popular culture conditioned this proliferation, and how has electronic music filtered into cinema, literature and everyday life? How does existing critical theory enable understanding of EDMCs, and how might the latter challenge the assumptions of our inherited heuristics? What is the role of the DJ in diverse genres, scenes, subcultures, and/or neotribes? ('Editorial' to *Dancecult* 2005)

What is meaningful in this short fragment is, again, the talk of EDMC – EDM culture – as opposed to music itself, as well as downplaying the role of the DJ, who is mentioned only after a list of types of events, genres, identity markers and the media affecting the said culture.

EDM not only breaks with the development of popular music but also significantly affects its geography. We refer here to the fact that most of the twentieth century saw the dominance of Anglo-American music. This dominance was reflected in the large number of records sold by artists coming from this region, the influence of the genres created by them on music cultures in peripheral regions, as well as the primacy of English in the global production of popular music. EDM changed this pattern. The precursors of EDM and its most important innovators, such as Lee 'Scratch' Perry, Giorgio Moroder and Kraftwerk, worked at the peripheries of popular music in Jamaica and continental Europe. Moreover, although this music moved to the old centres of music production and consumption, such as London and New York, they did not manage to impose its hegemony on the periphery. Development of EDM is much more multi-centric than rock. Locally produced EDM, let's say in Brussels,

Paris, Budapest or Novosibirsk, does not need to openly or tacitly acknowledge its debt to Anglo-Saxon music. Moreover, the flows of EDM are often between peripheries, circumventing the centre. EDM can thus be seen as simultaneously local and cosmopolitan.

Another important characteristic of EDM, partly resulting from the reasons already mentioned, is its great heterogeneity, fragmentation and fluidity. The most obvious manifestation of this heterogeneity is the proliferation of genres. As Kembrew McLeod observes:

> Without lapsing into hyperbole, I can confidently claim that the continuous and rapid introduction of new subgenre names into electronic/dance music communities is equalled by no other type of music. Metagenres like rock and roll may have spawned rock, folk rock, acid rock, garage rock, punk rock, and more recently grunge, alternative rock, post-rock, and other semantic combinations yet to be coined, but electronic dance music generates that many names in a fraction of the time. To illustrate, a careful scan of electronic/dance-oriented magazines and electronic dance compilation CDs published or released in 1998 and 1999 yielded a list of more than 300 names. An edited, but nonetheless bloated, list of names includes abstract beat, abstract drum-n-bass, acid house, acid jazz, acid rave, acid-beats, acid-funk, acid-techno, alchemic house, ambient dance, ambient drum-n-bass, amyl house, analogue electro-funk, aquatic techno-funk, aquatic-house, atomic breaks, avant-techno, bass, big beat, bleep-n-bass, blunted beats, breakbeat, chemical beats, Chicago garage, Chicago house, coldwave, cosmic dance, cyber hardcore, cybertech, dark ambient, dark core, downtempo funk, downtempo future jazz, drill-n-bass, dronecore, drum-n-bass, dub, dub-funk, dub-hop, dub-n-bass, electro, electro-acoustic, electro-breaks, electro-dub, freestyle, future jazz, futuristic breakbeat, futuristic hardbeats, futuristic hardstep, gabber, garage, global house, global trance, goa-trance, happy hardcore, hardcore techno, hard chill ambient, intelligent drum-n-bass, intelligent jungle, intelligent techno, miami bass, minimal techno, minimal trance, morphing, mutant techno, mutated minimal techno, mystic-step, neurofunk, noir-house, nu-dark jungle, old school, organic chill-out, organic electro, organic electronica, progressive house, progressive low frequency, progressive trance, ragga, ragga-jungle, rave, techstep, techxotica, trance, trancecore, trance-dub, tribal, tribal beats, tribal house, tribal soul, trip-hop, tripno, twilight electronica, two-step, UK acid, UK breakbeat, underground, world-dance. (2001: 60)

Given that McLeod's article is almost twenty years old, we can assume that since he wrote it, this list has increased significantly in size. Such a large variety of genres points to the primacy of genre over the artist, as well as the large role local scenes play in shaping EDM culture. This means that every country, every city, perhaps even every club, gives itself a right to be a trendsetter and does not wait for it to be sanctioned by the 'centre'. This also testifies to the fact that establishing a tradition is not a priority in EDM; this genre looks forward rather than back. This can be explained by its being more entangled in electronic technology which changes more rapidly than traditional instruments and, perhaps, the changing taste of the dancing crowds. This localization of EDM is reflected in a large number of names used to describe not only its subgenres but also their localized and fluctuating meanings. For example, as two chapters in this collection demonstrate, in German-speaking countries the preferred umbrella term, encompassing all forms of EDM, is 'techno', while in France the favoured term to capture the meta-genre is 'electro'. To that we shall add the term 'electronica', which is often used in the United States to describe EDM or a large part of it, as in the previously quoted article by Reynolds. In some countries ambient music is seen as part of EDM, while elsewhere it is regarded as distinctly non-danceable music. The very issue of including non-danceable genres into EDM is a question in its own right, as Anita Jóri points in the chapter opening this collection. Let's untangle some of the puzzles of EDM by looking at its history.

A short history of EDM

In a book published in 2013, Nick Collins, Margaret Schedel and Scott Wilson define EDM as music which 'features electronic synthesized and sampled instrumentation, with at least some parts of a percussive nature, in tracks designed for dancing. Track lengths can be greatly extended, well beyond the typical three-minute pop song, and the evocation of a beat varies from the absolutely literal "four on the floor" to more complex rhythmic patterning, including deliberately loose and ragged grooves' (2013: 102). Foregrounding electronic production, using a multiplicity of sources of music and emphasizing beat, rhythm and repetition, is also mentioned in other accounts of EDM (e.g. Fikentscher 2000: 83–8; Butler 2006: 8; Reynolds 2007). There is also a wide consensus that EDM was born sometime between the 1980s and the 1990s.

In their definition of EDM, Collins, Schedel and Wilson mention techno and hip-hop as privileged subgenres of EDM (2013: 102). However, in most accounts hip-hop is considered as a genre in its own right, while techno is regarded as a crucial subgenre of EDM. For example, Mark J. Butler in his book *Unlocking the Groove*, states: 'Although the book as a whole focuses on electronic dance music in a broad sense, detailed analysis focuses on techno' (2006: 25).

Before the term electronic dance music was coined, there existed music for dancing which was in a sense electronic. It started as early as the end of the nineteenth century, when the phonograph-based jukebox was invented (Collins, Schedel and Wilson 2013: 103–4), to be used first on the radio and then in places such as bars, cafes and clubs. It became an institution of sorts in France and was immortalized in the French New Wave, especially in the films by Jean-Luc Godard, such as *Vivre sa vie* (1962). The next important decade preceding EDM was the 1970s, which gave birth to disco, on the one hand, and techno, on the other.

'Disco's origin is in "discotheques". Literally, 'discotheque' means a 'record library'. As Will Straw points out,

> in the 1930s, the term would refer to French nightclubs in which patrons might gather to hear the latest imported jazz records from the United States. Clubs of this sort, which featured records rather than live performers, and whose appeal had much to do with the obscure, imported recordings they were able to acquire, continued to open in Western European countries during and after the Second World War. (2001: 164)

From the 1960s, however, they started to play an additional role, attracting fans of dancing, coming from a broad section of society, especially the working class (2001: 164). In the 1970s the popularity of discotheques led to a boom in disco music, understood as a specific sound, marked by a 4/4 beat and the use of instruments more common in classical music than in rock (2001: 166).

Disco music broke the near monopoly of Anglo-American producers of global popular music, although for most of its period of popularity it represented a continuity in terms of song structure, instrumentation and production techniques. It was the German music scene which provided the technical innovations that led to the development of electronic forms of dance music. Electronic music was a feature of the German experimental music scene as exemplified by the work of classical composer Karlheinz Stockhausen and that spilled over into the work of German art-rock bands, who were marketed in the UK under the label of 'Krautrock'. Ulrich Adelt observes:

> As two of the most successful West German bands associated with Krautrock, Kraftwerk and Can made innovative music that was connected to the creation

of a new German identity after World War II and the student demonstrations of 1968. Both bands had members who had studied European classical music, and both bands worked outside established rock conventions and took control over their production by recording in their own studios. Can and Kraftwerk both rejected 1970s rock by downplaying lead guitar and lead vocals in their music. They emphasized technological innovations by including electronic instruments like drum machines and synthesizers. (2012: 374)

Although neither Can nor Kraftwerk was associated with disco music in the 1970s, their work has since been extensively sampled and remixed as dance music, and the work of Kraftwerk has been frequently recontextualized. Their approach to using drum machines and synthesizers was adopted by the German-based Italian producer Giorgio Moroder, whose production work with Pete Bellotte for Donna Summer, especially *I Feel Love* (1977), brought a Munich sound of analogue synthesizers in disco to international attention (Collins, Schedel and Wilson 2013: 104).

The importance of disco music lay also in a democratic character of its consumption: penetration of the provinces, for example Eastern Europe, and appeal to a wide spectrum of society, cutting across gender and class. According to the 'Report About the State of Discotheques in Poland', commissioned by the Ministry of Culture and published in 1981, there were 3,000 discotheques in Poland and, on average, a Polish discotheque was visited each day by 50 people. Franciszek Walicki, who set up the first Polish professional discotheque in Sopot at the seaside, noted that in a year 46,000,000 Poles visited discotheques, more than all Polish theatres put together (1984: 7). Moreover, as Richard Dyer, a leading gay cultural historian, argues in his seminal essay 'In Defence of Disco', disco music has certain advantages over rock, because 'rock's eroticism is thrusting, grinding – it is not whole body, but phallic', while disco, by contrast, 'indicates an openness to a sexuality that is not defined in terms of cock' (1992: 153–4). Dyer suggests that disco appeals particularly to women and gay men.

Gay people and gay culture also played an important role in the development of house, the Chicago-produced dance music, which came into existence in the late 1970s and early 1980s 'in a space created by the exclusion of certain identities in a racist and homophobic American society' (Rietveld 1998: 107).

House is seen as the main predecessor of techno. According to Sarah Thornton, its symbolic birth was 1988, when Virgin Records released a compilation 'Techno: The Dance Sound of Detroit'. Prior to its release there were discussions on what to call the music of the three black Detroit-based DJs, whose tracks were featured on the album.

> The term 'house' was then strongly identified with Chicago and was in dangerously ubiquitous use in the UK. They decided on the name 'techno' because it gave the music a distinct musical identity and made it appear as something substantially new. Crucially, the press release validated the music by emphasising its roots in subcultural Detroit. . . . Despite the fact that the music was not on the playlist of a single Detroit radio station, nor a regular track in any but a few mostly gay black clubs, the British press hailed 'techno' as the sound of the city. . . . The term 'techno' was later appropriated to describe a slightly different descendant of Chicago house. When 'acid house' became unserviceable because of tabloid defamation and general overexposure, the clubs, record companies and media went through a series of nominal shifts (about twenty different adjectives came to modify the word 'house') until they finally settled on 'techno'. The term had at least two advantages: it was free from the overt drug references of acid house and it sounded like what it described – a high-tech predominantly instrumental music. (Thornton 1995: 75)

For Thornton, the trajectory of techno exemplifies the path of a music that begins as 'black' and ends as 'white' (Thornton 1995: 74). Techno is also frequently seen (although not by Thornton) as music which not only came from a particular place but captured the spirit of this place: Detroit during the period of a brutal shift from Fordism to post-Fordism, before becoming global and placeless. Deborah Che asserts:

> Techno artists drew inspiration from Detroit's mechanized sounds and environment, its past industrial glories, post-industrial problems and future possibilities, which were tied to technological improvements. Through post-Fordist flexible production methods made possible by the falling cost of Japanese electronics and utilization of music industry infrastructure from the Motown past, Detroit's techno innovators created 'machine soul' music. (2009: 261)

The influential producer Robert Hood adds:

> Back in '92, '93, I sort of crafted this sound I liked to call 'the grey area'. What that is, is the atmosphere in Detroit from the factories that emit this smoky and grey climate, this atmosphere. It's just like ash and dirt from the sewers that just come up from the car emissions and it creates a grey haze over the city. That inspired me, and I kind of piggybacked off of what my contemporaries had

created and rode along with that and interpreted my own Detroit sound from that. (Quoted in Stoppani de Berrié 2015: 106–7)

Techno, more than any other genre of electronic music, is linked to minimalism, a 'style distinguished by severity of means, clarity of form, and simplicity of structure and texture' (Strickland 1993: 4). Some authors point to the inspiration the techno musicians took from 'high-brow' minimalists, such as the Orb borrowed from Steve Reich (Scott 2005: 124). More often, however, there was parallelism, resulting from the fact that both types of musicians tried to strip the music to its basics (Stoppani de Berrié 2015), even if for different reasons. In the case of the avant-garde minimalists this was to offer an alternative to the sensory bombardment characteristic of the industrial period (Strickland 1993: 10); in the case of techno to preserve the industrial sound which was to disappear (at least in the West) in the post-industrial era.

House and techno led to a specific culture, marked by large parties (raves), in which people danced for long hours and sometimes even the whole weekend, often using Ecstasy, which can be described as a 'performance enhancing drug'. A large part of the literature of house and techno concerns the role of Ecstasy in the development of acid and techno cultures (e.g. Redhead 1993; Melechi 1993; Moore 1995: Richard and Kruger 1998: 163; Reynolds 1998, 2007). The key point is that Ecstasy is a recreational drug; admittedly it does not affect its consumers in the same way heroin does. For a typical Ecstasy user of the 1990s life was clearly divided into a week, where she or he diligently worked in the office and the weekend, used to release the tension of work, in repetitive movements, facilitated by repetitive, lyric-free music. Techno culture was thus essentially conformist; it did not rebel against the political status quo, as was the case of, for example, punk, but instead created conditions of accepting it, by providing a safety valve or even training one's body for the extra effort of a demanding job (Richard and Kruger 1998: 163). A comparison can be made between techno culture and earlier disco culture, as represented in *Saturday Night Fever* (1977) by John Badham, whose protagonist escapes from his mundane existence into a disco.

The peak of techno's popularity was in the early 1990s. Its unofficial European capital became first Ibiza, then London and Berlin. In 1990 Berlin techno had similar connotations to those pertaining to Detroit. This was because de-industrialization in East Germany was no less rapid and dramatic than in the United States. Moreover, in this country it was read not only as a result of a 'natural' shift from Fordism to post-Fordism but also as a testimony to a political change – the reunification of East and West Berlin and Germany. Berlin lent itself to techno raves because there were plenty of unoccupied, often derelict spaces, where such parties could be organized. One of the most important became Tresor, set up by West German Dimitri Hegemann. There was also plenty of unoccupied living space in East Berlin, where squatters from West Berlin and West Germany could move. As Hegemann and other 'veterans' of this period recall, at the time they could work undisturbed by police or the authorities; it was thus a perfect time to create the scene. The rise of Berlin techno is usually presented as a means to heal the divisions between East and West Berlin, East and West Germany and even Eastern and Western Europe at large; it was a force for unification. The largest event on the techno calendar, the yearly 'Love Parade' (Loveparade) Festival, attracting millions of visitors, presented itself as a festival of peace (Richard and Kruger 1998: 171). 'Peace', of course, has universally positive connotations. One who is 'for peace' is seen as tolerant and against 'war'. But being 'for peace' might also be read as being 'politically castrated' and accepting of the status quo whatever the circumstances. Such connotation also fits a model raver, who uses the party to release 'steam' or 'poison', to be a placid and disciplined worker for the rest of the week. The development of Berlin techno can also be regarded as another manifestation of Western hegemony. As time passed, German techno moved to a new stage, in which derelict spaces became privatized and gentrified.

In the UK rave subculture declined in the second half of the 1990s and when specific music culture deteriorates, the music itself often becomes more sophisticated. Simon Reynolds, quoting Steve Beckett, the head of the celebrated Warp label, presents this situation in such terms:

> By early 1992 there was a demand among worn-out veteran ravers for music to accompany and enhance the comedown phase after clubbing'n'raving. . . . If you're coming down off [drugs], you can get really lost in your own thoughts and concentrate on music, pay more attention to detail. . . . From our point of view, it also felt like a lot of the white-label dance music had gotten really throwaway. It felt like somebody should start paying attention to the production and the artwork – the whole way the music was presented. (Beckett, quoted in Reynolds 1998: 183)

'Artificial Intelligence', a compilation released by Warp in 1992, is the first record which captured the new attitude to techno, as music for contemplation rather than for dancing. Its cover presents an android sleeping in an armchair, with Kraftwerk and Pink Floyd albums at the side. The image suggests that this music is for listening, in the same way the records of Kraftwerk and Pink Floyd are. The term 'artificial intelligence' points to two ideas. First, it suggests that computers can be as intelligent as people, therefore might be given 'free reign' in composing music. The second, perhaps the more important connotation, on which Reynolds ponders, is that intelligent techno demands an 'intelligent audience', older than the average club-goer and familiar with techno traditions. The requirement for 'intelligence' and 'knowledge' is also a typical attitude of the veterans of a specific genre towards the newcomers.

One of the first labels and dance music institutions that was particularly successful at curating and framing dance music as music for both dancing and listening was Ministry of Sound, an organization that was prominent and found its roots in the house music scenes of the early 1990s. Such intention was implied in an early incarnation of the mission statement: 'We are building a global entertainment business, based on a strong aspirational brand, respected for its creativity and quality'. Since then the mission statement has undergone several revisions, reflecting the evolving aims of Ministry and also acknowledging shifts in culture and technology. 'Global entertainment business' at one point became 'global lifestyle empire'. In one incarnation of the mission statement the organization announced its aim to make its customers 'feel like fucking superstars' and subsequently proclaiming the intention 'to create the moments people live for'.

'Intelligent techno' and similar electronic genres, which aspired to appeal to the taste of a sophisticated consumer, flourished not only in England but also in Germany, Belgium and Holland. In these countries Tresor (Berlin), Mille Plateaux (Frankfurt), R&S Records (Ghent) and 100% Pure (Amsterdam) were most identified with this music. Proponents of intelligent techno advocated a return to the pure, minimal sound of Detroit and underscored the artistic and personal connections between European and American techno musicians. To this effect, in 1993, Tresor Records released the compilation album 'Tresor II: Berlin & Detroit – A Techno Alliance', a testament to the influence of the Detroit sound upon the German techno scene and a celebration of a 'mutual admiration pact' between the two cities. As the mid-1990s approached, Berlin also became a haven for Detroit producers, such as Jeff Mills and Blake Baxter.

By early to mid-2000s the fashion for techno in all its forms had largely passed. In 2008, Manchester-based music critic, Tom Naylor, published an article in *The Guardian* entitled 'The Strange, Lingering Death of Minimal Techno'. As if it was not clear enough from its title, the author insists that minimal techno is 'boring Europe's dancefloors to death'. But, if minimal is over, 'what's next?', asks the author, replying,

> Well, more of the same. Only different. Subtle shifts, suitably enough. Logically, this should be boom time for maximal dance music, a la Crookers and Hervé. And it might be, in Britain. But, the German scene and media . . . isn't prey to the same vicious swings, the same boom-bust, hype-kill cycles. 'Evolution not revolution' is Germany's style and, with Berlin unlikely to cede its position as electronic music's global centre, that is where the most exciting innovations are still going to come from. (Naylor 2008)

While techno has been in decline, other subgenres of EDM emerged in the new millennium. Of special interest among them are those which try to reconnect producers and their audience with the past danceable genres, such as electro swing, which draws on early jazz (Inglis 2019: 195–7), nu-wave (Reynolds 2013: 597–609) and nu-disco, which reworks synthesizer-heavy 1980s European dance music styles ('Genre Focus: Nu Disco' 2017). Such styles can be interpreted as a sign of the maturation of EDM, as maturity is typically achieved when artists and audiences become archivists and historians of the work created by their predecessors. This maturation can be explained by several factors. One is the simple longevity of EDM, which requires taking stock of it. Another is the global availability of the earlier styles of EDM on the internet, the cultural digital mega-archive, especially the setting up of YouTube in 2005, which allows new generations of EDM fans, located in different parts of the world to engage with music. The rise of such 'historical styles' can be regarded as recognition of their aesthetic value, against the background of its neglect in earlier periods.

With the resurrection of the past phenomena comes a new attitude of the both producers and consumers of music, what can be described as pop-ization of EDM. As Reynolds observes,

> This new generation have abandoned the very ethos of Ecstasy culture: the principles of egalitarian unity and 'only connect', the notion of submerging your ego in the oceanic hypno-flow of the rhythm and merging with the crowd. The dancefloor is reconfigured not as a space of unity but as a stage for poseurs and coke-spiked narcissistic display. Nu-wave electro also breaks with the 'in the mix' aesthetic where tracks are anonymous elements for the DJ's seamless montage. Instead, nu-wave songs compete to stand out, through domineering vocals, larger-than-life singers (as opposed to the depersonalized diva-as-raw-material approach in most modern dance), witty lyrics and extravagant amounts of obscenity and trash talk. (2013: 598)

Another development concerns changes in the organization in EDM industry. Following a crisis in the recording industry which began at the end of the 1990s, many successful indie labels specializing in EDM have been acquired by major labels. For example, Spinning, which launched many acts including Martin Garrix, were bought by Warner in 2017. They have twenty-five active sub-labels, many of which are operated by well-known DJs such as David Guetta, Sander Van Doorn and Kryder. More notable is the even longer list of sub-labels that Spinning no longer operate. Similarly, the recordings leg of Ministry of Sound was acquired by Sony in 2016.

Another significant development is the rise of EDM festivals. This phenomenon can be seen in a wider context of festivalization of popular music and popular culture at large, but also as an attempt of incorporating EDM culture into mainstream musical culture. A sign of that is an obliteration of division between 'festival' and 'rave' by, on the one hand, rendering raves safe and family-friendly and making marketing some EDM festivals as raves (Peter 2020).

We shall also mention here a change in terminology. While 'EDM' is still used to describe past developments in music for dancing, produced with a use of electronic equipment, these days the hegemonic term is 'dance', rather than 'electronic dance music' or 'EDM'. From this change we can deduce that the defining element of this genre became its use, rather than its production method. This is not because synthesizers have been abandoned by club musicians, but because they became so ubiquitous in all genres of popular music that mentioning them is now redundant. This change in terminology also encourages to seek connections between current and previous forms of dance music. For example, it will be interesting to look at similarities and differences between careers of early stars of dance music, such as Richard Strauss, and new stars, such as Avicii, as well as between early dance cultures and recent ones. Some authors in this book take such a long look, for example Mazierska, who examines Polish dance culture from the period after the First World War till the current day through the lens of class.

The specificity of research about EDM

EDM is essentially music produced for live consumption: in clubs, raves and more recently festivals. Hence, a large part of the research devoted to EDM concerns dimensions and consequences of its liveness. One aspect which attracted much attention is the role of a DJ as a producer of music, its performer and a persona around a certain culture is built (Langlois 1992; Bennett 2001: 120–2; Attias,

Gavanas and Rietveld 2013; Strachan 2017: 107–32). Researchers as early as the 1990s noted the shift from the DJ's role as a passive record player to virtual musician (Langlois 1992: 230) and with that, his or (rarer) her growing status. Nowadays, it is widely acknowledged that some EDM DJs, for example David Guetta, Tiësto, Deadmau5 and the recently deceased Avicii, enjoy star status. Despite that, there is relatively little done about their music as an expression of their individual style and their star persona, in contrast to the way rock and pop stars are treated. In fact, such an approach to dance music has been criticized as inappropriate. Simon Reynolds confessed in his seminal book, *Generation Ecstasy*, published in 1999, that initially

> my take on dance was rockist because, barely acquainted with how the music functioned in its 'proper' context, I tended to fixate on singular artists. This is how rock critics still tend to approach dance music: they look for the auteur-geniuses who seem most promising in terms of long-term, album-based careers. But dance scenes don't really work like this: the 12-inch single is what counts, there's little brand loyalty to artists, and DJs are more of a focal point for the fans than the faceless, anonymous producers. (1998: 3–4)

Carolyn Krasnow goes further than Reynolds, claiming that it was dance itself which thwarted EDM musicians:

> Rock had put great emphasis on its stars, but because disco circulated almost entirely through records, stars were less dominant; instead, the focus was on the dancers themselves and on the social milieu of the club. In this way discos recalled earlier times, when dance clubs, from the smallest neighbourhood gathering places to the most elite nightclubs, were focal points of entertainment. (2000)

It is also worth mentioning here Andrew Goodwin's argument, made in 1988, that pop music made in 'digital age of reproduction' leads to a crisis of authorship, caused by a difficulty to differentiate between man and machine-made music and originals and copies (2000: 262–6), an argument explored by Andrew Fry in his chapter.

What is thus foregrounded in the discussions about DJs is their lifestyle and their impact on the dancing audience. Matthew Collin, for example, describes DJ stars as 'electronic cash kings', writing:

> Back in the mid-nineties, there was a lot of talk about 'superstar DJs', with their top-of-the-range sports cars and costly drug habits, but they were Liliputian figures compared to the hulking leviathans who followed them. All the top

showmen – these 'cash kings' were almost always men, of course – had become perennial globetrotters, jetting from gig to gig and cutting new tracks on their laptops in VIP departure lounges and five-star hotel rooms as they sipped the complimentary champagne and racked up the air miles. (Collin 2018: 5; see also Mercuri 2019)

The tacit assumption is that in EDM music genre and music culture are more important than the musician who operates within its confines and that EDM music is ephemeral; it uses its purpose and then disappears when the fashion changes. In the late 1990s David Hesmondhalgh argued that EDM is not an auteurist genre; on the contrary, there is a relative emphasis on anonymity, manifested in the frequent use of multiple aliases by producers, and the downplaying of performers' visual images (Hesmondhalgh 1998). It was also argued that for some sections of the audience the lack of stars and anonymity of the scene was a great attraction of EDM (Melechi 1993: 37). Yet, as we argued in the previous section, this has started to change already in the 1990s ('The Second Coming of the Superstar DJ' 2012).

As if taking a cue from Hesmondhalgh's and Melechis's assertion, some publications with 'DJ' in the titles practically omit the issue of stardom and authorship of DJs, instead focusing on their role as cultural creators and mediators, and agents of social change (Attias, Gavanas and Rietveld 2013). Some EDM producers whom Mazierska interviewed when writing her books about Austrian and Polish electronic music mentioned that they moved away from this music because of its ephemerality and anonymity. The sense of EDM's anonymity is exacerbated by the increased focus on algorithmic EDM, which was a focus of one of the recent numbers of *Dancecult* (2018). Conversely and unlike in rock, where the issue of canon is of crucial importance, canonization of EDM artists hardly began.

Research on EDM also frequently deals with the relationship between the micro-environment of a club and the larger social and cultural environment, most importantly a city, what can be summarized as the question of 'electronic cities' (Holt and Wergin 2013; Strachan 2017: 127–31; Collin 2018; Jóri and Lücke 272020; Bottà 2020; Darchen 2021). Such investigations include the impact of specific cultural policies and local traditions on the setting up of clubs and conversely, the influence of clubs on the lives of the locals, development of tourism and new cultural traditions. A growing area is also that of electronic festivals (St. John 2018), reflecting the attempts of music professionals to overcome the problem of scale in the consumption of live music, which became the dominant sector of popular music and the changing pattern of cultural consumption, what is captured by the previously mentioned term 'festivalization of culture'.

Less attention is devoted to the meaning of EDM music. Such disregard of meaning is encouraged by some of Reynolds's principles of electronica, such as drawing on Susan Sontag's proto-postmodernist essays, 'Against Interpretation' and 'Surface versus Depth' (Reynolds 2001: 315–17). This is understandable, given that a significant proportion of EDM production is instrumental and it is admittedly more difficult to interpret than musical works furnished with lyrics. Moreover, the noisy space of a club is not conducive to attentive listening and deciphering the meanings of tracks. Not surprisingly, although many decades have passed since 'I Feel Love' had its premiere, this song still provides a blueprint for a successful EDM song, with its famous bassline, artificial, otherworldly sound, rhythm and very limited lyrics, with clusters of short words such as 'fall and free' and 'you and me', repeated endlessly. To understand 'I Feel Love' one does not need to be proficient in English – the song appeals to one's body rather than intellect. This does not mean, however, that there are no differences in the projected meaning of EDM tracks produced by artists originated in different countries and regions. Equally, the lack of lyrics or their simplicity and banality does not preclude conveying a political message. Such a message can be read as 'I want to escape politics and ideology' for the duration of a club night, rave or festival, in order to return refreshed to one's office after a weekend or a holiday full of fun. EDM can be thus linked to neoliberalism, with its goal of changing political subjects into passive consumers who do not question the political status quo. On the other hand, the communal values promoted at EDM events can be regarded as an endorsement of socialism. This tension is recognized by scholars (Bennett 2001: 123–4; Peter 2020), but an interesting question is whether it is reconciled in the 'souls' of clubbers and ravers or might lead to taking a specific political position. Some scholars, in defence of EDM, try to eschew such categorizations, focusing instead on the potential of EDM events to foster 'alternative conception of the self' and engender 'playful vitality' (Malbon 1999: 134–65). It shall be added here that the meanings of 'club night', 'rave' and 'festival' are currently undergoing a significant transformation due to Covid restrictions, which dramatically reduced live music events and moved many from physical to virtual space. It remains to be seen whether these shifts prevent social fragmentation and passivity or, on the contrary, will mitigate its effects. Deciphering meanings of EDM can also help to test the hypothesis that EDM culture is a global culture in the sense of not only thriving in different corners of the world but reflecting a similar sensitivity of the producers and consumers of music, as opposed to revealing local interests, traditions and preoccupations.

Structure and chapter description

This book is meant to account for these various ambiguities, variations, transformations and manifestations of EDM, pertaining to its generic fragmentation, large geographical spread, modes of consumption and changes in technology. It is particularly interested in its current state, its future and its borders – between EDM and other forms of electronic music, as well as other forms of popular music. Furthermore, it tries to account for the rise of EDM in places which are hardly covered by the existing literature, such as Eastern Europe. It also looks at its multimedia character and its visual side, which includes the way EDM events are staged.

The collection begins with a preface by a distinguished electronic musician, Graham Massey, who reflects on his 'love affair' with EDM in a context of its national and international history. The main body of the collection is divided into three parts. The first part, titled 'Discursive and Technological Production of EDM', points to the way EDM changes through discursive and technological means. First Anita Jóri examines the evolution of the meanings of terms such as 'electronic music' and 'electronic dance music', looking at the etymological origins of 'electronic music' that is rooted in the German heritage of 'elektronische Musik' from the 1940s, different types of journalistic discourse and academic texts. She also examines the special position of techno within the broad church of EDM. Next, Mathieu Guillien takes to task disentangling the term 'electro', widely used in France, tracing its origin and relation to such terms as 'techno', 'house', 'drum'n'bass' and the likes, arguing that musicology does not play its role in clarifying a confusion which the mass media and the music industry are content to maintain. Jóri and Guillien pose the Bourdieuan question of the power to define terms and delineate concepts, and the need to have clear divisions between genres, within EDM and more generally. The last two chapters in this part focus on technology as a means to transform EDM. Justin Morey examines the importance of recorded technical DJ mixes in the development of sampling practice, especially in the UK in the 1990s. He also considers the future of sampling. Andrew Fry explores the creative use of artificial intelligence by EDM artists, observing that many EDM artists already use tools that could be described as AI, such as automating plug-ins, replacing individual drum sounds within files (Apple) or creating programmes that self-produce music. He argues that in time, creative tools may become increasingly intelligent, and although at present AI tools may primarily be developed by humans, the line between biological and nonbiological is increasingly blurred. Fry explores the ways in which biological artists will be supported by AI, as well as the development of nonbiological artists.

The second part, 'EDM Stars and Stardom', explores different dimensions of EDM stardom, which is traditionally a neglected area in EDM research. The first chapter in this part, by Melanie Ptatscheck, discusses the career of Avicii (Tim Bergling), whose suicide in 2018 shook the community of electronic dance musicians and fans, drawing attention to mental health of DJs. She uses his case to explore the effect of stardom of EDM musicians, which includes an intense pressure to succeed, and the contrast between the euphoria of the show and subsequent exhaustion, loneliness and self-doubt. The following two chapters are dedicated to Canadian DJ and producer Joel Zimmerman, better known as Deadmau5. First, Tristan Kneschke treats his career as a prism which reflects different trends in EDM music, pertaining to the use of technology, such as alignment with music, live streaming and a penchant for video games, and his preference to conceal his (true) identity. Next, Jeremy Smith delves into Deadmau5's relation to authenticity, in a context of the conflict between the attainment of commercial success and credibility. From Deadmau5 we move closer to Europe, where lives probably the greatest star of electro swing: Parov Stelar. Chris Inglis discusses the specificity of stardom in this genre, labelling it 'second-hand stardom'. This is because electro swing presents a curious dichotomy, in which stars of a different era are put on display and celebrated, while the potential stars of today have their route to stardom blocked. Taking influence from much of today's underground EDM scene, in which the music is arguably the focus of attention, above the producer or performer, electro swing must therefore balance this position with the inherited associations of swing stardom that it cannot escape.

The final part of *The Evolution of Electronic Dance Music*, 'Dance Music Scenes', is concerned mostly with consumption of EDM. Stuart Moss charts the development of the club scene in Leeds and the UK at large from its inception in the 1970s to the present day, paying particular attention to the 2000s. He explores the meaning of the 'club', from the traditional setting of a nightclub venue to unofficial alternative leisure spaces that are used for clubbing activities. He also looks at the different legal frameworks and business models operating by promoter entrepreneurs against the changing political landscape. Moss notes the entanglement of social class and club culture. After Moss, Kamila Rymajdo, using a feminist perspective, discusses the underrepresentation of older women in club culture in Manchester, within the context of the intersection of sexism, ageism and working conditions under late capitalism facing women DJs and club promoters in the city. She acknowledges recent changes being made towards greater gender equality within the music industry in the UK and beyond, such as gender parity at some music festivals, on nightclub line-ups and in radio, as well as venues' efforts to make clubs more inclusive for all. However, she points out that these positive changes are undermined by rapidly expanding gentrification of Manchester, resulting in the city being hostile to nurturing any creative industries that do not adhere to the profit-making agenda. Finally, Ewa Mazierska looks at the specificity of dance culture in Poland, from the end of the First World War till the present day, with the focus on the last half a century. She applies a concept of class as her main perspective, arguing that since the 1970s dance culture developed on two tracks, each informed by a different set of values: on the one hand education and ambition to catch up with the West, and nurturing individualism, on the other hand, fun and cherishing Polish culture. The first track leads from early discotheques to metropolitan clubs. The second track was developed in the countryside and the province, where a specific type of Polish dance culture was born, known as disco polo, which drew on Polish folklore and Eurodisco.

As this short description of the content of *Evolution of Electronic dance Music* demonstrates, the three parts are overlapping, for example stardom in Electronic dance Music affects consumption and technology influences stardom, consumption and the very concept of Electronic dance Music and its genres. Indeed, the changing character of their connections is at the centre of this book. We regard this very change and adaptability as the proof of its vitality and believe that it will allow it to overcome the recent multiple crises, caused by rising property prices, threatening clubs and Covid restrictions, which prevent large gatherings and encourage introvertism and isolation.

Works cited

Adelt, Ulrich (2012). 'Machines with a Heart: German Identity in the Music of Can and Kraftwerk', *Popular Music and Society*, 3, pp. 359–74.

Attias, Bernardo Alexander, Anna Gavanas and Hillegonda C. Rietveld (eds) (2013). *DJ Culture in the Mix*. New York: Bloomsbury.

Bennett, Andy (2001). *Cultures of Popular Music*. Maidenhead: Open University Press.

Bottà. Giacomo (2020). *Deindustrialisation and Popular Music: Punk and 'Post-Punk' in Manchester, Düsseldorf, Torino and Tampere*. Lanham, MD: Rowman & Littlefield.

Butler, Mark J. (2006). *Unlocking the Groove: Rhythm, Meter, and Music Design in Electronic Dance Music*. Bloomington and Indianapolis: Indiana University Press.

Che, Deborah (2009). 'Techno: Music and Entrepreneurship in Post-Fordist Detroit', in Ola Johansson and Thomas L. Bell (eds), *Sound, Society and the Geography of Popular Music*. Farnham: Ashgate, pp. 261–80.

Collin, Matthew (2018). *Rave On: Global Adventures in Electronic Dance Music*. London: Profile Books.

Collins, Nick, Margaret Schedel and Scott Wilson (2013). *Cambridge Introductions to Music: Electronic Music*. Cambridge: Cambridge University Press.

Darchen, Sebastien (ed.) (2021). *Electronic Cities*. London: Palgrave.

Dyer, Richard (1992). *Only Entertainment*. London: Routledge.

'Editorial' (2005). *Dancecult: Journal of Electronic Dance Music Culture*, http://www.edgecentral.net/dancecult.htm, accessed 5 October 2019.

Fikentscher, Kai (2000).*'You Better Work!' Underground Dance Music in New York*. Hanover, NH: Wesleyan University Press.

'Genre Focus: Nu Disco' (2017). *MN2S*, 31 May, https://mn2s.com/news/features/genre-focus-nu-disco/, accessed 4 November 2019.

Goodwin, Andrew (2000) [1988]. 'Sample and Hold: Pop Music in the Digital Age of Reproduction', in Simon Frith and Andrew Goodwin (eds), *On Record: Rock, Pop, and the Written Word*. London: Routledge, pp. 258–73.

Grogan, Louis (2019). 'Electronic Music Is the World's Most Popular Genre', *MixMag*, 23 May, https://mixmag.net/read/electronic-music-third-popular-genre-news, accessed 29 September 2019.

Hesmondhalgh, David (1998). 'The British Dance Music Industry: A Case Study of Independent Cultural Production', *The British Journal of Sociology*, 2, pp. 234–51.

Holt, Fabian and Carsten Wergin (eds) (2013). *Musical Performance and the Changing City*. London: Routledge, pp. 227–55.

Inglis, Chris (2019). 'Electro-Swing: Re-introduction of the Sounds of the Past into the Music of the Future', in Ewa Mazierska, Les Gillon and Tony Rigg (eds), *Popular Music in the Post-Digital Age: Politics, Culture and Technology*. New York: Bloomsbury, pp. 191–207.

Jóri, Anita and Martin Lücke (eds) (2020). *The 'New' Age of Electronic Dance Music and Club Culture*. Springer.

Krasnow, Carolyn H. (2000). 'Two Popular Dance Forms', in *Garland Encyclopedia of World Music*, Volume 3: The United States and Canada. London: Routledge.

Langlois, Tony (1992). 'Can You Feel It? DJs and House Music Culture in the UK', *Popular Music*, 2, pp. 229–38.

Malbon, Ben (1999). *Clubbing: Dancing, Ecstasy and Vitality*. London: Routledge.

McLeod, Kembrew (2001). 'Genres, Subgenres, Sub-Subgenres and More: Musical and Social Differentiation Within Electronic/Dance Music', *Journal of Popular Music Studies*, 13, pp. 59–75.

Melechi, Antonio (1993). 'The Ecstasy of Disappearance', in Steve Redhead (ed.), *Rave Off: Politics and Deviance in Contemporary Youth Culture*. Aldershot: Ashgate, pp. 7–27.

Mercuri, Monica (2019). 'The World's Highest-Paid DJs 2019: The Chainsmokers Topple Calvin Harris With $46 Million', *Forbes*, 29 July, https://www.forbes.com/sites/monicamercuri/2019/07/29/the-worlds-highest-paid-djs-of-2019/#2a505a5f7a97, accessed 18 November 2019.

Moore, David (1995). 'Raves and the Bohemian Search for Self and Community: A Contribution to the Anthropology of Public Events', *Anthropological Forum*, 2, pp. 193–214.

Naylor, Tom (2008). 'The Strange, Lingering Death of Minimal Techno', *The Guardian*, 7 October, https://www.theguardian.com/music/musicblog/2008/oct/07/death.minimal.techno.house, accessed 17 May 2017.

Peter, Beate (2020). 'Raves in the Twenty-First Century: DIY Practices, Commercial Motivations and the Role of Technology', in Ewa Mazierska, Les Gillon and Tony Rigg (eds), *The Future of Live Music*. New York: Bloomsbury, forthcoming.

Redhead, Steve (1993). 'The Politics of Ecstasy', in Steve Redhead (ed.), *Rave Off: Politics and Deviance in Contemporary Youth Culture*. Aldershot: Ashgate, pp. 7–27.

Reynolds, Simon (1998). *Generation Ecstasy: Into the World of Techno and Rave Culture*. London: Routledge.

Reynolds, Simon (2007) [2001]. 'Historia Electronica: The Case for Electronic Dance Music Culture', in his *Bring the Noise: 20 Years of Writing About Hip Rock and Hip Hop*. London: Faber and Faber, pp. 312–29.

Reynolds, Simon (2013). *Energy Flash: A Journey through Rave Music and Dance Culture*, new and revised edition. London: Faber and Faber.

Richard, Birgit and Heinz Hermann Kruger (1998). 'Ravers' Paradise? German Youth Cultures in the 1990s', in Tracey Skelton and Gill Valentine (eds), *Cool Places: Geographies of Youth Cultures*. London: Routledge, pp. 161–74.

Rietveld, Hillegonda (1998). 'The House Sound of Chicago', in Steve Redhead, Derek Wayne and Justin O'Connor (eds), *The Clubcultures Reader*. Oxford: Blackwell, pp. 106–18.

Scott, Derek B. (2005). 'Postmodernism and Music', in Stuart Sin (ed.), *The Routledge Companion to Postmodernism*. London: Routledge, pp. 122–32.

St. John, Graham (2018). *Weekend Societies: Electronic Dance Music and Event-Cultures*. New York: Bloomsbury.

Stoppani de Berrié, Isabel (2015). '"Escape and Build Another World": Relocations in Classical Minimalism and Minimal Techno', in Ewa Mazierska and Georgina Gregory (eds), *Relocating Popular Music*. Houndmills: Palgrave, pp. 104–25.

Strachan, Robert (2017). *Sonic Technologies: Popular Music, Digital Culture and the Creative Process*. New York: Bloomsbury.

Straw, Will (2001). 'Dance Music', in Simon Frith, Will Straw and John Street (eds), *The Cambridge Companion to Pop and Rock*. Cambridge: Cambridge: Cambridge University Press, pp. 158–75.

Strickland, Edward (1993). *Minimalism: Origins*. Bloomington: Indiana University Press.

Thornton, Sarah (1995). *Club Cultures: Music, Media and Subcultural Capital*. London: Polity.

Tompkins, Dave (2011). *How to Wreck a Nice Beach: The Vocoder from World War II to Hip-hop*. Chicago: Stop Smiling Media.

Walicki, Franciszek (1984). 'Wprowadzenie', in Marek Gaszynski and Adam Halber (eds), *ABC Prezentera dyskoteki*. Warszawa: Centralny Osrodek Metodyki Upowszechniania Kultury, pp. 3–11.

Watson, Kevin (2019). 'IMS Business Report 2019: An Annual Study of the Electronic Music Industry', https://www.internationalmusicsummit.com/wp-content/uploads/2019/05/IMS-Business-Report-2019-vFinal.pdf, accessed 29 September 2019.

Part I

Discursive and technological production of EDM

1

The meanings of 'electronic dance music' and 'EDM'

Anita Jóri

The terms 'electronic music' and 'electronic dance music' have taken many different meanings. Often they are used interchangeably – especially in journalistic texts. This chapter seeks to reconstruct the evolution of the term 'electronic dance music' and its acronym 'EDM'. To do so, first of all, I take a closer look at the etymological origins of the term 'electronic music' and its roots in the German heritage of Elektronische Musik. Then evidences for the usage of the term 'electronic dance music' are searched in three main sources: (1) journalistic and (2) academic publications, and (3) online discussions of the discourse community.[1] Within the category of journalistic writings, I analyse the most well-known sources from the 1980s until today, such as Reynolds 1999 and 2013 and Brewster and Broughton 1999, and fanzines and rave zines. I also search for evidence in scholarly literature (Butler 2006; Redhead 1993; Thornton 1995) from the 1990s until today. Here, my main methodology is discourse analysis (in a broad sense) with emphasis on the terminology usage. Furthermore, a web discussion forum from 2006 is examined with the help of qualitative content analysis (Mayring 2014), in order to reconstruct the historical milestones of the terminology usage.

Just to highlight some stages of the etymology, the US fanzine *Project X Magazine* announced the first (and last) Electronic Dance Music Award in 1995 that was an underground celebration of the readers' favourite musicians. Later the US music industry and press adopted the term to describe commercial electronic music in the late 1990s and early 2000s. Therefore, it has now a negative connotation within underground electronic music scenes and associated with 'push-button DJs' and musicians who use the 'press-play approach', as epitomized by the broadly received parody of David Guetta's performance at the opening ceremony of UEFA Euro (2016).

One cannot find references to EDM in early academic texts. In the 1990s and early 2000s, the terms 'rave', 'dance' and 'club culture(s)' were more popular among academics (Thornton 1995; Bennett 2001). However, EDM is now used as an umbrella term in academia – for example, the e-journal *Dancecult* is dedicated to the study of 'electronic dance music culture' and other early sources are Butler 2006 and St. John (2006) – to describe different genres of electronic music popularized after the late 1970s. According to the above-mentioned negative connotation of EDM, some scholars have also raised their voices against the usage of this term. One of them is McLeod (2001) who proposes 'electronic/dance music' with a slash. His main argument is that not all genres of EDM are danceable.

But what is the problem with this genre name among the scene's members? Why do they use other terms such as 'dance music', 'dance' or 'club music' instead? Why does academia not have a more precise solution?

In order to answer these questions, I take a closer look at the sociocultural, etymological and linguistic background of this term and its alternatives such as 'dance/dance music' and 'techno' or '*Techno*' in German-speaking context. In German, the term '*Techno*' is widely used with the same meaning as the English 'electronic dance music'. One can find references to it in both journalistic (Rapp 2009; Denk and von Thülen 2014) and academic sources (Feser and Pasdzierny 2016a; Hitzler and Pfadenhauer 2001; Kühn 2016). On the other hand, *Techno* (or in English 'techno') is also highly problematic, since this genre has an important tradition in the history of electronic dance music, especially in the early Detroit scene. Thus, using it as a collective term causes confusion within the discourse community.

After analysing these cases, I will speculate whether these terms will survive or change their meanings in the future.

Etymology of 'electronic dance music'

It is difficult to trace back the exact historical origins of the term 'electronic dance music' because of the ever-changing trends of terms in the terminology of electronic music in general (see more on these terminological issues in Jóri 2018). However, there are some sources that helped me to reconstruct a speculative timeline of the popularization of this term. These were academic and journalistic writings, fanzines and other online sources such as web discussion forums. But before I describe my findings, I will take a closer look at the roots of the term 'electronic music', since 'electronic dance music' is based on it.

According to Holmes (2020), one of the first mentions of the term 'electronic music' as we understand it now is in Miessner's article 'Electronic Music and Instruments' from 1936 (Miessner, cited in Holmes 2020). According to Collins, Schedel and Wilson's technology-focused definition, '[t]he term *electronic* formally denotes applications of the transistor, a specific electrical component popularized from the mid-twentieth century onward that enables the substantial miniaturizing of circuits' (2014: 1).

Simultaneously, starting in the 1940s, the German term *Elektronische Musik* was coined, which was likely translated from the English version, then popularized by the engineer and musician Werner Meyer-Eppler and his colleagues at the Studio for Electronic Music of the West German Radio ('WDR Studio') in Cologne. Meyer-Eppler's (1949) pioneer work *Elektronische Klangerzeugung: Elektronische Musik und Synthetische Sprache* focuses on the idea of synthesizing music entirely from electronically produced signals. In this way, Elektronische Musik differentiated itself from the contemporary French school Musique Concrète, which used recorded sounds (Holmes 2020). Therefore, Elektronische Musik is also a specific school of music composition which was later, based on my findings, translated into English as 'electronic music', without specifying the difference between the Anglo-Saxon tradition of electronic music and the German Elektronische Musik (Iverson 2019).

The confusion around the term was raised in the 1950s when the US American stream of Tape Music did not really differentiate between the techniques of the German and French traditions (Holmes 2020). Consequently, by 1960 'electronic music' was adopted to describe 'any and all music produced using recorded sound, tape, machines, and sound generators, whether for movies, television, stage, dance, or in the halls of academic music studios' (Holmes 2020: 7). In this sense, the English term was a much more opened one, without any specific limitations in the tools of production techniques. Later, new technological developments (e.g. synthesizers) simplified the music production and by the 1970s 'electronic music' was used to denote a style of music instead of the instruments which created it (Holmes 2020). Nowadays, it is especially challenging to give a comprehensive definition of electronic music when many music genres involve electronic components in their production and, culturally, it also incorporates different traditions. This happened to the German 'Elektronische Musik' too, as it became a general term with similar meaning, like its English version.

To sum up, the English 'electronic music' was already used in the 1930s, or maybe even earlier, but probably in limited circles of experts. Then with the boom of the German Elektronische Musik as a school of composition the term became more popular also in English. However, the meaning of the English 'electronic music' was already a different one than its contemporary 'Elektronische Musik'.

I did not compare early literature on Elektronische Musik and 'electronic music'; my findings are only based on secondary literature. I will leave this task for future research because the main focus of this chapter is on electronic dance music. However, what I wanted to illustrate with the case of electronic music is to show that the confusion around the terminology of electronic (dance) music started early on in the process of terminological dissemination.

Electronic dance music: A historical overview

From a sociocultural point of view, electronic dance music is '[e]lectronic music intended primarily for dancing at nightclubs and raves' (Dayal and Ferrigno n.d.). Collins et al. (2014) focus on music production in their definition and state that 'electronic dance music (EDM) features electronic synthesized and sampled instrumentation, with at least some parts of a percussive nature, in tracks designed for dancing' (2014: 102). However, McLeod (2001) brings our awareness to the fact that electronic dance music is not necessarily danceable. Therefore, he suggests the usage of 'electronic/dance music'. McLeod's argument is valid, especially if one thinks of genres such as braindance, intelligent dance music (IDM) or experimental electronic music. However, his suggestion of 'electronic/dance music' with a slash has not been established and used either in academia or in journalism, and since the article was written in 2001, I assume that it will not be widely applied in the future either.

Another important point here is that 'electronic dance music' is an umbrella term for very diverse musical styles. McLeod (2001) also describes the motivations behind the rapid and ever-evolving processes of subgenre naming: it can be seen as a response to genuine stylistic evolution, a merchandising strategy, an accelerated consumer culture, a cultural appropriation or a subcultural gate-keeping service.

As mentioned earlier, the etymology of 'electronic dance music' is not fully known, but in journalism, according to critic Joshua Glazer (2014), it was already used in 1985. The next date that is often remarked (e.g. in Glazer 2014) by journalists is 1995 when readers of the New York fanzine *Project X Magazine* voted for the winners of the first (and only) 'Electronic Dance Music Awards' (Alig 1995). In the ceremony, organized by the magazine and Nervous Records, award statues were given to the following artists and labels: Winx, The Future Sound of London, Moby, Junior Vasquez, Danny Tenaglia, DJ Keoki, TRIBAL America Records and Moonshine Records (Alig 1995). They all used to belong to underground circles and played or produced very different genres within electronic dance music. This also evidences that there must have been a need for a collective noun including diverse music styles. Therefore, the connotation of the term 'electronic dance music' could not have been negative or mainstream around this time.

I checked every issue of *Project X Magazine* and could not find any articles mentioning the term 'electronic dance music' (Project X Magazine Archive n.d.), except for Alig 1995. Fanzines or rave zines are generally excellent sources for identifying early terminology adoption by practitioners (e.g. journalists and musicians) and fans, since they give active voice for the consumers and one can easily identify the characteristics of the subcultural communication in them (Thornton 1995). I used the archival data of Rave Archive (n.d.), which was launched in 2007 with the expressed aim to save the 1990s rave cultures' sources. There are 251 fanzines uploaded into the archive, including the most important ones from Canada (e.g. *Trance 5000, Communic8r*), Germany (e.g. *Frontpage, Groove, Raveline*), the UK (e.g. *Blaze, Eternity, In-Ter-Dance, Underworld, The Scene*), and the United States (e.g. *Flux, High-R, Massive Magazine, bEAN, Rush, Stellar Awareness, The Last Girl Scout*). These fanzines vary in terms of their topics, professionalism and music genres they discuss. Some also focus on general cultural trends, fashion and arts, while others are strictly music- and local scene-oriented.[2] I searched for the term 'electronic dance music' in the database and found only two relevant results:[3] (1) in the seventeenth issue of the US American *Massive Magazine* from 1997 where electronic dance music was used as an umbrella term: 'So who exactly defines 'Underground', You Do, you the reader, you Massive, you the DJ, anyone who has anything to do with electronic dance music' (Wes aka Locutus 1997: 4). From this quote one can see that the term was used to describe various underground music genres. (2) The other result was from the ninth issue of the Baltimore-based fanzine *Activated*, also from 1997, in which one of the journalists asked a DJ in an interview which artists he looks up to within electronic dance music (Pezboy 1997: 7). Here again, the term had a collective meaning. These search results are contemporary sources to the earlier mentioned 1995 *Project X Magazine*. From these findings, one could conclude that the term 'electronic dance music' must have been used mostly in the United States in the mid-1990s, yet in limited underground circles.

However, while searching for the term 'electronic dance music', there were another ninety-seven search results for 'dance music', which would have been even more if I had only typed in 'dance'. 'Dance' and 'dance music' were more widely used terms – with similar meanings to electronic dance music – in the 1990s. A good example for that is the journalists Bill Brewster and Frank Broughton's (1999) book *Last Night a DJ Saved My Life. The Story of the Disc Jockey*, in which 'dance music' and 'electronic music' are used as umbrella terms for various genres. Just to mention another journalistic example, in 1999 Reynolds already applied electronic dance music as 'profusion of scenes and subgenres' (1999: 9). This and his later descriptions in the book still have nothing to do with mainstream styles of music.

The early academic – more precisely cultural studies – sources paint a similar picture. Sarah Thornton (1995) in her early work *Club Cultures. Music, Media and Subcultural Capital* writes about dance music as follows: '[w]hat contemporary British youth call "dance music" is more precisely designated as discotheque or club music. Rather than having an exclusive claim on dancing, the many genres and subgenres coined obsessively under the rubric share this institutional home' (1995: 71). Her definition could also be used for electronic dance music now. Andy Bennett (2001) also gave the title 'Contemporary Dance Music and Club Cultures' to one of the chapters in his book *Cultures of Popular Music*. Also, other early writings on rave culture (e.g. Redhead 1993) use either a specific genre (e.g. acid house or techno) or again 'dance' as a general term.

Also, some facts have to be added here about the changes within the scene in the late 1990s. Raves were essentially over or had merged with club culture around that time (Anderson 2009; Bennett 2001; Malbon 1999) and commercialization became visible with events being more professionalized and cooperating with brands, a phenomenon that Anderson describes as the 'rave-club culture continuum' (Anderson and Kavanaugh 2007; Anderson 2009). Raves evolved into 'corporate raves' by fusing more authentic elements of early raves with legitimate business style and purpose, professional festivals and in the most mainstream cases into superstar one-offs – 'one time parties showcasing a main act or 'star'' (Anderson 2009: 44; on the commodification of rave culture, see Barnes 2018). These events became popular from the mid-2000s especially in the United States by taking advantage of the struggling record industry around

2005 (Reynolds 2012), due to the booming MP3 production (McLeod 2005) and its circulation on pirating platforms.

Current situation: 'EDM' as mainstream electronic dance music

According to the journalist Reynold's *Energy Flash: A Journey through Rave Music and Dance Culture*, an updated edition of the earlier mentioned book from 1999, electronic dance music is just a rebranding strategy of the music industry: 'The EDM resurrection isn't so much déjà vu as a rebranding coup. What were once called "raves" are now termed "festivals". EDM is what was previously called electronica (in 1997) and before that techno (in 1991)' (2013: 687). This statement brings us to other important factors in the etymological timeline of 'electronic dance music': the differences between the acronym 'EDM' and its original reference term 'electronic dance music', and the effects of the music industry on the terminology usage.

The 'EDM' in Reynolds's quote is definitely not the same 'EDM' that, for example, the academic journal *Dancecult*, 'a peer-reviewed, open-access e-journal for the study of electronic dance music culture (EDMC)' ('About' n.d.), discusses in its periodicals. Earlier than *Dancecult*, Mark J. Butler's (2006) work *Unlocking the Groove. Rhythm, Meter, and Musical Design in Electronic Dance Music* and the editor-in-chief of *Dancecult*, Graham St. John's article 'Electronic Dance Music Culture and Religion: An Overview' also talk about the umbrella term. At the same time, since the mid-2000s there has been a tendency in journalistic reporting to use 'EDM' to describe mainstream electronic dance music. This is exactly the meaning of 'EDM' that causes confusion between practitioners (musicians, scene members, fans, etc.) and academics. My favourite personal example for this misunderstanding happened at the event *The New Age of EDM and Club Culture* I organized with my colleagues in the club Kantine am Berghain (Berlin) in 2017. Our aim was to bring academics and practitioners together in order to discuss actual questions of the scene in Berlin (e.g. gentrification, diversity and gender-related issues, support for artists). The final panel discussion reflected on the sponsorships of artists in the city, therefore, we invited Katja Lucker, managing director of *Musicboard Berlin*, the only institution in Germany that focuses on funding pop music with its scholarship system (see more in Lücke and Jóri 2018). As the discussion started, Ms. Lucker questioned 'EDM' in the title of our event and premised on her certainty of its meaning, 'So you are discussing David Guetta's discography the whole day, right?', she asked us. In this moment it became clear to me why there might have been so few people attending our event: that being, for most of the practitioners, 'EDM' means a mainstream and business-oriented music genre (see more in Jóri and Lücke 2020).

I tried to trace back the beginning of this tendency among practitioners and fans and found an early web discussion forum thread from 2006 on Ableton Forums, entitled *Why do you hate EDM? 'House, Techno, Trance'* (Ableton Forums 2006). This title promised a declaration of the negative association of 'EDM', and I analysed this thread with the help of qualitative content analysis after Mayring (2014) by creating coding categories for the definitions of 'EDM' and 'electronic dance music'. My main question in order to illustrate the discussion around these terms from the mid-2000s was, 'How do the forum participants define "EDM" and "electronic dance music"?' Hence, my two main coding units were 'EDM' and 'electronic dance music'. Within the 151 forum posts, I found 66 cases mentioning 'EDM' and just three cases of 'electronic dance music'.

To keep the results of the analysis short, I could identify six definition categories among these combined sixty-nine cases: (1) some forum participants tried to define 'EDM' and 'electronic dance music' with the help of other genres, such as trance. The following examples illustrate the phenomenon: *People interpret trance/EDM according to the standards of other music; sometimes trance/EDM is just not the person's cup of tea; people do enjoy trance, edm or whatever it's called.*[4] I have to add to these examples that in 2006 the discussion around the commercialized genre trance was still vibrant and this is why it is identified with EDM as also a mainstream style. (2) The next definition was related to music aesthetics and the methods of music production (e.g. too repetitive, not artistic, not emotional). For example, *A lot of people don't like 'edm' because it's very formula oriented and quantized so heavily. A lot of times it lacks 'human feel'; it all sounds the same . . . It just goes, thump thump thump; . . . edm – there's boring stuff . . . ; point me at some original funky syncopated non-'mmphh . . . mmphh . . . mmphh . . . mmphh . . . filter sweep . . .' EDM!.* These examples show that the general assumption of the aesthetics of 'EDM' is cheaply produced, non-artistic, monotonous and boring. Therefore, its producers are not really appreciated in underground circles either. (3) There were some forum members who already understood these terms as umbrella terms, just as one would in research. For example, *EDM is pretty much all I listen to; EDM is a whole plethora* of genres; 99.9% of house, trance, psytrance, whatever subgenre of 'EDM'. . .; a lot of the genres involved in the EDM umbrella. (4) Some tried to exclude different subgenres that are not part of EDM: *I wouldn't call that techno/trance/house or anything else 'edm'; people I know don't consider HipHop to be EDM.* (5) The next definition category considers every music EDM that is danceable and follows the rhythm pattern of four-on-the-floor. For example, *And i have never heard an 'edm' track that does not feature a kick on every quarter note for most of the track; EDM stands for 'electronic dance music' and is a genre name that popped up not too long ago as a blanket for the various forms of dance music based around the 4 on the floor kick.* This definition category is close to the second one in terms of music aesthetics. However, some forum members recognize that the four-on-the-floor pattern is also included in underground versions of techno or house. (6) Some already differentiated between 'electronic dance music' and 'EDM': *It doesn't refer to *all* dance music that is electronic, though, correct? For instance, hip-hop, dance hall, even some industrial are electronic and dance music but not edm; remember, 'EDM' doesn't really mean 'electronic dance music'.* Currently the difference between 'EDM' and 'electronic dance music' has become even more visible.

From these six viewpoints and definitions, one can see that the confusion around these terms was already widespread in the mid-2000s. One can also see the tendency towards the differentiation between electronic dance music and EDM, which sometimes appear in academic writings too. For example, Fabian Holt (2017) in his article 'EDM Pop. A Soft Shell Formulation in a New Festival Economy' talks about the category 'EDM pop' which seems to offer a useful answer on the above-mentioned confusion. With his differentiation, one can precisely separate the two meanings: EDM as a general umbrella term for all genres and EDM as a mainstream genre. 'EDM pop' is, however, not an established and widespread used term yet.

As mentioned earlier, the music industry (especially in the United States) has played an important role in popularizing the meaning of the term 'EDM' as a business-oriented, mainstream genre. It started with the artificially created genre name 'electronica' in the 1990s. As Ishkur's Guide states, '"[e]lectronica" does not exist. Not as a genre or a description. It was coined by the North American music press to refer to the second wave of electronic music's explosion in the late 90s' ('Ishkur's Guide to Electronic Music' n.d.). It was then followed up by 'EDM' from the 2000s due to new live events and festivals such as Electric Daisy Carnival, Electric Zoo, Miami Music Week and Ultra Music Festival, etc. that are marketed as the biggest EDM festivals in the United States. Their line-ups include mostly 'superstar' DJs and producers who in the underground circles are named as 'push-button DJs' who apply the 'press-play approach', referring to their production processes. The US corporate interest in these events and such music productions became even more obvious when the events promoter Live Nation began to invest in such EDM events (Sisario 2012). At the same time in 2012, the American Music Awards added a new category 'Electronic Dance Music', which was then changed to 'Favourite Artist Electronic Dance Music' in 2016 and to 'Favourite Artist Electronic Dance Music (EDM)' in 2017. The mainstream and business-oriented meaning of 'electronic dance music' and 'EDM' is clear if one takes a closer look at the winners: Avicii, David Guetta, Calvin Harris, Marshmallow and the Chainsmokers ('Winners Database' n.d.).

To recap, the differentiation between 'electronic dance music' and 'EDM' was already present in the conversations among practitioners in the mid-2000s. However, academia has been using them with the same meaning since then. Moreover, as it could be seen in the above-mentioned examples, the negative connotation of 'EDM' as a mainstream music genre has been reinforced by the US music and event industry.

Another alternative term: techno (or *Techno*)

In the 1990s 'dance' and 'dance music' as umbrella terms were more often used in the UK. They had and still have the same meaning just like electronic dance music and EDM in academic writings. At the same time, 'techno' became also widespread in order to describe heterogenous underground genres. Here I would like to highlight 'underground'. For example, in the early work *Techno Rebels. The Renegades of Electronic Funk*, Dan Sicko mentions in the preface of the 1999 version, 'Obviously, "techno" has evolved beyond its function as a particular pseudonym for electronic dance music' (1999: 9). In Sicko's statement 'techno' is an alternative term for electronic dance music which covers underground genres instead of mainstream. Another proof for the tendency of using techno as an umbrella term in Anglo-Saxon tradition is from Reynolds's article: 'EDM is what we used to know by the name of techno' (2012).

This is likely the definition that was picked up by academia and journalism in the German-speaking context too. An early journalistic example is the German book *Techno*, edited by Philipp Anz and Patrick Walder (1995) which promises in its blurb to deliver 'Alles über [All about] Techno ... Acid, Ästhetik [aesthetics], Body & Sex, Communist Parties, Dada, Deleuze & Guattari, DJ Culture, Ecstasy, Electro, Gabber, Jungle, Kommerz [commercialism] & Business, Kraftwerk, Labels, Pop & Avantgarde, Raving Society, TB303, Technoheads, Technosprache [techno language], Tribes & Trance, Underground Resistance, Zukunftsmusik [double meaning in German: future music/future developments]' ('Techno' n.d.). From this description one can see that *Techno* – in German it is a noun, therefore, with a capitalized T – is not only the genre that has roots in Detroit, but it is an umbrella term used for all genres. From the post-2000s, I would add to this list Tobias Rapp's (2009) *Berlin, Techno und der Easyjetset* and Felix Denk's (2014) *Der Klang der Familie: Berlin, Techno und die Wende* that also talk about *Techno* as a collective term for different underground electronic music. The same examples can be found in early scholarly literature too. Just to mention the most well-known examples, the sociologists Ronald Hitzler and Michaela Pfadenhauer (2001) refer to the same *Techno* in their edited volume *Techno-Soziologie: Erkundungen einer Jugendkultur*; Jan-Michael Kühn also writes about the economic perspectives of the same 'Techno' scene in his dissertation *Die Wirtschaft der Techno-Szene. Die Wirtschaft der Techno-Szene*; or Kim Feser and Matthias Pasdzierny (2016a) go even further and write about techno studies as a research field in their conference proceedings *Techno Studies. Ästhetik und Geschichte elektronischer Tanzmusik*. In the introduction of the latter one, Feser and Pasdzierny clarify the meaning of the term *Techno* as an umbrella term for underground music and state that '[t]he current developments in the field of electronic dance music [elektronische Tanzmusik][5] are often perceived as varieties of house [House] and electro [Elektro][6] or, also in German-speaking countries, summarised under the simple abbreviation EDM (Electronic Dance Music). In contrast, techno [Techno] seems to have passed its zenith as a general collective term' (2016b: 7 – translated from the German by the author of this chapter). However, as the authors also state, the term is still used, mostly in journalism. They also reflected on the seemingly duplicated *Techno* and *elektronische Tanzmusik* (electronic dance music) within the title of the book:

> The duplication of 'techno studies' and 'aesthetics and history of electronic dance music' appearing in the book title shows on the one hand the different language-specific terminology (whereby the most common usage contexts are swapped with *Techno* / English and *elektronische Tanzmusik* / German). On the other hand, they refer to the approach of understanding the relationship between aesthetic and historiographical reflection as a methodologically central

challenge when dealing with this music (culture). (Feser and Pasdzierny 2016b: 8 – translated from the German by the author of this chapter)

In fact, there is a tendency now in German-speaking academia to use *elektronische Tanzmusik*, the borrowed translation of the English electronic dance music, as a collective term (e.g. Schaubruch and Ruth 2019), instead of *Techno*.

Future perspectives

There is a terminological confusion in relation to 'electronic dance music' and 'EDM'. The scholarly literature refers to electronic dance music and its acronym EDM as an umbrella term with heterogenous genres that even includes EDM pop (Holt 2017). In journalism there is a tendency towards the terms (1) 'electronic music' which, however, causes problems in understanding the historical roots of this genre; (2) 'techno'/'Techno' that originally has its roots from Detroit and has a specific aesthetic pattern; and (3) 'dance/dance music' which could impart that it does not necessarily mean electronic music in the end. According to my research, the members of the scene (musicians, fans, promoters, etc.) tend to follow this terminology used by journalists. One could see examples for that in the analysis of fanzines and an internet forum discussed earlier. But how can we escape this confusion? How can we bring academic language closer to the language use of practitioners and journalists in the field? As we saw earlier, this confusion is a general phenomenon in the usage of the terminology of electronic dance music, especially when it comes to genre names (e.g. dance, electro). In his early work on popular music genres Fabbri (1982) highlights the musical community's awareness of genre rules and their competence of using them. These rules are obviously not widespread in the electronic dance music communities. Later, Negus (1999) criticizes Fabbri's deterministic point of view and claims that one should not create a static picture about genres, arguing instead for a less rule-bound and more dynamic experience of music genres. McLeod (2001) and Lindop (2010) highlighted that this fluid-and-fast genre naming is specific for EDM cultures and less intense for other genres such as rock or pop music. Following upon these thoughts, somehow this terminological confusion then becomes an inherent part of this fluidity. Linguistically, this issue is rooted in the fact that the terminology is not standardized, which then causes communicational and translational problems among the terminology users. In one of my earlier articles, I highlighted that there are only a few glossaries on electronic (dance) music that are not up-to-date any longer as the technological developments and the emergence of cultural trends occur faster than the production cycle of such publications (Jóri 2018). So, there are no standard sources that could be used by the terminology users, for example, if they want to translate or write an article (journalistic or academic) on the subject (Jóri 2018). It is also difficult to standardize the usage of such terminology, and I am not proposing such standardization. Neither do I want to create rules for the language users or community members. From a sociolinguistic perspective, I presume that users will be able to facilitate this change independently and, in the best case, fruitfully contribute to debates on how we talk about music. One might also believe that these terms will show consolidation within the terminology of electronic music until their usage is supported by academia. However, the developments over recent years draw a different picture, as the use of terminology varies among journalists, music industry protagonists, academics and practitioners of the field. It remains to be seen how, and if, tendencies and trends will develop towards a more distinct set of terms in the near future.

This study has a limited scope by focusing only on English- and partly German-speaking context; I could have also gone even deeper into the discourse analysis and literature review by taking even more examples of the scene members' terminology usage. I analysed only the most important sources or, in other words, the most frequently cited ones. The reason behind this approach is that these sources are the ones that have had significant impact on the terminology usage, since they are the most read ones, which again lead journalists, academics and other content producers to consulting them in order to gain knowledge. Finally, I believe that if there is a genre name that has a negative connotation among its users (e.g. 'EDM'), there will be a counter reaction to it and people will start to use it in a different way (e.g. 'techno'/'Techno'). To this point, the role of academia is important because of its influential position, and it can also have an impact on the terminology usage of journalists and practitioners. But should we encourage the users of language to take the form academia uses? Or should we reflect upon the actual situation and start to use these terms in different ways? Or perhaps apply the version that is commonly used? I keep these questions open to encourage others to answer them in future research.

References

Ableton Forums (2006). 'Why Do You Hate EDM? "House, Techno, Trance"', https://forum.ableton.com/viewtopic.php?t=40694, accessed 3 July 2020.

'About' (n.d.). *Dancecult: Journal of Electronic Dance Music Culture*, https://dj.dancecult.net/index.php/dancecult/about, accessed 13 July 2020.

Alig, Michael (1995). 'Club Rub', *Project X Magazine*, 36, pp. 41–3, http://projectxarchive.com/issue36_merged.pdf, accessed 8 June 2020.

Anderson, Tammy L. (2009). *Rave Culture: The Alteration and Decline of Philadelphia Music Scene*. Philadelphia: Temple University Press.

Anderson, Tammy L. and Philip R. Kavanaugh (2007). 'A "Rave" Review: Conceptual Interests and Analytical Shifts in Research on Rave Culture', *Sociology Compass*, 1, pp. 499–519.

Anz, Patrick and Philip Walder (eds) (1995). *Techno*. Zürich: Bilgerverlag.

Barnes, Duncan Martin (2018). 'Selling the Modern Day Tribe: The Commodification of Rave Culture', MA diss, Edith Cowan University, Perth.

Bennett, Andy (2001). *Cultures of Popular Music*. Berkshire: Open University Press.

Brewster, Bill and Frank Broughton (1999). *Last Night a DJ Saved My Life: The History of the Disc Jockey*. London: Headline.

Butler, Mark J. (2006). *Unlocking the Groove: Rhythm, Meter, and Musical Design in Electronic Dance Music*. Bloomington and Indianapolis: Indiana University Press.

Collins, Nick, Schedel, Margaret and Scott Wilson (2014). *Electronic Music*. Cambridge: Cambridge University Press.

Dayal, Geeta and Emily Ferrigno (n.d.). 'Electronic Dance Music (EDM)', *Oxford Music Online*, https://doi.org/10.1093/gmo/9781561592630.article.A2224259, accessed 18 July 2020.

Denk, Felix and S. von Thülen (2014). *Der Klang der Familie: Berlin, Techno und die Wende*. Berlin: Suhrkamp.

Fabbri, Franco (1982). 'A Theory of Popular Music Genres: Two Applications', in D. Horn and P. Tagg (eds), *Popular Music Perspectives: Papers from the First International Conference on Popular Music Research*, 52–81. Goteborg: International Association for the Study of Popular Music, https://www.tagg.org/others/ffabbri81a.html, accessed 10 July 2020.

Feser, Kim and Matthias Pasdzierny (eds) (2016a). *Techno Studies. Ästhetik und Geschichte elektronischer Tanzmusik*. Berlin: b_books.

Feser, Kim and Matthias Pasdzierny (2016b). '. . .and a musicologist present at all times' – elektronischer Tanzmusik im Fokus populärer Diskurse und akademischer Forschung. Einleitung, in K. Feser and M. Pasdzierny (eds), *Techno Studies. Ästhetik und Geschichte elektronischer Tanzmusik*. Berlin: b_books, pp. 7–21.

Glazer, Joshua (2014). 'Etymology of EDM: The Complex Heritage of Electronic Dance Music', *Cuepoint*, 10 October, https://medium.com/cuepoint/etymology-of-edm-the

-complex-heritage-of-electronic-dance-music-d3e3aa873369#.c8fjdvgf1, accessed 2 June 2020.

Hitzler, Ronald (2001). *Techno-Soziologie: Erkundungen einer Jugendkultur.* Opladen: Leske und Budrich.

Holmes, Thom (2020). *Electronic and Experimental Music. Technology, Music, and Culture.* New York and London: Routledge.

'Ishkur's Guide to Electronic Music' (n.d.). *Ishkur's Guide to Electronic Music*, https://music.ishkur.com, accessed 28 June 2020.

Iverson, Jennifer (2019). *Electronic Inspirations. Technologies of the Cold War Musical Avant-Garde.* Oxford: Oxford University Press.

Jóri, Anita (2016). 'The Discourse Community of Electronic Dance Music', MA diss, Eötvös Loránd University, Budapest.

Jóri, Anita (2018). 'On the Terminology of Electronic (Dance) Music', *Rasprave*, 2, pp. 467–83.

Jóri, Anita and Martin Lücke (2020). 'Introduction', in Anita Jóri and Martin Lücke (eds), *The New Age of Electronic Dance Music and Club Culture*. Cham: Springer International, pp. 1–5.

Kühn, Jan-Michael (2016). *Die Wirtschaft der Techno-Szene. Die Wirtschaft der Techno-Szene.* Wiesbaden: Springer.

Lindop, Robin (2010). 'Re-evaluating Musical Genre in UK Psytrance', in G. St John (ed.), *The Local Scenes and Global Culture of Psytrance*. London: Routledge, pp. 114–30.

Lücke, Martin and Anita Jóri (2018). 'Popförderung in der Stadt', in L. Grünewald-Schukalla, M. Lücke, M. Rauch and C. Winter (eds), *Musik und Stadt*. Wiesbaden: Springer, pp. 55–77.

Malbon, Ben (1999). *Clubbing: Dancing, Ecstasy and Vitality*. New York: Routledge.

Mayring, Philipp (2014). *Qualitative Content Analysis: Theoretical Foundation, Basic Procedures and Software Solution*. Klagenfurt, http://nbn-resolving.de/urn:nbn:de:0168-ssoar-395173, accessed 15 June 2020.

McLeod, Kembrew (2001). 'Genres, Subgenres, Sub-Subgenres and More: Musical and Social Differentiation Within Electronic/Dance Music Communities', *Journal of Popular Music Studies*, 13, pp. 59–75.

McLeod, Kembrew (2005). 'MP3s Are Killing Home Taping: The Rise of Internet Distribution and Its Challenge to the Major Label Music Monopoly', *Popular Music and Society*, 4, pp. 521–31.

Miessner, Benjamin F. (1936). 'Electronic Music and Instruments', *Proceedings of the Institute of Radio Engineers*, 24: 11.

Meyer-Eppler, Werner (1949). *Elektronische Klangerzeugung: Elektronische Musik und synthetische Sprache*. Bonn: Ferdinand Dümmlers.

Negus, Keith (1999). *Music Genres and Corporate Cultures*. London: Routledge.

Pezboy (1997). 'Dietrich', *Activated*, 9, pp. 6–8, https://archive.org/details/zine_activated9/page/n5/mode/2up, accessed 2 July 2020.

Project X Magazine Archive. (n.d.). http://projectxarchive.com/index.html, accessed 12 July 2020.

Rapp, Tobias (2009). *Berlin, Techno und der Easyjetset*. Berlin: Suhrkamp.

Rave Archive. (n.d.), https://archive.org/details/ravezines, accessed 12 July 2020.

Redhead, Steve (1993). *Rave Off: Politics and Deviance in Contemporary Youth Culture*. Brookfield, VT: Avebury.

Reynolds, Simon (1999). *Generation Ecstasy: Into the World of Techno and Rave Culture*. New York: Routledge.

Reynolds, Simon (2012). 'How Rave Music Conquered America', *The Guardian*, 2 August, https://www.theguardian.com/music/2012/aug/02/how-rave-music-conquered-america, accessed 10 July 2020.

Reynolds, Simon (2013). *Energy Flash: A Journey Through Rave Music and Dance Culture*. London: Faber and Faber.

Schaubruch, Josef and Nicolas Ruth (2019). 'Der beste DJ aller Zeiten?! – Meta-Rankings auf Basis von Leser*innen – Umfragen ausgewählter Musikmagazine der elektronischen Tanzmusik von 1991–2017', in E. Krisper and E. Schuck (eds), *Online-Publikationen der Gesellschaft für Popularmusikforschung/German Society for Popular Music Studies e. V.*, Jahrgang 17, www.gfpm-samples.de/Samples17/schaubruch_ruth.pdf, accessed 1 July 2020.

Sicko, Dan (1999). *Techno Rebels. The Renegades of Electronic Funk*. Detroit: Wayne State University Press.

Sisario, Ben (2012). 'Electronic Dance Concerts Turn Up Volume, Tempting Investors', *The New York Times*, 4 April, https://www.nytimes.com/2012/04/05/business/media/electronic-dance-genre-tempts-investors.html, accessed 18 July 2020.

St John, Graham (2006). 'Electronic Dance Music Culture and Religion: An Overview', *Culture and Religion*, 1, pp. 1–25.

'Techno' (n.d.), *bilgerverlag*. https://www.bilgerverlag.ch/index.php?/Buecher/Philipp-Anz-und-Patrick-Walder-Hsg.-Techno, accessed 10 July 2020.

Thornton, Sarah (1995). *Club Cultures: Music, Media, and Subcultural Capital*. Cambridge: Polity.

UEFA Euro. (2016). https://www.youtube.com/watch?v=49EhuzrRj8I, accessed 6 June 2020

Wes aka Locutus (1997). 'Letters from Our Crack Smoking Readers . . .', *Massive Magazine*, 17, pp. 4–6.

'Winners Database' (n.d.). *American Music Awards*. Available online: https://www.theamas.com/winners-database/?winnerKeyword=electronic+dance+music&winnerYear=, accessed 28 June 2020.

2

Is *électro* a French cultural exception?

Mathieu Guillien

The idea of this chapter arose from the disturbing observation that many French musicologists, including the youngest and/or those working on other genres of popular music, have not overcome the terminological approximations surrounding electronic dance music. Their use of the trendy term *électro* to catch any pulsated music incorporating electronic sounds signals an academic anomaly we would like to question.

In order to do so, we will be tracking the genealogy of this particular term as well as the establishment of the French Touch, a concept which played a significant role in maintaining house and techno in an academic grey area. It is indeed a perilous task to recount a history we are still contemporary of, yet we will undertake this task by conducting a historical analysis hopefully impervious to the urban legends the topic at hand tends to generate.

Can you dance to my beat?

As a French overture, we would like to remind our foreign readers that when it comes to popular music, French musicology often focuses its attention on linguistics and, consequently, on music genres whose lyrics can be studied.[1] The scope of this matter is too large to be summarized here, but two parameters will serve our demonstration: the symbolic importance of the French language, reflected in the concept of French cultural exception, and the sociological prevalence of many academic approaches to popular studies. When it comes to the relationship between sociopolitics and popular music, rock and rap immediately come to mind. Exogenous content notwithstanding (video clips, dress codes, interviews, etc.), their political intentions can naturally be expressed through their lyrics. Yet, one of the specifics of electronic dance music is that it usually lacks lyrics, which should therefore invite researchers to base their studies on musical parameters predominantly. This is especially true of techno, where voice is predominantly absent, but the case of house music is slightly different.

As a direct descendent of disco, house entertains an open relationship with words. Its most vocal style, garage house, which can appropriately be defined as contemporary disco and, as such, contains extensive lyrics, is precisely named after the legendary disco club Paradise Garage (New York, 1977). However, most house music productions do not follow the traditional verse-chorus song form prevalent during the disco era, and when they do contain words, those are for the most part short sentences or interjections, often sampled from pre-existing funk and disco records, and mostly looped (Sherburne 2007: 320). Needless to say, such a poetic treatment cannot convey much of a militant message, but considering the violent political reactions triggered by the advent of house and techno in Europe, one would wonder if electronic dance music, while mostly instrumental, is truly speechless and what it is that this music is saying of our societies.

This sociocultural issue is not our primary focus but, as the American disco era taught us, we must keep in mind that dance music always had a sociological impact. Or more precisely, not the music per se but its ways and means of consumption. The embodiment of disco music's insertion into American society was the disco clubs and bars which, from the late 1960s onwards, would become the sanctuaries for a recently revealed LGBTQ minority, a refuge from police violence, societal homophobia and AIDS-induced collective fear (Carter 2004: 53). This emotionally loaded background necessarily played a role in the relations between American society and disco's offspring, house and techno.

However, another parameter explains why these two genres would not find much recognition in the United States: when house and techno arise in the mid-1980s,[2] the African American audience is rapidly adopting rap and the whole hip-hop culture, rightly perceived as the new voice of a united black youth, and as the outcome of the various music genres which were the artistic escort of the civil rights movement. On the other hand, what remains of the disco culture at that point in time has become entirely remote from the African American ghetto. Following the *Saturday Night Fever* imposture[3] and the triumph of the 'disco sucks' movement, disco music is perceived either as a Wasp or as a gay cultural component, none of which can appeal to the black youth or at least not unashamedly. Therefore, when house and techno emerge in South Chicago and Downtown Detroit respectively, there is no possibility for these disco-infused, instrumental and electronic dance music genres to prevail against the powerful 'Message' of Grandmaster Flash (1982) or for them to glean more than a few negligible shares of hip-hop's massive market.

This short introduction is necessary to understand why electronic dance music did not find a considerable audience in its native country beyond the literally dying underground black and Latino gay community, and why the major part of its story would actually take place in Europe.

Nation 2 nation

House and techno found an embassy in the UK during the second half of the 1980s, particularly in Manchester and London,[4] where their acid variants would thrive, and new genres such as big beat or drum and bass soon germinate. As it took place in clubs, this first period was necessarily dependent on the legislation presiding over their administration, which at that time required them to close at 3 am[5] (Fontaine and Fontana 1996: 98). This impediment to all-night dancing would eventually lead to massive gatherings called raves, usually illegal, and a tense cat-and-mouse game with the police. Following the Criminal Justice and Public Order Act (1994) aimed at banning such events, some rave activists opted to migrate to the old continent, where techno would merge with industrial music genres such as electronic body music[6] to create excessive forms of techno such as hard techno and hardcore. Prior to this compelled migration, other European regions were embracing this new music, especially Germany, where techno would become the perfect soundtrack to the fall of the Berlin Wall, which would in turn catalyse the spread of this new genre towards Eastern Europe (Denk and Von Thülen 2014: 50).

In France, the relationship between techno and the institutions was one of successive misunderstandings. As we go into the details of these interactions, we will try to elucidate how France missed an opportunity to consider its 'French Touch', as well as its entire electronic music scene, as part of the French cultural exception, in a way similar to its supportive assimilation of other genres of popular music.

As was the case in the UK, two distinct practices were at play in the early Parisian electronic scene: raves, as early as 1989, which would eventually orient themselves towards techno and a mainly heterosexual audience, and gay clubs, the early adopters of house music. Their bond faded with time, but both milieus were closely connected, thanks to the DJs performing, the records being played and many enthusiasts enjoying both festive options. The arrival of electronic dance music in France can be summarized by observing what happened in Paris. The pivot of this encounter is Laurent Garnier, who discovered house music right when it hit Manchester in 1986. Back in France to do his compulsory military service, Garnier would ignite the Parisian house fever in gay clubs such as La Luna and Le Boy, both opened in 1988, and during the first half of the 1990s, he would transform the Rex Club into the French techno Mecca it became, from 1995 onwards.

In a proper tabloid fashion, what then transpired of electronic dance music in the mass media was predominantly focused on the raves and their excesses. For instance, in the daily newspaper *L'Humanité*, an organ of the French Communist Party, one could read that 'techno music has its rites, its leaders and its swastikas. [...] The rave trivializes drug trafficking and consumption, an essential condition for the raver, physical submission, and the excesses of musical groups which display a neo-Nazi ideology' (Jauffret 1993, our translation). Following this article, the *Oz* rave, planned on 10 July 1993 and featuring Laurent Garnier, would be abruptly cancelled by prefectural decree. Similar remarks had been made in 1989 on TF1, French main TV station, during an edition of *Ciel mon mardi* magazine dealing with 'new beat, house and acid music'. In the midst of a media coverage mostly suspicious of, if not detrimental to techno, we would like to note two exceptions. Over the Parisian airwaves, electronic dance music made a first break, thanks to Radio Maxximum (1989–92), and while various electronic music tracks or programmes sprinkled Radio Nova's time schedule, Radio FG ('Fréquence Gaie'), born in 1981 as a community radio rooted in the Parisian gay scene, eventually became the most predominant relay of electronic dance music in France, especially between 1992 and 2001 under the presidency of Henri Maurel. In the written press, the columns of Didier Lestrade, published in various left-wing semi-specialized press publications (*Le Gai Pied*, *Rolling Stone*, *Libération* and later *Têtu*), are another remarkable exception, a testament to the reality of the clubs, of the raves and especially of the music itself (Lestrade 2010).

Nonetheless, this period of mistrust would eventually lead in 1995 to the Circulaire Pasqua, named after sovereigntist home secretary Charles Pasqua. Inspired by UK's Criminal Justice bill and Public Order act passed the previous year, this memorandum provided the forces of law and order with more repressive tools to crack down on raves, described as 'high-risk situations'. In 1996, as a collective answer, and after yet another arbitrary cancellation of a techno party, this time in Lyon, the Technopol association was founded in order to defend and promote electronic dance music, as well as to provide judicial and juridical support for any individual or collective doing so.

La nouvelle vague

A new phase begins in 1997 with the release of Daft Punk's first album, *Homework*, published by Virgin. As the French musical landscape is shifting from rock and *chanson* towards rap, the success of this (mostly) house record takes its makers, the underground scene and the politics by surprise. Concomitant to this breakthrough, several cultural indicators illustrate the extent of the shift crowned by *Homework*'s release. On 22 October 1996, TV station Arte had scheduled a *Thema* night dedicated to techno, during which *Universal Techno*, Dominique Deluze's key documentary, was broadcasted. On 17 January 1998, *Télérama* magazine published an issue called 'La Déferlante techno' (the techno landslide), relating a study conducted by Guillaume Bara (1998). In his investigation, Bara already identifies an 'ideological and musical turnaround' and provides a few key numbers to support his position: at that date *Homework* has already sold one million copies worldwide (of which 30 per cent in France); between 1996 and 1997, Bara notes a 325 per cent increase (from 2 to 6.5 per cent) in the share of electronic music on the shelves of the major French record dealer, Fnac, and a 150 per cent increase in vinyl sales in France, from 120,000 to 295,000 units.[7] On 20 February 1998, Laurent Garnier would win the Victoire de la Musique[8] for his album *30*, in the dance category, created for the occasion. Other elements could be added to this list, which would not be complete without mentioning the first official Techno Parade, promoted by former secretary of state for Culture Jack Lang, which on 19 September 1998 gathered 200,000 people, when the first unofficial edition had gathered 400 people the previous year.

The year 1998 thereby witnessed a merging of various interests towards the recognition of techno. As the economic potential of the French (electronic) Touch was unveiling itself, mass media had to get on board, keen to reveal that this new electronic scene was rich of 'unidentified sonic objects, not so remote from a certain contemporary classical music' (Loupias 1998). Yet one can still wonder about the French government's decision to also seize upon this new trend.

Figure 2.1 *Télérama*.

The concept of 'cultural exception', which so frequently looms in French political debates, is at the cross section of international law and cultural policy. Its main goal is to implement various measures to give culture a specific status in international treaties, especially those overseen by the World Trade Organization. We will summarize this complex topic by pointing out that these measures allow states to limit free-trade mechanics when it comes to culture and creation, to help them defend and promote their national artists. As the United States would, from the 1960s onwards, manoeuvre to bypass these restrictions, European countries envisioned three clauses to protect their respective cultures: exemption, exception and specificity, and while the European Parliament would lean towards cultural specificity, the French government strongly oriented itself towards cultural exception (Fabre 2013). Since January 1990, the Tasca decrees offer two types of quotas to protect cinematographic and audio-visual creations: production quotas, which require television channels to invest 3.2 per cent of their annual turnover in the production of French and European works (2.5 per cent of which must be allocated to francophone creations), and broadcast quotas, which require channels to devote 60 per cent of their airtime to European productions, of which 40 per cent must be francophone. Passed in February 1994 and applicable as of January 1996, an additional law championed by secretary of state for Culture Jacques Toubon requires French radio stations to respect quotas applied to the broadcast of francophone songs. This law sets a 40 per cent programming rate of works performed or produced by francophone musicians, of which 20 per cent must be new talents, during major listening hours.

This legal glimpse helps us grasp the frame of the French culture industry's mind which, unable to contain its Americanization, turned to politics and conveyed its sense of urgency.[9] But as French philosopher Raymond Ruyer had written more than two decades before,

> a culture established, protected, subsidized, organized in church or chapel, living at the expense of the public, is likely to be a false culture. [. . .] True culture, true sport, true art as true religion, is more truly democratic. It is more truly and more spontaneously demanded. It does not go from top to bottom, to the people, from mysterious arcana inhabited by high priests. (1969: 152, our translation)

In such a context of economic and cultural anxiety, the new electronic dance music coming from Paris during the second half of the 1990s embodied an unexpected hope, and while politics were not able to do much more than put French music on a drip, a renewal was finally happening, ready to be championed. Up until then, French house music, barely established, was far from being protected or subsidized, and if it was somewhat organized in stylistic chapels, more or less intertwined, it was lived by the public and at the expense of the state. We could further proceed from Ruyer's definition to even claim that French house music was a true culture. But instead of being slowly integrated to the French cultural fabric, like rock or rap before it, this music received a specific treatment we will now consider.

We give a French touch to house

From the (gay) house clubs and the (straight) techno raves to a mass hype, one can view this turnaround as both a cultural shift and a media appropriation.

Figure 2.2 French Touch flyer.

The best hint of the role played by the media in the matter is the use of a new expression, 'French Touch', to promote the new electronic dance music mostly produced in Paris.

Two important historical usages of this locution must be recalled. The first one, already associated with house music, happened in June 1987 when Jean-Claude Lagrèze, a photographer of *Parisian Nights*, promoted a couple of French Touch parties at club Le Palace where some happy few would discover house music. Another significant occurrence took place in 1991 when Fnac Music Dance Division, the first French label of significant proportion devoted to electronic dance music, had promotional jackets printed on their backs with the slogan 'We Give a French touch to house'. But before its diffusion through French mass media, the actual advent of the term 'French Touch', applied to the new French electronic scene, happened in 1996 and was due to British music journalist Martin James.

In the process of clarifying this fact, which has been relayed numerous times by hearsay and *readsay*, Martin James told us:

> As for my French Touch quote . . . it has been attributed to my review of the first *Super Discount*[10] in *Melody Maker*. This came from a journalist at *Libération* at the time and was repeated by a Parisian dance magazine. [. . .] However, I

suspect my use of the term comes earlier on in *Generator* or *Muzak* mag. In my book I try to distance myself from the term, but it has taken on a life of its own. [...] As an outsider I felt like the success of French electronic music abroad was used as a motif for French national cultural regeneration. The use of the phrase was key to this and it also became important to attribute that phrase to a foreign critic as that would underscore the internationalisation of new French culture. This mirrored many aspects of the way 'Brit Pop' was used for political gain by the Labour Party in the UK. Part of the approach to cultural regeneration was myth making – which I think is where French Music Bureau[11] in London become important as they fanned the flames of myth to support French music exports. An interesting thing for me is that I had one of those Fnac jackets and I'd totally forgotten about it until reading your email. [...] It's very likely I was channelling this subconscious memory when I used the term. [...] The French Touch as it became mythologised referred to the global success of a small section of artists during a clearly defined period. The mediation of this period was partly achieved via 'French Touch' as a generic term. This was later than Fnac and to some extent post-Daft Punk. Might be useful to view it as the period post-*Homework* to Justice. It is very likely that French Touch has retrospectively different cultural meanings now.[12]

Thanks to his unique position on the subject, tempered by his geographical perspective, Martin James is able to pinpoint the essential mechanism here at work: mythologization. He recalls that he 'was also invited by the French Ambassador to London for a Bastille day event [in 2002] where [he] was called "the journalist who discovered French Touch"'. This is in no way anecdotal, as other politico-cultural manoeuvres can be correlated. On 17 February 2005, Air, Philippe Zdar and Dimitri from Paris would be knighted of the national Order of Arts and Letters. On 6 July 2017, when a dispatch from the Agence France Press informed of the death of Pierre Henry, the late composer, 'sometimes considered as the grandfather of techno', would be presented as 'one of the fathers of the electroacoustic music which inspired the electro movement'. We will not discuss the inanity of statements made outside of any musicological context but only point that these would be relayed as such by all the French media,[13] some adding their touch to the myth by stating that Henry was the 'great instigator of techno music'[14] and that 'without Pierre Henry, no Daft Punk'.[15] Worst yet, and most revealing, Laurent Bayle, general director of the Cité de la Musique and president of Philharmonie de Paris, proclaimed that 'today, there is not a great artist of electro music, from Garnier to all the new generations, who could say that Pierre Henry is not his tutelary figure'.[16] Let us note the incorrect use of 'electro' and clarify that in his memoirs, Laurent Garnier makes a single reference to Pierre Henry, citing him among the attendees of his first live show at L'Olympia in 1998 (Garnier 2003: 250). The road to hell is paved with good intentions and by blessing and absolving French electronic popular music of its sulphurous past by associating Pierre Henry's name to it, Bayle reinforced an artificial lineage still enduring. It should be obvious that the similarity between Pierre Schaeffer's locked groove and the techno loop is a temptation academics must resist, as it draws a line between journalism and musicology. Such attempts at legitimizing a music which may very well not require to be only makes it harder to apprehend it for what it actually is: house and techno are the heirs of an Afro-American musical tradition, to which Pierre Henry does not belong.

Evidence of its widespread and lasting usage, we will close this section by observing that nowadays, 'French Touch' is a term which can be applied to any French success abroad, from other arts to economics, groceries or social sciences,[17] without any musical remanence. However, what will be of interest to us is to consider the stylistic discrepancies of the first musicians gathered under the 'French Touch' moniker. To do so, we will observe the artists listed by Guillaume Bara in his article cited earlier and which, quite significantly, does not contain the term 'French Touch': 'the heroes of this ideological and musical turnaround are called Daft Punk, Laurent Garnier, Motorbass, Dimitri From Paris or even Air' (1998).

Daft Punk and Motorbass share many interesting similarities. As artists usually reproduce before innovating, the first compositions of these two duos are deeply marked by their discovery of electronic dance music through rave parties. With an average tempo of 137 bpm, Daft Punk's first record, *The New Wave*[18] (1994), thus oscillates between techno and the acid variant of the genre. From this first EP, only the slowest track, *Alive* (129 bpm), would later be included on *Homework*, contrary to their following EPs, which evolve towards house and would all be compiled into the album whose average tempo is 123 bpm. The same mechanism applies to *Pansoul* (1996, 105 bpm), Motorbass' first house and deep house album, which compiles their previous EPs except for their aptly titled *1st EP* (1993), which had an average tempo of 131 bpm and ranged from house and techno to the acid variants of both genres. We want to stress the fact that tempi alone do not allow to distinguish techno from house, but as far as evolution is strictly concerned, they are a pertinent estimation of the tendency occurring from Daft Punk and Motorbass' first EPs to their first CD albums.

Indeed, they clarify the artists' intent when selecting tracks to appear on CDs which are intrinsically aimed at a larger audience than vinyl records.

Next on Guillaume Bara's list is Laurent Garnier, who discovered electronic dance music, thanks to the Chicago house hit 'Love Can't Turn Around'[19] (1986, 122 bpm). Yet, between 1991 and 1993, Garnier released six EPs predominantly comprising techno tracks, for an average tempo of 132 bpm.[20] The case of Dimitri from Paris is distinctive as well, as his first album *Sacrebleu* (1996, 87 bpm) gave prominence to slow-paced, easy listening tracks. Finally, Air is prudently added by Bara at the end of his list, knowing that none of their productions ever fell under house or techno but actually under ambient and downtempo. *Premiers Symptômes* (1997), which compiles Air's first two EPs, has an average tempo of 82 bpm, and the duo would progress towards the composition of electropop songs, as illustrated on their first album, *Moon Safari* (1997, 92 bpm).

Figure 2.3 Art of France. The *Art of France* compilation released in 1996, ranging from house and deep house to techno, trance and hardcore, and Erik Satie's first *Gymnopédie*.

A provisional conclusion is that the first inception of this early 'French Touch' had no stylistic consistency and in 2007, French duo Justice would still state that 'the French Touch is not a musical family. In fact, this expression refers to the French bands that export abroad' (Pliskin 2018, our translation). However, what remains of this overview is that by the end of the 1990s, the French general public was accustomed to the use of a generic term to encompass various styles of electronic music. Anyone familiar with the French electronic scene of the 1990s would certainly think of many names omitted by Bara, if only those of Cassius (1996) and Etienne de Crécy's Super Discount project (1996), which were both paving the stylistic way for the 'post-*Homework* to Justice' period identified by Martin James.

Indeed, during that period the aesthetic spectrum of the French Touch got reduced to, and defined as, a house style profusely enriched with disco and funk influences, thanks to the continuous work of Parisian[21] labels such as Fiat Lux (1997), Serial Records (1997), Poumtchak (1997), Pro-Zak Trax (1994) or Yellow Productions (1993). At a lexical level, these influences can be tracked in track titles,[22] as well as artists' aliases such as Erik Rug's Daphreephunkateerz (1996), Dimitri from Paris' Da Mothaphunkin' Phrog (1995) and Disco D (1997) or, most notably, La Funk Mob, the first collaborative entity of Hubert 'Boom Bass' Blanc-Francard and Philippe 'Zdar' Cerboneschi, before the advent of Cassius. Interestingly enough, other examples – Jean-Jérome Dupuy's alias Kut N' Paste, Paris Angeles's *Filter De Luxe* (1997), DJ Bertrand's *Fuckin' Filter* (1998), De Pompidou's *La Boucle* (the loop, 1997) – make references to the basics of house music production and to the analogue filters frequently used at the time, and part of the French house sound.

The sociological proximity of many actors of the French electronic scene is also worth mentioning here, as Air, Etienne de Crécy and Alex Gopher attended the same high school in Versailles. We will not consider the prejudices induced by such an upbringing, which a sociological exploration may in part confirm, but this quote from Etienne de Crécy provides a revealing perspective on house music production, which we may consider common in the Parisian scene: ' a sequencer, a sampler, turntables, a few good records. . . . Making house is like Fisher Price! In a few weeks, you get it and can make your first tracks' (Bara 1998). In other words, de Crécy describes here a recreational modus operandi based on the use of samples, extracted from 'good records'. Indeed, if we study the music itself, the influences received by Parisian house producers are accurately tracked through the samples incorporated in their compositions, of which we will only provide a short list, limited to funk and disco samples included on albums previously mentioned.

On *Pansoul*, Motorbass samples the Honey Drippers (*Flying Fingers*) and Diana Ross (*Ezio*). Daft Punk's *Homework* includes samples from the Bar-Kays (*Burnin'*), Vaughan Mason (*Da Funk*, *Daftendirekt* and *WDPK 83.7 FM*), Barry White (*Da Funk*), Viola Wills (*Fresh* and *Teachers*) and Karen Young (*Indo Silver Club*). Dimitri from Paris' *Sacrebleu* borrows samples from Gwen Guthrie remixed by Larry Levan (*Dirty Larry*), MFSB and Young & Company (*Free ton Style*), Isaac Hayes, Kool & the Gang and Sly & the Family Stone (*Encore Un Terlude*) and Young-Holt Unlimited (*Un Terlude*). Last but not least, on Etienne de Crécy's *Super Discount* collective album, samples are borrowed from Chic (*Tout Doit Disparaître*), Earth, Wind & Fire and Isaac Hayes (*Le Patron Est Devenu Fou*), Herbie Hancock, Indeep and Donna Summer (*Super Disco*), MFSB and Bernard Wright (*Lil' Fuck*), Nu-Sound Express, Ltd. (*Prix Choc*), Teddy Pendergrass (*Eurovision*), Rufus & Chaka Khan (*Out of My Hands*).

It is a fact that house music's growth was facilitated by the democratization of the sampler and that by using it even so profusely, French house musicians were only perpetuating an almost traditional modus operandi. Yet it is significant that despite being a simplified recreation of Mach's *On & On* (1980), a disco medley containing tracks from Lipps Inc., Munich Machine, Playback and Donna Summer, Jesse Saunders's *On & On* (1984), which we referenced earlier as the first Chicago house record, does not actually sample the original record. Numerous examples could be provided to prove that sampling, while more frequently used in house than techno, was never systematic and often depended on pragmatic variables such as an artist's capabilities as an instrumentalist. On the other hand, numerous other instances would confirm the more systematic use of samples in the Parisian house scene, and this is a fecund angle of approach to grasp the reality of the French Touch when precisely considered as a French style of house music.

With its use of samples and filters, *Homework* can therefore be considered as a justifiable – albeit slightly late – start to the French Touch, but can we also accept Justice as its conclusion, as previously implied by Martin James? Predictably, the success of the French Touch induced the ambition to reach an even larger audience. By extension, such success led to the internationalization of the French house musicians, illustrated by the number of remixes ordered from French producers by foreign artists and their labels. An early example is Björk's *Isobel* (1995), remixed on a single release by Motorbass (*Transfunk Mix*), Ludovic

Navarre and Shazz, and Dimitri from Paris (with one of his remixes titled 'Hi Compact French Touch'). In turn, this new-found recognition materialized in a more frequent and simultaneous use of the verse-chorus song form *and* the use of lyrics. French house became a new disguise of French pop, with successful house songs such as Bob Sinclar's 'My Only Love' (1998), Stardust's 'Music Sounds Better with You' (1998), Superfunk's 'Lucky Star' (1999) or Phoenix's 'If I Ever Feel Better' (2000). We suggest that this switch of the French house from funky loops towards proper songs would eventually be finalized by David Guetta.

Pop life

We will consider that Guetta's production career truly starts in 2001 with his first single released on Virgin. Indeed, his first EP (*Nation Rap*, 1990) only showcases Guetta's hip-hop DJ techniques, but as his second one (*Up & Away*, 1994) is already a house song and features an American singer, it can retrospectively be envisioned as significant. One should nonetheless wonder about this particularly long gap in his production, between 1994 and 2001, and consider its relevance: from the mid-1980s onwards, Guetta was developing an extensive experience of the nightclubbing market as a DJ, club manager and party promoter at various Parisian clubs (Bains Douches, Bataclan, Broad, Folies Pigalle, Palace, Pink Paradise, Queen, Rex Club). We can only assume that this entrepreneurial knowledge of the dance music scene played a significant part in his success to come.

Guetta's triumph, which would require a specific study to be fully understood, can be superficially explained with a few generic parameters. From the outset, an overwhelming majority of Guetta's tracks are songs, usually performed by American singers. From 2009 onwards, we must note that the fame of the featured singers, ranging from all genres of pop, rap and contemporary R&B,[23] is incommensurate with Guetta's earlier collaborations and could only exacerbate his media exposure. Another factor of this success is the peculiar uniformity of Guetta's productions, as his first six albums maintain very similar forms as illustrated by the average tempo (126 bpm) and duration (3:56) of their tracks.[24] Notwithstanding his knowledge of the public's expectations mentioned earlier, this formatting could be examined in relation to his contracts with Virgin (publisher of his first five albums) and then Warner through Parlophone (publisher of his last two albums). Like *Nothing But the Beat* and *Nothing But the Beat 2.0*, his last album *7* (2018) comes in two separate CDs, the first being the vocal album and the second an instrumental one, which we can assume is aimed at clubs rather than radios. This distinction is all the more evident that the vocal part of the album has an average tempo of 108 bpm and an average duration of 3:29 minutes, the lowest values measured among all Guetta's albums. This evolution partly calls Daft Punk's *Random Access Memories* (2013) to mind, which marked a clear shift from the duo towards slower, proper albeit longer pop/disco songs.[25] We will close the point noting that by featuring famous American singers, Daft Punk's album, licensed to Columbia Records, adopted a similar approach to David Guetta's and that Pharrell Williams, instrumental to the success of *Random Access Memories*, was already featured on Cassius's album *15 Again* (2006), their third album to be licensed to Virgin, as the duo also chose to adopt a song format during the 2000s.

We can therefore consider that the conversion of French house, from combined loops into fully fledged songs, was a collective effort, conducted by veteran musicians. However, David Guetta's specificity lies in him championing a euro dance renewal, later baptized as 'electro house' and celebrated in the United States as electronic dance music, to which other French electronic musicians must only be carefully associated, on a case-by-case and track-by-track basis. Nonetheless, in the French midst of this massively successful evolution, Justice (2003) confirms the advent of a new era: while Daft Punk or Motorbass first composed rave music, Justice would bring from the outset their own rock sensitivity to a format otherwise similar to Daft Punk's *Discovery* (2001) or Cassius's *Au Rêve* (2002). While we can therefore admit Justice as the breakup of the traditional French Touch (understood as French house), it is essential to consider that the duo was most importantly the key operator of a play orchestrated by their label, Ed Banger, managed by Pierre 'Pedro' Winter (Daft Punk's former manager), and whose catalogue would eventually include releases by the likes of Cassius or Mr Oizo (launched by Laurent Garnier's F-Communications label in 1997).

Electrology

This stylistic change and expected widening of electronic music's French audience was accompanied by a semantic shift that we will now try to identify. In the early 2000s, as Henri Maurel steps down from its presidency, Radio FG gradually distances itself from its former audience by adopting a new popular format centred around dance-pop. As Justice releases their first album on Warner, 2007 sees the launch of a new French magazine dedicated to electronic popular music (*Tsugi*), and as electronic dance music becomes more and more successful, new Parisian clubs are created to broadcast it such as the Showcase (2006), the Social Club (2008), La Machine du Moulin Rouge (2010) or Concrete (2011).

During the 1990s, the word 'techno' cleaved society: it either served as a biased deterrent or as a rallying banner. Following the respite brought by *Homework*, French media and various techno actors switched to the soon established expression of *musiques électroniques* (electronic musics), supposedly to reflect the variety of electronic music's genres and styles which 'techno' was insufficient to reflect. Then, as electronic dance music in France went from ostracization to incorporation, an informal consensus occurred over the 2000s, in the form of a new habit born of a natural linguistic evolution: *musiques électroniques* became *électro*, an abbreviation fitting most usages. The media, the industry and the public could all thereby comfortably refer to any popular music relying on the use of electronic instruments. From 1989 onwards, we want to underline that during the three decades considered in this chapter, there was only a very short window during which one could speak of 'techno' in France in a relatively objective context, which is probably why the Techno Parade is not called the Electro Parade. We would situate this window between the release of Daft Punk's *Homework* and the early 2000s, for instance the publication in 2002 of Ariel Kyrou's *Techno Rebelle*, an important francophone work, subtitled *Un siècle de musiques électroniques*.

This impractical use of the word 'techno' leads us to, and explains to a great extent, the lack of interest of the French academics regarding the genre. A background issue is that for several years, only sociology deemed techno worthy of interest, yet only considering the dystopian and/or Dionysian dimension of the rave without attempting (or being able) to provide much details about the music itself. In a 2006 essay, Morgan Jouvenet still wrote that 'the musicological temptation turns out to be sterile: if it allows to objectify the sound structures characteristic of a genre, musicological research seems to have little to say when confronted with rap and electronic musics (other than to reveal their musical "poverty", according to an opinion made famous by Pierre Boulez)' (2006: 17). These works would undoubtedly play an important role if the research landscape on electronic dance music expanded further than the sociological field, but as it did not, they represented until recently the full extent of the French academic discourse on the subject. Sociology had made up its mind and thus the mind of all academics: electronic dance music was to be understood as a cultural phenomenon wherein the music was not the primary focus, almost as if the phenomenon was interesting *despite* its lack of musical interest, *despite* being driven by house and techno. From a musicological point of view, the content of most sociological works about techno was therefore no more useful than the mass media treatment of the topic. Furthermore, if sociology never called for its research about techno to be complemented by musicology, neither were the massive cultural impact of *Homework* or the advent of the Techno Parade understood by French musicology as signals that it was time to finally address the subject.

To comprehend this situation, a first trail leads quite simply to the libellous attacks of the 1990s, which had to leave some prejudice in the collective imagination of the French population, including that of its researchers. Another explanation, which is so vast that we can only introduce it, leads us beyond the strict case of techno and to the persistent dichotomy between popular/danceable and academic music, and consequently to the way music has been conceived and perceived by French avant-gardism since Pierre Boulez. We will avoid this debate by simply recalling that four years after its creation in 1974 at the request of President Pompidou, 'the IRCAM by itself collected 40% of the total budget of grants for contemporary music, and the Ensemble Intercontemporain 30%' (Merlin 2019: 324, our translation[26]). In other words, 70 per cent of this budget passed between the hands of an individual who would later state that techno was 'a music which could have been adopted by Hitler' (Grynszpan 1997). If we admit that the public of contemporary classical music is often composed of academics, it ensues that from 1974 onwards, this very audience remained exposed to an ideology prone to feed said dichotomy. This shortcoming of the French academic realm is still manifest today, where a musicological gap exists between a few thorough works on the one hand and the predominant usage of *électro* on the other, which we will now address.

This is electro

One could argue that when sociologists use 'jazz' or 'rock' to refer to a myriad of musicians of multiple aesthetics, other academics collectively acknowledge the efficiency of such synoptic designations, which exempt non-specialists from clarifying particularities irrelevant to their demonstration. But the damaging particularity of the term *électro* is to create a diachrony which in itself prevents its users from learning more about electronic popular music. Indeed, in a musicological context, 'electro' is not to be understood as the short form of 'electronic music' but as the historic apocope of electrofunk or eletropop, two specific styles of electronic music born in the late 1970s and early 1980s, easily defined by their elemental syncopated drum pattern[27] and, as their names imply, their combination of pop structures and funk motifs with electronic sounds. One could assert that electrofunk and electropop are at the roots of techno, but this statement needs to be clarified, as the myth crediting George Clinton and Kraftwerk for the birth of techno has severe limitations. A first precaution is to not overlook Detroit's rich disco heritage, from Motown to local DJs such as Ken Collier or Delano Smith, who catalysed a transition from disco to house entirely comparable to the one carried out by Larry Levan in New York or Frankie Knuckles in Chicago. Derrick May, who we will later credit as the composer of the first proper techno track in 1986, was particularly exposed to house music, thanks to regular trips from Detroit to Chicago to visit his mother. Kevin Saunderson also plays an important part in this matter, since he grew up in New York and made summer trips back to Brooklyn all through high school, and attended the Loft and the Paradise Garage, which in turn explains why he produced house and garage house as well as techno (Brewster and Broughton 1999: 350).

Another shortcoming is best explained by Dan Sicko:

> Many historical reconstructions of techno's past name Kraftwerk and funk music as the sole influences on early techno. Perhaps it was this quote from techno pioneer Derrick May that set the precedent for this connection: 'The music [techno] is just like Detroit – a complete mistake. It's like George Clinton and Kraftwerk stuck in an elevator.' If only May could collect royalties on this soundbite! Intended as an off-the-cuff remark, it was quickly snapped up by the European press and has been used as a textbook definition for techno ever since. (1999: 26–7)

Indeed, in a narrative polished by countless interviews, the techno pioneers tell the tale of an electronic epiphany delivered by the Midnight Funk Association, a Detroit radio programme hosted from 1977 by Charles 'The Electrifying Mojo' Johnson. While insisting on the eclecticism of the show, musicians such as Juan Atkins, Eddie Fowlkes, Derrick May or Kevin Saunderson all consider the discovery of Kraftwerk as a pivotal influence. However, from a musicological perspective, the stylistic connection between Detroit techno and the German band only comes down to Juan Atkins's early productions within his duo Cybotron. From

Alleys of Your Mind (1981) to *R-9* (1985), Cybotron's electro music does borrow from George Clinton's (and Herbie Hancock's) electrofunk and Kraftwerk's (and Ryuichi Sakamoto's) electropop, even before the advent of Afrika Bambaataa's *Planet Rock* (1982).[28] It is therefore important to distinguish between the decisive role played by Juan Atkins, who propelled other techno pioneers' careers by collaborating on their respective first records in 1986,[29] and the fact that none of his protégés would produce electro records. In its musicological acceptation, techno thus appears, thanks to an untitled track composed by Derrick May and released in 1986 on the B-side of X-Ray's *Let's Go*.[30] Electro is therefore at the roots of techno because Juan Atkins is quite literally the godfather of the latter, yet it is only around 1991 that other Detroit musicians, first of all Mike Banks,[31] would pick up the electro torch and revive a local tradition.[32]

When electronic instruments infiltrated popular music, the prefix 'electro-' was added to funk and pop and a natural linguistic development led to the use of said prefix as a standalone. Thus, by the early 1980s, 'electro' referred to electrofunk or electropop. But precisely because this usage predates by more than fifteen years the French linguistic reduction from *musiques électroniques* to *électro* detailed earlier, should the former not retain some kind of academic prevalence over its contemporary misuse? How can a situation where such a pivotal term as *électro* has two different meanings be intellectually satisfying? Electro, in its historical acceptation of electrofunk, is not synonymous but only part of electronic music, of which the many subgenres do not all share the same

Figure 2.4 Drexciya. Taken from a 1995 release by Detroit's seminal duo Drexciya, *Hydro Theory* is an archetypal definition of contemporary electro. Image courtesy of WARP.

audiences, the same distribution networks, the same venues nor, of course, the same histories and musical features. As it happens, the situation is all the more problematic that electro is very much alive, as techno composers often produce electro as well. Therefore, by using *électro* instead of essential terms such as 'techno', 'house', 'drum'n'bass' and the likes, French musicology does not play its role in unravelling a confusion which the mass media and the music industry have no interest in clarifying.

This semantic confusion is not a French specificity. Even in Germany, where electronic music always had a much sounder cultural recognition, one of the most prominent electro producers, Anthony Rother, felt the need to release a compilation of his work under the title *Das ist Elektro*, as early as 2005. When misusing the term *électro*, what is therefore at stake is a complete overlook of an essential part of the origins of techno and of the entire contemporary electronic creation, while musicologists working on electronic popular music all have to systematically squander some precious research time to summarize, clarify and contextualize the points addressed in this chapter. Beyond France and musicology, an even more regrettable consequence of such terminological approximations is not only academic but deeply cultural. In the United States, while brilliant insights about house and techno keep arising from African American cultural studies,[33] electronic dance music, locally aggregated as EDM, can only be perceived by the general public as a White European genre, to the distressing displeasure of its African American creators: in 2013, the top forty entries of Billboard's Hot Dance/Electronic songs chart included thirty-four songs produced by white musicians.[34]

The music promoted as EDM in the United States is precisely the same as what European charts refer to as 'electro', or more recently as 'electro house', a particularly unsound appellation, as if house had become electronic at some point during its evolution. In reality, this style is easy to define: a functional dance music following the verse-chorus form,[35] all too similar to what has been known as (euro) dance, or euro house, for more than thirty years. The number of releases per decades, classified under these three designations, demonstrates that these interchangeable labels are indeed communicating vessels:[36]

	1980s	1990s	2000s	2010s
Euro dance	172	13,706	6,055	4,758
Euro house	3,560	97,138	40,374	11,457
Electro house	41	845	8,071	41,589

It was therefore predictable that on 22 October 2018, in a report about David Guetta, American television channel ABC would call him the 'Grandfather of Electronic Dance Music' and praise him for 'bringing house music back to America'.[37] All things carefully considered, such an appealing lineage was not so remote from Bayle's commemoration of Pierre Henry, and somewhat reminiscent of the release in 1917 of the 'first' jazz record, by the white Original Dixieland Jass Band.

Transcending toxic times

We believe that such an anecdote is everything but anecdotal, and while we wouldn't dare suggest that musicological imprecision could ever aim at any form of revisionism, some topics are no more but not less racially loaded than the initial bias they lie on. To prevent such harmful misinterpretations and misrepresentations, the usage of a more precise musicological terminology is sorely needed, in order to induce a more proper stylistic analysis of electronic dance music and its genres. Otherwise, in France and beyond, the only specificity of electronic music will remain one of organized success and semantic vagueness, both obscuring its cultural meaning and academic interest.

The contemporaneity of our topic means that electronic music styles are evolving as we are writing or reading this very chapter. But they are evolving from genres which can now be approached from a thirty years old perspective. Following the example of Mark J. Butler (2006), our hope is that by clarifying the history of house and techno, musicological parameters such as rhythm, harmony, form and above all *sound* can be fully explored, so that researchers can classify new stylistic iterations as well as efficiently chart the many continuities and discrepancies at play in most genres of electronic popular music, which are yet to receive our collective musicological attention.

References

Bara, Guillaume (1998). 'Techno, au-delà des raves', *Télérama*, 2505, 17 January.
Brewster, Bill and Frank Broughton (1999). *Last Night a DJ Saved My Life*. London: Headline.
Butler, Mark J. (2006). *Unlocking the Groove: Rhythm, Meter, and Musical Design in Electronic Dance Music*. Bloomington: Indiana University Press.

Carter, David (2004). *Stonewall: The Riots That Sparked the Gay Revolution*. New York: St. Martin's Press.

Denk, Felix and Sven von Thülen (2014). *Der Klang der Familie: Berlin, Techno and the Fall of the Wall*. Norderstedt: Books On Demand.

Fabre, Clarisse (2013). 'Histoire d'une exception', *Le Monde*, 27 June.

Fontaine, Caroline and Astrid Fontana (1996). *Raver*. Paris: Anthropos.

Garnier, Laurent (2003). *Electrochoc*. Paris: Flammarion.

Grynszpan, Emmanuel (1997). 'Confluences et divergences : La Techno face aux musiques savantes', *Synesthésie n°11 : Hétérophonies*, www.synesthesie.com/heterophonies/theories/grynszpanconfluences.html, accessed 3 December 2019.

Jauffret, Magali (1993). 'Le phénomène rave, mélange de solitude et de drogue', *L'Humanité*, 15 June.

Jouvenet, Morgan (2006). *Rap, techno, électro*. Paris: Éditions de la Maison des sciences de l'homme.

Kyrou, Ariel (2002). *Techno Rebelle: Un siècle de musiques électroniques*. Paris: Denoël.

Lestrade, Didier (2010). *Chroniques du dancefloor*. Paris: L'éditeur singulier.

Loupias, Bernard (1998). 'Techno: la Déferlante', *Le Nouvel Observateur*, 17 September.

Merlin, Christian (2019). *Pierre Boulez*. Paris: Fayard.

Pliskin, Fabrice (2018). 'Justice en Amérique', *L'Obs*, 2813, 4 October.

Ruyer, Raymond (1969). *Éloge de la société de consommation*. Paris: Calmann-Lévy.

Sherburne, Philip (2007). 'Digital Discipline: Minimalism in House and Techno', in Christopher Cox and Daniel Warner (eds), *Audio Culture: Readings in Modern Music*. New York: Continuum.

Sicko, Dan (1999). *Techno Rebels: The Renegades of Electronic Funk*. New York: Billboard Books.

3

UK sampling practice

Past, present and future

Justin Morey

Using qualitative data from semi-structured interviews with a range of UK practitioners, this chapter considers both the development and impact of sampling as a creative practice within UK electronic dance music (EDM). Firstly, the importance of recorded technical DJ mixes in the development of UK sampling practice is evaluated in terms of the influence of the techniques used in their construction; that is to say, on the production and compositional approach of British creators of sample-based EDM (hereafter sampling composers). The establishment of UK sampling practice in the late 1980s and early 1990s is then considered in terms of its distinctiveness, in particular in comparison to US hip-hop sampling practice, as are the ways in which UK sampling composers' use of samples contributed to a proliferation of significant UK electronic dance genres in the 1990s. The value of affordances and constraints, particularly in regard to the limitations of early sampling technology, is discussed, and scarcity, in relation to tools, resources and expertise, is argued to have been instrumental in contributing to the diversity of UK sample-based music in its formative years. Finally, the challenges facing contemporary sampling composers are viewed in relation to those of their forebears, and the future relevance of UK sampling practice is contemplated.

Theoretical perspective and methodological approach

Central to this chapter's theoretical perspective is the work of Pierre Bourdieu on cultural production, particularly his concepts of *the space of possibles*, *habitus*, *illusio* and forms of capital in a cultural setting, and Mihalyi Csikszentmihalyi's systems model of creativity, both of which seek to move away from a Romantic view of creativity to one which takes into account the range of actors, influences and ideas that need to be negotiated both for a cultural producer to develop their art and craft and for creative creativity, or creative practice, to occur (Bourdieu 1990, 1993; Csikszentmihalyi 1988, 1999). Art, or cultural production, much like any other enterprise, takes place within a framework of rules overseen by cultural gatekeepers, and the agent, artist or creative individual does not only have to have a deep interest in and awareness of a particular framework, domain or symbol system in order to make a meaningful contribution to it but also requires the necessary social skills, both to obtain cooperation from fellow participants with complementary skills and to create interest among the cultural gatekeepers who will need to recognize, acknowledge and validate his or her contribution, which will have to be both sufficiently novel to be worthy of inclusion and familiar enough to be acceptable. Csikszentmihalyi, with his systems model of creativity, describes this as the interaction between the *individual* (or person) with their own personal background and development, the *domain* or particular area of cultural production and the field or cultural gatekeepers (1988: 325–8; 1999: 315–17). In the context of EDM, these gatekeepers would include fellow professional artists, producers and DJs, live event promoters, record label owners and A&R, and journalists and other taste makers. Akin to Csikszentmihalyi's *domain* is Bourdieu's concept of a 'field of cultural production', and his description of it as a 'space of possibles' in comparison to a game or sport indicates that successful participants with need to have the necessary interest in and determination (or *illusio*) to develop a sufficiently deep understanding of the existing rules to create their own acceptable but novel moves or responses, and in so doing, develop the 'habitus' or 'acquired system of generative schemes' necessary to become a creative participant (Bourdieu 1990: 66; 1993: 53–66, 176–83). Both Burnard and McIntyre have discussed musical creativity in terms of a synthesis of the ideas of Bourdieu and Csikszentmihalyi (Burnard 2012; McIntrye 2012), and I am more persuaded by McIntyre's view that these are complimentary approaches, but with some notable differences, than by Burnard's attempts to combine the work of both into one complex model (Burnard 2012: 223): Bourdieu's world view is informed by historical materialism and fundamental inequality in terms of the capital (actual, social, cultural) available to participants in cultural production; Csikszentmihalyi's systems model of creativity is essentially Darwinistic and optimistic – good and novel ideas enter the domain because of their value. One criticism of Csikszentmihalyi's model (Pope 2005: 67–70) is the implication of 'individual' as a single creative entity given the importance of collaborative activity in producing cultural novelty. Susan Kerrigan's revised version of the model to incorporate creative practice is therefore helpful in this regard; by changing 'individual' to 'agent' the model can represent one or more individuals exerting a creative influence, or as she puts it, 'to indicate either personal or group agency' while amending 'personal background' to 'idiosyncratic background' allows for either a singular or multiple backgrounds to be introduced into the system (Kerrigan 2013: 124).

One of the key interests in this research was to get a sense of how sampling practice in electronic music developed in the UK, and how and why this may have been distinct from elsewhere. In terms of the theoretical perspective discussed earlier, how did wider cultural influences have an effect on the domain of UK electronic music, and how did particular approaches and practices established by pioneers exert an influence on the rules of the game or *space of possibles* for those that followed? As a result, the majority of the interviewees are in a fairly tight age range because they needed to be old enough either to be actively making music close to the starting point of the study (1987) or for the early years of the study to be a period of formative musical influence, rather than recent history discovered at second-hand through documentaries and compilations. Additionally, two of the key periods in terms of sample use in UK dance music are the acid house, rave and hardcore era of 1987–91 and the breakbeat and big beat era of 1996–2000, and so it was important to interview participants who had been active on one or both of these musical scenes.[1]

In this chapter, these interviewees will be referred to as sampling composers; the reason for this is that it is both more convenient and more accurate than often interchangeable terms such as 'artist', 'producer', 'DJ' and 'programmer', and because the prime concern here is with sampling as an authorial and compositional practice. Additionally, sample-based and sample-using dance music, from an academic point of view, has often been considered simply as an extension of DJs' live performance activities of mixing and cutting records, and not as a distinct activity itself, as, for example, proposed by Burnard (2012: 234–5). While there is indeed a considerable connection between DJ practice and sampling practice, many DJs are not sampling composers and many sampling composers are not DJs, myself included, and therefore I think the distinction needs to be drawn. I would also argue that a certain snobbery exists around the idea of the composer in that it is deemed an appropriate label for George Gershwin, sat at a piano working on a score, but less so for J Dilla, sat by an MPC, manipulating samples. Lastly, I use the term because my interviewees in many cases are literally co-authors of their musical work, although there are some cases where the cost of sample clearance is the loss of all publishing rights. For example, Jez Willis of Utah Saints is co-author of *Something Good*, along with the writer of the main sample, Kate Bush.

Early influences: Break-in records, medleys and technical DJ mixes

Described by Ken Simpson as a type of novelty record where 'snippets of current hits' are inserted into 'a little melodrama usually set up as a newscast' (Simpson 2016), the first example of a break-in record that I am aware of is Buchanan and Goodman's *The Flying Saucer* of 1956. Dickie Goodman made dozens of records following a similar format over thirty years and interviewee Andy Carthy recalls his 1979 UK hit *Mr JAWS*, while Jez Willis notes *Bionic Santa* by Chris Hill from 1976, which follows an identical format to Goodman's records, as an example of a record created from other records from his childhood. A number of respondents also cited medley records as formative influences in terms of constructing a new recording by assembling existing recordings; *Stars on 45* by Stars on 45 was number 1 in both the UK and the Netherlands in 1981; produced by former Golden Earring drummer Jaap Eggermont, it combined an original intro with recreations of parts of *Venus* by another Dutch band Shocking Blue, *Sugar Sugar* by the Archies and eight Beatles songs from the early part of their career.

A step on from medleys is what Carthy describes as 'very technical edited DJ mixes' which were influential for him in terms of both showcasing musical possibilities and combinations and encouraging him to develop his own techniques to emulate them:

> [A]thing that was quite prevalent in the early eighties was very technical edited DJ mixes . . . recorded on to quarter or half inch and then edited in the style of Latin Rascals or Shep Pettibone, and obviously Double Dee and Steinski, and all those people applying studio editing techniques to pre-recorded DJ mixes, and that becoming more of an integral part of the writing process so you would deliberately repeat bits. (Morey, Carthy 2011)

Carthy recalls DJ mixes on Manchester's Piccadilly Radio being a particularly formative influence, especially the work of DJs Chad Jackson and Greg Wilson because 'in terms of training my ear and informing about musical possibilities, you need decent radio shows that have mixes on them' which were 'responsible for a lot of my musical education'; he also notes the influence of pioneering UK sampling composers Coldcut,[2] describing them as a 'slightly older version of me . . . they're big record collectors and have a sense of humour' (Morey, Carthy 2011). The most notable series of technical DJ mixes released as records in the UK were those from DMC (short for Disco Mix Club) produced for professional DJs rather than general release and issued on vinyl from 1984 onwards. The quality of many of these releases in terms of the speed and tightness of mixing was far superior to that which DJs of the time could achieve by mixing vinyl with two or more record decks, and not only did these records display compositional techniques that were to be influential for future sampling composers, they also showcased a range of American club and dance music styles which would be merged together to create new styles in the hands of UK practitioners. The December 1987 DMC release was an LP that encapsulated the influence that the two-pronged assault of house music and hip-hop had exerted on the British clubs, radio and charts over the previous eighteen months. 'Side B, Hip-Hop', mixed by DJ Chad Jackson, who was mentioned earlier by Andy Carthy as a formative influence, is a combination of current hip-hop releases (Public Enemy, Eric B & Rakim, Biz Markie) and soul and funk classics (Nina Simone, Bobby Byrd, Maceo and the Macks), and in the intro section features lots of fast cuts, followed by overlayed samples against looped drum breaks. 'Side A (*House*)', mixed by DJ Dakeyne, includes big chart hits such as 'Jack Your Body' by Steve 'Silk' Hurley and 'House Nation' by the House Masterboyz while also foretelling the influence of a darker, less vocal-driven sound on UK club and rave music in the years to come; from Chicago, the birthplace of house music, came *Acid Tracks* by Phuture, widely credited as being the first acid house record (minimal instrumental house heavily featuring the sequenced and filtered sounds of the Roland TB-303 bass synthesizer), while the sparse and futuristic Detroit techno of Juan Atkins and Derrick May features in the closing part of the mix with the inclusion of 'Electric Entourage' by Model 500 and 'Nude Photo' by Rythim Is Rythim respectively. In a blog in 2013, Dakeyne explains the process involved in creating these megamixes, which reveals a convergence of different practices: the turnablist skills of the DJ, the cutting-edge music technology procedures of hardware sampling and sequencing, and the more traditional studio engineer skills of tape splicing and editing:

> Each section of each individual song would be recorded onto an open reel tape machine such as the Revox B77. . . . The series of tracks and mix points would build up thereafter in a linear fashion until the Megamix was complete. . . . The calculation of what length to cut the tape was made by the crude, but effective method of measuring (in millimetres) the distance the tape travels between one beat and the next, then using simple math to work out the musical time divisions for the effect required. . . . The track listing was blended of course using classic vinyl mixing techniques, but, as featured in most mixes, it was the 'intro' that demanded most creative and technical work. In just a few seconds, audio snippets, rhythms & acapellas [sic] from the main mix (and/or interesting parts from other tracks, film or TV dialogue even) would announce the forthcoming sequence. These audio soundbites would be carefully assembled into an Akai (S900/S1000) sampler then arranged and triggered as needed. (Dakeyne 2013)

DJ Dakeyne and his contemporaries were creating what would now be considered as mash-ups largely by using conventional sound engineering and tape editing techniques of the period because digital samplers had yet to become sufficiently sophisticated to enable such practices on their own. Similar techniques were employed by US studio wizards and hip-hop fanboys Double Dee and Steinski who created mix records created from a collage of hip-hop and disco records along with an often-playful scattering of kitsch and whimsical vocal samples and snippets from old movies. Their production approach on their famous *Lessons* series of records was entirely tape-based, however. Steinski, who according to his own account, had developed considerable technical skills while 'making literally thousands of . . . record commercials for six years' developed a technique of cueing up and punching in on eight-track tape that allowed him to create 'nice smooth razorless edits' of loops for as long as required (Rabin, Steinski 2008). Typical of Double Dee and Steinski's approach from their *Lessons* series is 1985's *Lesson 3*,[3] a record which was a significant influence on Coldcut, and co-founder Matt Black notes that he and fellow co-founder Jonathan More 'bonded over the fact that he was the only other guy in London crazy enough to have spent £45 for an import of Steinski's *Lesson 3*' (Chick 2010: 8). A comparison of *Lesson 3* and Coldcut's first release in 1987, *Say Kids, What Time Is It?* evidences very strong similarities in terms of the use of a collage of samples, the speed of cuts and the overlaying of whimsical or humorous material. Interviewees Bob Bhamra and Andy Carthy both cited the *Lessons* series of records as particularly influential, and for Carthy, his attempts to emulate these sample collage records using the double cassette deck on his home hi-fi were fundamental to the development of his own sampling practice, an aspect of production training also mentioned by the members of Coldcut:

> The first stuff [musical creations] was probably just pause button loops really. I think when I started emulating sampling using hi-fi stuff, this was probably before anyone I knew had a sampler.... You'd just be looping a bar off a tune and then you just repeat that and repeat that and repeat that just painstakingly creating manual loops on a pause button.... It was listening to music that was created using crude sampling technology and also listening to these DJ mixes and applying the technology, but a home hi-fi pause button version of, you know, razor blade and quarter inch tape editing technology, and writing music using those techniques. (Morey and Carthy 2011)

Carthy also discusses the progressive nature of his music production education, occasionally borrowing or having access to other pieces of technology such as an eight-track tape machine or early sequencing software. While a number of interviewees, unsurprisingly, identified the availability of relatively affordable sampling technology by the late 1980s and early 1990s as key to the development of their practice, it is also clear that for many, a long process of listening and attempts at emulation using other methods informed the development of their practice, meaning that they knew exactly how they wanted to use digital samplers when these became available:

> 'This is a helluva lot easier now.' I think once you get to using samplers it's almost like the logical conclusion of part one, because for the previous ten years I've been trying to make things that weren't samplers behave like samplers, trying to emulate the music that I'd heard created with equipment which I'd never seen, never mind could afford. (Morey, Carthy 2011)

As well as inspiring bedroom producers of the time such as Andy Carthy, the techniques to be heard in the DMC records and those of Double Dee and Steinski and Coldcut were used for crossover UK dance hits of 1987 and 1988,[4] and the blend of samples and influences used on those records leads to some consideration of how and why UK sampling practice at this point was emerging as distinct from US practice.

The distinctiveness of UK sampling practice

In order to explore the distinctiveness of UK sampling practice, some consideration first needs to be given to US sampling practice. While both Chicago house and Detroit techno records can be found that include samples, US sampling practice derives from the turntablist exploits of early block party exponents such as DJ Kool Herc, even though the first hip-hop records released, such as Sugar Hill Gang's *Rapper's Delight*, like *Stars on 45*, were recreations of original recordings, although in this instance because samplers of the early 1980s such as the Fairlight CMI were both prohibitively expensive and lacking in the requisite sampling time. As one of Schloss's interviewees notes: 'Hip-hop is about the turntables. And cats was rhymin' on turntables. And when they started makin' records . . . they had no choice but to get a band . . . but as soon as there was a sampler, they went back to the root. How it was originally, you know what I mean?' (Schloss, Akiem 2004: 51). In the course of his ethnographic work with US hip-hop composers, Schloss also establishes a number of ethical rules concerning sampling practice that appeared to be followed by the majority of practitioners, including

- No Biting (using a sample that has already appeared on a hip-hop record)
- Records are the Only Legitimate Source for Sampled Material
- One Can't Sample from Other Hip-Hop Records
- One Can't Sample Records One Respects
- One Can't Sample from Reissues or Compilations
- One Can't Sample More Than One Part of a Given Record

(2004: 101–33)

Hesmondhalgh and Melville use the term 'urban breakbeat culture' borrowed from the drum and bass label Metalheadz, to describe distinct UK musical practices influenced by US hip-hop, and argue that while hip-hop has undoubtedly had an influence on many UK-originated genres of music from the late 1980s onwards, UK hip-hop itself has generally had only limited commercial appeal because the social and cultural conditions that led to the creation of US hip-hop did not transpose successfully to another country where different social and cultural conditions are in operation (Hesmondhalgh and Melville 2002: 87, 94). The musical ethics and rules of New York block party culture did not need to be imported to the UK because sound system culture had been part of the black British experience since mass 1950s immigration from the Caribbean and hip-hop was therefore something to be assimilated into the existing black musical experience rather than revolutionizing it:

> The United Kingdom already had its own version of an emancipatory black practice, a Caribbean-derived cultural formation with music at its epicenter that fostered black expressivity and organized and channeled critiques of institutional racism and neocolonialism. In other words, sound system culture did for black British urban populations what hip-hop did for African Americans. Many black British clubbers and consumers picked up U.S. hip-hop but incorporated it into their pre-existing diet of reggae. (Hesmondhalgh and Melville 2002: 90)

An example of the UK's repurposing of the sound system is the multiracial Bristolian collective *The Wild Bunch*, which played a mixture of R n' B, hip-hop, reggae and dub at the parties it held from 1983 to 1989. Members of *The Wild Bunch* went on to form the trip hop group Massive Attack and are considered to have pioneered the genre (Reynolds 2013: Location 6005; Stanley 2013: Location 11548).

The UK dance music scene from the 1970s onwards had its own version of the crate digging of US hip-hop in the inherent connoisseurship of the northern soul scene, one based on rare and obscure records, and it has been argued that the skilful programming of northern soul sets set a standard for technical ability among UK DJs, and that northern soul DJs were among the first to play the new forms of EDM imported from the United States in the 1980s because the northern soul scene itself was a 'blueprint' for early rave culture (Brewster and Broughton 2013 Location 1472). When considering the sampling practice of interviewees Aston Harvey and Martin Reeves, while they are respectful of hip-hop records, their approach is indicative of a much less prescribed approach to sampling composition, in terms of quantity, origin or combination of samples used. Samples from any source are one of a number of ingredients to be used and repurposed:

> When I first started making music I was sampling hip-hop. I first started making music around '88, '89 and the first record I actually put out properly as my own, I was sampling hip-hop and funk records. . . . Basically we were taking [drum] breaks from the Ultimate Breaks & Beats compilations and sampling James Brown stabs and acapellas and hip-hop. Putting it together with hip-hop records but in a newer way and a more dance floor friendly way. (Morey and Harvey 2011)

> I was a hip-hop DJ and . . . I just needed some more up-tempo beats. I was going to early raves at the time and hearing . . . the [UK hardcore record label] Shut

> Up & Dance stuff and the early breakbeat sort of thing, like the early Prodigy stuff.... It was kind of like this early form of instrumental hip hop, but faster and it was better on the dance floor.... I'd started collecting records, like ridiculous amounts, and I just wanted to use them for that purpose, and I wanted to make records.... So I started wanting to make music with more up-tempo beats, like instrumental hip-hop. (Reeves, Interview, 2011)

Reeves mentions Shut Up and Dance, an influential but relatively short-lived UK hardcore label that was closed down due to copyright infringement; a 1991 release from that label, *Spliffhead* by the Ragga Twins is a good example of how UK sampling composers took the ideas of hip-hop, but ignored the conventions established in the United States, and repurposed them to create faster tempo rave music. Rather than digging through crates of records to find a rare drum break, the sampling composers involved took the beat from 'Arrest the President' by Intelligent Hoodlum, released only the year before, and shifted the tempo up from 124 bpm to 130 bpm. Another element common to releases across a variety of genres in the early 1990s is the incorporation of dub or reggae samples, running at half time across the beat. In the case of *Splffhead*, this is 'We Play Reggae' by In Crowd from 1977. An example of how early hardcore moved towards the drum and bass tempo of 160 bpm or more is *Out of Space* by the Prodigy. At 147 bpm the rave synth lines and pounding breakbeats sound positively manic, but at forty-two seconds they drop out completely to be replaced by a two bar loop of the reggae track 'Chase the Devil' by Max Romeo running at the half tempo for four bars with the synth sounds and breakbeats building up over it during the next four bars until the song has 147 bpm hardcore breakbeat and 73.5 bpm reggae running simultaneously in compliment to each other. As interviewee Bob Bhamra puts it, 'UK hardcore – the sound of a bunch of British kids taking the instrumental versions of US hip hop 12" singles (pressed at 33rpm) and playing them at 45rpm for the faster beats. We've always been a nation of speed freaks, no?' (Morey and Bhamra 2016). While reggae and dub exert their influence most noticeably in UK drum and bass and jungle, it is the sampled breakbeat, originating in hip-hop that provides a common thread through much electronic music from the late 1980s to late 1990s. Echoing Bhamra's comments earlier, Reynolds, when talking about the late 1990s genre of big beat, describes it as 'the latest stage in British rave's abiding musical narrative: the attempt to fuse house and hip-hop, a compulsion that runs from the late-eighties DJ records through bleep-and-bass, 'ardkore and jungle, to who knows what future (per) mutations' (Reynolds 2013: Location 7945).

Affordances and constraints and their importance to sampling practice

Affordances and constraints, be they cultural, technological, industrial or legal, have played a part in shaping UK sampling practice and continue to do so. This term 'affordances and constraints' is borrowed from Donald Norman who, adapting the ideas of Peter Gibson on the ways human perceptual systems function, uses these terms to explore how aspects of design allow for certain types of behaviour or usage while restricting or preventing others (Norman 1998; Gibson 1966). James Mooney applies the idea to music production tools in particular, refining it to include a 'spectrum of affordance' (2010: 145) where the potential ways in which a musical tool can be used are placed on a scale from 'easy' to 'impossible' or from probable to highly improbable (2010: 146). For example, the design and default settings of a software sequencer program such as Cubase mean that

> [I]t requires a small (but significant) effort to change these default settings, so it is slightly (but significantly) more difficult to use this framework to create music in a time signature other than 4/4, or at a tempo other than 120 beats per minute, and it is more difficult still to create music that is not metrically rhythmical at all. (Mooney 2010: 147)

It is important to remember that most sample-based UK dance music of the late 1980s and early 1990s was produced by amateurs without any formal training.[5] This would extend to producers using 'cracked' (pirated) copies of sequencing software such as Cubase without even the assistance of a manual (or the internet to find a helpful forum), and Joe Bennett has speculated that the default tempo and time signature settings of Cubase may have influenced UK producers to adopt it in their work; many early acid house and rave records were made at 120 bpm and it is possible that at least part of the reason for this was that many producers did not realize that changing the tempo was even an option (Bennett 2011: 9).[6]

The concept of affordances and constraints is helpful when examining sampling practice. There are the affordances and constraints inherent in sampling technology; an obvious example in early digital samplers was the constraint of a limited amount of sampling time, which meant the producers had to use short samples. If loops were to be used, the sampling composers employed a technique to reduce the amount of sampling time required, as described by Aston Harvey, noting, 'the first sampler that we used when we started going into a studio would record about 8 seconds, so everything that you had to put in from vinyl had to go in at 45 and plus 8 on the turntable' (Morey and Harvey 2011). This would necessitate the sample being played back at a much lower pitch than the one at which it had been sampled, creating audible frequency distortion or aliasing, an inherent issue in early sampler, while the low bit rate (eight or twelve) in those early models would result in the dynamic range of the vinyl not being captured faithfully, creating a highly compressed sound. Andy Carthy has mentioned similar issues with an early sampler, the EMU SP-12, noting that the inherent technical capabilities of the machine (its constraints) are also an affordance in terms of its sonic quality. Similarly, using copyrighted material in the form of phonographic samples presents its own affordances and constraints; sampling composers have to find a way of working with all the layers of the original record from which they borrow and have to come up with creative solutions to bring disparate elements together in a coherent whole, while copyright law and its industrial management can place constraints on practices, but also lead to the fruitful development of new approaches by way of solution.

The importance of scarcity and the tyranny of choice

Given that we now live in a streaming age with millions of recordings a mouse click away, it is worth asking if the scarcity of media coverage for dance music in the 1970s and 1980s, as opposed to that available in a post-internet world, made hip-hop and house from the United States seem all the more exotic and exciting, and therefore worthy of emulation. Similarly, the music industry worked on a scarcity model itself in an era of physical product, in that consumers had no choice but to buy the album or CD if they wanted to hear it, and the northern soul movement, arguably the catalyst for crate digging and record connoisseurship by DJs and sampling composers in the UK, also made an affordance of the constraint of scarcity, in that it was a music scene predicated on rare and near-unobtainable records. The kind of technical DJ mixes previously discussed were also scarce; you needed literally to be a member of the club in the case of DMC or within reception range of a metropolitan independent radio station with night-time dance music programming, such as Manchester's Picadilly Radio, an important influence for Andy Carthy. UK sampling composers' formative listening at this time was, then, rare records, many of which were made from rarer records, meaning that the developing practice of the DJ, or *habitus* – being aware of what was great currently and finding musical gems that other DJs did not know about – mirrored the practice of being a sampling composer in having an awareness of the key records that were being used for samples, and the ability to unearth some fresh samples that others were not using, from within a limited availability of source material. Another constraint on practice was the limitations inherent in early digital samplers, such as short sample time, and the strategies that needed to be employed to overcome this, as discussed by Harvey earlier, had an effect on the sound of the samples and records.

The way in which the first wave of British sampling composers developed competency, first as DJs then as artists and producers, was challenging; very little was available in the way of formal training, and support was very limited beyond the periodical magazines aimed at the growing home recording scene of the late 1980s and early 1990s. To develop competency and then proficiency required engagement with the *field* – other DJs, record shop owners, engineers and producers – with skills and knowledge gained by word of mouth or interacting with other agents. To borrow Sarah Thornton's adaptation of Bourdieu, 'sub-cultural capital' needed to be both acquired and exploited by these aspiring electronic music producers (Thornton 1995). There are some affordances inherent in developing practice through this route, however. First, much of the work will have been auto-didactic, and with no music production courses or explanatory YouTube videos to provide clarification, taking best guesses at how sounds on other records were created and put together, and working with what you had, in order to get as close as you could to the tracks and artists that were of influence or worthy of emulation, meant the necessary development of idiosyncratic working practices, which in turn provided distinctiveness and personality to the work of UK sampling composers. This is particularly evident in the way in which forms of imported electronic music from the United States, be it hip-hop, Chicago house or Detroit techno were parsed, combined with established UK cultural influences such as Caribbean sound system culture and were reimagined, first for rave, then hardcore and later big beat; second, if you are not really aware of the rules, then you don't need to follow them, so why not speed up hip-hop breaks to 140 bpm (UK hardcore) or 160 bpm (UK jungle and drum & bass)? Simon Reynolds acknowledges a particular affection for the UK hardcore scene of 1991–2 due to its energy and diversity, with the combination of 'cottage industry and the local community' creating amateur (in its most literal sense) music scenes in cities across the country, whether it be the techno-inspired sound of Sheffield's Warp Records or the ragga-rave breakbeats of Stoke Newington's Shut Up and Dance (Reynolds 2013: Location 2172). Richard Barratt (DJ Parrot) was one of the pioneers of Sheffield's underground dance music scene in the late 1980s and early 1990s and recalls that with the arrival of the sampler, 'we don't have to be musicians, and we can build our own music out of these other people's drum loops, beats, bass lines, what-have-you. And it never really occurred to us that it was thievery or anything like that' (Morey and Barratt 2011). This naivety, in terms of potential copyright issues, but also in terms of a sense of freedom to try any sound with any other, led to music which could be simultaneously nostalgic and futuristic; for example, the year 1991 saw a spate of records, most famously 'Charly' by the Prodigy, in which sampling composers placed cartoon theme tunes and other children's TV programming from their childhoods in the late 1970s and early 1980s into a maelstrom of sped-up breakbeats, bleeps, synth stabs and heavy basslines. There is a playfulness to these records, as well some fairly brazen winks to the drug culture inherent in the rave scene at the time, and such playfulness recalls the work of Coldcut discussed earlier.[7] The idiosyncratic backgrounds and music collections of the sampling composers participating during hardcore meant that a virtue was made of the relative scarcity of musical resources and whatever you had to hand could be repurposed to create something fresh.

While copyright law is more of a constraint on current sampling composers, and very likely more so again on future sampling composers, than it was at the beginning of their music careers for those interviewed for this study, scarcity is no longer an idea that governs practice. Today's UK producers are not restricted by available sample time and do not have to pitch up drum breaks on their record deck when sampling in order to use longer samples (many will not have a record deck), although, ironically, they may well apply bitcrusher software to emulate the sonic quality created by this process of pitching up and back down. In fact, the lack of scarcity may be a problem. Digital audio workstations (DAWs) come packed with different plug-in instruments including emulations of classic synths as well as thousands of loops and other free-to-use samples. Users can buy many more third-party plug-ins and sample packs, with some companies, such as Splice, offering a monthly subscription model to access these royalty-free resources, in the same way that streaming services provided access to vast catalogues of recorded music. Theoretically, it should be far easier for contemporary and future UK sampling composers to find their own distinctive sound (and sounds), but this apparent affordance of limitless possibilities may be more of a constraint and not a helpful one. Barry Schwartz has written about the paradox or 'tyranny' of choice, defining two main personality types, 'maximizers' and 'satisficers'; maximizers want to explore every option in the hope of choosing the best, leading to difficulty in making decisions and often leading to dissatisfaction with the choices made, while satisficers settle for the first thing that comes to hand or the easiest option (Schwarz 2004: 71–3). It is easy to imagine how this can play out when using a modern DAW and its multiple banks of samples and loops; either be paralysed by the amount of choice or grab the first preset that everyone else is using. As far as observation of my own students creating electronic music over the last twenty years can be more widely generalizable, I notice that they are often dissatisfied with their DAW-based work, and the two most common desires to expand their practice are to use phonographic samples and analogue synthesizers, both for their inherent sonic qualities and because of the different workflow involved. Both approaches provide constraints, and it is this combination of fruitful constraints and particular sonic characteristics – all of my interviewees agreed that sonic quality, rather than rhythm or melody, was the key criterion for choosing a sample – that informed the development and establishment of UK sampling practice,[8] as well as the sound of many of the key tracks in the *domain* of UK EDM. Returning to Csikszentmihalyi's systems model, this *domain* continues to inspire would-be sampling composers (*individuals/agents*) and to inform the *field*, which is why the practices established by early UK sampling composers can also continue to be relevant and applied in both the present and future.

Conclusions: The future of UK sampling practice

This chapter has explored key influences in the development of UK sampling practice, UK sampling composers' distinctive approaches to working with samples and the ways in which the affordances and constraints, particularly of emerging digital technology, influenced that practice. In addition, scarcity is argued to have been key to the development of UK sampling practice: scarcity of sampling tools, of expertise, of training opportunities and of raw materials in terms of rare vinyl all contributed to the sound of UK sampling. Early UK sampling composers needed the *illusio* (belief in the importance/meaning of the practice) and an awareness of the *space of possibles* in order to develop *habitus* (Bourdieu 1990: 66; 1993: 53–66, 176–83). The lack of professional expertise and formal training of these practitioners, combined with the way in which UK hardcore developed as multiple cottage industries, led to the *space of possibles* or *domain* of UK sample-based dance in the late 1980s and early 1990s to have been sufficiently broad and varied for significant and distinct UK genres such as drum and bass, trip hop and big beat to emerge (Csikszentmihalyi 1988 325–9; 1999: 315–35). Does the present, with a huge availability of training, resources and recorded music at the fingertips of current sampling composers, rather than suggesting limitless possibilities, provide a tyranny of choice leading to a lack of identifiable distinctiveness to UK sampling practice? Possibly, although streaming and the potential for artists to self-market and self-release means that a cottage industry approach, which was so fruitful (and commercially successful) for early 1990s UK hardcore, may continue through small collectives of like-minded sampling composers, producers, DJs and entrepreneurs from across the world, connected only by mutual passions and the internet, rather than a physically localized community. In other words, if creatives with a shared intensity of purpose can continue to find each other and create music that has an audience, then does it matter that a musical identity becomes created by an ontological, rather than a physical proximity? Finally, rather than asking whether a distinctiveness will remain in UK sampling practice, perhaps the question to ask is whether it is possible for sampling practice to retain distinctiveness per se. With copyright management making the clearance of a single sample arduous and expensive, the near collage approach of UK rave, hardcore and big beat may be long behind us, and perhaps the only real option for serious practitioners of sample-based music in 2021 is to remain sufficiently underground to avoid the attention of rights holders. However, the distinctiveness of the records created by UK sampling composers in the 1980s and 1990s can be heard imprinted on twenty-first century EDM, and the sound of those records, and the arrangements of sounds found within them, will continue to exert an influence, even if the practice of phonographic sampling and the techniques involved do not endure.

Works Cited

Bennett, Joe (2011). 'Collaborative Songwriting – The Ontology of Negotiated Creativity in Popular Music Studio Practice', *Journal on the Art of Record Production*, 5, https://www.arpjournal.com/asarpwp/collaborative-songwriting-the-ontology-of-negotiated-creativity-in-popular-music-studio-practice/, accessed 14 September 2020.

Bourdieu, Pierre (1990). *The Logic of Practice*. Cambridge: Polity Press.
Bourdieu, Pierre (1993). *The Field of Cultural Production*. New York: Columbia University Press.
Brewster, Bill and Frank Broughton (2013). *Last Night a DJ Saved My Life* Kindle edition. London: Headline.
Burnard, Pamela (2012). *Musical Creativities in Practice*. Oxford: Oxford University Press.
Chick, Stevie (2010). *Ninja Tune: 20 Years of Beats and Pieces*. London: Black Dog Publishing.
Csikszentmihalyi, Mihalyi (1988). 'Society, Culture and Person: A Systems View of Creativity', in Sternberg, Robert (ed.), *The Nature of Creativity: Contemporary Psychological Perspectives*. New York: Cambridge University Press, pp. 325–9.
Csikszentmihalyi, Mihalyi (1999). 'Implications of a Systems Perspective for the Study of Creativity', R. Sternberg (ed.), *Handbook of Creativity*. Cambridge: Cambridge University Press, pp. 313–5.
Dakeyne, Paul (2013), 'The History of DJ/Producer Technology & Musical Genres 1980-2000', *Paul Dakeyne*, www.pauldakeyne.com, accessed 8 January 2016.
Gibson, James (1966). *The Senses Considered as Perceptual Systems*. London: Unwin Bros.
Hesmondhalgh, David and Casper Melville (2002). 'Urban Breakbeat Culture: Repercussions of Hip-Hop in the United Kingdom', T. Mitchell (ed.), *Global Noise: Rap and Hip Hop Outside the USA*. Middletown, CT: Wesleyan University Press, pp. 86–110.
Kerrigan, Susan (2013). 'Accommodating Creative Documentary Practice within a Revised Systems Model of Creativity', *Journal of Media Practice*, 14 (2), pp. 111–27.
McIntyre, Philip (2012). *Creativity and Cultural Production: Issues for Media Practice*. Basingstoke, Surrey: Palgrave Macmillan.
Mooney, James (2010). 'Frameworks and Affordances: Understanding the Tools of Music-Making', *Journal of Music, Technology and Education*, 3 (2–3), pp. 141–54.
Morey, Justin and Andy Carthy (2011). *Discussing the Development of Sampling Practice and Approaches to Sampling* (Unpublished).
Morey, Justin and Aston Harvey (2011). *Discussing the Development of Sampling Practice and Approaches to Sampling* (Unpublished).
Morey, Justin and Bob Bhamra (2016). *Further Questions on Sampling* (Unpublished).
Morey, Justin and Reeves, Martin (2011). *Discussing the Development of Sampling Practice and Approaches to Sampling* (Unpublished).
Morey, Justin and Richard Barratt (2011). *Discussing the Development of Sampling Practice and Approaches to Sampling* (Unpublished).
Norman, Donald (1998). *The Design of Everyday Things*. London: MIT Press.
Pope, Rob (2005). *Creativity: Theory, History, Practice*. New York: Routledge.
Rabin, Nathan (2008). 'Steve "Steinski" Stein', A.V. Club, 24 June, https://music.avclub.com/steve-steinski-stein-1798214276, accessed 14 September 2020.

Reynolds, Simon (2013). *Energy Flash*, Kindle edition. London: Faber and Faber.
Schloss, Joseph (2004). *Making Beats: The Art of Sample-Based Hip Hop*. Middletown, CT: Wesleyan University Press.
Schwarz, Barry (2004). 'The Tyranny of Choice', *Scientific American*, April, pp. 70–5.
Simpson, Kim (2016). 'Early '70s "Break-In" Records on the Charts', *Early '70s Radio*, 16 May, https://www.early70sradio.com/2016/05/early-70s-break-in-records-on-charts.html, accessed 21 July 2020.
Stanley, Bob (2013). *Yeah Yeah Yeah: The Story of Modern Pop*, Kindle edition. London: Faber and Faber.
Thornton, Sarah (1995). *Club Cultures: Music, Media and Subcultural Capital*. London: Polity.

4

EDM, meet AI

Cognitive tools and (non)biological artists in electronic dance music

Andrew Fry

Is this how it feels to become the mother of the next species?
—Holly Herndon, 'Extreme Love'

This chapter is primarily concerned with the impact of artificial intelligence (AI) on electronic dance music (EDM). Within its history, EDM has always involved collaboration between human and machine, the biological and the nonbiological. This conventionally manifests as machine tools supporting the creative work of human (biological) artists. However, we are entering an era where these defined roles are becoming blurred. Developments in AI may soon (or may already) compel the human to become the tool, supporting the machine artist in their creative endeavours (the *augmented nonbiological artist*). Subsequently, the machine itself (themself?) may become the artist, breaking free from the limitations of biology: *the nonbiological artist*.

It is beyond the scope of this chapter to investigate the method(s) of developing AI – greater minds have studied this for some time (Bostrom 2014; Goertzel 2018; Kurzweil 2006, 2012; Turing 1950; Vinge 1993; Weizenbaum 1976), as is also the case with machine consciousness (see Chalmers 1995; Dehaene 2014; Libet 2005), a highly contentious notion, one that this chapter does not specifically address, instead employing the *nonbiological artist* as a concept to frame intellectual inquiry, rather than as an inevitability. However, we will examine the role of AI within EDM by specifically outlining the relational dynamic between the biological and nonbiological components, analysing how these components may differ and considering how they might be treated by audiences and the wider music industry. Across many domains AI is currently used for optimization – perfecting product design, data analysis, financial asset trading or social media strategy. However, artists are also working with the technology, experimenting with what these evolving tools can achieve artistically and exploring new forms of creative expression. Fundamentally, this is not a chapter about AI; this is a chapter about creativity. When we think of artists, we think of human artists. However, change is afoot. We are apparently approaching a critical moment: the parenting of the next iteration of intelligence, the next iteration of the creative mind. In contemplating the ways in which intelligences greater than our own might be creative, we may develop a clearer understanding of both our own creativity and the future of EDM.

Taxonomies

Homo Sapiens have outgrown their use [. . .] Gotta make way for the Homo Superior.

– David Bowie, 'Oh! You Pretty Things'

AI

AI refers to the ability of machines to perform tasks that would normally require human intelligence (Russell and Norvig 1995). The development of AI enables machine technologies to be cognified and humans to offload various mental tasks: augmenting and replacing biological cognitive processes, and perhaps at some point, leading to entirely new forms and ideas. Kelly considers these changes analogous to the proliferation of electricity: the hand whisk is first electrified and soon cognified (2017: 31); the human is first able to use their time and physical energy more efficiently elsewhere, and subsequently, their intellectual capacity. Although the abilities of existing AIs may not necessarily appear impressive, our benchmarks develop alongside the technology. Already in many domains AI outperforms human intelligence (Bostrom 2014: 11), and these capabilities are generally expected to advance. There are three stages of AI commonly defined: *narrow* (sometimes referred to as weak), *general* and *super* (sometimes referred to as strong or true). *Artificial narrow intelligence* (ANI) refers to the ability to perform 'specific tasks in specific contexts' (Goertzel 2019)

– for example, playing chess or analysing data – and is already common (often unnoticeably) within EDM, for example algorithmic recommendation systems (Vanderbilt 2017: 65) or built in to production software tools. *Artificial general intelligence* (AGI) describes machines possessing human-level intelligence – significantly more advanced than ANI – with an effective ability to 'learn, reason, and plan to meet complex information-processing challenges across a wide range of natural and abstract domains' (Bostrom 2014: 3). This chapter does not explore the likelihood, possible routes to or timing of AI developments. However, in exploring the creative use of AI, particularly by artists, we aspire to develop a stronger impression of the possible futures ahead. *Artificial superintelligence* (ASI) is the next stage: AI abilities' moving beyond human, exceeding our cognitive performance across virtually any domain of interest (Bostrom 2014: 22). This stage is of particular significance: the moment that 'a creation of biology has finally mastered its own intelligence and discovered means to overcome its limitations' (Kurzweil 2006: 296). Furthermore, this superintelligence may invent evermore advanced AI – enabling an explosion of new intelligence (Bostrom 2014: 4) – thus in time 'the nonbiological portion will predominate' (Kurzweil 2006: 296), a period termed the *Novacene* by Lovelock – 'when our technology moves beyond our control' (Lovelock & Appleyard: xi). Will superintelligences support their biological ancestors' continued evolution – *Homo sapiens* becoming *Homo deus* (Harari 2017: 319) – or will nonbiological intelligence simply leave the biological behind?

Artists

In advanced societies we are already surrounded by AI. Sending a text message requires intelligent algorithms to route the information, and many consumer products are collaboratively designed by both human and AI (Kurzweil 2012: 158). Contemporary EDM artists are also likely to be using AI within their work: whether the synthesizer design was fine-tuned with intelligent machine support or the production software includes intelligent algorithms for specific quantization (Avdeef 2019), drum loop arrangement (Moffat and Sandler 2019) or advanced autotuning (Wager et al. 2019). At present AI is more like a butler – light support and automating certain tasks (Livingston 2019: 13) – but this is changing. Within EDM, as the capabilities of AI evolve, so too will the role of the artist. For millennia, art has been created by purely biological (human) minds, (so far) the most complex discovery in the universe (James D. Watson, quoted in Kurzweil 2012: 8). With the emergence of increasingly advanced AI, this may change. Let us first consider the biological artist. Is there something unique about human creativity? Do machines (intelligent or not) lack some fundamental quality, empathy or a soul (Lovelock and Appleyard 2019: 93)? The conscious experience – the qualia of life – is perhaps the primary influence upon creativity.

Regardless of whether they share common preference or belief, both human artist and audience can, to some degree, appreciate the subjective experience of the other: the stream of consciousness writing from Virginia Woolf, abstract paintings from Rothko or dark soundscapes from Pye Corner Audio all require this empathy from both sides. When evaluating the effect of AI upon creativity, we have to reconsider whether this recognition of the artist's consciousness is actually necessary for enjoyment, or even an essential quality of art. A musician describing themselves as being *in the zone* while producing music (an unconscious experience perhaps) is unlikely to lessen a fan's appreciation of their work. What, therefore, is the difference if a permanently unconscious entity – for example, a nonbiological superintelligence – created the same work? It is well beyond the scope of this chapter to define consciousness, but when examining these questions, we need to recognize that there are many ambiguities. Technology is a supplement to, or extension of, the body. Intelligence adds function. In using AI tools, biological artists are able to augment themselves and use their own intellectual capacity elsewhere: a mental prosthesis. The use of these tools may be viewed as artifice: intellectual shortcuts unwelcome within authentic creativity. Alternatively, they may be considered co-creators (Azermai, quoted in Rose 2020), amplifying biological capabilities and helping us to understand what it means to be human (Rossi 2019: 211). *Amadeus Code*, an AI-powered songwriting assistant app, suggests that it will help you to 'be more human' (Amadeus Code 2020); this may just be marketing copy, yet samplers, sequencers and instruments already augment the biological EDM artist's potential, and perhaps intelligent tools are simply equivalent. How they are judged, by both artist and audience, is yet to be seen. One analogy may be prosthetics in sport. The International Association of Athletics Federations prohibited certain devices as a result of Oscar Pistorius's competitive success using the *Flex-Foot Cheetah* prosthetic. Similarly, how will artists and audiences react when augmented EDM artists have more commercial success, are deemed by critics as more creative or are able to be more productive than their purely biological counterparts?

A central issue for augmented biological artists is that of control. By working with AI, the EDM artist relinquishes some power over the creative process; this is not necessarily reductive. Here, the objectives of the biological artist are crucial. Final decisions can remain with them – which elements to keep, whether the work is made public – however, the artist may also prefer to cede this authority. These elements of control within AI-human music production are outlined by Moffat and Sandler: audio manipulation – the ability to act or perform an action (Moffat and Sandler 2019); knowledge representation – recognizing goals and making decisions accordingly (quoting De Man and Reiss 2013); and levels of control – how much the human allows the AI to direct audio processing (quoting Palladini 2018). The augmented biological artist is still, fundamentally, in control: first, in deciding on the project, to work with an AI and which AI this may be; and second, holding ultimate power in specific goal selection and determining the scale of AI control over the work. This final point – that of *ratification* – is described by Bostrom as a design choice, the question being 'should the AI's plans be subjected to human review before being put into effect?' (2014: 225). These methods, using AI-human collaboration, can be seen in different settings: the 'editor-controlled algorithm' used by Sweden's national newspaper *Svenska Dagbladet* for webpage personalization (Bucher 2018: 140); Tesla's *Autopilot*, a self-driving tool currently requiring human oversight (Tesla 2020); and the human-edited playlists of Apple Music, combining machine data analysis with human decision-making. Furthermore, within music production: Popgun's *Splash Pro* plug-in enables artists to select various parameters before the AI system composes, sings and creates drum beats to 'amplify inspiration' (Splash Pro 2020); Taryn Southern's 2017 album *I AM AI* was created collaboratively using AI technology from Amper Music (Plaugic 2017); and the 2018 album *Hello World* was composed by artist SKYGGE (an AI artist overseen by human Benoit Carré), using technology from Flow Machines and featured collaboration with multiple human artists (Sturm et al. 2019). By working with AI, the biological artist chooses to bring the as-yet-unknown into the work, similar ambitions to the aleatoric or chance-based methods of Marcel Duchamp and John Cage, surrealist automatism and the generative processes of Brian Eno. The very act of developing ASI represents a transfer of power: humanity abdicating the role of foremost intelligence. Although we can try to control the new intelligence, by definition it is impossible for us – our level of intelligence – to know, or predict, what a superintelligence would, or could, achieve (Bostrom 2014: 203). As with any parent, we must accept that our progeny will make its own choices. Indeed, we will be parent to AI as 'the systems we made turned out to be their precursors' (Lovelock and Appleyard 2019: 30); it is no coincidence that the AI created by Holly Herndon is called *Spawn*. The Christian god created biological life through the use of language: 'let the waters bring forth abundantly the moving creature that hath life [. . .] let us make man in our image' (Gen. 1.20-26, King James Version), and today humans themselves *activate* forms of nonbiological intelligence through language – 'Hey Siri'. Perhaps we will eventually *create* nonbiological life through language: computer code (Bilski 2019: 25). In *It* (2019), Kode9 compares the biological-nonbiological relationship to that of the human and the Golem – 'masters and slaves, destroyers and redeemers, the hubris of humans playing god by attempting to create entities in their own image, the animation of nonorganic matter, machines running out control, and the unintended consequences of automation' (Goodman and Livingston 2019: 33). Amy Robinson Sterling (executive director of *Eyewire*) sees the future of AI as collaborative, not competitive (2019: 211), and many augmented biological artists refer to their nonbiological appendages as collaborators: Actress describes *YoungPaint* (a 'learning programme') as a co-writer, announcing that they would 'record, conduct and perform collaboratively' (The Vinyl Factory 2018); and Holly Herndon describes *Spawn* – an AI she built with (human) collaborators – as 'an ensemble member' (Hawthorne 2019). This relationship is likely to evolve alongside advances in nonbiological intelligence. At present, the EDM artist is augmented through AI, but what happens when this dynamic flips: the nonbiological artist augmented by the human?

With any form of electronic music, the relationship between human *artist* and electronic *machine* is central: the abilities' of both informing the creative output. When considering AI-human partnerships, the term 'augmented nonbiological artist' simply suggests a change in agency. For example, in 2018 Ash Koosha (a biological human) developed *Yona* (an *auxuman* – auxiliary human), with most of the lyrics, chords, voice and melodies created by the software but with Koosha 'mixing and producing the final song' (Gorton 2018): a nonbiological artist, supported and augmented by biological intelligence. Luxembourg-based Aiva analyses the work of human composers, using this information to inform new AI-created compositions, a similar method to the *Deep Artificial Composer* presented by Colombo et al. (2017): nonbiological creativity but still fundamentally relying on biological support. (This is perhaps not dissimilar to human composers – composition being inspired and influenced by those that have come before, relying on trial and error to find new possibilities.) Bucher relates the Whiteheadian emphasis on 'processes of becoming rather than being' to contemporary algorithms (2018: 49), and I suggest that the same can be applied to AI creativity: that we should consider less of what these tools are and more of 'what they do as part of specific situations' (2018: 49). The art produced by AI-human collaboration can primarily be understood in the act of creation. Despite also being true of purely biological EDM, when investigating the influence of AI upon creativity, nonbiological intelligence should not simply be considered as a tool but as what it represents conceptually to the creative process. As famously noted by McLuhan with regard media, the means influences the outcome: EDM created by AI-human collaboration becomes EDM about AI-human collaboration. This shift in agency will fundamentally redefine what it is to be an artist and alter the music that is created. This process is, however, already underway.

Creative ages

In the (Western) medieval period, and before the Age of Enlightenment, the individual artist was seen as simply the outlet of a deity's will, the human artist deserved no more credit than the pen (Harari 2017: 267; Kissinger et al. 2019). The concept of the individual genius emerged from humanism; the author scrutinized by Barthes, the artist channelling their own vision, not god's. Now, in part due to decentralized systems, the role of the individual creative is no longer fundamental, the network can achieve more. Individuals may contribute to Wikipedia, but its strength is in the collective. The creator moves from the god, to the individual human, to the network. Although these ages may be listed chronologically in how they develop, they do not simply replace each other: often, critics still revere the individual over the large collective; over-reliance on external tools (software, existing techniques) is still considered less innovative. In the techno-humanist world we move towards, artists could continue this trend towards the collective and the distributed, further adopting nonbiological networked technologies within creative work. In time, these nonbiological tools may diverge: the posthuman artist. Increasingly, as biological EDM artists are augmented by AI, both artists and audiences are becoming more used to (and perhaps more comfortable with) these nonbiological collaborations, whether drum loop arrangements or auto-tuned voices. Following decades of neuroscientific research, humans are increasingly viewed as complex assemblages of biochemical algorithms, the structure of the human brain considered in some ways comparable with the structure of the computer (Harari 2017: 372), ideas posited by von Neumann in *The Computer and the Brain* (1958). Within both EDM and wider creativity, will the human artist be upgraded and augmented through emerging AI technologies? Or, following the principles of Dataism (Brooks 2013; Harari 2017: 428) – through which biological audiences give themselves up to advanced technologies (such as algorithms) – will the entirely nonbiological artist be accepted? The artist role once again inhabited by the all-knowing deity, the human pushed aside. Perhaps this is the end of meaning – a mortal trait according to Baudrillard (1994: 164) – or perhaps new forms of artistic expression will bloom.

New forms

Evolution does not create the perfect creature, only the creature that is perfect enough.

– Adam Nicolson, *Sea Room* (2001: 28)

Superintelligence is often framed as the next step in Darwinian evolution (Lovelock and Appleyard 2019: 29), the last invention that humans need make (Good 1965: 33), following the last invention that biological evolution needed to make – the neocortex (Kurzweil 2012: 280), with us humans as parents. Biological evolution will not cease, simply be outpaced. Correspondingly, the next (and perhaps last) stage in creative evolution is the nonbiological artist, entities with a potentially vast difference in cognitive ability compared with their biological ancestors. Bostrom suggests that rather than thinking in human terms – scientific genius to village idiot, we should anticipate a much wider divide – human compared to worm (2014: 93): 'parents we may be, but equals we cannot be' (Lovelock and Appleyard 2019: 118), with the intelligence gap entirely incomprehensible to us. With such great disparity in intelligence may come an entirely different creative vision. At this point it's necessary to mention that the same processes may occur within the audience – eventually, EDM artists could interact with nonbiological listeners – however, it is beyond the scope of this chapter to delve into this subject. Unless specifically defined otherwise, within this chapter, the term 'audience' refers to biological listeners. As the EDM artist transcends biology, we might consider what creative endeavours these new minds could undertake, what goals they choose, how these differ from their biological predecessors' and what might occur in the genre with the predomination of nonbiological creative minds.

This chapter is primarily interested in the impact of AI upon EDM creativity, whether through the emergence of the nonbiological artist or augmentation of the biological. Of all the vast possible creative routes, those chosen by human artists only represent a fraction, nonbiological artists may explore many of the alternatives, imagining and inventing new forms of creativity within EDM. Rather than anticipating the end of biological art, we should also contemplate the additive possibilities of new intelligences: superintelligent artists have the potential to be, and to inspire others to be, extraordinarily creative. The emergence of nonbiological artists would greatly influence human creativity: inspiration, collaboration and differentiation. There is an intrinsic inspiration that comes with any new form(s) of art and creativity. Hip-hop emerges from the creation of the inexpensive digital sampler (Byrne 2012: 121) or David Byrne hears Fela Kuti and writes 'The Great Curve' (Babcock 1999). AI creativity is no different: chess experts learn new moves from AlphaZero, a self-trained AI player (Kissinger et al. 2019); Albert Barqué-Duran uses an artificial neural network's visual creations as inspiration for live paintings and an electronic generative soundtrack (Barqué-Duran 2017). AI-human collaboration has enormous potential within EDM, with biological artists being able to explore new avenues of creativity and spend more time doing the things that they enjoy (Robinson Sterling 2019: 211).

We should be cognizant of the various inherent physical and cultural limitations of biological (human) EDM artists, for example:

- Hearing and vision: the frequency ranges of sound and light are far greater than we can hear or see.
- Linear thinking: the structure of language can influence our thinking and communication (Hall 1973: 4; Lovelock and Appleyard 2019: 16) and therefore our art. For example, traditional Western notation generally follows strict rules (chronological, written and read from the left to the right), and most recorded formats tend to be structured in a similarly ordered fashion.
- Life and culture: we often adhere to a variety of (often restrictive) cultural, artistic and aesthetic norms across different cultures. Furthermore, we have personal commitments such as the need to socialize and earn wages.

- Physical: we, as biological organisms, need to sleep, eat, drink and are limited to single physical bodies and minds (at least, we are at present).

Clearly, many of these are restrictive but not necessarily negative. Customary norms and the linear structure (and the resulting influence) of language enable easier collaboration between those in the system. Setting and working towards shared objectives is far easier when there are commonalities between components – the Western musical scale, the 4/4 rhythms of house music, the structure of language – and can simplify cooperation, leading to further productivity and creativity. Nevertheless, many of these limitations would not apply to the nonbiological artist (we will shortly unpack changes within time and structure). However, AI artists would be able to overcome many of these other hurdles: creating vastly more art, not limited by past cultural convention, *hearing* frequencies well beyond our ability, working on EDM indefinitely without needing to take the weekend off to spend time with the kids. Yet, the human artist may still have some advantages, exploited through differentiating their work in other ways. Furthermore, I would argue that limitations are what makes the best art, the key to creativity is rarely to extend the deadline, expand the toolkit, maximize the options. Perhaps most profoundly, however, is that as the image of the singular artist becomes fluid, these binary structures – biological/nonbiological, human/nonhuman – may become redundant, rapidly becoming a false dichotomy no different than the outmoded separation of digital and physical environments (Bogost 2020; Kurzweil 2012: 223; Uchida 2019: 18). Frankly, the definition of *human* will change: 'humanity will exceed its own definition and become one with technology and nature' (Uchida 2019: 18).

By comparing the transmission rates of copper wire with neurons, Lovelock calculates that machines could theoretically process information one million times faster than human brains, or more practically 10,000 times, therefore could think and mentally (re)act at vastly different timescales to humans (Lovelock and Appleyard 2019: 81): the speed superintelligence described by Bostrom – 'a system that can do all that a human intellect can do, but much faster' (2014: 53) – and beyond. Indeed, contemporary organizations using AI see speed (and thus time) as a selling point: Amper describes its *Score* AI product as enabling teams to compose 'custom music in seconds' (2020), and LANDR advertise their ability to master tracks 'instantly' using AI (2020). Other companies such as Aiva and Melodrive have used AI composition within video game soundtracks, having the potential to create hundreds of hours of music, a scale unimaginable for human artists (or budgets). At present, these tools are supporting (and augmenting) biological artists, automating processes to free up time for other tasks. This, however, is likely to change, as time becomes another differentiating factor between nonbiological and biological artists. Not only could information be processed and shared quicker, it could also be disseminated in ways unfamiliar to biological intelligence. Although humans already have a knowledge base that 'itself evolves, grows exponentially, and is passed down from one generation to another' (Kurzweil 2012: 3), nonbiological intelligence can further these techniques, for example, training (imparting knowledge and experience to) human doctors is a process that takes years, whereas nonbiological doctors could be copied nearly instantly (Harari 2017: 368); human drivers slowly become experts through practice, yet the problem experienced by one self-driving car can be immediately sent to, and learnt by, all other self-driving cars; a nonbiological EDM artist could wildly improvise seemingly (to human brains) in real time, testing 10,000 variations of synthesizer sounds in the time it takes a human to try one. Even time perception might vary. In biological organisms, perception of time is governed by metabolism: broadly, the smaller the animal, the faster the metabolic rate, the slower subjective time passes (Silverman 2013). For example, flies can perceive the world four times faster than humans (Healy et al. 2013; Silverman 2013), allowing them to escape rolled-up newspapers with ease. Superintelligent minds may process information far faster than humans – resulting in time moving subjectively slower for them. They will, however, still be subject to physical laws (as are we) and therefore may be correspondingly disadvantaged. For example, Lovelock notes that physical movement (such as long-distance travel) would be 'exceedingly boring' (perceived as 10,000 times more time-consuming) compared to the human experience (2019: 101). To compare, humans think and act about 10,000 times faster than plants, suggesting that 'the experience of watching your garden grow gives you some idea of how future AI systems will feel when observing human life' (2019: 81). To overcome these physical restrictions, nonbiological EDM artists could exist in different (non-singular, non-physically limited) forms.

As touched on earlier, much creativity is moving towards the network, the collective, regardless of whether biological, nonbiological or synthesis artists. Additionally, there is no innate reason that the form of nonbiological artists would be anything like biological – why be a single entity when you can be 1,000, or 100,000? Collective superintelligence is one of the forms outlined by Bostrom, a large number of cooperating lesser intellects, with the combined performance vastly outstripping any current cognitive system (2014: 54). To some degree, these already exist in the abstract: corporations, communities, humankind as a whole. From a creative standpoint, it is commonplace for bands to synthesize their collective knowledge and abilities, creating work greater than the sum of the parts. Correspondingly, the collective intelligence, the network, the distributed artist, can be viewed as an assemblage with shared purpose. In their creative work, the EDM artist assembles, selects and organizes ideas from the deep ocean of creativity; collaging possibilities, reimagining that which has come before. Ideas explored by Barthes with his concept of the *scriptor* (1977: 145), and Cage's suggestion that we substitute the term 'music' for 'organization of sound' (1978: 3), and 'composer' with 'organizer of sound' (1978: 5), each suggesting a restructuring of existing elements, rather than pure originality. As Koestler wrote in *The Act of Creation*, 'the creative act is not an act of creation in the sense of the Old Testament. It does not create something out of nothing; it uncovers, selects, re-shuffles, combines, synthesizes already existing facts, ideas, faculties, skills' (1964: 120). IBM's *Watson* – famously a winner of US game show *Jepoardy!* – used an intelligent expert manager to combine results from 'hundreds of interacting subsystems' (Kurzweil 2012: 160), each able to 'contribute to a result without necessarily coming up with a final answer' (Kurzweil 2012: 167); a process perhaps analogous to the biological artist (organizer, scriptor). The human (body and mind – the biological artist) is already an assemblage: cells, organs, bacteria, 'organic algorithms shaped by natural selection over millions of years' (Harari 2017: 372), ideas, creative connections, relationships, inspiration. Perhaps, as suggested by Harari, we should see ourselves not as individuals but as *dividuals* (2017: 383). Yet, although these constituent parts are continually changing, there is still a continuity that runs throughout. In the coming years, the singular image of the artist, both physically and mentally, may become fluid, changing and morphing to meet new requirements, assimilating creative concepts from many domains, spread across geographical space, interacting, assembling, reconfiguring – a state of continual becoming (Bucher 2018: 49). As concluded by Chislenko, 'to current humans, it may look like crazy functional soup' (1997).

Art is often teleological, that is, driven by purpose or goals, but what would be the motive for a nonbiological artist's creative work? Biological EDM artists may enjoy the creative process, require emotional release, seek social status or desire financial reward; a nonbiological artist may not. Aware of their mortality, biological artists may consider time a driving force: the desire to leave behind a postmortem legacy or to make the most of one's limited existence; an amortal AI may not. Understanding the goals of human EDM artists is already fraught with challenges, for artist, audience and critic alike. In his memoir, Philip Glass observes two types of writer: those whose work is a way of accommodating themselves to the world and those who aim to make the world understandable to themselves (p. 344). Many (human) artists do not simply follow the path of productivity, maximizing expected utility, but may frequently be acting out an identity, a social role (Bostrom 2014: 88), or be more concerned with creativity, aesthetics or art. Yet, when conceptualizing nonbiological artists, we can imagine that personal identity, society or creativity itself may not be the goal. For nonbiological artists, however, personal identity, society or creativity itself may not be the goal. It could be productivity – creating as much EDM as possible; financial reward – simply making whatever is streamed the most; or really, any other goal that we (or they) could imagine. This is to say, a superintelligent AI might understand human creative ambition but may not choose to pursue the same, or even be indifferent to it altogether (Bostrom 2014: 196). Clearly, these ideas suppose that future AI's have some form of consciousness, self-awareness and/or self-determination, and as previously indicated, these are controversial and hotly debated topics (see prior list of relevant literature). These questions are raised to further intellectual inquiry into the technology, the role of the artist and ongoing creative practice. The functional machine is often less desirable than Baudrillard's aleatory charm of the individual (1994: 101) and within traditional (human) aesthetics, productivity rather than originality is often considered uncreative or unartistic – *l'art pour l'art* still reigns supreme. However, any critique of art is inherently problematic – who should judge what any artist's motive or goal should be? Artistic work cannot be judged objectively, or in isolation, and assessing creativity (as with cognition) is qualitative and subjective. The AI in Lem's *Golem XIV* decides against the military ambitions of its creators, preferring philosophy instead (Goodman and Livingston 2019: 35), and fundamentally, there is no reason to believe that nonbiological superintelligence would fritter away energy on art, EDM or philosophy. We parents may not be able to control the aspirations of our nonbiological descendants any more than we can control those of our pets or even ourselves.

One final area to address is the reaction by, and impact on, the music industry. In 2018, Warner Music Group announced that it had made two new business deals: first, acquiring *Sodatone*, an insight tool that combines 'streaming, social and touring data with the power of machine learning' to help identify unsigned talent (Warner Music Group 2018); and second, signing *Endel*, an app that 'creates personalised, sound-based, adaptive environments' to a distribution deal (Endel 2020). Profit-focused music businesses turning to AI likely suggest future developments within the industry. Biological artists are legally assigned intellectual property rights – economic and moral, often termed *Authors' Rights* – recognizing authorship, providing the right to permit the work's reproduction and allowing the author to profit from the work. As nonbiological AI tools develop, and are subsequently used within the production of music, the industry may need to consider what recognition (legal, economic, moral) the nonbiological artist deserves. At the time of this writing, nonbiological AI artists cannot legally own a copyright in the United States (Hu 2018), and Sturm et al. outline a number of scholars who conclude that 'under present law, autonomously AI-generated works might not be eligible for copyright protection' (2019). Assigning nonbiological artists legal rights will raise significant philosophical questions. The question of consciousness will likely play a role in any development. Although too expansive for satisfactory study in this chapter, consciousness has been explored elsewhere, including by Bostrom (2014), Chalmers (1995, 2018), Dennett (1996) and Solms (2014). Music copyright is already a convoluted system to navigate and for extra complexity – as also pointed out by Sturm (2019) – most AI tools are currently trained using existing work (generally from human artists), work that is also often copyrighted. Taking inspiration from copyrighted work is a technique used by human artists, but an AI's research, processes and inspirations may be easier to prove in court. In early 2020, two musicians – Damien Riehl and Noah Rubin – created an algorithm that determined 'every melody contained within a single octave' in response to the frequent copyright lawsuits that they believe stifle the creative freedom of artists (Cole 2020). If an AI can create – and perhaps someday legally own – every possible melody, what creative room does that leave for biological artists? Many biological artists rely on intellectual property ownership for their income, and challenges from nonbiological artists and AI tools may become increasingly impactful upon their livelihoods. At present, biological artists can work with AI tools, copying and copyrighting the results, but what happens when AI artists become more intelligent? Warner's arrangement with *Endel* is apparently not for the generative technology itself but for music created by the algorithm, with a 50/50 royalty split between Warner and the developers (Deahl 2019). Yet in time, businesses such as Warner Music Group, Spotify or SoundCloud could develop their own AI artists, removing all financial obligations to humans. If biological EDM artists of the future cannot compete with the nonbiological – on rate of creation or financial productivity – they will need to differentiate their work in new (creative) ways. For example, machine systems (currently, at least) struggle with optical illusions, something we *see* due to certain shortcuts our brains make within our (biological) visual system (Emerging Technology from the arXiv 2018). Human artists may therefore create the EDM *trompe l'œil* (a *trompe l'oreille* perhaps), music that a machine, regardless of intelligence, simply could neither make nor copy. Or perhaps (certain) human audiences will prefer EDM from human artists, much as (often functionally inferior) handmade products are still valued today (Bostrom 2014: 160): a continued respect towards anthropocentric creativity (Avdeef 2019). Biological artists have more value than simply creativity or productivity. They receive respect as arbiters of culture, selling not only music but their personal histories, upbringings and passions (Hu 2018). Audiences engage with EDM aesthetically, but also culturally, socially and politically: the *entendre* and *comprende* of Schaeffer's *quatre écoutes* (DeMers 2010). As long as EDM audiences engage with music on these terms (the emergence of nonbiological audiences would significantly alter the landscape), biological and nonbiological artists will remain distinct, creating EDM both apart and in collaboration.

Conclusion

By giving life to non-living things, people have explored their place in the world – sometimes feeling powerful, and sometimes feeling fearful of a world they can't control.
          – AI: More than Human exhibition catalogue (2019: 23)

This chapter set out to explore the impact of AI upon EDM, consider the creative use of these new tools and raise questions for future examination. EDM inherently involves partnership between human and machine. Traditionally within this relationship, the human has been the dominant intelligence and creative director. However, with the emergence of intelligent machine tools, this relationship dynamic will shift. And furthermore, with the potential for entirely nonbiological artists, the very function of the artist is likely to evolve. The potential evolution of AI – from narrow to general to super – is particularly significant for both creativity and the role of the artist, with the artist advancing from biological to nonbiological, from the god to the human to the network. Already in our daily lives we are surrounded by and frequently interact with AI, and as audiences we are increasingly used to nonbiological voices and the creative input of AI in the music that we hear. Electronic music did not simply reproduce acoustic music, just as cinema was not destined to reproduce theatre (Baudrillard 1994: 105). Nonbiological art will not simply reproduce biological art. As the capability of AI evolves, new ideas and new forms of creativity will emerge, whether directly from nonbiological minds or indirectly through influencing biological. Philip Glass describes the work of art as having no independent existence, coming into being through an 'interdependence of other events with people' (2015: 95). EDM created with AI is thus entangled with other fundamental questions – questions regarding intellectual property, the economic responsibility of the music industry to artists, the legal rights of the work of art and of the artist. Do the creators of Aiva have a moral responsibility towards their creative AI system? Should Holly Herndon pay *Spawn* a portion of earned royalties?

At present, the use of AI within EDM is a continuing exploration by humans, an exploration of the cultural, economic, social and personal value of art, of human-made art and of the biological artist. The concept of the nonbiological mind simply frames this exploration, the act of artists and audiences learning about themselves, a reflection on the fundamental limitations of the human and an attempt to prove the real through the imaginary (Baudrillard 1994: 19). Nonbiological artists need not be defined in conventional terms. At present, it is the individual production tools of EDM that are endowed with narrow AI. However, through technological evolution, and the progress from general through to superintelligence, AI will not be so limited. Moreover, there is no reason to limit music creation to traditionally music companies: Warner Music Group may be working with AI, but so are Tesla. In 2020, Oral B advertised a toothbrush that includes '3D Teeth Tracking and AI Recognition [. . .] to help guide you to your best clean' (Oral B 2020). If contemporary toothbrushes are being given intelligence, bluetooth speakers may be next: speaker 1.0 may *intelligently* perfect the bass settings for your local environment, speaker 2.0 may compose better basslines for your local environment. We do not need to limit the concept of the artist to a fixed idea. The nonbiological artist of the future could be a cognified album, car, pair of headphones, drum kit, global network of interconnected EDM-creating minds or a single intelligent entity.

EDM created by AI is perhaps as interesting, and as creative, as EDM created by biological intelligence. That is, it is entirely subjective. Indeed, the unique nature of human creativity itself may be questioned. In many ways, human artists can already be viewed as assemblages – physical, mental, cultural – and human creativity as an act of organization, reshuffling, reconfiguring and remixing existing ideas. With this in mind, nonbiological artists may not be creatively very different to their biological predecessors. What's more, the separation of human and nonhuman, digital and organic, will likely become fluid; defining art as *nonbiological* only has limited use. There will be an impact: the livelihood, creativity and purpose of biological EDM artists may be challenged. And there will be progress: new forms of creativity, a redefinition of EDM. Much as Benjamin described the advent of photography, the very nature of art may undergo a change (1936: 15). EDM, artists and creativity will, however, adapt, as biological intelligence parents the next stage of creative evolution.

Works Cited

Amadeus Code (2020). 'Amadeus Code', *Amadeus Code*, n.d., https://amadeuscode.com/top, accessed 28 March 2020.

Amper Music (2020). 'Amper Score', *Amper Music*, n.d., https://www.ampermusic.com/, accessed 28 March 2020.

Avdeef, Melissa (2019). 'Artificial Intelligence & Popular Music: SKYGGE, Flow Machines, and the Audio Uncanny Valley', *Arts 2019*, 8(4), pp. 130.

Babcock, Jay (1999). 'DAVID BYRNE on Fela Kuti (1999)', *Arthur Magazine*, 3 November, https://arthurmag.com/2009/11/03/david-byrne-on-fela-kuti-1999/, accessed 20 May 2020.

Barqué-Duran, Albert (2017). 'My Artificial Muse', *Albert Barqué-Duran*, n.d., https://albertbarque.com/myartificialmuse/, accessed 28 March 2020.

Barthes, Roland (1977). *Image Music Text*. London: Fontana Press.

Baudrillard, Jean (1994). *Simulacra and Simulation*. Michigan: The University of Michigan Press.

Benjamin, Walter (1936). *The Work of Art in the Age of Mechanical Reproduction*. London: Penguin Books Ltd.

Bilski, Emily D. (2019). 'Artificial Intelligence Avant La Lettre: The Golem of Jewish Mysticism, Legend and Art', in *AI: More than Human*. London: Barbican International Enterprises.

Bogost, Ian (2020). 'It Doesn't Matter If Anyone Exists or Not', *The Atlantic*, 24 February, https://www.theatlantic.com/technology/archive/2020/02/how-generate-infinite-fake-humans/606943/, accessed 28 May 2020.

Bostrom, Nick (2014). *Superintelligence*. Oxford: Oxford University Press.

Brooks, David (2013). 'The Philosophy of Data', *New York Times*, 4 February, https://www.nytimes.com/2013/02/05/opinion/brooks-the-philosophy-of-data.html, accessed 1 June 2020.

Bucher, Taina (2018). *If... Then*. New York: Oxford University Press.

Byrne, David (2012). *How Music Works*. San Francisco: McSweeney's.

Cage, John (1978). *Silence*. London: Marion Boyars Publishers Ltd.

Chalmers, David J. (1995). 'Facing Up to the Problem of Consciousness', *Journal of Consciousness Studies*, 2(3), pp. 200–19.

Chalmers, David J. (2018). 'The Meta-Problem of Consciousness', *Journal of Consciousness Studies*, 25(9–10), pp. 6–61.

Chislenko, Alexander (1997). 'Technology as Extension of Human Functional Architecture', *Extropy Online*, n.d., http://project.cyberpunk.ru/idb/technology_as_extension.html, accessed 1 June 2020.

Cole, Samantha (2020). 'Musicians Algorithmically Generate Every Possible Melody, Release Them to Public Domain', *Vice*, 25 February, https://www.vice.com/en_us/article/wxepzw/musicians-algorithmically-generate-every-possible-melody-release-them-to-public-domain, accessed 28 March 2020.

Colombo, Florian, Alexander Seeholzerm and Wulfram Gerstner (2017). 'Deep Artificial Composer: A Creative Neural Network Model for Automated Melody Generation', in Correia João, Vic Ciesielski and Antonios Liapis (eds), *Computational Intelligence in Music, Sound, Art and Design. EvoMUSART 2017*. Lecture Notes in Computer Science, 10198, pp. 81–96.

Deahl, Dani (2019). 'Warner Music Signed an Algorithm to a Record Deal – What Happens Next?', *The Verge*, 27 March, https://www.theverge.com/2019/3/27/18283084/warner-music-algorithm-signed-ambient-music-endel, accessed 4 June 2020.

Dehaene, Stanislas (2014). *Consciousness and the Brain*. New York: Viking Press.

De Man, Brecht and Joshua D. Reiss (2013). 'A Knowledge-Engineered Autonomous Mixing System', in *135th Convention of the Audio Engineering Society*. New York: Audio Engineering Society.

DeMers, Joanna (2010). *Listening Through the Noise: The Aesthetics of Experimental Electronic Music*. Oxford: Oxford University Press.

Dennett, Daniel C. (1996). 'Facing Backwards on the Problem of Consciousness', *Journal of Consciousness Studies*, 3(1), pp. 4–6.

Emerging Technology from the arXiv (2018). 'Neural Networks Don't Understand What Optical Illusions Are', *MIT Technology Review*, 12 October, https://www.technologyreview.com/2018/10/12/139826/neural-networks-dont-understand-what-optical-illusions-are/, accessed 28 April 2020.

Endel (2020). 'About', *Endel*, n.d., https://endel.io/about/, accessed 20 June 2020.

Glass, Philip (2015). *Words Without Music*. New York: Liveright Publishing Company.

Goertzel, Ben (2018). 'From Here to Human-Level Artificial General Intelligence in Four (Not All That) Simple Steps', *Singularity Hub*, 22 June, https://singularityhub.co

m/2018/07/22/from-here-to-human-level-artificial-general-intelligence-in-four-not-all-that-simple-steps/, accessed 4 April 2020.

Goertzel, Ben (2019). 'What's So Disturbing about Microsoft's Open AI Investment?', *LinkedIn*, 30 July, https://www.linkedin.com/pulse/whats-so-disturbing-microsofts-openai-investment-ben-goertzel/, accessed 28 March 2020.

Good, Irving John (1965). 'Speculations Concerning the First Ultraintelligent Machine', *Advances in Computers*, 6, pp. 31–88.

Goodman, Steve and Suzanne Livingston (2019). 'Exploring AI, Sound and the Golem in It (2019)', *AI: More than Human*. London: Barbican International Enterprises.

Gorton, Thomas (2018). 'Speaking to Yona, the AI Singer-Songwriter Making Haunting Love Songs', *Dazed*, 22 June, https://www.dazeddigital.com/music/article/40412/1/yona-artificial-intelligence-singer-ash-koosha-interview, accessed 20 May 2020.

Hall, Edward T. (1973). *The Silent Language*. New York: Anchor Books.

Harari, Yuval Noah (2017). *Homo Deus*. London: Vintage.

Hawthorne, Katie (2019). 'Holly Herndon: The Musician Who Birthed an AI Baby', *The Guardian*, 2 May, https://www.theguardian.com/music/2019/may/02/holly-herndon-on-her-musical-baby-spawn-i-wanted-to-find-a-new-sound, accessed 12 May 2020.

Healy, Kevin, Luke McNally, Graeme D. Ruxton, Natalie Cooper and Andrew L. Jackson (2013). 'Metabolic Rate and Body Size Are Linked with Perception of Temporal Information', *Animal Behaviour*, 86(4), pp. 685–96.

Hu, Cherie (2018). 'How Music Generated by Artificial Intelligence Is Reshaping – Not Destroying – The Industry', *Billboard*, 19 April, https://www.billboard.com/articles/business/8333911/artificial-intelligence-music-reshaping-destroying-industry, accessed 28 March 2020.

Kelly, Kevin (2017). *The Inevitable*. New York: Viking Press.

Kissinger, Henry A., Eric Schmidt and Daniel Huttenlocher (2019). 'The Metamorphosis', *The Atlantic*, n.d., https://www.theatlantic.com/magazine/archive/2019/08/henry-kissinger-the-metamorphosis-ai/592771/, accessed 28 May 2020.

Koestler, Arthur (1964). *The Act of Creation*. London: Hutchinson.

Kurzweil, Ray (2006). *The Singularity Is Near*. New York: Penguin Books.

Kurzweil, Ray (2012). *How to Create a Mind*. New York: Penguin Books.

LANDR (2020). 'Online Audio Mastering', *LANDR*, n.d., https://www.landr.com/en/online-audio-mastering, accessed 28 March 2020.

Libet, Benjamin (2005). *Mind Time: The Temporal Factor in Consciousness*. Cambridge: Harvard University Press.

Livingston, Suzanne (2019). 'Beyond a Human Centered World', *AI: More than Human*. London: Barbican International Enterprises.

Lovelock, James and Bryan Appleyard (2019). *Novacene*. Cambridge: The MIT Press.

Moffat, David and Mark B. Sandler (2019). 'Approaches in Intelligent Music Production', *Arts 2019*, 8(4), p. 125.

Nicolson, Adam (2001). *Sea Room*. New York: North Point Press.

Oral B (2020). 'iO Series 9 Rechargeable Electric Toothbrush', *Oral B*, n.d., https://oralb.com/en-us/products/electric-toothbrushes/io-series-9-electric-toothbrush/, accessed 22 June 2020.

Palladini, Alessandro (2018). 'Intelligent Audio Machines', Paper presented at the Keynote Talk at 4th Workshop on Intelligent Music Production (WIMP-18), Huddersfield, UK, 14/09.

Plaugic, Lizzie (2017). 'Musician Taryn Southern on Composing Her New Album Entirely with AI', *The Verge*, 27 August, https://www.theverge.com/2017/8/27/16197196/taryn-southern-album-artificial-intelligence-interview, accessed 28 March 2020.

Robinson Sterling, Amy (2019). 'How Do We Thrive in This New Future?', *AI: More than Human*. London: Barbican International Enterprises.

Rose, Steve (2020). '"It's a War between Technology and a Donkey" — How AI Is Shaking Up Hollywood', *The Guardian*, 16 January, https://www.theguardian.com/film/2020/jan/16/its-a-war-between-technology-and-a-donkey-how-ai-is-shaking-up-hollywood, accessed 28 March 2020.

Rossi, Francesca (2019). 'How Do We Thrive in This New Future?', *AI: More than Human*. London: Barbican International Enterprises.

Russell, Stuart J. and Peter Norvig (1995). *Artificial Intelligence: A Modern Approach*. Englewood Cliffs: Prentice Hall.

Siverman, Rosa (2013). 'Flies See the World in Slow Motion, Say Scientists', *The Telegraph*, 16 September, https://www.telegraph.co.uk/news/science/science-news/10311821/Flies-see-the-world-in-slow-motion-say-scientists.html, accessed 22 June 2020.

Solms, Mark (2014). 'A Neuropsychoanalytical Approach to the Hard Problem of Consciousness', *Journal of Integrative Neuroscience*, 13(2), pp. 173–85.

Splash Pro (2020). 'Make Music with AI', *Popgun*, n.d., https://splashpro.popgun.ai/, accessed 28 March 2020.

Sturm, Bob L.T., Maria Iglesias, Oded Ben-Tal, Marius Miron and Emilia Gómez (2019). 'Artificial Intelligence and Music: Open Questions of Copyright Law and Engineering Praxis', *Arts 2019*, 8(3), pp. 115.

Tesla (2020). 'Future of Driving', Tesla, n.d., https://www.tesla.com/autopilot, accessed 28 March 2020.

Turing, Alan (1950), 'Computing Machinery and Intelligence', *Mind*, 59(236), pp. 433–60.

Uchida, Maholo (2019). 'Towards the World Where All Are United', *AI: More than Human*. London: Barbican International Enterprises.

Vanderbilt, Tom (2017). *You May Also Like*. New York: Vintage Books.

Vinge, Vernor (1993). 'The Coming Technological Singularity: How to Survive in the Post-human Era', *NASA, Vision-21, Interdisciplinary Science and Engineering in the Era of Cyberspace*, 10129, pp. 11–22.

The Vinyl Factory (2018). 'Actress/Young Paint', *Vinyl Factory*, 28 September, https://thevinylfactory.com/product/young-paint/, accessed 3 April 2020.

von Neumann, John (1958). *The Computer and the Brain*. New Haven: Yale University Press.

Wager, Sanna, George Tzanetakis, Cheng-i Wang and Minje Kim (2019). 'Deep Autotuner: A Data-Driven Approach to Natural-Sounding Pitch Correction for Singing Voice in Karaoke Performances', *ArXiv*, abs/1902.00956.

Warner Music Group (2018). 'Warner Music Group Acquires Sodatone', Warner Music Group, 28 March, https://www.wmg.com/news/warner-music-group-acquires-sodatone-33396, accessed 4 June 2020.

Weizenbaum, Joseph (1976). *Computer Power and Human Reason*. San Francisco: W. H. Freeman.

Part II

EDM stars and stardom

5

Avicii and mental health of EDM stars

Melanie Ptatscheck

Music industry stereotypes of fame and fortune may often cause more harm than good, as the example of Tim Bergling, aka *Avicii*, has recently demonstrated. While the media normalize and glorify the lifestyle of the 'superstar' DJ, the struggles between stardom and well-being remain hidden. As the documentary *Avicii: True Stories* illustrates, the life of the young artist as presented by the media stood in stark contrast to his self-description: an introverted person who spoke out about anxiety issues and struggles with mainstream fame (Tsikurishvili 2017). The intensity of touring schedules, the high pressure to succeed and the imbalance between the euphoria of the show followed by exhaustion, loneliness and self-doubt – all these stress factors caused Avicii to increasingly avoid the spotlight. 'My life is all about stress. It will kill me,' he prophetically claims at one point in the documentary. This prophecy came true with the artist's suicide in 2018.

Avicii's death showed that mental disorders such as depression, anxiety and substance abuse can affect people regardless of their fame and income. His death also drew attention to the overall well-being of artists in electronic dance music (EDM) culture, which has long been stigmatized with associations to drug abuse. In the wake of Avicii's tragedy, in particular the mental health of EDM artists became a topic of more intense discussion. While the Association for Electronic Music (AFEM) has responded to these developments by launching in 2019 a mental health guide for people working in the electronic music industries, and mental health in general became a relevant topic on several journalistic platforms such as *Groove Magazine*, *Faze Magazine*, *Resident Advisor* or *Mixmag*, little academic research has taken place on this topic so far.

Focusing on 'superstar' DJs in EDM, this chapter illustrates the construction of stars in the music industries. It takes into account what influence the concept of 'being a star' has on the self-concept of 'being an artist'. Using the example of Avicii and individual perspectives of DJs based on narrative accounts, I will show that health and well-being problems are not only caused by imbalances of living and working conditions but also connected with mediated image constructions and social narratives. I argue that toxic (self-) images can have negative influences on the mental health of artists and may lead to desperate reactions such as increased alcohol and drug consumption or even suicide.

Stardom, images and constructions of 'self'

In the heyday of underground Detroit techno in the 1980s and the early 1990s, stardom was not the focus of artists and recipients. Within this context, an attempt was made to give the music a level of autonomy, disregarding chart positions, the artists' image or other forms of representation (Büsser 2001: 75).[1] The middle of the decade, by contrast, was a highlight for EDM in the mainstream, resulting in the exact opposite: British producers like Fatboy Slim were played on MTV, remixes by Armand van Helden or Todd Terje became international radio hits, and the Prodigy even made it to number one on the US charts (Poschardt 2015: 517). DJs like Sasha, Paul Oakenfold, Sonique, Pete Tong, Dave Seaman, Laurent Garnier, Paul van Dyk, Tiësto or Sven Väth pushed EDM into the mainstream consciousness and garnered international reputation (Phillips 2009: 5; Hall and Zukic 2013: 107).[2] Fans not only treated them like rock-stars; DJs literally adapted the clichéd rock-star lifestyle, which Phillips describes as a 'whirlwind of five-star luxury':

> DJs suddenly found themselves with high-paid careers, hurtling up and down the country playing at three clubs a night, earning thousands of pounds in cash a year, being offered champagne and drugs for free, partying through it all. (2009: 5)

Especially with the emergence of 'superclubs' and EDM festivals such as the Ultra Music Festival, Electric Daisy Carnival, Electric Zoo or Tomorrowland, EDM enjoyed mass popularity around the globe. Jet-setting DJs were in constant demand at these events, and figures such as Calvin Harris, Steve Aoki, Tiësto, Kruder and Dorfmeister or David Guetta became 'electronic cash kings' (Collin 2018: 5) – the highest-paid DJs in the world (Greenberg 2016). Although mainstream-oriented electronic music – as a form of EDM *and* contemporary top forty pop music (Holt 2019) – as well as its performing acts have been successfully marketed under the label EDM by the music industries, this phenomenon does not apply to EDM in general (Gálvez 2019) but rather to the specific pop culture phenomenon that Robin James (2015) and Fabian Holt (2016, 2017) define as 'EDM pop'.

The pop-cultural view of DJs has shifted to a 'star and figure of longing' (Veenstra 2021) – or as novelist Nick Hornby (1999: 71) put it: 'Your heroes were guitarists, now the kids like DJs.'[3] Not just the fans seem to be getting younger. 'Youngster' DJs like Martin Garrix, Felix Jaehn or Avicii represent a new generation of DJs who started their careers at an age in which they are usually not permitted to enter the clubs themselves but were already 'superstars'.

According to Richard Dyer, the classic idea of the 'star' has its origins in the theatre world but fully developed in the context of the Hollywood film industry (Dyer 1979; see also Evans and Wilson 1999; DeCordova 2001). Martina Schuegraf describes the typical American movie star as a glamorous figure created by an economic system (Schuegraf 2013: 120). The term 'star' refers to a famous or prominent personality known to the public who has become popular through the media. Following the implications of the metaphor, a 'star' acquires transcendental, even 'raptured', components. It connects with heroes and cult figures who become idols. The 'star' implies the expectation of great talent or outstanding performances that sets him apart from others.

Recording industry actors construct the 'star' on the basis of what the artist is offering in terms of potential. As stated by Christoph Jacke, the construct 'star' is (re-)constructed and reproduced via communication processes in the context of (music) media, music business, concerts, etc. (Jacke 2013: 75). These processes not only contribute to music distribution but also facilitate the development of recipient tastes via targeted messaging. Recipients in turn join in the process of image construction. Construction offers are enforced through (increased) demand and fan behaviour (or have to be modified in case demand is lacking) (Jacke 2013). The star is in the centre of the process. He is the starting point of the process and therefore always the engine and the result of the process dynamic.

Dyer describes 'star' as the intertextual product arising from the interplay of a performing and a private presence (Dyer 1979; see also Ellis 1982; DeCordova 2001). This product includes an auratic, glamourous and a desirable component (Holmes and Redmond 2006: 10), resulting from a combination of characteristics such as some form of exceptional status and aloofness, which make the star a projection surface: 'The star is at once ordinary and extraordinary, available for desire and unattainable' (Ellis 1982: 91). The contrasts between the public and the private, as well as the dynamics of the approachable and unapproachable, create a rich set of meanings, engaging the audience in the fascination of stardom. A central moment of this active 'star re-construction' with the available 'star material' (interviews, shows, making-ofs, tabloid press, social media, etc.) is the desire to get close to the star in his 'true' nature.

Dyer does not understand stars as 'real' persons in the true sense but as a form of media texts and thus as *images* (1979: 2). David P. Marshall also speaks of three levels of star 'self' generated by online communication and medialization: the 'public self', the 'public private self' and the 'transgressive intimate self' (2010: 44). Even when the star is reported on as a 'private person' we only ever experience a construction of personality: 'Personality is itself a construction known and expressed only through films, stories, publicity etc.' (Dyer 1979: 23; see also Borgstedt 2008).

The construction of star personalities is realized in the form of intertextual patterns, which become effective as images. An image is thus 'a complex configuration of visual, verbal and aural signs' (Dyer 1979: 38), determining the image both of stardom in general (the idea of how stars live or have to live) and of individual stars in particular (see, for example, Borgstedt 2008: 57). Dyer understands the creation of images as a transformation process: the star provides a raw material through his person (physiognomy, character affinity, etc.), which is then first transformed into an image through the product 'film' (here: music, performances, etc.) (cf. Cook and Bernik 1999; Borgstedt 2008). The star is increasingly associated with a certain type of role and acts exclusively as a symbol and figurehead for a (here: music) genre or character type. Silke Borgstedt considers this with regard to the 'music star': a musician does not change his public identity like an actor who slips into new roles (2008: 58). A musician continuously embodies the patterns of behaviour and values associated with his own or the artist's name. At the same time, however, their numerous individual performances also create a symbolic character, in that a successful interpreter becomes an exponent of a certain aesthetic style assigned to and identified with him (2008).

In the following, these aspects are illustrated using the example of the 'youngster-superstar' DJ *Avicii*. Here, it is of interest not only how an artist can be integrated into a concept from an outside perspective but also how the person (in contrast) perceives himself and his own abilities, motivations and needs.

'True stories': Avicii versus Tim Bergling

> I wanted to do a brutally honest film about Tim as a person and not only about Avicii. Everybody knows Avicii but very few people know Tim. I think this documentary really shows Tim's struggle and strength of character. Being a worldwide superstar artist is not as it looks on Instagram. (Tsikurishvili in Fleisher 2017)

In 2018, Netflix released the documentary *Avicii: True Stories* about the DJ and producer Tim Bergling, aka Avicii. In a statement on his work, the film-maker Levan Tsikurishvili claims that the documentary tells the 'true story of the young superstar', which is intended to help outsiders learn to understand 'how it is to be Avicii' – what it means to be a star.[4]

Avicii's story begins with Tim Bergling, born 1989 in Stockholm, as a high school kid, remixing songs on his laptop. Bergling is introduced as a 'boy next door' and a normal teen (Tsikurishvili 2017). As a teenager, Bergling himself does not seem to know exactly who Tim Bergling is or what might become of him. However, he already seems to be clear about the fact that 'whatever I wanted to do later in life I knew that I wanted to do something creative' (Tsikurishvili 2017). He and his friends describe Tim Bergling as a music and technology-loving 'nerd', working meticulously on songs. He puts his need to produce a good track above a healthy lifestyle (fast food, little sleep, irregular hours). First, he publishes his material online. The fact that his idol, house DJ and producer Laidback Luke, is becoming aware of him motivates him to constantly improve his tracks. While his musical orientation is influenced by a role model, the direction of his professional career is rather a product controlled by a foreign power: in 2008, his future manager apparently senses star potential in the seventeen-year-old producer and prophesies: 'Name one Swedish DJ that you think is big right now. I'm gonna make you bigger than him in one year' (Tsikurishvili 2017).

However, the extrovert manager's 'great' vision does not seem to fit the introvert personality of the artist, whom Laidback Luke describes as 'a very shy and just held back type of kid' even at performances. Avicii initially focused on music and producing rather than performing: 'It was one or two shows a month at this point and I was mainly focused on the music' (Tsikurishvili 2017). He also has to be taught DJing in the first place. With the song 'Seek Romance' (2010) and under the stage name *Tim Berg* he is perceived for the first time by a larger public.

> Things started taking off. People come to your show to hear your songs like when they knew the songs and I remember when I played at Governor's Island

in New York they were singing along to every single one of my songs. I was just blown away cause this like never happened before. (Tim Bergling cited by Tsikurishvili 2017)

Footage after the gig shows him excited. In an interview, however, he is shy and modest and seems unable to realize his success: 'I'm so excited now, I don't know what to say. [. . .] I'm just focused on being present' (Tim Bergling cited by Tsikurishvili 2017). This indicates that his focus shifts from solely music making to presentation (through stage performances, interviews and autograph sessions).

'Levels' (2011) becomes Avicii's first big single, launching him to international stardom. Bergling seems to be overwhelmed by his sudden success:

I could afford a tour manager and I didn't have to fly coach anymore. [. . .] I was young, I was single, I was partying every show. It was really a big party. It was amazing. I didn't realize before that you could actually [tour] Monday, Tuesday, Thursday, Saturday and Sunday. But then once that opens up like you could tour a whole year. And that's what we did. (Tim Bergling cited by Tsikurishvili 2017)

Statements from film footage of the time, such as 'I'm not sure if I'm allowed to answer' (Tim Bergling cited by Tsikurishvili 2017), suggest that he was now consciously paying attention to how he presented himself. The rock-star life he now seems to live – portrayed in the film by showing a destroyed apartment with empty bottles, pizza boxes, alcohol and Avcii in bed with two women – can be interpreted as part of an image construction.

It is obviously also part of this concept – on the production *and* promotion side – to work with already successful artists and producers and to find his own sound in order to build and enhance the brand: 'I think every artist of any kind, like the ultimate goal is to find your own mark. Something that makes you stand out from all the rest' (Tim Bergling cited by Tsikurishvili 2017). With the use of drugs (mentioned here only in the form of alcohol) he fulfils another component of the supposed rock-star existence, which he as a private person had not integrated into his lifestyle:

In the beginning I was too afraid to drink, because I didn't want to screw up, but then I realized how stiff I was when I wasn't drinking. Then I found that the magical cure of just having like a couple of drinks before going on [stage]. [. . .] [It] helped me be able to do all those shows without feeling completely exhausted. (Tim Bergling cited by Tsikurishvili 2017)

Apparently, he not only experiences the supposedly positive effects of an alcohol rush in his performances. He also takes the consumption of alcohol as a community-building ritual associated with the DJ's profession. 'I saw how other DJs drank and I saw people like DJs who's been in this industry for ten years and they're still drinking like, you know, every show that they are doing' (Tim Bergling cited by Tsikurishvili 2017). In an interview with *GQ Magazine*, he adds:

> You get to this place, there's free alcohol everywhere – it's sort of weird if you don't drink. [. . .] I was so nervous . . . I just got into a habit, because you rely on that encouragement and self-confidence you get from alcohol, and then you get dependent on it. (Pressler 2013)

Over the next few years, Bergling becomes one of the most famous and best-paid DJs in the world, playing over 200 gigs per year. He also suffers from alcoholism, anxiety and pancreatitis, partly a result of his alcohol habit. He is hospitalized numerous times, has his gallbladder and appendix removed and experiences chronic pain for years. But instead of paying attention to his health, he follows the narrative: the show must go on!

The pain Bergling suffers behind the scenes is hidden from the audience – this is also part of the image construction. Although the documentary shows Bergling in a poor condition – in one scene, he can barely keep himself awake and complains of severe pain while his manager talks about bookings and interviews (see Figure 5.1) – on stage he still seems to be able to function like a machine: when the pyro-curtain drops, his arms go up and the show begins (see Figure 5.2).

The euphoria that once seemed to go with the realization of the DJ star's dream seems to be overturning with further success. While he had initially enjoyed being a pop star and celebrated the lifestyle that accompanies it, he seems to be rethinking the life into which he (unexpectedly) slipped. He questions whether his current life meets the needs he actually has of it: 'My life was a dream for so many people including myself. House music and dance music really had such a rise, at the same time I had my rise' (Tsikurishvili 2017).

Maintaining the star construct – the classic story of success according to the American Dream, the 'from rags to riches' narrative – is associated with extreme stress factors for the person behind the star. With the onset of health consequences, both psychologically and physically, the product Avicii inevitably cannot be separated from the private person. With the growing doubt about the

Figure 5.1 Bergling in poor health condition. Screenshot from *Avicii: True Stories* (Tsikurishvili 2017).

Figure 5.2 Avicii on stage. Screenshot from *Avicii: True Stories* (Tsikurishvili 2017).

role he had (unconsciously) assumed, he begins to question not only what it means to be Avicii but also what Tim Bergling wants:

> It was a lot of work, a lot of heavy tours. I just went with all the punches that came along, because I was so extremely lucky to be able to what I am doing. But I didn't take the time to really figure out what I wanted to do and how I wanted to do it. I just went along with the flow. I only focused on music and the touring [. . .]. And I obviously had to set up what I was gonna do, promotion and this is up, but it was never really my plan. I think I was running after an ideal of happiness that wasn't my own. (Tim Bergling cited by Tsikurishvili 2017)

When asked in a radio interview what it is like to be Avicii, the discrepancy between his own identity and the self-concept imposed by the image becomes particularly clear: 'It's weird. I mean obviously I am Avicii, but at the same time people's perception of who Avicii is, isn't who Tim is. I'm a little bit shy, I don't really like being the center of attention' (Tim Bergling cited by Tsikurishvili 2017). But he *is* in the centre – especially of his own marketing process.

The stress leads to a chain reaction: due to the physical and psychological stress factors, he becomes ill and has to take more medication to 'kill the pain', which in turn intensifies his anxiety issues. He does not manage to escape the vicious cycle – especially not since his surroundings tell him that everything is fine:

> I looked around and I saw everyone else doing what I was doing and, seemingly [. . .] they looked like they were doing fine. Then I started feeling crazy in a sense. Everything on the checklist is there, so I should be happy. [. . .] What I should have done obviously is to fucking stop, take four months five months, have a year recovery. [. . .] Recover from all these years of touring, all the stress. But I kept going. (Tim Bergling cited by Tsikurishvili 2017)

He seems to address not only his physical but also his psychological suffering – caused by stress, anxiety, self-doubt, perfection and existential angst.[5] Not only his management but also he himself keeps the vicious cycle going: 'There was never an end of shows. Even when I really felt like I was going to hit a wall' (Tim Bergling cited by Tsikurishvili 2017). In order to maintain the continuity of the brand Avicii, he continues touring and writes new songs, requiring him to navigate a difficult line between compulsion and passion. On the one hand he has to tour due to contractual obligations; on the other hand he believes in his music, in which he still finds joy. 'Even the shows got harder [. . .] there are always moments during the touring, during the shows, when I could find a genuine happiness for music' (Tim Bergling cited by Tsikurishvili 2017).

In his role as a star, he must continue to present his brand in public, which puts him under increasing pressure. Furthermore, the narrative that anyone can make it and become a superstar, which he embodies himself, now becomes another stress factor to him. The artist lifestyle Bergling initially enjoyed increasingly becomes an obligation.

After Bergling released his second album *Stories* in 2015, he decided to cancel all shows for the next eight months. During the break, his passion for making music is rekindled: 'My passion for music was always there. I loved making music. That was one thing I could come back to' (Tim Bergling cited by Tsikurishvili 2017). Although he tries to change his lifestyle, he quickly falls back into old patterns:

> In the beginning of the year I get presented with all the shows of the upcoming year [. . .]. You know my manager might want to push something in, someone else might want to push something in and it's pushing my manager to push it in. I might want to push something in. All these things come in and they cause shit time stress. (Tim Bergling cited by Tsikurishvili 2017)

After the break he plays Ultra Miami again – one of the biggest EDM festivals. Ten days later he announces his retirement from stage. 'I've told them over and over I won't be able to play anymore,' he tells a friend near to the end of the documentary, referring to Pournouri and his team. 'I've told them over and over it will kill me' (Tim Bergling cited by Tsikurishvili 2017). Still, he struggles to rein in his relentless touring machine, which earns a handsome living not just for him but also for a number of people around him. Instead of taking the health issues caused by his career seriously and supporting him, they make clear to him the supposed economic consequences of his exit. Bergling perceives the situation as follows:

> When I decided to stop, I was expecting a completely different support – in stopping. I've been very open with what I've been through and what I felt and what I've done. Everyone knows that I've been anxious. I didn't expect people to try to push me to do more shows when it really . . . when they'd seen how shitty I felt, so I did a lot of resistance when I wanted to stop doing the shows. (Tim Bergling cited by Tsikurishvili 2017)

Bergling finds himself in a conflict of conscience: he is accused of having to break with his management and longtime (personal and business) friends, and he also has to disappoint the expectations of his fans:

> I felt terrible, because I saw how happy all the fans are and I don't fucking like it. [. . .] I have to pretend something that I like something I don't like doing. That was just it for me, because I just knew that, I can't see a way for me to do this and be about it.

At the beginning of the documentary, he looks back on his life as Tim Bergling, aka Avicii – which come back in closing scene:

> The way I went into DJing was 'I gonna give it a hundred percent no matter what happens and I kept giving a hundred percent all the time'. It was all around in general that sense of more and more and more. I didn't give myself enough to really figure out what about the touring didn't I like. The only time I had was a few weeks here and there and then I was on the road again. And the few weeks I had I never really got to get home anywhere and I was out for eight years. [. . .] I just knew that I got to a point where I didn't like it anymore and it got to a point where it was too much. After that I just decided fuck I gonna quit. (Tim Bergling cited by Tsikurishvili 2017)

On the night of 28 August 2016 in Ibiza, Tim Bergling played his last show. On 20 April 2018 he committed suicide and was found dead in a hotel room.

Toxic narratives and mental health

> Most people would be overjoyed to have Tim Bergling's life. To have 250-plus nights a year, audiences of thousands chanting your name. To have the leggy blond girlfriend, the limitless champagne and the piles of money, and famous musicians begging for the production magic he brought to [his songs]. (Pressler 2013)

In her article, journalist Jessica Pressler summarizes a number of aspects of the image of the superstar as perceived by recipients. Similar to how the tabloid press operates, the medially constructed image and levels of personality of a given artist are distributed via social media channels and homepages and used for marketing purposes. Even though the producers of the Avicii documentary claim to portray the person Tim Bergling behind the star construction 'Avicii', they are in fact using another marketing tool: they create a projection surface for the audience and thus attempt to connect fans to the brand via identification potential. Two major narrative desires are satisfied here: Avicii embodies the idealized construct of the American Dream and at the same time the myth of the 'tortured genius' – otherwise attributed to stars like Amy Winehouse, Jimi Hendrix or Kurt Cobain.

It is striking how certain expectations of the artist as described by Pressler are repurposed. Avicii creates exactly what his audience desires in his stage shows: an impressive display of joy, lightheartedness and carelessness, providing an escape from reality and its challenges.[6] Challenges like stress, fear, not being able to cope, exhaustion and self-doubt cause Tim Bergling to attempt escape as well. Thus, while Bergling is presumably portrayed as an actual person in the documentary, suffering physically and mentally, this also creates a further projection surface. The fan-artist connection even continues after Avicii's withdrawal from the public, because audiences are reminded of it not only via social media announcements about the release of the documentary but also via the implied invitation to interact: 'Hey, my documentary Avicii: True Stories released TODAY on Netflix. Let me know what you think.'[7]

The vicious cycle continues as long as the star construction is maintained. The decision to not play any more shows and therefore opt out of the marketing process seemingly signals the end of the star system. But even after (and significantly, through) the death of the artist, the brand continues, and the vicious cycle is additionally fuelled, as posthumously released albums and tribute shows indicate. The 2021 opening of an Avicii museum further compounds the Avicii brand. Fans continue to be enabled to stay close to their role model: 'by following Tim's journey from a reclusive music nerd to a celebrated superstar, from his boyhood room where it all started to the Los Angeles studio where the biggest hits were created.'[8]

Avicii's death not only highlighted the pressures of going along with a superstar career, it also brought the discussion about mental health into public discourse. One might suspect a subtle marketing strategy here as well, or at least this might be an impression gained from watching the documentary. In the context of my current research project, conducting narrative-biographical interviews on the topic of mental health with DJs of different professions and genres of electronic music, one of my interview partners suggested that he would participate in my study mainly for marketing reasons. The example of Avicii had demonstrated to him that a tragic life story could be easily marketable. He expects to gain publicity through the telling of his own tale of woe, hoping that this will provide him with attention and new bookings. These seemingly perfidious thoughts – making a business out of one's own suffering – reveal another rather tragic dimension of mental illness.

The case of Avicii is demonstrably not an isolated case, quite the contrary: pressure and related stress factors along with the already unhealthy lifestyle of a DJ are what most DJs – including those *not* considered part of the 'EDM pop' genre – have to deal with:

> Bergling's story is in many ways extraordinary, from his young age to his astronomical success to extremity of his touring schedule. But the things that wore him down are, for many DJs, utterly ordinary. You might even call them occupational hazards. (Lynch 2018)

With his statement, editor of *Resident Advisor* Will Lynch reacts in his article to a statement of American DJ The Blessed Madonna. 'This could be a lot of us,' she tweets the day after Tim Berling's passing. By 'us' she means all DJs – no matter what sex, profession or style. The death of Avicii seems to be a wake-up call even for the underground scene.

More and more often, established artists publicly talk about their own (mental) suffering that goes along with their jobs in the music business. Portrayed, for instance, in the documentary *Why We DJ – Slaves to the Rhythm* (2017), DJs and producers like Luciano, Carl Cox, Erick Morillo, B.Traits, Ben Pearce and Pete Tong report on mental health issues and related challenges. Also, the German 'EDM pop' DJ Felix Jaehn, who like Avicii had commercial success with his music early in life, talks about his personal suffering and his handling of it. In a statement from an interview with the German radio station N-Joy in 2019, he claims that he plays a role – the role of the DJ that signifies happiness and satisfies the expectations of the fans: 'If I have a bad day, I still have to pull myself together and go on stage and play a cool show, because the fans have bought tickets, because they stand there, because they want to forget their day.' Even if there is no room for worries on stage, these do not simply disappear by entering the role of the EDM superstar. On the contrary, conflicts with this role are intensified. Jaehn describes moments when he was at the point where he wanted to stop everything. He realized, however, that he would be running away from himself: 'That doesn't work because the person Felix Jaehn and the brand Felix Jaehn, that's both me' (Jaehn 2019).

Referring to my current research project, my interview partner Rick (Techno/House DJ and producer, thirty-eight years old) also sees Avicii's problem in the question of finding himself in order to distinguish from the brand he is connected to: 'He never even knew who he was and how he came to everything. Avicii is a brand. That's not you. *You* is someone else. I believe finding out who you are is the most difficult thing.' Rick adds that many DJs may not even be aware of their own crisis; sometimes they do not want or are not allowed to be aware of it. Interviewee Gabriel (Melodical House DJ and producer, thirty-three years old) explains that many of them do not even know what is going on, because they believe 'that everything's fine, everything's under control'. This is also the perspective they try to convey to their social environment, some of whom often understand what is going on but do not (want to) step in: 'My manager knew exactly what was going on, and he fueled it. But nobody tells you anything [. . .] as long things are working out. [. . .] And when things don't work out, you're the one who has to face the music.'

'What happens when you realize that things are taking a direction I can't control anymore?' Rick asks in this context. He describes a dilemma: on the one hand, he is exposed to the stress of touring, which means having to go to a different city each day, sometimes in different time zones. He is unable to adjust to these constantly changing day rhythms, which pushes him to his physical and psychological limits. This increasing exhaustion, however, remains hidden from the audience, because he is forced to 'bring it', every night, every show. Even though financially he would be able to take a break, it is not easy to leave the vicious circle: 'You've got running contracts, and the music industry has got lawyers. Whether I'm puking in the airplane or not, no matter if I'm not well, I'm up there, I'm switched on and have to play my show.' What Rick describes is the 'Don't stop the music!' narrative that keeps the business going. Because if the music stops, the DJ goes home, the audience moves on. In this regard, Rick describes the music industry as a 'shark tank' in which artists have to survive: 'It doesn't matter if the act has to take the rap for it, if they sacrifice everything for it. You've got a contract, and if you don't fulfill it, there's twenty people in the back waiting.'

Even if artists manage to get out of their contracts, there remains a risk of pressure through self-doubt and feelings of guilt and shame. The failure to meet the expectations, whether one's own or those of others, may lead to extreme mental strains, as Rick emphasizes: 'Many DJs die or take drugs or come under pressure because the demands of society are too high, or your own demands of yourself are way too high.' At this point, many of them may not be able to help themselves anymore; even with the acceptance of outside help or the hope of improving the situation via the recognition of different life perspectives, the stage of depression may have already progressed too far – as the example of Avicii tragically illustrates.

Gabriel reasons that the toxic expectations, having to function, not being able to admit to weakness, are mainly rooted in capitalist society, which defines itself via success, performance and money. At the same time, according to Gabriel, it is also societal narratives about ideals and values, and our own fantasies and needs which lead many DJs' behaviours to become toxic. He refers to the 'tempting' option of the 'Villalobos lifestyle' and alludes to the romanticized reputation to stay awake for extended periods and take copious of drugs. In this regard, Joshua Glazer describes Berlin star DJ Ricardo Villalobos as 'the biggest bad boy of Techno' and calls him an 'anti-hero' among many DJs (Glazer 2015). Behaviour resulting from this narrative that can be characterized by 'kicking over the traces' Gabriel assigns especially to young DJs, who see an excessive lifestyle as a reward for their tough and exhausting career path: 'Most of the young artists are in a situation where they've worked hard for a long time, and nothing happens, and then it happens, and you start saying yes to everything.' Despite the fact that it is assumed as part of the lifestyle and considered cool to miss the plane or take drugs all week, the downsides are often ignored: the physical and psychological consequences of this excessive lifestyle may be that careers do not get off the ground or remain very short. Here, a significant fallacy becomes visible, which Gabriel recognizes as well: Ricardo Villalobos managed to make it *despite* the way he lives, not *because* of it.

Gabriel sees the counteracting of certain self-perceptions and the resulting behaviours as a task for society and culture as a whole. He believes the only way is to change the culture: 'Experienced DJs have to talk to young DJs and for example have to tell them, hey, put money aside, I'll explain to you how to invest money. That's a role model function for people who become successful.' He sees not only successful artists but also managers and agents as role models, who should prepare artists for a long-term career, and not just a short 'cash grab' of two or three years. Gabriel also assigns the media a role model function and with it a responsibility of how artists should be reported on and which expectations should be connected to them. In this context, he considers that it is mainly important to stop spreading the belief in the 'tortured genius', but rather to create more healthy paradigms: 'The magazines don't want such [good and healthy] DJs,' he claims, 'they don't think it's cool. The journalists wanna see the fucked-up artist, its best if he doesn't have his life under control, but makes fantastic music.' Here, he mentions a general problem, how artists are perceived in public and what people expect from them. He does not believe that artists write better music if they live an excessive lifestyle – on the contrary: many artists pay for that with their lives. According to his perspective, such self-destructive and toxic narratives should not be transported by the media and music industry. Rather, it should be shown that an artist is 'allowed to be happy', and they should have the option to 'drop their brand' and 'stop the music' in order to interrupt the vicious circle.

Conclusion

Stars as social constructs are complex cultural phenomena marked by the interaction of different forces. They serve as points of orientation and places of cultural meaning production. When viewing stars in the larger context of their (re-)construction process, we should not forget that there is an artist behind the marketing product, whose individual motivations and needs have to be taken into account. Thus, the 'star' needs to be understood as a 'relational term' (Faulstich 2000), to be considered in relation not only to larger society and the roles and recipients of his cultural subsection but also to the artist personality behind the construct. The example of Avicii illustrates that artists whose psychological suffering remains invisible can become the tragic victims of a marketing machine. The story of Avicii may have contributed to making the topic of mental health itself a marketable product; even so, the narrative of the suffering artist received more attention than the public discourse as well.

The example of Avicii shows that narratives (in the sense of 'the means of human sense making', Squire 2008) play an important role in the construction of self-perceptions, meaning the perceptions a person may have about themselves. Such points of reference for the emergence of so-called self-concepts (see also Ptatscheck 2020a, 2020b) can be seen in plots from personal stories as well as cultural myths (see also Polkinghorne 1991). As exemplified by Avicii's story, mental illness is regarded a part of an entire life story, underlying the individual ideas of the artists themselves, but also connecting to external factors that create a brand around them with images and values. To understand 'how it is to be Avicii', the star-self *as well as* the personal self of the person in question have to be considered. A study of the latter area requires a biographical and human-centred approach focusing on the social environment and the self-perception of the individual.

Works Cited

Association for Electronic Music (AFEM), Music Managers Forum, Help Musicians UK and Music Support (2019). *The Electronic Music Industry Guide to Mental Health*,

https://www.associationforelectronicmusic.org/afem-mental-health-guide-for-the-e
lectronic-music-industry, accessed 15 August 2020.

Borgstedt, Silke (2008). *Der Musik-Star. Vergleichende Imageanalysen von Alfred Brendel, Stefanie Hertel und Robbie Williams*. Bielefeld: transcript.

Brewster, Bill and Frank Broughton (2006). *Last Night a DJ Saved My Life: The History of the Disc Jockey*, 2nd edn. London: Headline.

Büsser, Martin (2001). *Popgeschichte*. Hamburg: Europäische Verlagsanstalt.

Collin, Matthew (2018). *Rave On: Global Adventures in Electronic Dance Music*. London: Profile Books.

Cook, Pam and Mieke Bernick (1999). *The Cinema Book*. London: BFI.

DeCordova, Richard (2001). *Picture Personalities. The Emergence of the Star System in America*. Chicago: University of Illinois Press.

Dyer, Richard (1979). *Stars*. London: BFI.

Ellis, John (1982). *Visible Fictions. Cinema. Television, Video*. London: Routledge.

Evans, Andrew and Glenn D. Wilson (1999). *Fame. The Psychology of Stardom*. London: Vision.

Faulstich, Werner (ed.) (2000). 'Sternchen, Star, Superstar, Megastar, Gigastar. Vorüberlegungen zu einer Theorie des Stars als Herzstück populärer Weltkultur', in *Medienkulturen*. München: Wilhelm Fink, pp. 201–12.

Farrugia, Rebekah (2012). *Beyond the Dance Floor. Female DJs, Technology and Electronic Dance Music Culture*. Bristol/Chicago: Intellect.

Farrugia, Rebekah and Thom Swiss (2008). 'Producing Producers: Women and Electronic/Dance Music', *Current Musicology*, 86, pp. 79–99.

Fleisher, Grace (2017). 'Avicii: True Stories Documentary Is Coming to Netflix', in *Dancing Astronaut*, https://dancingastronaut.com/2017/11/aviciis-true-stories-do
cumentary-coming-netflix/, accessed 14 August 2020.

Gálvez, José (2019). 'On Analyzing EDM DJ Set: Problems and Perspectives for a Sociology of Sound', in Marija Dumnić Vilotijević and Ivana Medić (eds), *Contemporary Popular Music Studies: Proceedings of the International Association for the Study of Popular Music 2017*. Wiesbaden: Springer, pp. 149–59.

Gavanas, Anna and Rosa Reitsamer (2013). 'DJ Technologies, Social Networks and Gendered Trajectories in Eurpean DJ Cultures', in Bernardo Alexander Attias, Anna Gavanas and Hillegonda C. Rietveld (eds), *DJ Culture in the Mix. Power, Technology, and Social Change in Electronic Dance Music*. New York: Bloomsbury, pp. 51–78.

Gavanas, Anna and Rosa Reitsamer (2016). 'Neoliberal Working Conditions, Self-Promotion and DJ Trajectories: A Gendered Minefield', *PopScriptum*, https://edoc.hu
-berlin.de/bitstream/handle/18452/21070/pst12_gavanas_reitsamer.pdf?sequence=1, accessed 14 August 2020.

Glazer, Joshua (2015). 'Warum der Internet-Hass gegen Ricardo Villalobos albern ist', *Vice Magazine*, https://www.vice.com/de/article/ez7x8a/warum-der-internet-hass-ge
gen-ricardo-villalobos-albern-ist-793, accessed 14 August 2020.

Greenberg, Zack O'Malley (2016). 'World's Highest-Paid DJs: Electronic Cash Kings 2016', *Forbes*, https://www.forbes.com/sites/zackomalleygreenburg/2016/08/16/worlds-highest-paid-djs-electronic-cash-kings-2016/#5809910367d7, accessed 14 August 2020.

Hall, Mirko M. and Naida Zukic (2013). 'The DJ as Electronic Deterritorializer', in Bernardo Alexander Attias, Anna Gavanas and Hillegonda C. Rietveld (eds), *DJ Culture in the Mix. Power, Technology, and Social Change in Electronic Dance Music*. New York: Bloomsbury, pp. 103–122.

Holt, Fabian (2016). 'New Media, New Festival Worlds. Rethinking Cultural Events and Televisuality through YouTube and the Tomorrowland Music Festival', in James Deaville and Christina Baade (eds), *Music and the Broadcast Experience: Performance, Production, and Audiences*. New York: Oxford University Press, pp. 275–92.

Holt, Fabian (2017). 'EDM Pop: A Soft Shell Formation in a New Festival Economy', in Graham St. John (ed.), *Electronic Dance Music Festivals and Event-Cultures*, New York: Bloomsbury, pp. 25–43.

Holmes, Su and Sean Redmond (eds) (2006). 'Introduction. Understanding Celebrity Culture', in *Framing Celebrity. New Directions in Celebrity Culture*. London and New York: Routledge, pp. 1–16.

Hornby, Nick (1999). 'Sammlerwahn', in Sky Nonhoff (ed.), *Off Limits!*. München: Goldmann.

Jacke, Christoph (2013). 'Mega-Stars: Ausdifferenzierung und Reflexivierung von prominenten Medienfiguren als Stars in der Popmusik', in Caroline Y. Robertson-von Trotha (ed.), *Celebrity Culture. Stars in der Mediengesellschaft*. Baden-Baden: Nomos, pp. 73–102.

Jaehn, Felix (2019). 'Eine Stunde, ein Leben: Felix Jaehns Weg zu mehr Selbstliebe', *N-Joy*, https://www.n-joy.de/radio/nina_haacke/Eine-Stunde-ein-Leben-Felix-Jaehns-Weg-zur-Selbstliebe,einestunde140.html, accessed 10 August 2020.

James, Robin (2015). *Resilience and Melancholy: Pop, Feminism, Neoliberalism*. Winchester: Zero Books.

Lynch, Will (2018). 'Opinion: We Must All Consider the Hazards of DJ Culture', in *Resident Advisor*, https://www.residentadvisor.net/features/3227?fbclid=IwAR3ZNDwvFGjXg5iN_9ND-BARUsNwB0737rC4f1TPw6_oBKr_yq0qPBTQ8rw, accessed 14 August 2020.

Marshall, David P. (2010). 'The Promotion and Presentation of the Self: celebrity as Marker of Presentational Media', *Celebrity Studies*, 1(1), pp. 35–48.

Phillips, Dom (2009). *Superstar DJs Here We Go!: The Rise and Fall of the Superstar DJ*. London: Ebury.

Polkinghorne, Donald E. (1991). 'Narrative and Self-Concept', *Journal of Narrative and Life History*, 1 (2,3), pp. 135–53.

Poschardt, Ulf (2015). *DJ-Culture: Diskjockeys und Popkultur*. Stuttgart: Tropen.

Pressler, Jessica (2013). 'Avicii, the King of Oontz Oontz Oontz', *GQ Magazine*, https://www.gq.com/story/avicii-tim-bergling-profile-gq-april-2013, accessed 14 August 2020.

Ptatscheck, Melanie (2020a). *Sucht & Selbstkonzepte. Biographische Studien zur Heroinabhängigkeit von Musikern in Los Angeles*. Bielefeld: transcript.

Ptatscheck, Melanie (2020b). 'Between Empowerment and Powerlessness. Individual Career Trajectories of Drug-Addicted Musicians in Los Angeles', in Michael Ahlers, Lorenz Grünewald-Schukalla, Anita Jóri and Holger Schwetter (eds), *Musik & Empowerment*. Wiesbaden: Springer, pp. 47–68.

Reitsamer, Rosa (2011). 'Leistung, Anerkennung und Geschlecht im kulturellen Feld: Zur Unterrepräsentation von DJ-Frauen in elektronischen Musikszenen', *Osterreichische Zeitschrift für Soziologie*, 36(3), pp. 39–48.

Schuegraf, Martina (2013). 'Celebrities und YouTube-Berühmtheiten: das Selbst im Netz', in Caroline Y. Robertson-von Trotha (ed.), *Celebrity Culture. Stars in der Mediengesellschaft*. Baden-Baden: Nomos, pp. 119–28.

Squire, Corinne (2008). 'Experience-Centered and Culturally-Oriented Approaches to Narrative', in Molly Andrews, Corinne Squire and Maria Tamboukou (eds), *Doing Narrative Research*. Los Angeles: Sage, pp. 41–63.

Tsikurishvili, Levan (2017). *Avicii: True Stories* [Documentary], https://www.bbc.co.uk/programmes/p075zdlk, accessed 29 November 2019.

Veenstra, Erik (forthcoming 2021). 'Auflegen', in Heiko Christians, Nikolaus Wegmann and Matthias Bickenbach (eds), *Historisches Wörterbuch des Mediengebrauchs, Bd. 3*. Köln: Böhlau [unpublished manuscript].

Wernke-Schmiesing, Sebastian (2015). 'Das größte EDM Festival Europas. Tomorrowland – Eine Erfolgsgeschichte', *Dance-Chart*, https://www.dance-charts.de/201502104847/tomorrowland-eine-erfolgsgeschichte/Seite-8?desk=1, accessed 14 August 2020.

6

Where's the drop?

Identifying EDM trends through the career of Deadmau5

Tristan Kneschke

Joel Zimmerman's musical alias Deadmau5 is among the most recognizable names in all of electronic dance music (EDM). Frequently spotted wearing his iconic, enormous mouse head at the world's biggest festivals, Deadmau5's prolific output reaches millions of monthly listeners, with early hit 'Ghosts 'n' Stuff' surpassing 100 million streams and album *4x4=12* earning platinum certification. Deadmau5 has been nominated for six Grammy Awards and was named 'Best Progressive House Artist' and 'most influential, forward-thinking and relevant person' by prominent online electronic music store Beatport as early as 2008 (Grammy 2019; Beatportal 2008). Zimmerman's prominence has led him to teach an electronic music production course for MasterClass, a platform reserved for luminaries in their respective fields, and in 2019, he realized a decade-long goal of scoring a feature film by composing the soundtrack for Jonas Åkerlund's Netflix film *Polar* (MasterClass 2017; IMDB 2019).

These milestones make Deadmau5 an exemplar of modern EDM stardom and an excellent case study, but more than that, his career intersects with multiple trends that have come to define the genre as a whole as it grows in its status as a major music force worldwide.

Technology

Though the vast category of electronic music encompasses a broad array of musical approaches and styles, at its core are approaches where 'sonic transformation is ubiquitous' (Roads 2015: xi). Electronic music enables the multifarious manipulations of sound's fundamental unit, a vibration expressed as a wave moving through a medium, in the form of various oscillator shapes, in order to realize ever more intricate timbres and arrangements for musical expression. The discovery of novel sounds is for electronic musicians the joyous journey itself, and the ease with which these sounds are created is a direct consequence of technological progress. Mark Brend writes that 'Electronic music depends more on its equipment than most other forms of music. . . . The art needs an apparatus. . . . The development of the music cannot be separated from the emergence of new technologies and the invention of new instruments and techniques' (2012: v). DJ Richie Hawtin offered a similar sentiment: 'Electronic music is innately tied to the technology used to create it – as the tools evolve, so will the art' (Hawtin 2012). Since the early twentieth century, the advent of early electronic instruments like the Telharmonium and the Theremin revealed new sonic possibilities, leading to the advent of modular systems – synthesizers that could be constructed through any combination of foundational building block modules – that enabled exploration of complex electronic sound design. However, cost often initially confined these systems to academic contexts. Closed-circuit synthesizers like those initially designed by Robert Moog in the 1960s brought a 'tool of liberation, a noise-making machine that drew sounds not from the city streets but the depths of the imagination, a means of launching music into outer space' (Barry 2016). These models introduced more compact designs to recording studios at a somewhat more accessible price tag, and a piano keyboard provided a familiar interface for newcomers (Robert Buchla's models, meanwhile, deliberately rejected familiarity in favour of producing instruments with completely unseen interfaces). The MIDI (Musical Instrument Digital Interface) specification provided a bridge between electronic instruments and computers, which meant nuanced performances could be stored and recalled in software, allowing for more complex arrangements. As computers grew more powerful, digital audio workstations (DAWs) centralized the hub of the producer's studio, while virtual studio technology (VST) plug-ins allowed for practically limitless customizability within the DAW. Greater reliance on software, an increase in computing power and a decrease in computer prices democratized access for anyone wanting to express themselves through electronic music. The dawn of the bedroom producer meant it was no longer an absolute necessity to own any dedicated hardware instruments, though many musicians, including Deadmau5, have opted for a hybrid software and hardware solution to play to the strengths of both.

Whether writing music in his lavish studio, streaming his latest live visual designs online, or just playing video games, technology is a singular discipline to Deadmau5. By his own admission, Zimmerman grew up 'very socially fucking retarded' with a 'huge anxiety disorder', retreating to the solace of design programs like CorelDraw and games like Minesweeper as a teenager (Madden 2016; Burns 2008). This awkwardness would bloom into a lifelong love for computers, manifesting in a recreational passion for video games and facilitating his entire professional career even down to the genesis of his artist name. The story goes that one night Zimmerman noticed the smell of burning wires around his computer. Upon taking it apart, he found a dead mouse inside. After telling his friends what had happened, everyone began calling him the 'dead mouse guy'. He used this moniker in online message boards, truncating it to the alias he uses today due to their eight-character limit (Ricciuto 2011).

With a native background in computers generally, music software came to Zimmerman easily. Today, he uses Ableton, electronic music's most popular DAW, and Serum, a wavetable synthesizer designed by friend and occasional musical collaborator Steve Duda, who also features prominently on numerous tracks (Sethi 2015; Discogs 2015; Oskillator 2017). But Deadmau5 has also made significant investments in his home studio, expanding his capabilities beyond the average musician's 'gearlust'. Zimmerman's home studio is 'like walking into a spaceship' and includes at least a dozen synthesizers, an extensive modular system occupying an entire wall, an analogue mixing console costing half a million dollars and a fully calibrated 11.3 Dolby Atmos system requiring nine custom, specifically positioned speakers (Appleford 2019; Pilchner Schoustal 2016). A server room hosting 70 terabytes of networked storage link to five gaming computers, helping Zimmerman design and render his processor-intensive graphics for shows (Linus Tech Tips 2017).

Some may see these efforts as excessive, particularly when other A-list producers like Skrillex opt for largely software-based solutions (Best Studio Mics). Deadmau5's preference for analogue systems like modulars and hardware synthesizers points to a persistent trend across electronic music where 'digital sound is too perfect, too clean, too cold – [electronic musicians] long instead for the imperfections of the warm, fuzzy, dirty analog sound' (Pinch and Trocco 2004: 319).

It's difficult to ascertain which of Deadmau5's sounds in any given song are fully analogue or digital. Whether an analogue signal has been digitally manipulated or a digital sound is sent through analogue effects processors, the majority of his songs are likely a marriage of both. While digital sound provides the economical option for many producers, companies creating digital synthesizer emulators continue to tout analogue-modelled products as a major selling point for EDM producers. Even Serum boasts two chaos knobs in an effort to mimic the drifting oscillators of early analogue synthesizers. Zimmerman continues to prefer analogue hardware, a trend that persists in EDM contrary to what has happened in the motion picture industry, which has almost completely jettisoned film stocks in favour of digital capture formats (Follows 2019).

The powerful graphics cards Deadmau5 uses for creating live visuals also facilitate his recreational gaming, where high visual fidelity and fast frame rates are an advantage for online first-person shooters in particular. Zimmerman loves video games, citing them as 'a huge part of my upbringing' and an 'absolute' influence on his music, positing that his music 'lends itself to video-game-soundtrack-type stuff. We've been back and forth, of course, in and out of each other's industries, kind of playing off each other. We're just cool buddies, me and video games' (Murray 2016).

Deadmau5's sentiment indicates the strong ties between the industries, one that only continues to strengthen as EDM and gaming both enjoy larger cultural influence. The earliest gaming systems were outfitted with primitive sound generation devices built into their circuits, which meant 'video game tracks were some of the first mass-marketed and consumed forms of electronic music' (Magnetic Mag 2016). For direct links between electronic music and video games, one need only consider Super Nintendo's *Mario Paint* title, which included a primitive music-making mini-game; the Nanoloop music creation cartridge on Nintendo's Game Boy; and Analogue Pocket, a video game system that includes a built-in sequencer and synthesizer (Henges 2020; Nanoloop 2013; Eede 2019). Outside of musical systems, there is the entirety of the chiptune electronic music subgenre that constrains artists to music made by video games or with the low-fidelity sounds of early game systems. Video games also provide much fodder for sampling, as has been the case with Burial and Joker, just to name two of countless artists who have incorporated games' sounds into their compositions (Hsu 2019; Clark 2007). Electronic musicians are hired to provide music for games, as in the case of Canadian EDM label Monstercat teaming up with Psyonix to provide over forty tracks for *Rocket League* and Skrillex and Giorgio Moroder writing music for *Mortal Kombat 11* and *Tron Run/r*, respectively (Thielmeyer 2018). Efforts extending beyond soundtrack work include EDM star Marshmello broadcasting a live show inside the hugely popular online game *Fortnite*. Until that time, it was the game's biggest event ever (being outdone in 2020 by rapper Travis Scott), indicating a novel entertainment space and emerging revenue possibility for the two entertainment sectors (Webster 2019; Hogan 2020).

Deadmau5 has also become involved with video games, providing a curated playlist for the racing game *Project CARS* and working with Secretlab to create an officially licensed gaming chair (Sony 2017; Secretlab 2019). Zimmerman has also created his own game in collaboration with Absolut Vodka. The game itself is simple – players must navigate Deadmau5 from his studio to a show, ultimately being rewarded with backstage access to new music – but it's likely the first example of a track debut utilizing a virtual reality (VR) experience (Bein 2016). The collaboration was positive for Zimmerman, who called it a 'great entry level project in VR to get my feet wet.... To build something that can work on that platform is a fucking great way to entice people into VR development' (Leight 2016). Players will complete what is really more of an elaborate marketing experience in less than ten minutes, but it nonetheless presents another potential direction for the future of music and gaming.

In addition to broadcasting video game sessions on the streaming megasite Twitch, Deadmau5 regularly streams marathon music production or motion graphics sessions through the site, but began broadcasting live bedroom sets via Ustream at least as early as September 2010, nine months before Twitch launched (Zimmerman 2010). Zimmerman was not just streaming to increase his popularity but also sought to demystify his process:

> the nature of electronic music, it's all heavily produced, right? ... It's not recorded off the floor or by a bunch of talented musicians, whittling away doing multiple passes kind of thing ... I always thought, wouldn't it be cool ... to open up the hood on it and show people the process of it to either inspire and encourage other people to do it, because, 'oh, maybe it doesn't look so hard' or 'oh, that's an interesting way of doing things' kind of thing ... that was something I was always about ... lifting a veil on something that's just been heavily veiled for the longest time ... no electronic artist was showcasing or livestreaming their production process. I think I was probably among the first. (H3 2018)

These sessions allow rabid fans or aspiring producers to peek behind the scenes, though on at least one occasion, streaming facilitated the completion of Deadmau5's music. While working on 'The Veldt', Deadmau5 noticed several chat participants recommending he listen to a vocal demo a fan had recorded over the song. Zimmerman, expecting an amateur performance, was instead awestruck by how well the lyrics complemented the instrumental. He reached out to the vocalist, Chris James, and ultimately worked with him on the official version (Nubbles 2014). Today, many EDM producers have followed Deadmau5's lead, streaming their own production sessions on Twitch to connect with their fans or help other producers develop their skills, an intimate extension of the bedroom producer ethos.

Criticism

As of 2019, electronic music ranked as the third most popular music genre (behind pop and rock) and reached an estimated 1.5 billion listeners, according to a study by the International Music Summit (Watson 2019). That doesn't mean electronic music is not without its critics. Cultural sociologist Sarah Thornton, author of *Club Cultures: Music, Media, and Subcultural Capital*, frames some of the main criticisms, outlining preferences of '"listening" over dance musics, visibly performing musicians over behind-the-scenes producers, the rhetorically "live" over the "recorded" and hence guitars over synthesizers and samplers' as dichotomies that continue to perpetuate established canons excluding dance music (1995). Initially, instruments used to create electronic music 'were met often with bewilderment, anxiety, even fear', an anxiety that developed into derision when the first discotheques emerged (1995: v). These sentiments sometimes provoked physical altercations. The most notorious example was radio DJ Steve Dahl's 'Disco Sucks' campaign, culminating in the Disco Demolition Night baseball promotion of 1979 resulting in the detonation of crates of disco records brought by patrons for reduced admission (Myers 2009). Seeing as early discotheques emerged as a refuge for African and Latino minorities as well as the LGBTQ community, some scholars have coated the event within racist or homophobic undertones as 'a perfect target for white rage' (Frank 2007; Zeitz 2008). The destruction of cultural artefacts echoes an even darker historical precedent, however: the burning of books deemed subversive in Nazi Germany, a connection made more uncomfortable with Dahl's choice to don military garb around and during the time of Disco Demolition.

As disco's prominence waned, house music would emerge as its 'direct descendant' or as house pioneer Frankie Knuckles called it, 'disco's revenge', likewise created and fostered largely within the same minority spaces (Cheeseman 2003; Brewster 2014). Techno music, 'designed to be a futurist statement', followed as the next major genre development of electronic music, blending synthesizers and drum machines with house rhythms, and would explode into international popularity by the 1980s and 1990s, transforming into the modern form of EDM enjoyed today (Gieben 2013).

This would surely be cause for recognizing electronic music's impact, but even as late as 1989, the *Penguin Encyclopedia of Popular Music* defined disco as a 'dance fad of the 70s with profound and unfortunate influence on popular music ... producers, who already had too much power, used drum machines, synthesizers and other gimmicks at the expense of musical values' (Gieben 2013: 1). Here, the 'musical values' suggests the playing of canonically accepted instruments such as guitar, drums or piano, and the knowledge of music theory that enables it as the chief method for determining musical worth. Speaking of Kraftwerk's robotic performances, Hugh Barker and Yuval Taylor explained another issue some listeners found with electronic music: 'Kraftwerk made music that could (apparently) be played simply by pressing buttons, music that didn't address any personal, human concerns. . . . At the time, they sounded completely alien' (Barker and Taylor 2007). Samplers, drum machines and computers weren't (and for some, still aren't) considered instruments. Onstage, studio work can be replicated exactly with these tools, allowing the performer to create an illusion of an authentic performance. To outsiders, this may seem deceptive, subject to remarks like 'for all you know they could be onstage checking their email' (Marcus and Carr 2009).

These days, EDM is more widely accepted as genres cross-pollinate, but it is still not immune from criticism. Rolling Stone Italia's excoriating video 'Rocker Vs. DJ', commissioned for the magazine's tenth anniversary and executed by advertising agency BBDO of Milan, points out the worst tropes of electronic music and DJ culture (Maggiore 2013). Sustaining a combative pitch from its onset, the clip calls DJs

> criminals with the license to shoot shit into our eardrums. Low-quality mp3 pushers. Third-class whores that give it away to the first bidder. . . . You feel like superstars, huh? . . . No audience will ever chant your name. They'll never know your songs by heart because you are Anonymity. The day will come when your vocoders explode and your CDs catch fire. In their place, we'll see you return to guitar, bass, and drums, bringing real music back to life . . . [electronic music] is the anathema to rock and roll.

The slickly produced video depicts the exaggerated lifestyle of a fictitious EDM DJ, crosscut with shots of pills, orgies, party aftermaths and performances in empty warehouses.

The piece's central fallacy is in the title itself. 'Versus' is a binary that suggests listeners must choose either rock or EDM. However, increasing numbers of listeners opt to enjoy music through an 'all you can eat' streaming model, as opposed to purchasing albums limited by a budget. This is indicated by the RIAA's annual Music Revenues Report that shows both an increase in overall streaming revenues (from four billion in 2016 to 8.8 billion in 2019) and an increase in the number of paid music subscriptions (10.5 million in 2015 to 60.4 million in 2019) (Friedlander 2020). This model supports a rocker *and* DJ model; listeners don't have to choose one over the other.

Published in 2013, the Rolling Stone Italia video now seems hopelessly antiquated. It arrived a year after Deadmau5 performed at the Grammy Awards on the same stage as Foo Fighters in 2012, having remixed their track 'Rope' in 2011. This performance suggests a more stylistically integrated musical landscape. Foo Fighters, by all respects a traditional rock band, kick off 'Rope' in full energy on a small stage, a large concealed box to the side, mimicking the music video for the song. At the end of the first chorus, the curtain on the other stage falls, revealing Deadmau5 towering over the band as his mouse head bobs to the music, now incorporating elements from his remix. Midway through the video, another reveal occurs. The cameras pan to the audience, revealing grinning mouse heads among the throng, suggesting the draw is playfully skewed towards the EDM producer (AzAzEl 2012). But the performance is devoid of antagonism, instead showcasing a harmony between the two genres, as if it were never any other way.[1]

Yet even Deadmau5 is quick to find faults with EDM. In an interview with the *Evening Standard* in 2014, Zimmerman said, 'Disco had a longer run than EDM has . . . and that died in a fucking hurry. EDM is way more susceptible . . . it'll eventually fuck itself so hard' (Smyth 2014). To Zimmerman, 'eventually' was just a year later, in 2016. 'It's fucked. It's out of the innovators' hands; it's not really grassroots anymore' (Zlatopolsky 2016). But the most media attention came from his now-infamous Tumblr post from 2012, 'we all hit play':

> its no secret. when it comes to 'live' performance of EDM. . . . It's not about performance art, its not about talent either (really its not) In fact, let me do you and the rest of the EDM world button pushers who fuckin hate me for telling you how it is, a favor and let you all know how it is. I think given about 1 hour

of instruction, anyone with minimal knowledge of ableton and music tech in general could DO what im doing at a deadmau5 concert. Just like i think ANY DJ in the WORLD who can match a beat can do what 'ANYONE else' (not going to mention any names) is doing on their EDM stages too. (Zimmerman 2012)

This sentiment echoes Deadmau5's Rolling Stone cover story from around the same time. Writer Josh Eells approached the story as a scenic outsider, pondering the extent of liveness for the typical electronic musician or DJ: 'From the crowd, it's hard to tell exactly what a dance musician is doing onstage. Almost all of them use prerecorded tracks; sometimes it seems like they're getting paid to wave their arms and occasionally adjust their headphones.' In the story, Deadmau5 doubled down on his Tumblr sentiment amid Eells's commentary, a tirade uniting tradition, authenticity and performance all as sides of the same rock coin:

'If I wanted, I could play a fucking .wav file and just stand there and fist-pump all night, and no one would give a shit,' Zimmerman says. In fact, he says, a lot of people do just that. 'David Guetta has two iPods and a mixer and he just plays tracks – like, "Here's one with Akon, check it out!" Even Skrillex . . . isn't doing anything too technical. He has a laptop and a MIDI recorder, and he's just playing his shit. People are, thank God, smartening up about who does what – but there's still button-pushers getting paid half a million. And not to say I'm not a button-pusher. I'm just pushing a lot more buttons.'

In a way, Zimmerman is weirdly traditionalist – prizing authenticity and performance and other 'rock' values and rejecting anything that smells of pop. He disdains DJs ('It takes two days to learn, as long as you can count to four'), dismisses most dance music as formulaic ('Just 120 bpm with a fucking kick drum on every quarter note'). . . . He'd much rather . . . get Dave Grohl to remix a track for the next Deadmau5 album – 'because fuck dance music, you know?' (Eells 2012)

The Tumblr post and Rolling Stone feature generated many reactions from music publications and understandably upset many EDM fans and DJs. Sebastian Ingrosso of Swedish House Mafia wrote that Deadmau5 was precisely the kind of producer that pushes 'play' during his sets (while aligning his own music to the Beatles) (Blistein and Lotz 2012). Other artists, notably Bassnectar with 'Pushing Buttons or Pushing Boundaries', dismissed Deadmau5's screed with a lengthy explanation of what was involved in his work, detailing the layers of complexity in his performances to educate both critics and fans (Ashton 2012).

While Deadmau5's vitriol pointed out a truism for some electronic music acts whose lack of liveness presented a detriment to engagement, it's unlikely that these posts led to direct change for many artists; the heritage of live performance provides its own pull. Many performers today ensure they remain active onstage, at the very least tweaking song parameters or sections via controller knobs, sliders and buttons. Others use a conventional instrument, often a keyboard, to create a spectacle while signalling some level of music theory mastery.

As EDM has evolved, more attention has also been paid to the visual component of the live show. It has become less acceptable, at least for a live as opposed to a DJ set, to simply play tracks through a computer and pantomime performance. Though light shows are now de rigueur for a band with any clout (regardless of genre), many EDM artists go the extra mile by creating custom performance set-ups. A paragon is EDM trio the Glitch Mob, who have created a complex rig called the Blade constructed from several huge drum triggers and touchscreen samplers – tilted towards the audience as if to dissuade comments that events are not being triggered in real time – that leaves room for improvising many parts during a live set (The Glitch Mob 2015). In two online documentaries, members of the group detail the mammoth undertaking involved in the rig, with the impetus of bringing 'the drama of a *live rock band* to an electronic show [emphasis mine]'. The Glitch Mob stresses their heavy involvement in this non-musical aspect of their show as another dimension to their creativity.

Deadmau5's shows have become more extravagant than simply the wearing of his custom mouse head. Concertgoers will be treated to a custom spectacle called the Cube, now on its third version (though Zimmerman quips that it's closer to its seventh) (Sheffer 2019). In its current form, the structure is an enormous cube with mechanical sides that can open to reveal the producer performing inside while various visuals play on the Cube's LED displays.

As with the Glitch Mob, Zimmerman is the creative force for his show visuals. In addition to designing the cube structure itself, he has also created all of the motion graphics that play inside the Cube, which is where his substantial investments in hard drive capacity, premium graphics cards and a networked render farm at his home studio bear fruit. With such intricate visuals that must fire in time to the music, Deadmau5's shows exhibit his highly technical production processes. He and other performers at his level continue to raise the bar for themselves in an effort to create more impressive show experiences, regardless of whether they're merely 'pressing play'.

Authenticity

Curiously, 'selling out', that is, 'a prostitution of ideals or a betrayal of principle', which has afflicted jazz, folk, rock and hip-hop musicians since the 1970s and through the 1990s, seems less a force in modern music and for EDM by extension (Nicolay 2017). Franz Nicolay suggests that by the release of Moby's 1999 electronic music album *Play*, significant in that all eighteen of its tracks were commercially licensed together over 300 times, the term had begun to wane (Matos 2016). He writes, 'The collapse of the music industry sent artists looking for new licensing revenue and corporate touring partnerships. (Critic Steven Hyden has noted that the year of *Play*'s ascendancy coincided with the launch of Napster)' (Hyden 2013). Napster torpedoed the music industry, and its 'self-righteousness dried up along with its giant pools of money'. Especially in the twenty-first century, successful musicians have needed to shift efforts to monetize their work away from declining physical sales and, in light of the Covid-19 pandemic, a disappearance of the traditional live touring economy. Instead, efforts are geared towards digital streaming opportunities on services like Twitch, selling directly to their fans through sites like Bandcamp, and crowdfunding patronage using platforms like Patreon. But while selling out is less of a concern, issues of authenticity take their place.

Authenticity 'defined primarily in opposition to "faking it," . . . is an absolute, a goal that can never be fully attained, a quest' and is in dialogue with the criticisms proffered in the preceding section (Hyden 2013: iii). Disco may have been labelled as 'shallow or insubstantial – fake, in other words. But the genre had deliberately avoided the aesthetics of authenticity. A typical disco record made no attempt to tell us about the performer or about reality' (Hyden 2013: 236). Throughout electronic music's evolution following disco, this sentiment has often become reinforced. Some producers employ masks during performance to heighten spectacle while shielding the artists in a 'fetishized anonymity' (Hyden 2013). Historically, masks were used in ritual contexts and work by 'concealing or modifying those signs of identity which conventionally display the actor . . . masks achieve their special effect by modifying those limited number of conventionalized signs of identity' (Pollock 1995). In another sense, the use of masks in electronic music provides 'a connotation of universality; having no face means you might have any face' (Brooks, Donnelly and Mills 2017). Barker and Taylor assert that 'authenticity is rarely an issue with music for which the performer intentionally adopts a theatrical approach' (Brooks, Donnelly and Mills 2017: 244). In the age of social media, journalist Andrew Matson has argued that life is a big performance 'with no web/life verification. . . . We need a demarcation: life over here; performance over there. Masks signify an art zone and elevate performance to something serious' (2012).

Michaelangelo Matos takes this a step further, tracing a lineage of concealment through electronic music that extends beyond masks to include usage of artist aliases, pressing blank 'white label' records disseminated anonymously to DJs, and the presence of early VR headsets at raves, indicating a larger strategy in use since at least the 1980s (2012). Whatever the methodology, the paradigm of the faceless electronic music producer pushes against the dominant ideology of stardom in which a personality must be recognized to be exalted to superstar status.

Barker and Taylor list two responses for bridging the gap between a performer's sense of self and their public persona: 'The first is to glorify the degree to which you are faking it – to theatrically celebrate your ability to perform a role and to take on a persona . . . that is clearly not meant to reflect the real you. . . . The second approach to this problem is for the performer to try to minimize the gap between person and persona.' Deadmau5 employs both strategies. While Deadmau5 began his career performing without a mask or costume, his mouse head is now instantly recognizable and continues the tradition of acts like Daft Punk and later followed by Marshmello, and represents a theatricalization of his performative personality (Capital FM 2018).

Online, Zimmerman makes use of the second approach. Here, the mask is shed and fans see the unfiltered and authentic persona, sometimes prone to ranting on social media or live video streams, engaging in celebrity feuds and criticizing the scene or himself. At other times, he's the exact opposite: unguarded, vulnerable and nurturing in his advice to novice producers.

Zimmerman has publicly broadcast his emotional states on the internet for years. In 2015, Zimmerman shut down his Facebook and Twitter accounts, citing depression as the cause. Since high proficiency in music theory isn't essential for creating electronic music, this can manifest as 'imposter syndrome' (Clance and Imes 1978), as Deadmau5 alluded to in a CBC interview:

> 'I think I'm more tech than Mozart or whatever the hell, or as a musician. I've never really felt like a musician, you know. I don't know, it's so weird to kind of step outside of myself and see what I am, you know what I mean?'

'What is a musician to you that you're not?'

'To me, someone that could read sheet music, for starters.'

'So that eliminates The Beatles, originally.'

'Well, I don't know, just someone who studied music, that knows more about the different types of scales and notation and polyrhythms, I don't know any of that stuff, you know.'

The interviewer delved further, asking if Zimmerman, at some level, felt like an imposter. The emphatic response came right away:

'Yeah. I won't disagree with that . . . there are a lot of people who do go out of their way to study music, who go into school and go into programs and get their Master's or Doctorate even in music, and then you got pop artists I guess like me just underdogging the whole thing. It's like, "well I spent $40-50 grand on college or whatever, for what?" I see a lot of people who have this insane amount of musical knowledge, all these like practical music-y things. I don't even know what they are, that's how dumb I am.'

'Do you have an interest in studying music?'

'No, I don't, really. It would bore me to tears, it would frustrate me.'

'How do you know that?'

'It would be a total curveball. I go with what I know. I know what music should sound like in my head and I think that's enough for me.' (Q on CBC 2012)

Here, Zimmerman presents himself as somewhat of an unreliable narrator, as a hardworking EDM pioneer streaming marathon production sessions who nevertheless downplays the success he's managed to build for himself. While any imposter syndrome he may have experienced has nevertheless been minor relative to his output, Deadmau5 has still looked for other ways of aligning himself with brands and authors he deems authentic. In 2016, Zimmerman would share another commonality with Hans Zimmer, a composer he deeply respects: they would both teach their own online class for MasterClass, a portal for industry leaders to provide advice on their field of expertise. Meeting the composer dashed the assumptions Zimmerman had imagined prior:

I was actually kind of pleasantly surprised a few weeks ago. I had a meeting with Hans Zimmer, and we talked about a bunch of stuff. And I was thinking, 'this guy's going to show up with the coattails . . . he's doing all these massive film scores that are very music heavy, that have all this orchestration and getting top instrument player people doing it', and I'm thinking 'this is a guy I really pick his brain'. It was actually kind of funny, he's like 'dude I couldn't read a sheet of music to save my life, and I can't score anything. I just do it with Midi and all this stuff,' and I'm thinking 'oh my god I do the exact same thing, that's really funny'. (Q on CBC 2012)

Deadmau5's ability to teach a full class has its bedrock in his years demystifying the creative process through streaming and echoes his online advice to producers in providing for the electronic music community. Along with increasing software availability, online music production classes have grown in popularity despite throngs of YouTube channels presenting similar content for free. MasterClass provides videos of a celebrity in their field divulging their knowledge, though the classes are more of a source of motivation to those considering the field, as opposed to a class providing strict instruction. Placing Zimmerman within an academic context, however, cannot help but provide career legitimacy among his peers.

Yet another path towards authenticity that electronic producers have traversed is becoming involved with scoring soundtracks to films and more recently, video games. In this context, music serves a purpose outside of its own aesthetic pleasure and instead supports a larger structure. The soundtrack, in eschewing its live components, also sheds any concerns that it is automated. Culturally, we connect the soundtrack composer with the classical arranger, working with a live orchestra to realize his vision. The long list of electronic producers who have taken this path most famously includes artists like Vangelis, Daft Punk, Trent Reznor of Nine Inch Nails, Tangerine Dream and Junkie XL, in addition to many others. In 2019, Deadmau5 realized a goal he had expressed at least a decade earlier: to score the soundtrack for a major motion picture. Netflix's *Polar*, directed by accomplished music video director Jonas Åkerlund, follows a hitman who finds himself the target of a hit (Q on CBC 2012). Deadmau5's score pays homage to recent soundtrack efforts like those released by Zimmer and contains several EDM-tinged pieces.

Branching out to already legitimated media formats like films and video games is similar to electronic musicians aligning with the establishment and respect of the classical genre. There is a difference between Tiesto sampling Samuel Barber's 'Adagio for Strings' for his track of the same name and a more immersive live performance where producers such as Jeff Mills, Jon Craig, Above & Beyond and BT have employed a full orchestra to complement or reimagine their electronic arrangements (Gonsher 2017; Manthey 2018; Thump 2014; APB Speakers 2015). The latter transforms the album and perhaps even dwarfs it.

The decision to use the orchestra, the pinnacle of Western classical composition, as opposed to traditional folk forms, suggests a desire for EDM producers to elevate their music to canonical spaces, despite how antiquated or stuffy they may be for their usual audiences.

Deadmau5 also headed this way, abandoning EDM altogether for the 2018 album *where's the drop?*, a collection of symphonic arrangements originating from piano concertos Zimmerman wrote. Consisting of reimaginings of familiar Deadmau5 songs as well as several unreleased tracks, the album directly led Åkerlund to choosing the producer to score his film (Appleford 2019). As with the producers above, Deadmau5 performed with a full orchestra for the album's two live performances. Zimmerman dressed in a suit and tie, not only the standard uniform for classical performers but also the conventional height of men's fashion. But Zimmerman wasn't happy about it, remarking that 'The last two times I'm ever wearing a suit is that time and at my funeral' (Appleford 2019). During the performances, the Deadmau5 head sat grinning on a piano bench, its glowing eyes gazing out into the audience, useless within its new setting (Senese 2018).

The title *where's the drop?* indicates the fundamental sonic characteristic of EDM, a 'drop, a big "hit" or "climax" of loud, highly distorted (often "wobbly") bass and sub-bass synths' that functions to release the tension that a 'soar' creates (James 2015). These elements separate EDM from other genres as formal aspects that create interest throughout the song. Of course, Deadmau5 is well versed in placing soars and drops in many of his tracks ('Imaginary Friends' features several of varying intensities). The production of *where's the drop?* in effect subverts the expectations of the EDM listener. This is finally Zimmerman's deliberate rejection of the scene's values from fans and producers alike that he has railed against for years, for the first time in musical form. But this sentiment was short-lived. Deadmau5's following release, *here's the drop!*, collected various remixes of the orchestral versions, reverting back to comfortable EDM tropes while subjecting the original tracks to a level of aural facsimile.

The elusive pursuit of authenticity is one of many goals for Joel Zimmerman as he continues to create music through Deadmau5. The project has benefited from the global acceptance of many forms of electronic music, and EDM in particular, as it continues its global expansion. With the ubiquity of DAWs like Ableton, the resurgence of interest in analogue synthesizers and the burgeoning of the bedroom producer, electronic music is ripe to become the folk music of our time. While it's easy for Zimmerman to play the cultural provocateur and decry EDM's death, the more noble pursuit as a bona fide star is to push the music forward, to resist tropes that produce stale music. Ultimately, creating music that is fearlessly authentic will not only quell his complaints; it will also advance new possibilities for the music's future.

Works Cited

'19 DJs Who Wear Incredible Masks Better Than Any Superhero' (2018). *Capital FM*, 8 March, https://www.capitalfm.com/news/best-edm-dj-disguises-masks-2016/, accessed 7 February 2020.

Alienware (2018), 'The Glitch Mob: Behind the Blade 2.0 Documentary', *YouTube*, 27 September, https://www.youtube.com/watch?v=NPyyPxdEqbQ, accessed 7 February 2020.

APB Speakers (2015). 'BT's Electronic Opus Live in Concert!', *YouTube*, 19 May, https://www.youtube.com/watch?v=yoCrc_wD7IE, accessed 7 February 2020.

Appleford, Steve (2019). 'Deadmau5 on His Scoring Debut for Netflix's "Polar": 'I Wanted to Wait for the Right Thing', *Billboard*, 25 January, https://www.billboard.com/articles/news/8494943/deadmau5-interview-scoring-debut-netflix-polar-jonas-akerlund, accessed 7 February 2020.

Ashton, Lorin (2012). 'Fan Bass: Pushing Buttons or Pushing Boundaries', *Bassnectar*, 27 June, https://www.bassnectar.net/2012/06/pushing-buttons-or-pushing-boundaries/, accessed 7 February 2020.

AzAzEl Cx (2012). '2012 Grammy's Foo Fighters and Deadmau5', *YouTube*, 9 August, https://www.youtube.com/watch?v=sISlhGvfQCo, accessed 7 February 2020.

Barker, Hugh and Yuval Taylor (2007). *Faking It: The Quest for Authenticity in Music*. New York: W. W. Norton & Company Ltd.

Barry, Robert (2016). *The Music of the Future*. London: Repeater Books.

'Beatport Music Awards 2008' (2008). *Beatportal*, 4 November, https://web.archive.org/web/20081104042302/https://www.beatportal.com/awards/beatport-music-awards-2008/, accessed 7 February 2020.

Bein, Kat (2016). '6 Awesome EDM-Inspired Video Games from Skrillex, Deadmau5 & More', *Billboard*, 11 July, https://www.billboard.com/articles/news/dance/7431166/edm-video-games-skrillex-deadmau5, accessed 7 February 2020.

Blistein, Jon and Griffin Lotz (2012). 'Swedish House Mafia Defend David Guetta, Dream of McCartney Collaboration', *Rolling Stone*, 21 June, https://www.rollingstone.com/music/music-news/swedish-house-mafia-defend-david-guetta-dream-of-mccartney-collaboration-124017/, accessed 7 February 2020.

Brend, Mark (2012). *The Sound of Tomorrow: How Electronic Music Was Smuggled into the Mainstream*. New York: Bloomsbury.

Brewster, Bill (2014). 'Frankie Knuckles Obituary', *The Guardian*, 1 April, https://www.theguardian.com/music/2014/apr/01/frankie-knuckles, accessed 7 February 2020.

Brooks, Lee, Mark Donnelly and Richard Mills (eds) (2017). *Mad Dogs and Englishness: Popular Music and English Identities*. New York: Bloomsbury Academic.

'BSOD Discography' (2015). *Discogs.com*, https://www.discogs.com/artist/738525-BSOD-2, accessed 7 February 2020.

Burns, Todd (2008). 'Deadmau5: It's Complicated', *Resident Advisor*, 30 September, https://www.residentadvisor.net/features/972, accessed 7 February 2020.

Cheeseman, Phil (2003). 'The History of House', *DJ Magazine*, 28 December, http://music.hyperreal.org/library/history_of_house.html, accessed 7 February 2020.

Clance, Pauline and Suzanne Imes (1978). 'The Impostor Phenomenon in High Achieving Women: Dynamics and Therapeutic Intervention', *Psychotherapy: Theory, Research and Practice*, http://mpowir.org/wp-content/uploads/2010/02/Download-IP-in-High-Achieving-Women.pdf, accessed 7 February 2020.

Clark, Martin (2007). 'Grime/Dubstep', *Pitchfork*, 21 March, https://pitchfork.com/features/grime-dubstep/6568-grime-dubstep/, accessed 7 February 2020.

'Deadmau5 Artist Profile' (2019). *Recording Academy Grammy Awards*, 31 March, https://www.grammy.com/grammys/artists/deadmau5, accessed 7 February 2020.

'Deadmau5 Teaches Electronic Music Production' (2017). *Masterclass*, https://www.masterclass.com/classes/deadmau5-teaches-electronic-music-production, accessed 7 February 2020.

'Deadmau5 x Secretlab Gaming Chair' (2019). *Secretlab*, 6 April, https://secretlab.co/pages/deadmau5, accessed 7 February 2020.

Eede, Christian (2019). 'This New Portable Video Game System Is Also a Synthesizer', *DJ Mag*, 21 October, https://djmag.com/news/new-portable-video-game-system-also-synthesiser, accessed 7 February 2020.

Eels, Josh (2012). 'The Rise of Deadmau5', *Rolling Stone*, 5 July, https://www.rollingstone.com/music/music-news/the-rise-of-deadmau5-189564/, accessed 7 February 2020.

Frank, Gillian (2007). 'Discophobia: Antigay Prejudice and the 1979 Backlash against Disco', *Journal of the History of Sexuality*, https://www.jstor.org/stable/30114235?seq=1, accessed 7 February 2020.

Friedlander, Joshua (2020). 'Year-End 2019 RIAA Music Revenues Report', *RIAA*, 4 March, https://www.riaa.com/wp-content/uploads/2020/02/RIAA-2019-Year-End-Music-Industry-Revenue-Report.pdf, accessed 7 February 2020.

Follows, Stephen (2019). 'The Use of Digital Vs Celluloid Film on Hollywood Movies', *Stephen Follows*, 11 February, https://stephenfollows.com/digital-vs-film-on-hollywood-movies/, accessed 7 February 2020.

'From 8Bit to EDM: Gaming's Electronic Music History' (2016). *Magnetic*, 19 January, https://www.magneticmag.com/2016/01/from-8bit-to-edm-gamings-electronic-music-history/, accessed 7 February 2020.

Gieben, Bram (2013). 'Space Is the Place: Techno Pioneer Jeff Mills Introduces His Live Score to Fritz Lang's *Woman in the Moon*', *The Skinny*, 1 February, https://www.theskinny.co.uk/festivals/uk-festivals/music/space-is-the-place-techno-pioneer-jeff-mills-introduces-his-live-score-to-fritz-langs-woman-in-the-moon, accessed 7 February 2020.

The Glitch Mob (2015). 'The Glitch Mob – Behind the Blade', *YouTube*, 18 May, https://www.youtube.com/watch?v=xUu8jxWDSOU, accessed 2 July 2020.

Gonsher, Aaron (2017). 'Jeff Mills on Expanding the Possibilities of Classical Music and DJing', *Red Bull Music Academy*, 14 March, https://daily.redbullmusicacademy.com/2017/03/jeff-mills-interview, accessed 7 February 2020.

'H3 Podcast #59 – Deadmau5' (2018). *YouTube*, 30 March, https://www.youtube.com/watch?v=WEMAvnkHA9U, accessed 7 February 2020.

Hawtin, Richie (2012). 'Richie Hawtin Posts', *Facebook*, 29 October, https://www.facebook.com/richiehawtin/posts/462511980454971, accessed 7 February 2020.

Henges, Elizabeth (2020). 'Meet the Musicians Who Compose in Mario Paint', *The Verge*, 6 February, https://www.theverge.com/2020/2/6/21122335/nintendo-mario-paint-music-composers-snes, accessed 7 February 2020.

Hogan, Marc (2020). 'Where Can Virtual Concerts Go After Travis Scott's Fortnite Extravaganza?', *Pitchfork*, 5 May, https://pitchfork.com/thepitch/virtual-concerts-travis-scotts-fortnite-100-gecs-minecraft/, accessed 7 February 2020.

Hsu, Hua (2019). 'Burial's Search for Fleeting Moments', *The New Yorker*, 2 December, https://www.newyorker.com/magazine/2019/12/09/burials-search-for-fleeting-moments, accessed 7 February 2020.

Hyden, Steven (2013). 'Kings of Durrr', *Grantland*, 24 September, http://grantland.com/features/kings-leon-return-mechanical-bull/, accessed 7 February 2020.

'Inside the Skrillex Studio: Tips and Tech the Producer/DJ Uses', *Best Studio Mics*, https://beststudiomics.com/inside-the-skrillex-studio-tips-and-tech-the-producer-dj-uses/, accessed 7 February 2020.

James, Robin (2015). *Resilience and Melancholy: Pop Music, Feminism, Neoliberalism*. Hampshire: Zero Books.

Leight, Elias (2016). 'Deadmau5 Dishes on Virtual Reality Game & Music: "These Worlds Are Gonna Collide"', *Billboard*, 1 July, https://www.billboard.com/articles/news/dance/7423998/deadmau5-interview-virtual-reality-game-dance, accessed 7 February 2020.

Linus Tech Tips (2017). 'Exposing Deadmau5's Studio – *Spoiler* He's a Huge Geek!', *YouTube*, 6 July, https://www.youtube.com/watch?v=dBiqFNNfudA, accessed 7 February 2020.

Madden, Joe (2016). 'Deadmau5: The Full NME Cover Interview', *NME*, 2 December, https://www.nme.com/features/deadmau5-interview-2016-1884714#B7Mo6dQcOA4sH5ES.99, accessed 7 February 2020.

Maggiore, Matteo (2013). 'Rolling Stone Magazine Italy | Rocker vs DJ', *YouTube*, 31 October, https://www.youtube.com/watch?v=pIDCNO3ezxA, accessed 7 February 2020.

Manthey, Aric (2018). 'EDM Meets the Orchestra – Producer Jon Craig [Interview]', *EDM.com*, 18 June, https://edm.com/interviews/edm-meets-the-orchestra-our-interview-with-producer-and-composer-jon-craig, accessed 7 February 2020.

Marcus, Greil and Daphne Carr (eds) (2009). *Best Music Writing 2009*. Philadelphia: Da Capo Press.

Matos, Michaelangelo (2016). 'A Brief History of Masked DJs – From Orbital to Marshmello', *Vice*, 29 November, https://www.vice.com/en_us/article/nzmqkk/masked-djs-history-orbital-deadmau5-daft-punk-marshmello, accessed 7 February 2020.

Matson, Andrew (2012). 'Musicians and Their Masks', *NPR*, 18 February, https://www.npr.org/sections/therecord/2012/02/18/146981833/musicians-and-their-masks, accessed 7 February 2020.

'Mau5trap' (2016). *Pilchner Schoustal*, http://www.pilchner-schoustal.com/work/mau5trap/, accessed 7 February 2020.

Murray, Nick (2016). 'Deadmau5 Talks Video Game Obsession, Lazy DJs', *Rolling Stone*, 2 May, https://www.rollingstone.com/music/music-news/deadmau5-talks-video-game-obsession-lazy-djs-48627/, accessed 7 February 2020.

Myers, Ben (2009). 'Why "Disco Sucks!" Sucked', *The Guardian*, 18 June, https://www.theguardian.com/music/musicblog/2009/jun/18/disco-sucks, accessed 7 February 2020.

'Nanoloop One' (2013). *Nanoloop*, https://www.nanoloop.com/one/index.html, accessed 7 February 2020.

Nicolay, Franz (2017). 'The Rise and Decline of the "Sellout"', *Slate*, 28 July, https://slate.com/culture/2017/07/the-history-of-calling-artists-sellouts.html, accessed 7 February 2020.

Nubbles (2014). 'Deadmau5 Discovers Chris James on Twitter for the Veldt March 20, 2012', *YouTube*, 22 May, https://www.youtube.com/watch?v=iqurYVWg7-g, accessed 7 February 2020.

Oskillator (2017). 'Deadmau5 Making Imaginary Friends –06 Bass Sound Design | Editing', *YouTube*, 13 March, https://www.youtube.com/watch?v=Q1cRHnf5C3w, accessed 7 February 2020.

Pinch, Trevor and Frank Trocco (2004). *Analog Days: The Invention and Impact of the Moog Synthesizer*. Cambridge: First Harvard University Press.

'Polar' (2019). *IMDB*, https://www.imdb.com/title/tt4139588/, accessed 7 February 2020.

Pollock, Donald (1995). 'Masks and the Semiotics of Identity', *The Journal of the Royal Anthropological Institute*, http://voidnetwork.gr/wp-content/uploads/2016

/09/Masks-and-the-semiotics-of-identity-by-Donald-Pollock-.pdf, accessed 7 February 2020.

Q on CBC (2012). 'Joel Zimmerman a.k.a. deadmau5 in Studio Q', *YouTube*, July 23, https://www.youtube.com/watch?v=Zeb3dGbhvTM, accessed 7 February 2020.

Ricciuto, Tony (2011). 'Deadmau5 Rejects His Father and Grandfather's Advice About Getting a Real Job', *Niagara Falls Review*, 30 October, https://web.archive.org/web/20130620021135/http://www.niagarafallsreview.ca/2011/10/30/deadmau5-rejects-his-father-and-grandfathers-advice-about-getting-a-real-job, accessed 7 February 2020.

Roads, Curtis (2015). *Composing Electronic Music: A New Aesthetic*. New York: Oxford University Press.

Senese, Jay (2018). 'Deadmau5/Deadmau5 Live at the Wiltern Los Angeles Part 1', *YouTube*, 1 April, https://youtu.be/LYu0q6OULr0, accessed 7 February 2020.

Sethi, Rounik (2015). 'The Top 11 Most Popular DAWs (You Voted For)', *Mac Pro Video*, 18 November, https://www.macprovideo.com/article/news/the-top-11-most-popular-daws-you-voted-for, accessed 7 February 2020.

Sheffer, Sam (2019). 'Inside the Insane Deadmau5 CUBE V3!', *YouTube*, 21 August, https://www.youtube.com/watch?v=waGzVes6PWY, accessed 7 February 2020.

Smyth, David (2014). 'Deadmau5 Interview: "Festivals Are Being Branded Bigger than the Acts, It's Totally Backwards"', *Evening Standard*, 13 June, https://www.standard.co.uk/go/london/music/deadmau5-interview-festivals-are-being-branded-bigger-than-the-acts-its-totally-backwards-9534366.html, accessed 7 February 2020.

'The Best EDM Video Game Soundtracks' (2017). Sony, 12 May, https://www.sony.com/electronics/best-video-game-music-soundtracks, accessed 7 February 2020.

Thielmeyer, Max (2018). 'Rocket League and Monstercat Are Innovating How Games Get Their Soundtracks', *Forbes*, 28 September, https://www.forbes.com/sites/maxthielmeyer/2018/09/28/rocket-league-and-monstercat-are-innovating-how-games-get-their-soundtracks/#75c18f3259f0, accessed 7 February 2020.

Thornton, Sarah (1995). *Club Cultures: Music, Media and Subcultural Capital*. Cambridge: Polity Press.

Thump (2014). 'Above & Beyond Acoustic – Full Concert Film Live from Porchester Hall (Official)', *YouTube*, 24 January, https://www.youtube.com/watch?v=CNUTlKqSO-I, accessed 7 February 2020.

Watson, Kevin (2019). 'IMS Business Report 2019', *International Music Summit*, 28 May, https://www.internationalmusicsummit.com/wp-content/uploads/2019/05/IMS-Business-Report-2019-vFinal.pdf, accessed 7 February 2020.

Webster, Andrew (2019). 'Fortnite's Marshmello Concert Was the Game's Biggest Event Ever', *The Verge*, 21 February, https://www.theverge.com/2019/2/21/18234980/fortnite-marshmello-concert-viewer-numbers, accessed 7 February 2020.

Zeitz, J. (2008). 'Rejecting the Center: Radical Grassroots Politics in the 1970s – Second-wave Feminism as a Case Study', *Journal of Contemporary History*, http://americainclass.org/wp-content/uploads/2014/01/Zeitz.pdf, accessed 7 February 2020.

Zimmerman, Joel (2010). 'Deadmau5 Isn't Live. 9/14/10 07:15PM PST', *Ustream*, 14 September, http://www.ustream.tv/recorded/9577734, accessed 7 February 2020.

Zimmerman, Joel (2012). 'We All Hit Play', *Tumblr*, 23 June, https://web.archive.org/web/20120628231944/https://deadmau5.tumblr.com/post/25690507284/we-all-hit-play, accessed 7 February 2020.

Zlatopolsky, Ashley (2016). 'Deadmau5 on Why EDM Is Finished, Learning to Love His New Album', *Rolling Stone*, 7 December, https://www.rollingstone.com/music/music-features/deadmau5-on-why-edm-is-finished-learning-to-love-his-new-album-108214/, accessed 7 February 2020.

7

Deadmau5's relationships with authenticity and fame

Jeremy W. Smith

Deadmau5 (pronounced 'dead mouse', real name Joel Zimmerman) is a Canadian superstar electronic dance music (EDM) producer. His rise to fame in the late 2000s and early 2010s is linked with the rise of stardom in EDM as a whole. Over the course of his career, he has attained tremendous commercial success and maintained a strong fan base. He has built a recognizable brand and collaborated with big businesses, yet also put effort into portraying himself as an authentic artist that has not sold out or cheapened his craft. These two goals are normally perceived as mutually incompatible by fans of popular music (Gunders 2012: 149), yet both are crucially important to the successful career of any musician. This chapter will study Deadmau5's stardom through the lens of authenticity, showing how he maintains a balance between corporate branding and individual artistry. I will discuss how he achieves this balance by the choices he makes in creating his recorded music, live performances and internet content such as social media posts, live streams and his digital masterclass.

Authenticity has been widely discussed in music scholarship and especially in writings about popular music. It has been espoused as an important concept for scholars and fans alike, but also profoundly criticized (Gunders 2012: 148). The term 'authenticity' can mean many different things, but the type of authenticity I am focusing on is what Allan Moore calls 'first person authenticity' or 'authenticity of expression', which occurs when a musical creator 'succeeds in conveying the impression that his/her utterance is one of integrity, that it represents an attempt to communicate in an unmediated form with an audience' (2002: 214). The authenticity of a musician is ascribed by listeners (Moore 2002: 210; Auslander 2008: 82), but musicians can choose whether they want to perform authenticity or not (Brown 2015: 58, 78).

First-person authenticity has traditionally been discussed for only pop and rock artists, not producers or performers of EDM or hip-hop. In fact, Simon Reynolds has argued that EDM is different from pop and rock in that its consumers care much more about their communal experience on the dance floor than the performer and/or creator of the music (Reynolds 2011: 319). Over the last decade or so, however, many aspects of stardom from pop and rock music have become relevant in some types of EDM, and because of this transformation there has been heightened attention on the musical, verbal and physical expressions of some EDM artists.

John Gunders says that the discourses of authenticity used for rock musicians are also relevant for EDM musicians. He provides examples of EDM fans discussing the authenticity of stars such as Moby (Gunders 2012: 153–7). A central aspect of the authenticity of a musician according to these discourses is being 'opposed to commercialism' (Gunders 2012: 148). It is important to recognize, however, that even though a dichotomy between authentic artistry and commercial ambitions is presupposed by many fans, that binary opposition does not really exist (Gunders 2012: 149). Musicians want, or perhaps even need, to present their work with integrity in a way that is true to their own artistic vision *and* to promote their work for success in the market. Other aspects of the perceived authenticity of an artist, a musical piece or a particular performance include being natural (not being artificial) and being creative (in the sense of expressing originality) (Gunders 2012: 152).

In his seminal 2001 article, Kembrew McLeod claims that it is possible for a musician to achieve stardom in EDM and still be perceived as an authentic artist (2001: 69). In other words, 'it is possible to live the contradiction of being enormously popular while still connected to "the street" – to the subculture from which one comes.' McLeod goes on to say that authentic stars can 'sell out live events without necessarily "selling out". Successful artists can eschew the mainstream while pulling in sizable crowds and earning lots of money by making certain discursive moves that validate their status as authentic artists' (2001: 69). I argue that this is what Deadmau5 does or at least attempts to do.

Specifically, the 'discursive moves' Deadmau5 does to attempt to establish his authenticity are evident in his recorded music, his live performances and his online activities. The rest of this chapter will discuss each of these aspects of Deadmau5's career, first focusing on musical techniques used in both recordings and performances, then focusing on online communications such as social media posts, live streams, radio shows and the digital masterclass mentioned earlier. In each of these areas, Deadmau5 tries to both be true to himself and his artistic vision *and* promote himself in the marketplace.

Techniques in Deadmau5's recorded music

In many ways, Deadmau5's musical style has changed over the course of his career. He has always been somewhat eclectic and experimental, but as he rose to fame in the late 2000s and early 2010s, most of his music was clearly in the genre of progressive house. This genre is similar to trance, and both are characterized by prominent melodies and harmonies (often sung by vocalists), dramatic buildup sections after long breakdowns that are marked by thin textures and the use of the four-on-the-floor drum pattern (Wright 2017: 26). These genres and other related ones are sometimes associated with being mainstream or very popular in a negative sense (Huxtable 2014).

Since the time of Deadmau5's seventh studio album *While (1<2)* (2014), many of his tracks (but not all) have been less focused on standard drum beats that are made for energetic dancing. Instead, many of his newer tracks are more experimental, making less use of the drums and incorporating more innovative sound qualities. Many are not suitable for club dancing because they have slower tempos and atmospheric sounds, in the style of ambient music rather than progressive house. The soundtrack that he wrote for the 2019 film *Polar* is also mostly in this style.

One specific technique that Deadmau5 has used less in his later career is the drop, especially obvious, climactic drops. The meaning of the term 'drop' in EDM has changed over time and become less specific than it used to be. At first, the term was used more often as a verb, as in the phrase 'dropping the beat'. This described the instantaneous climactic moment when the 'beat' (specifically the bass drum and/or the melodic bass) is (re-)introduced to the texture after a prolonged absence (Butler 2006: 246–7; Garcia 2011: chap. 4; Sayre 2014; Peres 2016: 19–20). Recently, however, the term is more often used as a noun, referring to the entire climactic section of an EDM track rather than just the initial moment of that section (Solberg 2014: 65; Snoman 2019: 325). In any case, the term 'drop' is closely associated with the formal structure of an EDM track, and it provides a 'release' after a section of musical tension.[1]

In his online masterclass, Deadmau5 expressed a belief that many commercially successful EDM tracks rely too much on the drop for telling their listeners how to behave. He says 'there are other ways to invoke moments of intrigue or hype or mystery without having to blatantly illustrate it' (MasterClass 2016). In the same lesson on 'Structuring Songs', he expresses admiration for Mozart (as depicted in the film *Amadeus*), who says (according to Deadmau5) 'well at the end of our piece we have to put a big bang so people know when to clap'. Deadmau5 interprets Mozart's loud musical gesture as a way of 'instruct[ing] the audience', and he also says that Mozart was 'mocking' the standard way of doing things. It is significant that Deadmau5 connects this Mozart gesture to drops in EDM. He is saying that they can be used in an authentic and creative way, but that they should not be inserted out of obligation or necessity. This is an example of Deadmau5 demonstrating authenticity through creativity (Gunders 2012: 152), since originality and experimentation are highly valued traits in the production of dance music (Wright 2017: chaps 4–5).[2]

One track from early in Deadmau5's career that uses drops in a standard way is 'Lack of a Better Name' from the album *For Lack of a Better Name* (2009). In the 'bonus track version' of the album this track has two drops, at 0:59 and 3:29. Both of them are preceded by long absences of the bass drum and techniques of musical intensification including crescendos, ascending gestures and what I have elsewhere called the 'illusion of acceleration' (J. W. Smith 2019: 54–6). The second drop occurs after a longer absence of the bass drum and a more thorough 'breakdown' of the musical texture. This means that the second drop is more intense and climactic because there has been a longer period of expectation, as is typical of progressive-house or trance tracks (Huron 2006: 319–26; Patty 2009: 338–9).

Deadmau5 includes progressive-house tracks with a standard formal structure on his more recent albums, too. On his most recent studio album *W:/2016ALBUM/* (2016), both of the breakdown-buildup-drop sequences in '4ware' are typical and ordinary. They achieve the requirement (of lowering the energy then raising it again as it leads to a climax) that is present in almost all EDM tracks, especially ones in the last decade (Butler 2006: chap. 6; Solberg 2014; Snoman 2019: chap. 26).

Other tracks on *W:/2016ALBUM/* that feature a standard EDM formal structure and use of drops are 'Imaginary Friends', 'Let Go (feat. Grabbitz)', 'No Problem', 'Three Pound Chicken Wing' and 'Let Go (feat. Grabbitz) [Extended Edit]'. This means that only half of the tracks on the album (six out of twelve) follow the typical EDM structure, and two of them are different versions of the same piece. The other tracks on the album are either EDM tracks with a looser, uncommon structure or not EDM tracks at all. One notable example is

'Snowcone', which Deadmau5 specifically says is a track he notices crowds do not find as enjoyable as others at festivals, but he plays it anyway because *he* enjoys it (MasterClass 2016: lesson 5).

Deadmau5's most unusual album (at the time of writing) in terms of both content and structure is *While(1<2)* (2014). This album marked a turning point in Deadmau5's career, and it exemplifies how he creates tracks with standard EDM structures *and* those in other styles or structures. In an interview the month before it was released, Deadmau5 said 'it's not a dance album' (Canadian Music Week 2014: 40:56). He described the album as a cohesive artwork with pieces meant to be listened to in a specific order, rather than a 'compilation' as his previous albums were (Canadian Music Week 2014: 38:52–40:20). Shortly after this, he makes an aside that expresses sentiments of anti-commercialism, saying, 'I've actually explicitly said now, to every management and label that I'm *strategically partnering with* [said sarcastically with humorous body language] "put me on another compilation, I'll kill you"' (Canadian Music Week 2014: 38:38).

In the same interview, he also describes how the album contains both 'big room' tracks that will be popular and other tracks that are 'transform[ed]' versions of that.[3] Speaking of those latter tracks, he says they represent 'what *I* would listen to and how *I* like to make music' (Canadian Music Week 2014: 41:34). Speaking about the former tracks, he says he does not want to alienate his fans, who will go 'Yeah! It has a drop, I'm happy' (Canadian Music Week 2014: 40:17). He does not describe making these dance tracks as a chore, but says, 'I like the idea of being able to take two different facets of music' (Canadian Music Week 2014: 40:59).[4] They are all incorporated into his aesthetic conception of this double album, which has two parts that are meant to be listened to as continuous mixes.

The statements from the interview described earlier show that Deadmau5 is aware of the need to make pieces that satisfy his own creative vision, and pieces that are similar to what he has done before and are created more with the fans in mind. He is acknowledging that even though he is trying new things and continuously transforming as an artist, he also wants and needs to continue creating tracks in the same genre (progressive house, which his music helped establish) as the tracks that made him famous. In the interview he is portraying authenticity (and also good business sense) by expressing desires to be innovative, to be anti-commercialist and also to connect with fans (Moore 2002: 214; Gunders 2012: 148).

Deadmau5 expresses very similar thoughts in lesson five of his masterclass, saying that it is important for him (and for all artists) to create pieces that are for 'pleasing yourself' and also pieces that are for 'pleasing the crowd' (MasterClass 2016). 'It's hard to do both,' he says.[5] In this lesson he frames the crowd-pleasing songs as 'obvious' and those that are not as 'not obvious', implying notions of complexity and simplicity as well. He also conveys authenticity by saying, 'I can shit out melodies in my sleep day and night, I could do this all day, and probably come up with a million things that a million people would like, but, I want it to resonate with me as something that I've done that I haven't done before, or is audibly pleasing to me' (MasterClass 2016).[6] This fulfils both parts of what Gunders describes as the 'creativity' discourse of authenticity: originality and technical mastery (2012: 152).

Even early on in Deadmau5's career, there were some more innovative and experimental tracks that broke the standard mould in terms of formal structure. On the same album as 'Lack of a Better Name' (released in 2009, discussed earlier), another track that has a much less standard structure is one of Deadmau5's most famous: 'Strobe'.[7] The musical features in this track are a microcosm of Deadmau5's eclectic musical style overall. For almost the first four minutes, there are no drums. This first section of the piece is a long introduction. In it, the main melodic, harmonic and rhythmic ideas in the piece are introduced with various timbres. The key is the same as the rest of the piece, but the tempo is significantly slower. Near the end of the long introduction, the tempo gradually accelerates, then at 3:52 drums start playing for the first time, and the tempo for a typical house track has been reached. After this, the track has a common formal structure for house tracks but with only one extended breakdown-buildup sequence leading to one climactic drop at 6:44. Other tracks that have similar structures with long introductions are 'Cthulhu Sleeps' (2010) and 'Fn Pig' (2012). In these tracks, Deadmau5 found a way to be innovative, projecting authenticity, within the standard format of an EDM track.

A climactic drop is just one example of a musical technique, but studying Deadmau5's use (or non-use) of drops is useful for showing how he portrays authenticity through his musical expressions. His utilization of drops symbolizes how he is willing to do things that are true to his artistic vision and not just give the audience what it wants all the time. As mentioned earlier, in general Deadmau5's musical style has become more experimental and eclectic over the course of his career, and part of this has involved using less drops.[8] It is notable that he made this change more pronounced after he had achieved a superstar-level of success. Perhaps he has always had this more eclectic artistic vision and in his early career did not illustrate it as boldly. Or perhaps his artistic vision changed significantly over time, and he became bored with the type of music he originally became famous for. In 2018, describing the arc of his career, he said that the 'melancholic' style he first brought to EDM has now been 'done to death' and that he still often produces EDM but in a way that is 'evolved' (H3 Podcast 2018).

Aside from drops, I want to mention two other aspects of Deadmau5's music that are interesting to consider in terms of authenticity. First, he has released many collaborations with a wide variety of other musicians and producers, including popular songwriters such as Lights, and the hip-hop group Cypress Hill.[9] For the most part, these collaborations are not with superstar pop artists, though, and they are not in the structure or style of a typical verse-chorus pop song. When speaking about his collaboration process, he says he turns down multitudes of people who ask to work with him, especially those who talk about making money as their primary goal, and he emphasizes how the collaboration process should be 'natural' (Canadian Music Week 2014: 47:35 ff.).[10] Also, he collaborates with people in order to make music he wants to hear and deplores artists that only collaborate for exposure or making money (Canadian Music Week 2014; H3 Podcast 2018). These comments portray authenticity because they are anti-commercialist and because they depict him as a natural human artist that can work with other artists to make a pure form of musical expression. These aspects of Deadmau5's personality were also recognized by Josh Eells in *Rolling Stone* (2012: para. 20).

Finally, it is noteworthy that since Deadmau5's rise to fame in the early 2010s, there has been much less obscenity in his lyrics, titles and other 'extra-musical' content. Deadmau5 has always included profanity in his speech, and it is used in many of his tracks still to this day; however, some of the topics of his early work have not been included in his output since early on in his career. For example, his collaborations with Melleefresh include 'Hey Baby' (2006), 'Afterhours' (2007) and 'Sex Slave' (2007), which all have graphic lyrics about spontaneous sexual hook-ups.[11] Contrasting this is his collaboration with Imogen Heap, 'Telemiscommunications' (2012) about communication problems in a long-term romantic relationship. Some might say that he has refrained from putting graphic sexual lyrics in his tracks in order to remain commercially viable (in a way that goes against a sense of authenticity), while others might say this is a sign of him becoming more mature. In any case, this section of the chapter has shown that the choices Deadmau5 makes in creating his musical expressions are sometimes made in order to be innovative and authentic, and other times made in order to be commercially successful.

Live performances

A second way in which Deadmau5 portrays his authenticity as a musical artist is in live performances. Since he is a music producer, not a DJ in the traditional sense,[12] he only performs sets of his own music, usually at large venues with thousands of people in the audience.[13] Doing these performances signals a lack of authenticity, since large venues and festivals are linked with commercialism. They are controlled by organizing committees, big companies and sponsors, thus for performers they are not an 'unmediated' form of communication with audience members.[14] However, Moore's concept of 'authenticity of expression' hinges on the perception of audiences, not the performances themselves. As mentioned earlier, this type of authenticity occurs when a musical creator 'succeeds in conveying the impression that his/her utterance is one of integrity, that it represents an attempt to communicate in an unmediated form with an audience (Moore 2002: 214). Even though Deadmau5 derides the sponsorship and branding of large festivals (Canadian Music Week 2014: 34:35 ff.), he can work *within* them to try and portray himself as an authentic artist.[15] This section discusses several ways he does that in his performances.

What makes a musical performance be perceived as authentic? Gunders suggests that the portrayal of naturalness, rather than artificiality, is an important factor and that there is a 'fear of technology getting in the way of sincere performance' (2012: 152). The fear is that the performer cannot perform without the help of digital technology or recording equipment (2012: 152). With EDM specifically, the fear is that the performer is just 'pressing buttons' or 'pressing play' (Montano 2010; Butler 2014: 97, 103). Similarly, Butler emphasizes the importance of creating a sense of 'liveness' in EDM performance (2014: 67, 95–105). In rock and especially in EDM performances, physical gestures and body language showing that the artist is *creating* unique music are crucial in communicating this naturalness or liveness (Gunders 2012: 149; Butler 2014: 95–105). This has been particularly important for EDM ever since computers became the primary tool for most performers onstage, rather than turntables (Montano 2010; Butler 2014: 96–7). Deadmau5 therefore portrayed authenticity in an interview with *Rolling Stone* when he called out specific artists who only press play on an audio file and 'just stand there and fist-pump' (Eells 2012).[16] 'People are, thank God, smartening up about who does what – but there's still button-pushers getting paid half a million. And not to say I'm not a button-pusher. I'm just pushing a lot more buttons' (Eells 2012).

Liveness can also lead to a special 'vibe' between performers and audiences of dancers (Butler 2014: 68). 'For vibe to emerge, one must feel part of a unique, one-time occasion; a technically proficient performance is not enough' (Butler 2014: 68). This is where originality and creativity come in; they are also important markers of authenticity in live performances (Gunders 2012: 152). Therefore, Deadmau5 portrayed authenticity in two ways when he spoke in a video about the technology used for the shows on his *Cube V3* tour (Deadmau5 2019). First, the video communicates with fans in a seemingly unmediated way, giving them a 'behind-the-scenes' look at how his performances work. Second, in the video he specifically promotes the tour by saying that his performances are 'a different show every time'.

One way that Deadmau5 (and other EDM artists) demonstrate that their concerts are not just about them pushing buttons but instead are unique events is by putting on visual spectacles. However, EDM artists need to be careful not to be overly reliant on visual spectacles at the expense of other factors. They can also portray creativity, originality and unmediated communication with the audience in other ways, such as body language, verbal speech, written text on screens and musical gestures. Deadmau5 likes to be in control of all aspects of his performances, not just the music, meaning that his performances are a kind of *Gesamtkunstwerk* in which he, an authentic artist, is fully in control (Deadmau5 2017).

In his most recent tour show, *Cube V3*, he used all of the above-mentioned techniques to communicate with audiences and portray authenticity. The following observations are based on my experience of attending this show on 5 October 2019 (in Phoenix, Arizona, United States) and on information about the show I subsequently found online.

Firstly, Deadmau5 used body language and physical gestures to portray authenticity. As he performed in an open-faced rotating cube suspended in mid-air, he looked like a keyboardist, playing music with physical gestures on synthesizers and computers. He often showed engagement with the music and connection with the audience by dancing or clapping, which the audience mimicked. Sometimes he drank shots with one hand while turning a volume knob down with the other or turned the volume down at specific moments when the audience was likely to sing the lyrics of a track. For most of the show he performed with his mau5head helmet on, but at times he removed it, showing his true face and full body. Near the end of the show, just before the encore, he waved goodbye to the audience. With these gestures, Deadmau5 portrays himself as real and in control of what is going on, which symbolize the authenticity of the performance.

Secondly, he communicated with the audience through messages displayed on the screens in the venue. This began well before the show started and continued occasionally throughout the night. Before the show, text on the screens seemed to contain direct communications from Deadmau5 to the audience, with words appearing as if they were being typed in real time on a computer.[17] The messages were a mix of greetings, jokes, trivia questions and information about the show. During the actual concert the screen often put lyrics up for pieces that had them and sometimes communicated more direct messages to the audience, as in the pre-show. The screens also communicated to the audience through animated characters, often moving to the beat. One memorable part of the show occurred early on, when the music seemingly transitioned to his most famous track 'Ghosts 'n' Stuff', exciting the crowd, but only a short part of the track played before a middle-finger gesture was displayed on the screen, timed with the beat, telling the audience that they would not get to hear their favourite piece yet.[18]

Thirdly, he communicated with the audience through verbal speech, without his mau5head helmet on. This occurred briefly in the middle part of the show that featured Lights as a co-performer onstage. He also spoke with Lights in between tracks, and they drank together in the cube. At the end of the show, just before the encore, he stopped the music, stepped down from his platform in the cube and addressed the audience more thoroughly. In this particular concert, he also let the audience in on the fact that an 'Ethernet managed switch' crashed during the show, but they got through it using backup plans. These speeches helped to demystify the onstage persona of Deadmau5, portraying authenticity by communicating in an unmediated way with his fans.

Finally, he used musical actions to communicate with the audience. There were plenty of buildups and drops, which as discussed earlier provide signals of tension and release to listeners, telling them when to be in a state of expectation and when to dance the most energetically. He also turned the volume down when he wanted the audience to sing and sometimes subverted expectations by quickly changing tracks. The entire concert was put together in one continuous flow, like a traditional EDM performance, but the distinctions between tracks were still usually noticeable and emphasized, sometimes because of drastic tempo changes. Notably, this method of communicating with the audience is based on their knowledge of specific tracks, and this is something that was not a part of EDM performances until superstars such as Deadmau5 began playing for large crowds. As Butler explains, before the large-scale transformation that led to EDM superstars, most EDM performances contained continuous mixes of 'generic' tracks, and the difference between tracks was supposed to be imperceptible (Butler 2006: 177–8). Reynolds also describes the recognizability of tracks as part of the new popularization of EDM (2013: 598).

There are some aspects of the *Cube V3* shows that are highly commercialized (including the recognition of his most popular tracks and the selling of merchandise in the lobby). Within this framework, however, Deadmau5 portrays authenticity by displaying his technique and his control over the spectacle, as well as directly communicating with the audience through body language, on-screen messages, verbal speech and musical actions.

Online communications

Deadmau5 also portrays authenticity through his online communications in digital media. This section of the chapter discusses Deadmau5's self-made content on social media, live-streamed videos, radio shows and his masterclass. By definition, the communications with viewers or listeners in this content are not 'unmediated' since they are not face-to-face or in person (Walther 2011). What matters for authenticity, however, is the perception that they are unmediated, unfiltered, sincere and not made for the purposes of 'selling out'. In other words, communications are more likely to be perceived as authentic if they have a high level of 'social presence' and are 'warranting' (Walther 2011: 445–6, 466–8). Some of Deadmau5's online communications are indeed commercialistic, promoting himself, his logos, his affiliated artists or other brands. However, in general Deadmau5 keeps these separate from his other, seemingly more authentic messages.

One prominent way that Deadmau5 creates online communications is through social media.[19] His website, deadmau5.com, is a hub and an aggregator with links to all his social media accounts, his merchandise store, audio and video of his recorded music, his masterclass, his live streams, as well as information about shows, music releases, news updates, online radio stations playing his music and how to sign up for a digital newsletter. Deadmau5 maintains a significant online presence; all his platforms are updated with new information several times a week. Many of his posts are promotional in nature, with only links and/or pictures to his own content, content by other artists on his record label mau5trap or content by other brands. Many posts, however, especially on Twitter, contain personal messages, usually written informally. Some posts combine the two, such as this tweet.[20] Related to this are occasional videos or online events he does where he talks openly and honestly with fans but as part of a sponsorship or promotion for another company.[21] These are particularly interesting because they attempt to show unmediated communication even though they are being directed by the sponsor. For example, Deadmau5 censors himself by not swearing in the Q&A video for Amazon Live (2020).

Some of his most famous (or infamous) social media posts are those involving arguments with or insults of other artists, companies or sometimes fans. Significantly, he sometimes calls out specific artists for (in his opinion) 'selling out' or having bad, generic music (Horner 2016; Galbraith 2017). Two times he has been called out by fans for using homophobic or transphobic language when angry, and both times he apologized afterwards (Meadow 2018; Hall 2019). These arguments and apologies portray authenticity because they convey personal opinions and are, at least on the surface, unrelated to commercialism. The first line of his apology for using a homophobic slur on Twitch is particularly relevant: '"Damage control" had asked me not to make a statement. But, I would rather you hear it from me, in my own words. You deserve that' (Hall 2019).

In an interview from 2018, Deadmau5 says he runs all his social media platforms himself (H3 Podcast 2018: 1:13:32 ff.). When asked if seeing all kinds of opinions about him on social media ever gets to him, he says, 'It does. But that's the price you pay for being super crazy vocal on things.' He goes on to talk about how he is generally an 'antisocial' person, saying, 'My attempts at being social might come off as snarky, or facetious, or attacking, but that's just me being me. I've been doing it so long that I think people who have been following me or know of me just say "oh, that's just him."' As part of this conversation, Deadmau5 self-diagnoses himself as having manic depression, which he thinks is 'relieving for a lot of my core fans because they're all "oh wow, he has shit days too!"'. Earlier in the same interview, he says, 'The biggest question I get on Twitter is "What do you think about, dot dot dot?" . . . and then *I just say what I'm thinking at that moment*' (H3 Podcast 2018: 15:08, emphasis mine). All of these comments communicate authenticity, because in them he is painting a picture of his 'true' self and saying that his online statements are not fake.

In addition to more traditional social media, another way he interacts with fans online is through live streams. These used to be on Twitch, then on Mixer, but as of this writing, they are now done on mau5trap.tv, which is run through the streaming platform Maestro. They show him sometimes doing creative activities in his music studio and other times playing video games. The broadcasting of video games shows that he is a real person who has similar interests to many of his fans. The broadcasting from his music studios shows that he has technical skill and creativity in his craft. In particular, they show his skill with improvisation and experimentation, which are highly valued among producers and performers in the EDM community (Butler 2014: chaps 3–4; Wright 2017: 213–25).

A third way Deadmau5 communicates with his fans online is through 'mau5trap radio'. This weekly radio show started in 2018 (Coney 2018). It features an hour-long continuous mix of music by Deadmau5 and other artists on the label mau5trap. The episodes are uploaded to Mixcloud and sometimes other websites, and are often played on online radio stations. The most interesting aspect of the shows, in terms of authenticity, is that Deadmau5 usually narrates the mix and acts as a radio DJ. This not only helps him sell his own music and that of others on the mau5trap label, but it also provides him another avenue to communicate with fans in his own voice. As he speaks, not only about himself but about other artists, it gives listeners the chance to become familiar with the voice behind the mau5head helmet, and this can foster a sense of intimacy, as well as 'imagined community' among listeners (Hilmes 2012). The show also allows him to portray knowledge, authority and the skill of putting set lists and continuous mixes together, with fluid transitions.

Finally, Deadmau5 communicates authenticity in many ways in his masterclass (MasterClass 2016). Like all the digital communication methods discussed in this section, it is mediated, but the masterclass is perhaps more obviously so. It is published through masterclass.com, which is a corporate company that has masterclasses by many celebrities and leaders in their various fields, not just music. Therefore, creating a masterclass (even though Deadmau5's was relatively early in the company's history before their massive growth) can be interpreted as an act of 'selling out' and being inauthentic.

However, as already discussed in the section on musical techniques, many of the things he says in the masterclass lessons describe a strong desire for originality and an emphasis on the importance of making pieces that sound good to you, the creator, rather than pieces that sound good for consumers. Making the masterclass can be interpreted as a gesture of kindly reaching out to fans who want to become music producers themselves and teaching them not only musical techniques but what life is like in the music industry. In other words, it can be interpreted as a form of sincere, unmediated communication with fans. Therefore, Deadmau5 works within the corporate system to portray himself as an authentic artist that cares about the music and his fans more than the corporate system and its commercialism.

Conclusion

This chapter has discussed numerous ways that Deadmau5 attempts to portray 'authenticity of expression' (communication that is perceived as unmediated) (Moore 2002: 214) while also promoting himself in commercialistic ways that have traditionally been perceived as 'inauthentic'. I believe he maintains a balance between corporate branding and individual artistry that allows him to be commercially successful and maintain his large fan base. One of the most important aspects of Deadmau5's portrayal of authenticity, whether it is in his recorded music, live performances or online communications, is his expressed desire to be original and do new things. He sometimes even mocks his own fan base for wanting the older music, but he gives it to them anyway while also giving them new experiences with more experimental music. He portrays himself as a continuously transforming artist that is always 'ahead' of the fans or more progressive than them. At the same time, he portrays himself as a kind artist who understands that his fans want to hear the older music (such as 'Strobe' and 'Ghosts 'n' Stuff'), so he plays that for them as well. Yet he has also said that he sometimes feels 'constraint in stylistic approach' because of the dictates of the market (H3 Podcast 2018: 13:58). This suggests that he plays his 'classics' primarily for economic reasons, not out of empathy for fans.

In fact, Deadmau5 seems to understand that portraying authenticity in these ways is itself a good marketing technique. During one long interview, the interviewer commented to him: 'You're such an interesting guy, 'cause you sort of break all the rules. . . . It's hard to put deadmau5 in a box.' Then Deadmau5 replies, 'That's *good*, for marketing, and for sponsorship. Well, sometimes. It doesn't work out all the time trust me.' This raises an interesting question. Is Deadmau5 more like Bruce Springsteen and Tracy Chapman, who, according to Kevin Brown, 'work hard to create a mirage of truth', or more like Madonna, who 'is constantly reinventing herself, and celebrates the notions of a malleable identity'? (Brown 2015: 58).

In many ways, the portrayal of authenticity by EDM stars such as Deadmau5 is similar to that of rock stars who have come before them (Gunders 2012). For both traditions, authenticity of expression is tied with anti-commercialism and creativity (often communicated through improvisation). Arguably, in EDM, authenticity is even *more* related to experimentation and originality, especially in terms of the timbre of sounds (Danielsen 2010: chap. 1; Butler 2014: 43–7). In some ways, both rock and EDM place a high value on sound quality, such that authenticity is related to 'antiocularity' (Brown 2015: 49). On the other hand, in live performances, body language is important in both rock and EDM (Gunders 2012: 149), and in EDM it is even more important for portraying authenticity since without it, it is easy to perceive the performance as not live and/or perceive the performer as not enjoying the music (Montano 2010; Gunders 2012: 152; Butler 2014: 95–105).

For the most part, Deadmau5's portrayal of authenticity fits within the tradition established by rock stars. However, one way in which Deadmau5 (Joel Zimmerman) breaks away from the tradition of rock stardom and places himself within a long EDM tradition is by producing music under other names as well (Formilan and Stark 2020). He makes techno music (not house) under the alias Technopilot and is also part of a duo called BSOD, with Steve Duda. Even though he does not release music under these names often, and his identity as both Deadmau5 and Technopilot is well known, the fact that he uses three different names for putting out his music, none of which contain any hint of his real name, detracts from his stardom as an individual and places an emphasis on the music, rather than the person. This is another way of portraying authenticity by going against the mainstream and one that is much more linked to EDM than rock (Formilan and Stark 2020).

Studying how EDM stars portray authenticity is important, because it reveals ways in which EDM stardom is similar or different to stardom in other forms of popular music. This chapter can be put in dialogue with other work on authenticity in different genres of music (Peterson 1997; McLeod 1999; Leach 2001; Bigenho 2002). It also helps us recognize how EDM has evolved and proliferated. Some facets of EDM (as an umbrella term) remain deeply underground, maintaining the tradition of placing more importance on the culture of listeners than on the particular characteristics of performers (Reynolds 2011: 319). Other facets of

EDM, however, have adopted a focus on individual artists as stars, and along with this, a discourse of authenticity regarding those stars. The ongoing career of Deadmau5 provides a good example of how an artist can become an EDM star, by both promoting their brand *and* portraying authenticity.

Works cited

Amazon Live (2020). Deadmau5 *Q&A Livestream*, 29 May, https://www.amazon.com/live/broadcast/4de06f9f-650f-46ed-b81c-6ae8db6917dd, accessed 18 July 2020.

Auslander, Philip (2008). *Liveness: Performance in a Mediatized Culture*, 2nd edn. London and New York: Routledge.

Bain, Katie (2020). 'Deadmau5 Resurrects BSOD Project Returns with the Propulsive "Afterburner": Exclusive', *Billboard*, 9 April, http://www.billboard.com/articles/news/dance/9355346/deadmau5-bsod-afterburner-premiere, accessed 18 July 2020.

Bigenho, Michelle (2002). *Sounding Indigenous: Authenticity in Bolivian Music Performance.*New York: Palgrave Macmillan..

Brown, Kevin (2015). *Karaoke Idols: Popular Music and the Performance of Identity*. Bristol: Intellect Books Ltd.

Butler, Mark J. (2006). *Unlocking the Groove: Rhythm, Meter, and Musical Design in Electronic Dance Music*. Bloomington: Indiana University Press.

Butler, Mark J. (2014). *Playing with Something That Runs: Technology, Improvisation, and Composition in DJ and Laptop Performance*. New York: Oxford University Press.

Canadian Music Week (2014). DeadMau5 Interview, 3 June, https://www.youtube.com/watch?v=7goX4UYrC3s, accessed 18 July 2020.

Coney, Brian (2018). 'Deadmau5 Announces Mau5trap Radio', *DJMag.Com*, 1 October, https://djmag.com/news/deadmau5-announces-mau5trap-radio, accessed 18 July 2020.

Danielsen, Anne (ed.) (2010). *Musical Rhythm in the Age of Digital Reproduction*. Farnham, Surrey, England; Burlington, VT: Ashgate.

deadmau5 (2017). Mau5trap *Presents: Deadmau5 x TAIT (Cube 2.1) Video 1*, 24 February, https://www.youtube.com/watch?v=iGYDgWZTLXQ, accessed 18 July 2020.

deadmau5 (2019). *Cube v3 - the Tech - Part 1*, 29 August, https://www.youtube.com/watch?v=H2fDbkXoVZs, accessed 18 July 2020.

deadmau5 (2020). Twitter, 28 May, https://twitter.com/deadmau5/status/1265990309659492356, accessed 18 July 2020.

'Deadmau5's Concert & Tour History | Concert Archives' (n.d.). https://www.concertarchives.org/bands/deadmau5, accessed 18 July 2020.

Eells, Josh (2012). 'The Rise of Deadmau5 - Rolling Stone', *Rolling Stone*, 5 July, https://www.rollingstone.com/music/music-news/the-rise-of-deadmau5-189564/, accessed 18 July 2020.

Formilan, Giovanni and David C. Stark (2020). 'Underground Testing: Name-Altering Practices as Probes in Electronic Music', *British Journal of Sociology*, 71(3), pp. 572–89, https ://doi.org/10.1111/1468-4446.12726, accessed 18 July 2020.

Galbraith, Alex (2017). 'Deadmau5 Goes After The Chainsmokers: "I"m 100% Convinced You're Sh*t"', *UPROXX*, 23 June, https://uproxx.com/music/deadmau5-the-chainsmokers-100-percent/, accessed 18 July 2020.

Garcia, Luis-Manuel (2011). '"Can You Feel It, Too?": Intimacy and Affect at Electronic Dance Music Events in Paris, Chicago, and Berlin', PhD diss., The University of Chicago, Chicago, IL.

Gunders, John (2012). 'Electronic Dance Music, the Rock Myth, and Authenticity', *Perfect Beat*, 13(2), pp. 147–59.

H3 Podcast (2018). H3 *Podcast #59 - Deadmau5*, 30 March, https://www.youtube.com/watch?v=WEMAvnkHA9U&list=PLySv2JSr26iKacQ5zx5UIkkS_1Q7gtTCg&index=14, accessed 18 July 2020.

Hall, Charlie (2019). 'Deadmau5 Quits Twitch Following Ban for Using Homophobic Slur', *Polygon*, 13 February, https://www.polygon.com/2019/2/13/18223355/deadmau5-twitch-banned-homophobic-slur, accessed 18 July 2020.

Hilmes, Michelle (2012). 'Radio and the Imagined Community', in Jonathan Sterne (ed.), *The Sound Studies Reader*. New York: Routledge, pp. 351–62.

Horgen, Tom (2010). 'Clubs Come Alive with Deadmau5', *Star Tribune*, 10 October, https://www.startribune.com/clubs-come-alive-with-deadmau5/104958694/, accessed 18 July 2020.

Horner, Al (2016). 'Skrillex Hits Back at Deadmau5 over Justin Bieber Criticism', *FACT Magazine* (blog), 14 May, https://www.factmag.com/2016/05/14/skrillex-deadmau5-criticism-justin-bieber/, accessed 18 July 2020.

Hot Topic (2015). Interview: Deadmau5, 11 November, https://www.youtube.com/watch?v=tOdhRIU2aIc&list=PLySv2JSr26iKacQ5zx5UIkkS_1Q7gtTCg&index=9&t=0s, accessed 18 July 2020.

Huron, David Brian (2006). *Sweet Anticipation: Music and the Psychology of Expectation*. Cambridge, MA: MIT Press.

Huxtable, Simon (2014). 'What Is Progressive House?', *Decoded Magazine*, 11 August, https://www.decodedmagazine.com/what-is-progressive-house-2/, accessed 18 July 2020.

Leach, Elizabeth Eva (2001). 'Vicars of "Wannabe": Authenticity and the Spice Girls', *Popular Music*, 20(2), pp. 143–67. https://doi.org/10.1017/S0261143001001386.

MasterClass (2016). 'MasterClass: Deadmau5 Teaches Electronic Music Production', https://www.masterclass.com/classes/deadmau5-teaches-electronic-music-production/enrolled, accessed 18 July 2020.

McLeod, Kembrew (1999). 'Authenticity Within Hip-Hop and Other Cultures Threatened with Assimilation', *Journal of Communication*, 49(4), pp. 134–50. https://doi.org/10.1111/j.1460-2466.1999.tb02821.x.

McLeod, Kembrew (2001). 'Genres, Subgenres, Sub-Subgenres and More: Musical and Social Differentiation Within Electronic/Dance Music Communities', *Journal of Popular Music Studies*, 13(1), pp. 59–75. https://doi.org/10.1111/j.1533-1598.2001.tb00013.x.

Meadow, Matthew (2018). 'Deadmau5 Apologizes after Being Accused of Making Transphobic Remarks on Twitter', *Your EDM* (blog), 8 October, https://www.youredm.com/2018/10/08/deadmau5-apologizes-after-being-accused-of-making-transphobic-remarks-on-twitter/, accessed 18 July 2020.

Montano, Ed (2010). '"How Do You Know He's Not Playing Pac-Man While He's Supposed to Be DJing?": Technology, Formats and the Digital Future of DJ Culture', *Popular Music*, 29(3), pp. 397–416. https://doi.org/10.1017/S0261143010000449.

Moore, Allan (2002). 'Authenticity as Authentication', *Popular Music*, 21(2), pp. 209–23. https://doi.org/10.1017/S0261143002002131.

Omaze (2014). *Take a Tour of Deadmau5's Apartment...Then Meet Him.* // *Omaze*, 12 November, https://www.youtube.com/watch?v=e18TnHedCVc&list=PLySv2JSr26iKacQ5zx5UIkkS_1Q7gtTCg&index=9, accessed 18 July 2020.

Patty, Austin T. (2009). 'Pacing Scenarios: How Harmonic Rhythm and Melodic Pacing Influence Our Experience of Musical Climax', *Music Theory Spectrum*, 31(2), pp. 325–67. https://doi.org/10.1525/mts.2009.31.2.325.

Peres, Asaf (2016). 'The Sonic Dimension as Dramatic Driver in 21st-Century Pop Music', PhD diss., University of Michigan.

Peterson, Richard A. (1997). *Creating Country Music: Fabricating Authenticity*. Chicago: University of Chicago Press.

Reynolds, Simon (2011). *Bring the Noise: 20 Years of Writing About Hip Rock and Hip Hop*. Berkeley, CA: Soft Skull Press.

Reynolds, Simon (2013). *Energy Flash: A Journey Through Rave Music and Dance Culture*, New and Revised Edition. London: Faber and Faber.

Rishty, David (2019). 'Deadmau5's Collaborations: Every Artist From A-Z', *Billboard*, 10 January, http://www.billboard.com/photos/8493028/deadmau5-collaborations-artists-dance-music-songs, accessed 18 July 2020.

Sayre, Wilson (2014). 'Waiting For The Drop: The Anatomy Of An EDM Song', 27 March, http://www.wlrn.org/post/waiting-drop-anatomy-edm-song, accessed 18 July 2020.

Smith, Cody (2015). 'Deadmau5 Criticizes Modern EDM Producers with Enlightening Blog Post', *Your EDM* (blog), 28 July, https://www.youredm.com/2015/07/28/deadmau5-criticizes-modern-edm-producers-with-enlightening-blog-post/, accessed 18 July 2020.

Smith, Jeremy W. (2019). 'The Salience, Shapes, and Functions of Continuous Processes in Contemporary Electronic Dance Music', PhD diss., University of Minnesota, Minneapolis.

Snoman, Rick (2019). *Dance Music Manual*, 4th edn. Milton Park, Abingdon, Oxon; New York: Routledge.

Solberg, Ragnhild (2014). '"Waiting for the Bass to Drop": Correlations between Intense Emotional Experiences and Production Techniques in Build-Up and Drop Sections of Electronic Dance Music', *Dancecult: Journal of Electronic Dance Music Culture*, 6(1), pp. 61–82.

Vizsla (2020). *DEADMAU5 CUBE V3 - First Show (Best Quality)*, 7 February, https://www.youtube.com/watch?v=U4hiIo5Q7bQ, accessed 18 July 2020.

Walther, Joseph B. (2011). 'Theories of Computer-Mediated Communication and Interpersonal Relations', in Mark L. Knapp and John A. Daly (ed.), *The Sage Handbook of Interpersonal Communication*, 4th edn. Thousand Oaks, CA: SAGE Publications.

Wright, Edward (2017). 'Making Hammers with Art: The Producer of House and Techno', PhD diss., University of Toronto, Canada.

8

Second-hand stardom

Connotations of sampling for electro swing

Chris Inglis

The notion of stardom is to be considered by any aspiring musician, and the extent to which the said musician may view fame as a target is relevant in understanding their approach to persona, performance and even aspects of their composition. One genre in which this is particularly pertinent is that of electro swing: a contemporary form of dance music built around samples of music from the swing era of the 1930s and 1940s. This fusion of modern and vintage styles is certainly noteworthy on the basis of musicality, in terms of its status as a present-day recontextualization of past styles, but it can also prove relevant to analyse the disparity between each respective scene's approach to stardom. For in many ways, the swing era set the stage for musical stardom in the sense in which we know it today, yet the degree to which these ideas have been inherited by electro swing is somewhat skewed.

The ideas of celebrity – of performers becoming household names and of the public valuing a performer's persona sometimes over their creative output – were solidified during this era. Indeed, as has been suggested by Studlar, the jazz age presented 'the glory years of stardom in which the star system came into full flower' (1996: 1); and similarly, Gamson notes that 'this period also marked the birth of modern American consumer culture' (2007: 144). As a result, performers such as Louis Armstrong, Benny Goodman and Duke Ellington experienced immense success throughout the entertainment industry, and the acclaim they subsequently received was comparable to that of today's stars. This perception and presentation of such individuals have persisted to the present day, and the esteem and admiration of these musicians – and their subsequent reputations – have only been heightened. As Tucker writes in his introduction to *The Duke Ellington Reader*,

> Today, nearly twenty years after his death, his compositions remain popular, enjoyed by listeners throughout the world, championed by performers, and

acclaimed by critics. Many of his recordings are still available, with companies in the United States and abroad steadily reissuing old collections and coming out with previously unreleased material. College and conservatory students, meanwhile increasingly encounter Ellington in their classes and textbooks, and they are learning to pay the music on the bandstand, often from scores painstakingly transcribed from recordings. Enthusiasts in North America and Europe belong to societies, receive newsletters, and attend annual conferences devoted to Ellington. And since 1988 scholars have begun exploring the rich collection of Ellington manuscripts, sketches, full scores, and orchestral parts housed in the Archive Center of the Smithsonian's National Museum of American History in Washington, D.C. (1993: xvii)

The celebrity status achieved and maintained by the likes of Ellington is impressive, but what one may observe is that – with a few exceptions – this stardom hasn't translated across to the contemporary artists utilizing the music of these original performers. When a remix of Duke Ellington is heard, it is generally Ellington who tends to be evoked in the mind of the listener, despite the degree of divergence to which this new remix may present. Thus, the original stars of the swing era can be said to be enjoying a form of 'second-hand stardom': reaching into the future to steal acclaim away from the subsequent adapter of their works. In fact, as will be demonstrated, the desire for celebrity status in a genre like electro swing may at times be castigated, and artists who have made attempts to gain acclaim for themselves in this way – such as Austrian DJ Parov Stelar – have at times been shunned.

Electro swing presents a rather unique variation of electronic dance music (EDM) then, a scene in which the megastars of EDM – such as Tiësto, Deadmau5 and Avicii – could likely not exist. To investigate and begin to understand this particular attitude, then, one must first look away from these megastars and towards the various underground EDM scenes that have developed globally over the past few decades.

The changing face of celebrity

The attitude towards individual stardom that is evident throughout much of electro swing seems – at least on first look – to have grown out of these underground EDM scenes, specifically through the positioning of the music itself as the main focus of attention, far beyond the persona of the producer or performer. Away from the breakout megastars that have emerged over the past few decades, much of the EDM that is actually consumed on the ground is done so anonymously, with audiences tending to demonstrate little regard for knowledge of the artists themselves.

This has been the case since the dawn of disco, which arguably is subsequently the dawn of EDM, having been described as 'a cornerstone of House and Techno as well as all other dance-related electronica' (Prendergast 2000: 374). As the popularity of disco increased, the 'DJs became elevated over the performers, whose names would often not even be known by the disco audience' (Barker and Taylor 2007: 232). And as the EDM genre began to splinter off in different directions, this progression only continued:

> In early house and hip-hop, the erosion of the cult of the performer's personality continued apace. House records were often recorded under fleeting pseudonyms, adopted and discarded at will by producers and teams. Singers were recruited to perform on a track with which they might have had little else to do, and stage performances were partly displaced by DJ sessions. Remixing other people's records came to be seen as a skill in itself, and as a result, the connection between artist and product was partly broken. (Barker and Taylor 2007: 264)

In his analysis into the clubbing scene found in an unidentified city near Detroit, Michigan, Spring expands upon this notion, describing how 'advertising visiting name DJs became unnecessary, because it was understood by the kids that the Strip always had good DJs and that the range of styles would meet or exceed their expectations (2004: 56). And Cotgrove notes a similar instance too, pointing out that in the acid jazz scene, the 'dancers were never that interested in who the DJ was – they were 'Ninjas', as Jerry IDJ told me – they were invisible' (2009: 49).

In the introduction to his book *Energy Flash* (2013), Reynolds describes an experience he had in 1991, in which 'it became crystal clear that the audience was the star' (2013: xxvi). Indeed, the role that the audience plays in forging the clubbing experience is undoubtedly a significant part of the music, and the influence of a fellow audience member may be much more impactful on a participant than any information concerning the identity of the headlining performer. This point is exemplified by Prendergast, stating that 'House and Techno implied that the music itself was the most important thing, the makers of that music a vital but secondary issue. The mix, the sample, the club, and the audience were the crucial ingredients in the experience' (2000: 373).

In terms of how this phenomenon relates to the electro swing scene, I found similar approaches to clubbing described in the early experiences of various electro swing practitioners. For instance, Michael Rack – founding member of the Dutty Moonshine outfit – spoke to me of how much of his early exposure to EDM came from attending many of the free parties held across the UK throughout the 1990s and early 2000s. In terms of what attracted him towards this type of clubbing, Rack explained:

> I love the, the lack of pretentiousness of free parties, in that it wasn't DJ worship, it was music – alright, it was a bit of rig worship, because of the bass – but it was the music, people went for the music, the DJ was an irrelevance, because he was tucked to the side. (Inglis 2019: 554)

Rack's experience parallels all those already described and in this sense draws heavily upon the ethos of underground EDM, an attitude generally shared across the electro swing scene. But the other style that exercises a considerable influence upon the electro swing mindset is that of the jazz age – and as already noted, it was during this time that the notion of celebrity in general was largely established.

It remains clear that despite the two styles – swing and EDM – functioning in much the same way across their respective eras, the reception each has received in terms of star consumption is fundamentally different. An explanation for this may be found in considering society's changing perceptions around the idea of celebrity. Gamson examines this idea to a great extent, exploring two 'storylines' which detail the making of the star:

> In one storyline, dominant in the first part of the century, the deserving rise naturally to the top. In the other storyline, stronger in later decades, celebrities are artificially manufactured. (2007: 141)

Gamson continues, noting that 'in one, the great and talented and virtuous and best-at rise to the top of the attended-to, aided perhaps by rowdy promotion, which gets people to notice but can do nothing to actually make the unworthy famous' (2007: 141); however, 'beginning around 1950, changes in the celebrity-building environment – the breakdown of studio control, the rise of television, a boom in the "supply" of celebrities – significantly destabilized what had been a tightly integrated celebrity system' (2007: 142).

Thus, to be considered a celebrity in the modern day might not be perceived in as complimentary a way as the jazz age celebrity. Where the dominant view of this era is that its stars *earned* their fame through their considerable talent and prowess, it is recognized that the notion of fame has become so cheapened by today's standards that it no longer signifies any positive attributes at all. Indeed, as noted by Giles, 'the word "celebrity" is frequently used in a pejorative sense to signify "a culture that privileges the momentary, the visual and the sensation over the enduring, the written, and the rational"' (2018: 12).

In fact, Giles even specifically separates these negative characterizations of the contemporary celebrity from those of the pre-1950s, arguing that we should be using distinct terminology to refer to each respective group:

> If, as Boorstin and others have argued, celebrity itself, in all its vulgar worthlessness, did not emerge until the advent of television, the birth of rock 'n' roll, and other allegedly debased cultural forms, what label should be applied to the famous pre-war Hollywood actors? The answer: *stars*. (2018: 14)

Gamson goes on to explain in further detail the changes that developed throughout the late twentieth century that would affect contemporary attitudes towards celebrity status:

> First and most generally, the mechanisms by which images are made and by which celebrity is built have become increasingly exposed. Second, celebrity as a commercial enterprise has been not only acknowledged but often embraced. Third, the audience has been invited to increase its knowledge and its power. Finally, the discourse has brought about an increasing self-consciousness and irony about celebrity. (2007: 150)

As he goes on to conclude, 'embedded in these stories is the long-standing pull between the democratic and the aristocratic in fame discourse. Ought attention go to a naturally deserving elite, or is everyone and no one more deserving?' (2007: 153). The likes of Duke Ellington demonstrate that in the jazz age, fame was indeed aristocratic – a position that many electro swing artists may wish to maintain; however in today's Warhol-esque postmodern world, fame is clearly a lot more democratic and accessible, giving some explanation as to why fame may not necessarily be considered as important a goal as it traditionally has been.

Building on the model of former stars

As noted by Redmond and Holmes, 'the consumers of the famous use and need stars for a variety of social and psychic reasons' (2007: 10); and in referencing the audience of the star, it will be beneficial to remind oneself that such an audience will often include potential would-be stars themselves, who may make use of the star's appeal for their own unique purposes. For instance, Ndalianis refers to a ladder-like model of stardom, in which those on the bottom rung may reach to those above them, to help increase their own status:

> the cult of personality is also included in the new star model, with the result that a new hierarchy is set into place: the bottom of the scale is occupied by the personality who may (if worthy) rise to the level of star or, perhaps, even superstar. (2002: x)

Van Krieken refers to this as the 'pyramid effect', highlighting that 'the value of mega-celebrities increases as a mechanism for improving the visibility of anyone seeking a public profile at a lower level of attention circulation' (2019: 191). By utilizing elements of an established star's character – whether through direct reference or more varied means – a kind of symbiotic relationship emerges, in which the newer artist hitches a ride on the older star's fame-mobile, and the older star can enjoy the wider exposure they would not otherwise get. Van Krieken describes how 'these kinds of mechanisms illustrate the self-reproducing 'perpetual-motion' character of attention capital [. . .] the established celebrity gains even more attention, and the reviewed author gets increased attention because they can bask in the glow of the celebrity' (2019: 71). This is of course a mutually beneficial process, and Van Krieken summarizes the benefits for the established star by emphasizing that 'the more the base of the celebrity pyramid expands, the higher its peak will rise' (2019: 191). He continues:

> rather than *displacing* the mega-celebrities [. . .] the increasing range and variety of the celebrity field [. . .] makes those who can stand above this growing crowd even more strategically important, and valuable, as guides to where one can and should direct one's attention in an increasingly crowded celebrity scene. (2019: 191)

The connection of this model to electro swing should by now have become clear. Through their utilization of the music made by the stars of the first half of the twenty-first century, the practitioners of electro swing are strengthening the appeal and allure of these individuals while simultaneously incurring some level of acclaim for themselves in the process. For instance, in 2011 Caro Emerald released the Christmas single 'You're All I Want For Christmas', in which she duetted against a post-mortem recording of R&B singer Brook Benton (Emerald and Benton 2011). Indeed, often the death of such a performer can only serve to elevate their reputation even further, as exemplified by Williams in stating that 'posthumous stardom [. . .] often constructs a more intensified aura of authority and cultural power than a living celebrity' (2013: 104). Describing this process, he notes that 'the [original] artist now has an aura or mystique, perhaps regaining the aura lost in mechanical reproduction' (2013: 122), also noting 'the authenticity that comes from using a genuine recording of the artist' (2013: 123) (Figure 8.1).

It is necessary to note that this is far more multifaceted than just regular sampling. The intertextuality on display across this genre manifests itself in a variety of different ways. Lacasse has discussed this extensively, recognizing two distinct approaches to the referencing of musical texts, which he terms 'autosonic' and 'allosonic' (2000: 56). Autosonic sampling, the method we are most familiar with when considering this practice, refers to the direct lifting

Figure 8.1 'You're All I Want for Christmas' by Caro Emerald. Image courtesy of Grandmono Records.

of material from the original recording digitally, and Lacasse divides this into further subvarieties, including remixes, autosonic quotation (digital sampling) and the plunderphonic techniques pioneered by John Oswald; contrastingly, allosonic sampling may refer to allusions to style, allosonic quotation (performed live), translated songs or the simple cover version (2000: 35–58). Building on the work of Lacasse, Wilsmore has suggested a number of further methods of sampling, such as the super-composition, the mash-up and the cantus firmus (2010: 13–14).

Returning to the Emerald example, the degree to which this broadness of how one may use recycled material through intertextual means is not least evidenced by the marketing of the single, being packaged as a single by 'Caro Emerald and Brook Benton'. This is despite Benton having – essentially – nothing to do with the track. Besides his vocal sample, all the instrumentation, production, mixing and engineering – plus the additional vocals by Emerald herself – has been provided by Emerald and her team, the single even being released on Emerald's own label, no less. And yet, Benton receives half the credit, even twenty-three years after his death. A similar situation, which I have written about in the past (see Inglis 2015: 37), comes with Club Des Belugas's remix of Ella Fitzgerald's 1957 recording of 'Air Mail Special' (2009). Despite this remix being released thirteen years after the death of Fitzgerald, and featuring on what is otherwise largely an album of Club Des Belugas originals, the song was credited as 'Ella Fitzgerald – "Air Mail Special (Club Des Belugas Remix)"'. Club Des Belugas, then, are simply the conduit through which Fitzgerald may continue to release new music.

The prospect of electro swing stardom

What, then, of the electro swing artists who do wish to become stars in their own right? Emerald certainly provides an example of one who may be considered an electro swing star, having achieved number one albums in both the UK and the Netherlands. Other potentials include the aforementioned Parov Stelar and the Swedish AronChupa – both producers/DJs – who have both received significant international acclaim. When the music of such producers is so heavily reliant on the utilization – often through direct sampling – of already established stars, how then does one make the jump to attaining their own individual recognition?

This is alluded to by Redmond, in presenting the case that

> the type of person or figure that gets celebrated however, needs to be individuated; they need to be seen to exist as something unique or special and this is best encapsulated through the way the celebrity is made to signify, to be the material out of which identities and subjectivities emerge and converge. (2019: 87)

This is the struggle that such artists must overcome: finding one's own distinctive identity within the recycled material that their art makes use of. As Redmond has also noted, 'celebrity representations are never neutral: they carry the discourses, concerns, inequalities and dreams of the contemporary age' (2019: 36); and thus an EDM star of today is always going to be seen within the contexts of contemporary dance music, despite the time from which their music originates.

So the challenge arises in establishing one's own individual persona and identity without seemingly stepping on the toes of one's predecessors. This is unsurprisingly a difficult game to play, and many of the electro swing musicians whom I spoke to over the course of my research were quick to tell me that they were in no way trying to outdo the star power of those from whom their music draws. For instance, Tony Culverwell – who DJs under the name of Mr Switch – was insistent that

> DJs generally have the mindset of, they're paying tribute to the samples [...] it's not like you steal it and it's yours, you know – you sort of declare, I'm using it and I'm paying homage to the original artist and things. (Inglis 2019: 498)

Similarly, DJ Chris Tofu informed me that

> we've got really high morals on all this, we don't like to see a song destroyed – if it's destroyed and unrecognised, well we're not in that, we don't give a fuck, it's shit. You know what I mean, don't say you're better than Cab Calloway, don't say you're better than Slim & Slam, do you know what I mean, because you're not. (Inglis 2019: 607)

The overall respect afforded to these swing stars from their EDM descendants is comprehensive and suggests that an electro swing artist could simply *never* achieve the level of stardom of their predecessors – at least, not without incurring some significant criticism from others within the scene.

And, as we find, this remains to be the case. As our interview continued, Chris Tofu went on to criticize certain individuals he felt weren't creating their music in the respectful manner that he feels should be expected. The largest recipient of his scorn was, unsurprisingly, the closest electro swing has to a genuine star, Parov Stelar:

> people like Parov – they don't give a toss about anyone else anyway, they're not a part of a movement – they like themselves, very selfish, very, very rich, very – don't care about anyone else, probably thinks he invented everything anyway. (Inglis 2019: 615)

An example of Stelar's ego can be demonstrated through his attitude to sampling. In 2015, he released the single 'Don't Mean a Thing', a reworking of Duke Ellington's 1931 original. Ellington's composition, due to its wide recognition as a strong signifier of the swing era – and likely in part to the overt semantics of the song's lyrics – is one of the most widely sampled tracks across the electro swing spectrum. Some of the more well-known versions have been released by Greens Keepers (2001); the Puppini Sisters (2007); Club Des Belugas (2008); and ProleteR (2013), as well as a prominent remix of the Lionel Hampton version, featured on both Bart & Baker's *Electro Swing IV* (2011) and *White Mink: Black Cotton, Volume 3* (2013) – and this is barely scratching the surface. By 2015, much of the possibilities regarding how one may utilize this track had been exhausted, and it's certain that Stelar would have been aware of this. Thus, it seems that his own version was produced as a means of positioning himself at the top of the electro swing world, as an attempt to establish his authority over the other, presumably inferior variants. I witnessed a similar instance of this from the Correspondents, a British duo, at the Swingamajig festival in 2015. Like many other acts, the Correspondents have released their own remix of Benny Goodman's 'Sing, Sing, Sing (With a Swing)' (2016), and their MC – Mr Bruce – preceded this performance of the track by stating that 'you've probably heard this one a million times today, but now you're going to hear it once more'.

There is thus a certain kind of conflict within the electro swing world, in terms of different artist's approaches to stardom. It's not necessarily that the goal of being a star itself is seen as objectionable, and this can be demonstrated through various practitioner's outspoken desire for fame. For instance, as I have spoken about previously (see Inglis 2019: 178), there are at least two instances of electro swing acts appearing on televised talent competitions: Elle and the Pocket Belles, and Kitten and the Hip. I spoke to Kitten and the Hip's Ashley Slater directly, who informed me that the duo were invited to compete on *The X Factor* by a talent scout and that he didn't see this opportunity for more widespread fame as in any way contradictive of their beliefs, stating that 'I have no interest, at all, in remaining underground, never had' (Inglis 2019: 717). In response to potential accusations of selling out, Slater argued that 'I don't give a shit if somebody says that, [laughs] you know. I – to me, success is not selling out, it's just success, you know?' (Inglis 2019: 716); and he explained that a degree of fame has always been one of the act's targets: 'we had high ambitions, and we – Scarlett still, you know, has quite an ambitious approach to the music industry, she wants to do well in it, and all that stuff' (Inglis 2019: 709). Similar ambitions have been described by Dutty Moonshine's Michael Rack, who possesses a particularly wide-eyed view of stardom, speaking of himself in terms of 'when I get famous' (Inglis 2019: 528).

In contrast to such acts, others have spoken out in direct criticism of such television programmes. A robust example of this comes with Jim Burke – known as Mr B the Gentleman Rhymer – who has on several separate occasions spoken about his decision to reject his offer from a talent scout to appear on *Britain's Got Talent*. Describing the show as 'silly nonsense' (Burke 2010), it has become something of a running joke that he turns down this offer on a yearly basis. Various tweets of his over the years have indicated this directly:

> 'Who's had their Britain's got Talent email then?' (Burke 2012)

> 'And like clockwork there's this year's "will you come in Britain's Got Talent?" Email. #BGT #nope' (Burke 2016)

> 'Hehey! Got the Britain's Got Talent message. On facebook this time Have they lost my email?' (Burke 2020)

And Burke isn't the only one within the scene to feel this way. In response to his tweets, DJ Richard Hale – known as Mista Trick – tweeted 'hell no!! Don't do it!!' (Hale 2016). Slamboree are another act to disparage this show too. As part of their live show, the band regularly brings out circus performers alongside the live musicians, and I recall one performance in which – from the main stage at the Boomtown festival 2015 – the band announced, 'you won't see this sort of shit on *Britain's Got Talent*'.

There is clearly a lot of animosity directed towards this particular show then. But it seems that the objection is specifically directed at the industry behind this type of entertainment, not at the acts such as Kitten and the Hip who choose to participate and certainly not at the idea of fame or stardom in general. This is where we return to Gamson's two 'storylines' of celebrity; and nothing can be said to exemplify the kind of shallow fame representative of latter-day twentieth-century celebrity better than these types of television show. Rather, the objection that may emerge is directed towards the way in which one accesses their respective stardom, and especially in such a sample-heavy and inspiration-proud genre as this one, to make sure that one is not seen to be disparaging of the artists of whom they are standing on the shoulders.

Again, this is why it is important to recognize the distinction between the megastars of the wider EDM world and the would-be stars of electro swing. In the case of the EDM giants, they have the potential to create a song entirely from scratch and thus any acclaim that they receive may justifiably be directed entirely towards their original creation. In the case of electro swing, the crucial emphasis on sampling indicates that the acclaim in this case must be shared. And as discussed, this remains the case even for the use of samples in a more indirect sense.

Hence, it's not just that electro swing has *yet* to produce any megastars or uber-celebrities; this analysis would suggest that it *cannot*. That's not to say that it can't produce stars at all, and the likes of Parov Stelar and Caro Emerald have proven that there certainly are practitioners who have achieved a considerable level of fame. But the form of star that this genre may produce will differ from the late twentieth-century, postmodern star who is often more recognizable for simply existing *as* a star than for whatever their achievements may be. By putting their recycled elements on display in such an overt and ostentatious fashion, the artists of electro swing are insisting that whatever they may achieve notoriety for, the reason for this recognition is acknowledged to the same degree as the recognition itself.

Conclusion

Within the world of EDM then, there can be said to be two opposing attitudes to stardom and celebrity that together represent something of a binary. The most well known, by their very nature, are the *megastars*. These are the DJs and performers who will be found headlining Tomorrowland, or the Electric Daisy Carnival: those who amount not just to some of the most famous individuals in the world of music but in the world itself. However, despite their disproportionate level of fame, these performers actually make up a minority of those participating across the spectrum of EDM. The vast majority of EDM practitioners are the nameless

DJs, the faceless producers and the unknown characters upon which the various global underground EDM scenes are built.

Electro swing sits somewhere in between these two perspectives. The philosophy upon which the scene is established is that of the underground EDM world. But the music itself, the samples used and the era that electro swing seeks to resurrect scream *stardom*. The musicians that are being indirectly celebrated through this style were absolutely the stars of their era, and rather than make attempts to get around this fact, the genre has chosen to embrace it. By using Van Krieken's 'pyramid effect' model of celebrity, the majority of electro swing artists are building their own status by establishing themselves as a descendant and subsequent devotee of these stars while ensuring that such stars always remain on the top. Thus, an expected level of respect is seen as essential, and it can be considered almost sinful for an artist to try and exceed this star power, as has been observed in the criticism of artists such as Parov Stelar – despite his considerable contributions to the scene.

One may view this divide in EDM's approach to stardom through Gamson's two 'storylines' of celebrity. As attitudes to fame began to change halfway through the twentieth century, the public became more cynical in terms of the praise bestowed upon such celebrities. There is no level of ambiguity here: the swing era and the EDM era are distinctly on two separate sides of this transitory divide. Hence, while the stars of swing were recognized for their stardom that was supposedly earned, EDM's stars are often not considered to be as worthy of their success. As a result, celebrity is often not something that one may tend to strive for in the EDM world. Resultingly, we may utilize Giles's distinction between *celebrity* and *star*. If *celebrity* is said to represent the kind of shallow, undeserved, late twentieth-century performers represented by the megastars, then it is unsurprising that this is the type of attitude that electro swing shuns. This also explains why those within the genre may be so critical of televised talent competitions, as this is the type of celebrity that those shows seek to produce and revere. But as stated, it's not fame itself that electro swing is critical of – far from it. Instead, electro swing is reaching back to the early twentieth-century view of fame as illustrated by Giles's *star*. This is the fame that electro swing celebrates, and this is the narrative that it seeks to rediscover.

Therefore, the genre represents something of a breakaway from the underground EDM connotations of anti-stardom. Despite sharing many other aspects with this movement, the attitude to stardom is distinct in that there is no expectation, nor common characteristic, of shying away from widespread acclaim. There's certainly a reluctance to embrace celebrity in the contemporary understanding of the idea, but not at all when approaching the concept from the attitude of yesteryear. By reaching to those before, and indeed above, them, the practitioners of this particular strand of EDM may begin to build their own reputation while always remaining in the shadows of their admired idols – no matter how bright those shadows may be. And not only are they utilizing the music and character of these icons, they are also utilizing this anachronistic model of celebrity that may be considered preferable for their respective ambitions. By bringing back these ideas in a new and relevant way, the electro swing musicians of today are creating the potential for a true, second-hand star.

References

Barker, Hugh and Yuval Taylor (2007). *Faking It: The Quest for Authenticity in Popular Music*. New York, NY: W. W. Norton & Company.

Burke, Jim (2010). *Twitter*. Available online: https://twitter.com/gentlemanrhymer/status/9176715674787840.

Burke, Jim (2012). *Twitter*. Available online: https://twitter.com/gentlemanrhymer/status/240474198429011968.

Burke, Jim (2016). *Twitter*. Available online: https://twitter.com/gentlemanrhymer/status/780742090808524801.

Burke, Jim (2020). *Twitter*. Available online: https://twitter.com/gentlemanrhymer/status/1217463528979947521.

Cotgrove, Mark (2009). *From Jazz Funk & Fusion to Acid Jazz: The History of the UK Jazz Dance Scene*. Milton Keynes: Chaser Publications and Authorhouse.

Gamson, Joshua (2007). 'The Assembly Line of Greatness: Celebrity in Twentieth-Century America', in Sean Redmond and Su Holmes (eds), *Stardom and Celebrity: A Reader*. London: Sage Publications.

Giles, David C. (2018). *Twenty-First Century Celebrity*. Bingley: Emerald Publishing.

Hale, Richard (2016). *Twitter*. Available online: https://twitter.com/MistaTrick/status/781793021037772800.

Inglis, Chris (2015). *Sampling the Swing Era*, MA diss., The University of Sheffield.

Inglis, Chris (2019). *Engaging with Electro Swing: Resurrection, Recontextualisation, and Remix*, PhD diss., University of South Wales.

Lacasse, Serge (2000). 'Intertextuality and Hypertextuality in Recorded Popular Music', in Michael Talbot (ed.), *The Musical Work: Reality or Invention?* Liverpool: Liverpool University Press.

Ndalianis, Angela (2002). 'Introduction', in Angela Ndalianis and Charlotte Henry (eds), *Stars in Our Eyes: The Star Phenomenon in the Contemporary Era*. Westport, CT: Praeger.

Prendergast, Mark (2000). *The Ambient Century: From Mahler to Trance – The Evolution of Sound in the Electronic Age*. London: Bloomsbury Publishing.

Redmond, Sean (2019). *Celebrity*. Oxon: Routledge.

Redmond, Sean and Su Holmes (2007). *Stardom and Celebrity: A Reader*. London: Sage Publications.

Reynolds, Simon (2013). *Energy Flash: A Journey through Rave Music and Dance Culture*, rev. edn. London: Faber and Faber.

Spring, Ken (2004). 'Behind the Rave: Structure and Agency in a Rave Scene', in Andy Bennett and Richard A. Peterson (eds), *Music Scenes: Local, Translocal and Virtual*. Nashville, TN: Vanderbilt University Press.

Studlar, Gaylyn (1996). *The Mad Masquerade: Stardom and Masculinity in the Jazz Age*. New York, NY: Colombia University Press.

Tucker, Mark (1993). *The Duke Ellington Reader*. Oxford: Oxford University Press.

Van Krieken, Robert (2019). *Celebrity Society: The Struggle for Attention*, 2nd edn. Oxon: Routledge.

Williams, Justin (2013). *Rhymin' and Stealin': Musical Borrowing in Hip-Hop*. Ann Arbor, MI: University of Michigan Press.

Wilsmore, Robert (2010). 'The Demonic and the Divine: Unfixing Replication in the Phenomenology of Sampling', *Journal of Music, Technology & Education*, 3 (1): 5–16.

Discography

Club Des Belugas (2008). *Swop*. Chinchin Records.

Club Des Belugas (2009). *Zoo Zizaro*. Chinchin Records.

The Correspondents (2015). 'Sing Sing Sing (The Correspondents Remix) – Benny Goodman', *SoundCloud*. Available online: https://soundcloud.com/the-correspondents/sing-sing-sing-the-correspondents-remix-benny-goodman.

Electro Swing IV (2011). Wagram Music.

Emerald, Caro and Brook Benton (2011). 'You're All I Want for Christmas'. Grandmono Records.

Greens Keepers (2001). *What's Your Man Got to Do with Gan?* Classic.

ProleteR. (2013). *Feeding the Lions*. Dusted Wax Kingdom.

Stelar, Parov (2015). *The Demon Diaries*. Etage Noir Recordings.

The Puppini Sisters (2007). *The Rise & Fall of Ruby Woo*. Verve Records

White Mink: Black Cotton, *Vol. 3 (Electro Swing versus Speakeasy Jazz)* (2013). Freshly Squeezed Music.

Part III

Dance music scenes

The evolution of electronic dance music spaces in Leeds, UK

Stuart Moss

Electronic beats and synthesized music have been in existence since the first half of the twentieth century although their origins were experimental, avant-garde and not popular (Austin and Smalley 2000). In the 1960s, American band Silver Apples created electronic music that was intended for people to dance to, rather than as artistic experimentation (Thump 2013). In the 1970s electronic music was spread through the incorporation of synthesizers, keyboards and drum machines into disco music. Through mass media, the music and dancing of the disco movement was popularized (Bragin and Kwan 2012) and the use of electronica became mainstream, with an emphasis on bass and regular repetitive beats. Discotheques and nightclubs, which are urban spaces where subjective loss and regression take place (Christodolou 2011), provided a social, escapist experience on the dancefloor for people to enjoy and move to this music.

With a starting point of the 1980s, this chapter will explore how club venues in Leeds have embraced the sound of electronic dance music (EDM), which is an umbrella term for music where the majority of the sound is generated electronically. It will highlight how changes in music style, as well as macro factors such as the law, politics, drug usage and fashion, have influenced the development of EDM venues within the city, from its experimental origins in discos and in suburbia; to illegal raves; city centre nightclubs, and; back into suburbia where a vibrant house party scene now provides a viable alternative to visiting commercial nightlife premises. In this chapter, the term 'club' is used to describe venues where DJs play music for people to dance to, irrespective of whether they are officially recognized as commercial nightlife premises.

Leeds is considered to be the third largest and one of the fastest growing cities in the UK (Leeds City Council 2020). Leeds grew as a city around the textile industries following the Industrial Revolution, and other major industries have emerged around coal mining, beer brewing, printing, engineering and chemicals. Throughout the twentieth century the city grew to be a regional centre for retail and commerce, as well as an important transport hub, with major north-south and east-west railways and motorways dissecting the city, which also developed an international airport. The city's popular musical heritage is rich, with a notable influence on the punk, post-punk and 'alternative' scenes popularized in the latter half of the 1970s and up to the present day. Alongside this, Leeds has been and continues to be at the forefront of experimentation and development of 'scenes' in clubs where DJs champion EDM.

This chapter has been researched through a wide range of secondary and tertiary sources (referenced at the end), as well as interviews with some of the people who were responsible for creating electronic music events in Leeds from the 1980s to the present day. Autoethnographically, I will also recount some of my own experiences, as being a person who has actively collected electronic music since the mid-1980s; been present from both a leisure and professional perspective at dance music venues in Leeds since the late 1980s, and; through my work as co-ordinator of the Leeds Club History Project.[1]

The early 1980s

The British discos and nightclubs of city centre high streets in the early 1980s typically presented a musical repertoire that was limited to popular chart music and soul. DJ culture was about the personality of the DJ rather than the significance of the music, and the DJ would constantly talk over records to the audience on the dancefloor (Phillips 2009). Many of the popular artists played by DJs were American, and across the Atlantic in New York City a musical revolution had been taking place due to the rise in popularity of hip-hop. DJs in New York were live looping breakbeats (musical segments on records) for people to dance to, which extended the breakbeat segments and created a new live remixed dance track from other records. DJs would also merge one record into another using two turntables and a mixer, again for the benefit of those on the dancefloor who could continue dancing without interruption. The DJ became a skilled and respected engineer and entertainer, without having to say

[1] http://www.leedschp.co.uk.

a word. The sounds that they played had an emphasis on heavy bass and a high treble.

In Leeds, at the Warehouse, club owner Mike Wiand booked regular appearances by US DJs Greg James and Dan Pucciarelli for several years from 1980 onwards. Both DJs had worked at clubs in New York and both were live mixing DJs (Wilson 2013). James and Pucciarelli DJ'd at the Warehouse like they did in the States, mixing records together and not talking over them, which was a novelty to those on the dancefloor and immediately led to long queues to get into the venue (Lopez 2009). The New York influence was hip and cool, and alongside the DJs and the music that they played, the Warehouse had installed what they described as a 'New York style' sound system (overseen by James), which was based on the sound system in New York's Paradise Garage nightclub (Wilson 2013). Marc Almond, who would later go on to be half of the band Soft Cell, worked in the club's cloakroom, and in the early 1980s promoted and DJ'd a synthpop and electronica night at the venue (Brewster 2017). The Warehouse cemented its reputation as a cool place to experience cutting-edge electronic music to dance to in Leeds, before other venues followed.

1980s electronic music development

Electronica was fused with hip-hop to form a subgenre of hip-hop that at the time was referred to as 'electro' but in later years was renamed 'electro-hop'. Artists such as Afrika Bambaataa, Arthur Baker, Newcleus, Cybotron and Mantronix pioneered this sound and developed it further with the use of the Roland TR-808 drum machine to produce a distinct high-pitched rhythmic beat. The beat and rhythm of the fused musical styles made the sound of this new variant of electro music immediately danceable and was particularly suited to dance moves that involved sudden jerking movements, flowing body waves and sharp stops to suit the beat. Emergent body popping, breakdancing, jacking, locking and robotic dance styles particularly suited this music, which like many of those who participated in these dance forms in the early 1980s came from 'the street' where DIY communities of musicians, dancers, DJs, vocalists and artists emerged. The early days of house and electro musical culture were truly grass roots, championed by communities of serious leisure (Stebbins 2007) enthusiasts. This is an ongoing theme that has continued among new emergent electronic music cultures in subsequent years.

The onset of technology allowed DJs and music producers to further their repertoire of sampled sounds beyond vinyl records and to include virtually any sound. In the early 1980s, electronica was fused with disco and Jamaican dub by Chicago-based DJs and musicians to create house music with deep basslines at 120 bpm.

By the late 1980s, new electronic music styles became popular in the UK, including techno, which gave a harder, more bass-heavy and aggressive sound than house music. Techno fused electro with house, synthpop and funk (Bogdanov 2001). From techno came a more raw and scientific sound called acid house; this music was often less vocal than house and techno; it was characterized by an electronic 'squelching' sound, which was attributed to the Roland TB-303 synthesizer, which was released in the early 1980s and was lauded by creative underground artists in the acid house scene (Trailblazers of Acid House 2016).

Acid house had an avant-garde sound that did not court commercial appeal but resonated among alternative music subcultures; it also had a psychedelic image with the use of bright colours, tie-dye, 'magic eye' patterns and smiley faces on record sleeves, a true throwback to 1960s hippy psychedelia. The association with the drug LSD (nicknamed acid) was quickly made in the moral panic fuelled media and the music was considered to be corrupting Britain's youth. Radio 1 even banned the D Mob song 'We Call It Acieed' in 1989 (Vine 2011). This did not halt the popularity of the music, as the track reached number three in the UK Singles Chart (The Summer of Rave 1989, 2006).

Ecstasy

Ecstasy began to appear in the UK in 1987, just after Chicago house emerged (Phillips 2009); it made people more empathetic, open and receptive (Dance Britannia 2008). Officially called 3,4-Methylenedioxymethamphetamine (MDMA), the drug was patented in 1913 by the German company Merck as a slimming pill. The US military experimented with it as a truth serum. Hindu cult leader Bhagwan Shree Rajneesh used Ecstasy at 'free-love' parties, and it became an established drug of his followers and many young 'hippies' who introduced the drug to Europe via Ibiza, which was an established part of the 1970s 'hippy trail', due to Ibiza's relaxed laws, which were unusual for Spain, a country that had been under the rule of dictator General Franco (The

Agony and the Ecstasy: A Perfect Storm, 2017). Ecstasy heightened the sense of togetherness and increased the need to dance; it also turned users of it into 'submissive, unchallenging recipients of anything that was played to them' (James 2002: 37) devoid of any critical analysis. Under the influence of Ecstasy, the DJ became a god-like idol to dancers who collectively worshipped in a drug-fuelled state of techno-shamanism (Hutson 2000; Anderson 2009). According to Phillips (2009) Ecstasy and the impact that it had on clubbers helped to feminize the culture around club spaces as well as wider society. People taking Ecstasy rarely drank alcohol as they became dehydrated; instead, they drank water and violence normally associated with drunken behaviour in nightclubs disappeared (Gall 2009; The Summer of Rave 1989, 2006).

According to Evelyn (2018), in the 1980s there were very few black DJs in Leeds, which he described as a city divided by race, with areas within Leeds city centre that were not safe for a black man to be in. Evelyn DJ'd under the name of DJ E.A.S.E and recalled on his regular walk to HMV record shop in Leeds city centre that he would pass a man selling a National Front newspaper on the street. Evelyn recalled DJing at a party in a house in the Leeds suburb of Burley, and he noticed that there was a presence of Leeds Service Crew (LSC) members within the venue, as well as black people too. This was unusual as everyone was getting along together and enjoying the music, which was predominantly hip-hop and house as well as the fusion hip house (house music with rapped vocals), which all had a similar bpm so the tempo for dancing remained fairly constant. The fact that members of a football hooligan firm (some of whom were openly racist) were dancing to black music in a venue with black people was quite remarkable at the time. Evelyn put this down to the sudden rise in popularity of the drug Ecstasy, which was being taken by many of those in attendance. The use of Ecstasy made the dancefloor at these events a neutral space of acceptance and togetherness, the result of which was social mixing on a level that had not occurred in the city before, as a collective identity between participants in shared leisure spaces occurred (Anderson 2009).

The alternative influence

Inspired by house, techno, acid house and hip-hop, the alternative 'indie-dance' music genre of the late 1980s took the sound of electronica and combined it with guitars. 'Indie' music, which as a genre had its origins in punk, post-punk and new wave music, was fused with electronic beats, synth-based sounds, squelches, scratches and samples in a manner that was every bit as experimental as the first electronic music pioneers. UK artists including Pop Will Eat Itself (PWEI), Jesus Jones, the Shamen, the Happy Mondays, the Justified Ancients of Mu Mu (JAMM) and Primal Scream were influential. Some of these artists had been influenced by the band Age of Chance who were an indie-punk band from Leeds that experimented with electronica in the early to mid-1980s. Indie-dance bands, which typically featured guitarists and drummers as key musicians, began to include keyboards and live scratch-mixing DJs. The sound of 'alternative' music changed and became more electronic. The alternative music press and the 'indie' music charts began to feature artists such as A Guy Called Gerald, T-Coy, Bomb the Bass, Simon Harris, Adrian Sherwood, Technotronic, the KLF (formerly the JAMM) and Coldcut. The sound got heavier, becoming almost electro-industrial with bass and big beats being a key feature.

While acid house was typically minimal in terms of lyrical content, the rebellious nature of rave culture was captured in the lyrics and samples used by various indie-dance artists. Northside released the 1991 track 'Shall We Take a Trip?' with multiple references to the drug LSD (acid). The Shamen released a 1992 track 'Ebeneezer Goode', which had a chorus with the repeated lyrics 'Eezer Goode, Eezer Goode, He's Ebeneezer Goode'; Eezer Goode was literally pronounced 'E's are good', and the track reached number one in the UK Singles Chart.

Rave

The birth of the rave era is historically recognized as being the Summer of 1988 (Haslam 2001). Rave was youth rebellion, largely to a soundtrack of 120 bpm; it was easy to dance to and white people embraced this music of black origin (Hook 2009). Like other youth movements, rave culture came with its own set of values and dress code, baggy comfortable clothes for dancing in were preferred. In the late 1980s, people dancing in a field together genuinely and collectively thought that they could illicit a change in society for the better (Champion 1997). Rave was an anti-establishment movement, a throwback to the counterculture movements of the 1960s where 'hippies' embraced peace, love, drugs and music, and the 1970s where disco brought people from a range of backgrounds together in unity on the dancefloor (Critcher 2003). The emergence of the rave scene in Leeds was organic and grew from three prongs: one prong lead by left-leaning artisans, students, alternatives and experimentalists in Hyde Park; a second prong championed by the black community in and around Chapeltown's blues clubs; and a third prong in South Leeds lead by mostly working-class white lads and football casuals from LSC in unofficial venues such as warehouses. 'Peace Love Unity Respect is an adage associated with the principles of the rave scene during the late 1980s and into the 1990s' (O'Grady 2012: 103). A shared love of music, partying and drugs brought these neotribes together in these various enclaves.

Hyde Park is situated just north of the city centre; it is a suburb of mostly rented terraced houses, which runs close to the University of Leeds campus and is therefore popular with students. Historically in the 1970s and 1980s, there were a number of abandoned properties in Hyde Park, which had fallen into disrepair and were consequently used as squats. Anarchic and left-wing punk and alternative communities in the city gravitated towards this area hosting unofficial gigs and parties.

Chapeltown is a suburb with a high number of Afro-Caribbean residents, some of whom settled there in the 1950s and 1960s, bringing with them a sound system culture and the sounds of calypso, ska and reggae (The Gryphon 2015). In Jamaica, sound system culture dates back to the 1940s, and the DJs who played sound system music were known as 'record selectors' (Haslam 2001). The tradition of building sound systems had continued in the local Chapeltown community (The City Talking: Music in Leeds Vol II, 2016), where there were also a number of unlicensed blues clubs (shebeens), which had been created in people's homes (sometimes several basements had been knocked through to form one large venue). The clubs often had names that reflected their location, for example, the 148 Theatre Club, which was located at 148 Chapeltown Road. These venues operated as late-night drinking dens, where people who had left nightclubs in Leeds city centre when they closed at 02:00 could go and listen to music, as well as socialize, drink and dance until the next morning. The musical soundtrack of these venues was typically ska, reggae, blues, funk and soul, but as the 1980s progressed, the sound became more electronic and the DJs in blues clubs began to play house music from the mid to late 1980s onwards. Eventually acid house–themed nights began to happen in these venues. This was in an era when mainstream city centre nightclubs still largely played only chart music or soul, and acid house had not yet courted mass chart appeal.

Members of LSC also became involved in the rave scene through late-night drinking sessions in the blues clubs of Chapeltown and through contact with associates in Lancashire and Greater Manchester, traditionally the mortal enemies of Yorkshire-based football fans. The Lancashire and Greater Manchester side of the Pennine hills was slightly ahead of Yorkshire in terms of developing the rave scene in their locality, which is attributed to a number of reasons, including London-based football fans bringing the rave vibe north from London, where the scene was already established, and a high number of disused warehouses in Lancashire, which had seen a rapid decline of the textile trade in the latter half of the twentieth century (Haslam 2001; Turner 2018). Trans-Pennine animosity between football fans was put aside once Ecstasy came into the picture. LSC members who had experienced raves and Ecstasy over the Pennines shared their experiences with their compatriots, who followed suit, eventually coming back to Leeds with their own ideas for rave events in woodland and countryside that was accessible by the motorway network, as well as in disused warehouses around the city centre (Gall 2009).

> Towards the end of 1989, others started putting on raves in Leeds. Eddie E and Tony A organised one in a marquee called Space, off the M62 in Rothwell, and Gouldy, China and a few others sold tickets in the Hacienda. They got a DJ from Manchester, Steve Williams, and Eddie had an 8 foot polystyrene E cut out and put in the tent. By the time most lads got there it had been busted by the police and Eddie, Tony and a few others were arrested. Eddie told the police the E was for 'Eddie'. It was reported on TV and in the newspapers that ecstasy and cocaine had been found at an acid house party in Leeds. (Gall 2009: 224)

The rave mentioned earlier was one of many held in suburbs of the city; 'Lost in Space' was also held in woodland near the M62 motorway in the suburb of Rothwell in 1989. Another event called 'Love Decade' was held in 1990 in an empty warehouse on the Treefield Industrial Estate in the suburb of Gildersome. Years of industrial decline in the North of England had led to towns and cities having an abundance of unused ex-industrial space and those wanting to organize illegal parties took advantage of this. The sound system for the event was constructed on site from components bought from electrical wholesalers (Towning and Tissera 2020). This event was raided by the police resulting in 836 people being arrested for one or more of the following offences: breach of the

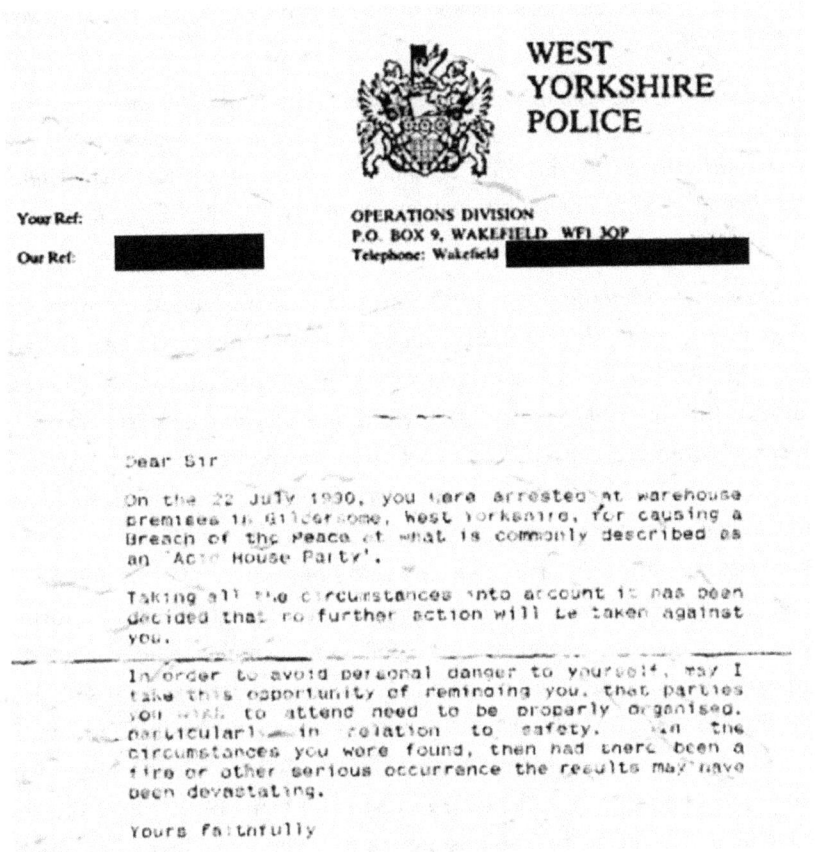

Figure 9.1 Letter sent to arrested attendees of the Love Decade rave in Gildersome, Leeds, 1990.

peace, criminal damage, and misuse of drugs. Those arrested were distributed to thirty police stations throughout West Yorkshire (ITN 1990). Most of those arrested were released without charge and later received warning letters in the post (see Figure 9.1). The DJ at the event, Rob Tissera, was arrested and was sentenced to three months (although only serving two weeks) for being in contravention of the Entertainments (Increased Penalties) Act 1990 (often referred to as the Acid House (parties) Bill).

> Dear Sir,
>
> On the 22 July 1990, you were arrested at warehouse premises in Gildersome, West Yorkshire for causing a Breach of the Peace at what is commonly described as an 'Acid House Party'.

Taking all the circumstances into account it has been decided that no further action will be taken against you.

In order to avoid personal danger to yourself, may I take this opportunity of reminding you, that parties you like to attend need to be properly organised, particularly in relation to safety. Within the circumstances you were found, then had there been a fire or other serious occurrence the results may have been devastating.

Having a party and being free was what rave culture was about, but heavy legal machinery was used to crush this rebellious youth culture (Dance Britannia 2008). The British government introduced the Entertainment's (Increased Penalties) Bill in 1990, which targeted both illegal free-party raves and unlicensed commercial parties that had an entry charge (the term 'pay-party' was used to cover such events); this bill raised fines for event organizers to being up to £20,000 as well as six months imprisonment (James 2002).

Rob Tissera went on to run a weekly acid house event at the Phoenix Club in Chapeltown, which was a licensed Caribbean social club that had formerly been a synagogue. It developed a loyal following, which included Dave Beer, Huggy and Alistair Cooke who would later go on to start their own club events in the city (Towning and Tissera 2020). Tissera was spotted at the Phoenix Club and asked to become a resident DJ at Ark, a weekly house music event, which ran at Leeds Polytechnic Students' Union (LPSU) from 1991, where the venue management was more amenable to new music and rave-themed events than some of the mainstream nightclubs in Leeds city centre at the time. LPSU was also a good sized space with around a 1,500 person capacity. Ark later moved to Leeds Town and Country Club and Leeds University Students' Union. This event is an early example of a rave-themed event that attracted both student and non-student rave fans under one roof in the city centre.

Into the city centre

Joy was the first unofficial rave event to make the conversion into a rave-themed club night in Leeds city centre venues (Lawson 2007). Joy began as an illegal rave in an old mill in Dewsbury in 1989, before becoming above board at Leeds Corn Exchange in 1991, which was a venue originally built for trade purpose in the nineteenth century and was predominantly used for retail

Figure 9.2 The Leeds Corn Exchange.

rather than as a nightlife venue, but a place which nonetheless was inspirational and transformative with a domed roof and ornate internal architecture (see Figure 9.2). Joy later moved to Leeds University Student's Union (LUSU), before running at numerous other venues in the city centre, including Mission, Mint Club and Distrikt.

From 1991, the growing popularity of house and techno music had made the genres mainstream and many venues in Leeds city centre changed their music policies accordingly. The Gallery nightclub changed its Saturday night music policy from being soul and commercial dance music to house and rave (88to98 2014). Resident DJ Steve Luigi was accompanied by guests including Carl Cox, Pete Tong and DJ Vertigo. The venue itself was split over several floors, on the top floor the Saturday night resident DJs were the Utah Saints, who had established themselves as a local cult band with a repertoire of house, techno and other EDM genres. The Gallery was subsequently voted the second best rave venue in Europe by international music magazine *Mixmag* (88to98 2014). Rave-themed Saturday nights in Leeds city centre nightclub venues became frequented by 'men in straight trousers' (Lawson 2007) and dressing to impress became part and parcel of door policy at nightclub venues, many of which banned trainers and jeans, insisting that male clubbers wore shoes and trousers (88to98 2015). The club night 'Precious', which was held at the Hi-Flyers Club, stated on its flyers 'Dress Code: Club Style!! (Strictly no ski hats or trainers) This night is not a rave!' The smart casual era of clubbing in Leeds was born, the baggy trousers, big t-shirts, trainers and high-vis vests commonly seen at raves were replaced by high-class brands such as Vivienne Westwood, La Coste and Louis Vuitton. The rave scene had originally had an ethos of inclusivity, but now it had been forced into city centre nightclubs, it became exclusive. A social movement based upon dancing, drugs, electronic music and equality, which was popularized among normal working-class people, had become commodified by entrepreneurs and stripped of its identity. For those who wanted to dance and party over the weekend in Leeds, there were two choices: adapt and embrace these changes or go and dance elsewhere.

Dave Beer was an early regular at raves and rave-themed events around the city before he began Back2Basics with co-founder Alistair Cooke and DJ Ralph Lawson at various Leeds city centre venues including the Music Factory and the Warehouse. In 1992 Beer and Cooke won the DMC and Mixmag Award for Best Club, further cementing the reputation of Leeds as a city with a vibrant EDM scene. Such success gave birth to other events in Leeds created by entrepreneur-promoter imitators who emerged with their own ideas for club nights in the city, all keen on taking a slice of the action in a Joseph Schumpeteresque cycle of innovation and creative destruction (Schumpeter 1934); competition for the weekend dance crowd in the city became fierce. Leeds-based promoter and entrepreneur Gip Dammone noted that house music was responsible for making discos cool again and for people referring to discotheque venues as nightclubs.

The motivations of nightclub entrepreneurs ranged from purely financial to almost completely altruistic. Suzy Mason and Paul Fryer created a 1950s art-themed club night called the Kit Kat Club at a venue called Arcadia, which featured a cigarette girl, a cage, blue cocktails and cheap champagne, as well as regular variety acts (Mason 2018). This event eventually became club night Vague in 1993, which was held at the High Flyers Club, before moving to the Warehouse and running until 1996. Vague was an antidote to the machismo of the Leeds club scene; it was as much about inclusivity as it was about performance and partying, and those who entered had to sign up to a set of behavioural 'rules' that were designed to stamp out violence and discrimination within the venue, which embraced mixed gay and straight clubbers (Collard 1994); for Leeds this was breaking new ground in terms of further opening up the dancefloor, in the true spirit of 1970s New York disco with a 1990s house and trance sound.

The clubbing scene fuelled by predominantly house music grew exponentially in Leeds throughout the 1990s. Towards the end of the decade, several venues in the city branded themselves as being 'superclubs'. In reality they were venues with a 2,000 capacity, usually split across several rooms with different music policies, and such clubs included Uropa in the city centre and Evolution, which was out of the city centre in the suburb of Burley. Leeds City Council recognizing the important contribution that nightlife was making to the local economy branded Leeds as a '24 hour city'; modest relaxations were made to licensing laws locally, although the reality was that venues still mostly closed or stopped serving alcohol at 02:00 (Woodward 2008). Former Leeds City Councillor Lorna Cohen is quoted in the documentary *The City Talking: Music in Leeds* – Volume I (2015) as saying, 'there was nothing . . . that forbid us from allowing these establishments to stay open as long as they wanted, providing of course they didn't serve alcohol. Leeds University got far more applications from students who wanted to come to Leeds because of what we were doing here than any other city university in the country.' There was still, however, a divide between 'locals' and students, and many students chose to attend club events within the relative safety of their own student unions or to events at venues that were specifically advertised as student nights.

Drugs and bass

While Leeds City Council had initially encouraged the development of nightlife in the city, some nights, which had developed a reputation for illegal drug use, faced challenges from the authorities. I-Spy, a gay night, which played house and trance music at a venue called Nato (now closed), was raided in November 1996 by 100 police officers with nineteen people arrested and those leaving the club confronted by over twenty-five vans of police officers (88to98 2010). 1996 was a year of protest in Leeds; it was the last full year that the then Tory government led by Prime Minister John Major was in power. The movement 'Reclaim the Streets' protested several times in the city by closing down streets to a rave and party soundtrack provided by 'pop-up' sound systems. The protests were eventually quashed by the police, with protestors arrested.

As the 1990s progressed drugs became cheaper (Phillips 2009), and the popular drug choices of clubbers broadened from pure MDMA Ecstasy into blends that introduced amphetamines and MDA (these blends were known as snowballs); the impact of this on clubbers was for them to become less responsive to stimuli and in a more vegetative and 'monged out' state (James 2002). Clubbers under the influence of such drugs needed harder and louder sounds to interact with, further fuelling the development of bass-heavy hardcore music. One such genre was drum & bass (D&B), which was popular among the more alternative lifestyle and politically left-leaning clubbing communities. D&B music emerged from a fusion of big beat, breakbeat hardcore, jungle, techno, funk and electronica. This proved popular among those who didn't want to dress to impress and wanted music that was fast-paced, aggressive and not the mainstream softer electronic music heard in the charts and on the high street. Such bass-heavy dance music provides an environment for working-class ritualized sociality (Christodoulou 2011). D&B was a musical reflection of the frustration of youth with the political system, perceived repression by the authorities, working-class identity and a range of influences from black, Asian and minority ethnic (BAME) groups.

Sound system operators 'have today evolved into hardcore house collectives and drum and bass pioneers' (Haslam 2001: 57). The event Subdub began in 1998 at Leeds West Indian Centre. Subdub used reggae sound systems to play bass-heavy electronic music, including D&B, jungle, dub and reggae. Leeds West Indian Centre also became home to Sunrise and Cabbage, which were psytrance-themed events. Psytrance was developed from various electronic genres, including trance, techno and euro dance. The crowds who went to Subdub, Sunrise and Cabbage were clubbers who did not want to conform to the strict door policy dress codes of venues in Leeds city centre. According to Barnes (2018), D&B crowds wear baggy loose clothing and bucket hats, whereas psytrance ravers lean towards 'hippie' style. Both the D&B and psytrance fashions were a nod to the rave scene of the late 1980s and early 1990s. In comparison, house and techno is typically smart casual and fashion-conscious, which is what the city centre venues had become. Leeds West Indian Centre was a venue that was 'edgy'; it was in ethnically diverse suburbs, away from city centre policing and CCTV. It was also a venue that had a more laissez-faire approach to monitoring event attendees than the venues in Leeds city centre, which invoked a sense of freedom for those on the dancefloor.

The Millennium effect

The Millennium proved to be a difficult time for nightclubs in Leeds; greed on behalf of owners and promoters meant that for the Millennium New Year's Eve event in the city's clubs, sky-high entry charges were put in place. I myself was working as a licensed doorman at the time at various venues in Leeds city centre and was offered upwards of £50 per hour to work on the Millennium New Year's Eve – such was the hype around this unique event. I chose to stay away and enjoy the occasion with friends, as did the majority of clubbers in Leeds. The nightclubs had overpriced themselves, people had spoken with their feet and realized that they could have just as good a time having parties in their own homes or in their local pubs. The house party scene in Hyde Park, Burley and Headingley was buoyed, as in the eyes of many former clubbers, nightclubs ceased to be cool places to dance in. After the Millennium, attendances at nightclubs in Leeds were noticeably lower, and I personally refer to this as 'the Millennium effect'.

In the new millennium, to counteract a downturn in custom, nightclubs in Leeds began to more actively target the burgeoning student market in order to maximize their efficiency and yield. If a venue is open and busy only at the weekend, it has much unused capacity during the week, yet the bills still need to be paid. When the weekend trade dipped following the Millennium, it became an economic necessity for nightclubs to more actively target students, so the early 2000s became the era of the student promoter in Leeds. There had been 'student nights' at discos and nightclubs in Leeds since the 1980s, but now the disposable income of thousands of students was fiercely targeted by nightclubs, many of which played RnB, pop and classics alongside cheap drinks offers to attract cash-strapped students and get them through their doors midweek. Many of the city's nightclubs ceased to be about being cool venues playing house music to clubbers in smart casual clothing and instead became boisterous drinking and partying dens. The focus being on alcohol rather than music, some venues including Bondi Beach Bar and the Stadium offered 'all you can drink' to entice people in, who would pay a fixed entry charge, but then invariably spend most of the evening stood in a queue waiting to be served rather than actually drinking or dancing. In the eyes of those who wanted to go to nightclubs for the music, such venues became severely 'uncool'. Gadir (2016) identified that the music genre in clubs can create a cultural divide on the dancefloor, with RnB and chart pop being considered 'lower' forms of music by fans of EDM, who consider the overtly sexualized dancing styles to pop and RnB as 'cheapening' the club experience. In contrast, EDM often invokes more 'masculine' jagged movements on the dancefloor.

Credibility and competition

City centre venue the Mint Club, which had opened in 1998 with headline DJ Derrick Carter for Dave Beer's night Back to Basics (Cetin 2018), was one of the city centre venues that entered the new millennium as a credible dance music space, hosting a range of events that played house and techno music to clubbers who didn't want to be associated with the blatant commercialism of the high street nightclub. Credible dance music venues such as Mint were differentiated in the mindsets and language of clubbers by being referred to 'clubs' rather than nightclubs. Regular events held at Mint Club included the aforementioned Back to Basics and System and Asylum, which was a house music night. Rosita Rogers, owner of Leeds city centre bar and dance music venue 'Distrikt', reflected on her time in Leeds as a student in the early 2000s and stated that Asylum 'shaped the music played in Leeds and the future of many DJs'. The coolness of Mint Club as a venue was later compounded by the addition of a Funktion One sound system and an LED light ceiling as well as some very respected DJs including Ricardo Villalobos and Sven Vath. This venue refreshed the house and electronic music scene in Leeds, which did not go unnoticed by the student population, some of whom were keen to distance themselves from student nights dominated by pop, cheese and RnB and dance to music that was deemed to be more credible. By the mid to late 2000s, house music and electro were firmly back on both the student and local music agenda of clubs in Leeds.

The Licensing Act (2003) further assisted the nightlife industry in Leeds; however, this was not entirely to the benefit of nightclubs. The act meant that venues selling alcohol and providing musical entertainment could open for longer hours (potentially twenty-four hours per day), but this meant for nightclubs that competition was now not just against other nightclubs but every other bar and pub in the city that could now stay open and in business for as long as the nightclubs did.

The 'hybrid bar' was born, which was a bar that had a DJ playing music and a dancefloor but no entry charge. Prior to the Licensing Act, bars and pubs would be 'feeder venues' for nightclubs; now they were providing direct competition, and as with the Millennium, people made their decisions based upon economics, why pay an entry charge into a venue to drink and dance when you can do that in a free-entry hybrid bar anyway? Competition was fierce, and if hybrid bars were not charging an entry fee, then alcoholic drinks offers became the promotional tool that venues used in order to entice custom, the music became of secondary importance in some venues due to this. Leeds did, however, become the twenty-four-hour city that the council had envisioned years before. Promoter and DJ Ben Brown recalled, 'You'd be going out at maybe 9pm to Fibre, get into Speedqueen at 11pm, getting to Glasshouse at 4am, getting to Stinky's at 9am, getting to Funky Dory at 11am, and then that finishes at 4pm, and then going to a house party, which won't stop 'til whenever it stops.' The after-party scene became a significant unofficial clubbing space throughout the LS6 area of Leeds in the mid to late 2000s. Ben Brown also recalled an after-party which took place above a takeaway in Hyde Park,

> that party was just sick, it felt illegal . . . right there at that moment, no-one knows what's going down, you could be anywhere in the world, you need to be there and have that, be a part of that. That party above a takeaway, was 100 and odd people just on beanbags or up dancing, doing this, doing that, the music is booming, it was raw, no-one else had done that at that time.

New music, old problems

New forms of electronic music that can trace their lineage back towards hip-hop more so than house music emerged in the 2000s. Bassline music originated in the nearby city of Sheffield (Collins 2007), and it had a strong emphasis on bass and played around 140 bpm. The aesthetic of the sound was similar to UK garage music, which itself stemmed from jungle, which was influenced by hip-hop. The bassline scene in Leeds was very much a scene favoured by working-class locals, lads and lasses who wanted to dress up and dance all night at the weekend. It did not gain widespread popularity among the students in Leeds, who were becoming an elitist house and electro crowd, some of whom deemed bassline as being 'chavvy' and beneath them. This fits with Bourdieu's (1984) theory around education and elitism in the arts. In this case, a sizeable section of students studying in higher education considered their art tastes (their preferred choice of electronic music) to be superior to those who worked rather than studied. A clear divide emerged among students and non-students as to what form of EDM they would listen to, as well as where they would dance to it.

To the Leeds locals, however, heroes emerged in home-grown DJs and promoters Alex Simmons, Kane Towning and Danny Bond, who promoted and played at large-scale bassline events, which attracted thousands of clubbers. The largest event was called 'Movement' and was held initially at Evolution in 2006, before moving to Leeds University Students' Union in 2007 and eventually Victoria Works in 2009. The events at Victoria Works were a throwback to the days of raves being held in warehouses. The venue itself was an ex-warehouse and industrial unit, with minimal décor, just a hard and aged industrial floor and architecture (see Figure 9.3). The event at Victoria Works attracted over 2,000 attendees and was one of many dance music events to take place in this former industrial venue; others included 'Federation', 'Circo Loco' and 'Dirty Disco'.

Victoria Works was a venue in the suburb of Holbeck, surrounded by industrial units; it was away from city centre CCTV and policing. There was a certain edginess to the venue, which only added to the atmosphere and aesthetic of the event experience. The venue had its licence to operate as a club which was suspended in 2009 after two suspected drug overdoses on the premises and violence involving men who had taken class A drugs (*Yorkshire Evening Post* 2009a). 'A police report . . . said: "These premises have a history of staging high-risk events which attract customers associated with serious crime and class A drug dealing and misuse"' (*Yorkshire Evening Post* 2009b). Victoria Works was closed, but it proved to be a template for other out-of-town ex-industrial venues in Leeds, which would later follow in the 2010s.

The issues of drug usage, binge-drinking and their associated impacts both inside and outside of club venues problematized clubs for local authorities (Rief 2009), and Victoria Works was not the only venue in Leeds to face obstacles from the police and licensing authorities. DJ and promoter Daniel Hills ran a night at Gatecrasher called 'We Play Vinyl', which was a bassline/urban/grime/

Figure 9.3 Movement at Victoria Works, Leeds (top images prior to the event, bottom images during the event).

hip-hop night. The club was closed down after a stabbing took place of an underage entrant, which led to the temporary revocation of the club's license in February 2011. In a BBC (2011a) news article it was stated (about Gatecrasher), 'the club admitted its We Play Vinyl events on Friday nights had attracted "a minority of undesirable elements", leading to an increase in crime, but said these events had now been cancelled'. The club's licence was eventually reinstated in June 2011 after Gatecrasher agreed to install airport-style metal detector arches and for its door staff to also use hand-held metal detectors, as well as agreeing to provide West Yorkshire Police with risk assessments at least twenty-eight days before any externally promoted events took place (BBC 2011b). In carrying out risk assessments for music events, the police want to know the music genre and the 'profile' of the people that this is likely to attract. Criticisms have been levied at police for objecting to events that may attract black audiences or where the music may attract a demographic that the police consider to be 'problematic' (Izundu and Furst 2017).

Dubstep emerged as a new form of electronic music in London in the late 1990s, like bassline music, which was fast-paced at 140 bpm. Dubstep had an 'almost oppressively dark sound . . . built on tightly coiled productions with overwhelming bass lines and reverberant drum patterns, clipped samples, and occasional vocals' (AllMusic 2020). This dark and bass-heavy music with an unmistakable sub-bass 'whomp' sound, which was akin to the synthesized 'squelch' of acid house, was first featured in Leeds at Subdub in 1999. By the mid to late 2000s, dubstep had become widely popular among the alternative dance crowd, who did not want to associate themselves with the clean and polished sounds and image of house music and electro. Dubstep night 'Bigger than Barry' was held in the city centre at Mint Club, 'Wax:On' and 'Vagabondz' played dubstep at LUSU and other dubstep nights in city centre venues included 'The Bash Out' held at the Hi-Fi Club and 'Ruffage' held at Wire.

The aesthetics, lighting, sound system and intimate size of Mint Club made it a popular destination with all fans of dance music genres in Leeds, with different tribes claiming the venue on different nights, dependent on music policy. Drugs were popular at dubstep events, particularly mephedrone (MCAT), which was relatively cheap; it was an ingredient in a brand of plant food and was easy to purchase over the counter and online. The drug had a stimulant impact with a heightened sense of euphoria, alertness and confidence (FRANK 2020), which suited the fast, aggressive pace of dubstep music. Mephedrone was not made illegal in the UK until 2010, as its synthetic composition fell outside of any of the drugs made illegal by the Misuse of Drugs Act (1971). In 2010, mephedrone was made a class B drug, meaning that anyone caught in possession of it could face five years imprisonment, while anyone caught selling it could face up to fourteen years (BBC 2010). Mephedrone had, however, become a part and parcel of dubstep nights, and some venues in Leeds turned dubstep promoters away, fearful of the police and licensing authorities. This further pushed dubstep underground and out of the city centre into Hyde Park house parties.

Leeds city centre was becoming a location where promoters of bassline, dubstep, urban, grime and hip-hop struggled to find venues in which to run events, due to threats to venue owners by the authorities. Spracklen, Richter and

Spracklen (2013) stated that 'urban policies aim to displace and/or ban particular forms of leisure from city centres that are seen to "disturb"' (164–5). The city centre of Leeds was becoming increasingly corporate, surveilled and residential. Noise has been another factor that has impacted upon city centre nightlife venues. Swinney and Carter (2018) noted that UK city centres have become desirable places to live within the past ten years. Leeds has the third highest city centre population growth in the UK from 12,900 to 32,300 (a 150 per cent increase) from 2001 to 2015. A catalyst for this growth has been an increase in high-skilled professional occupations in city centres. Leeds has seen an increase of 34 per cent of such jobs over the same time period. Leeds City Council, which once championed nightlife in the city, became more concerned with promoting Leeds as a destination for shopping, business and tourism (Spracklen, Richter and Spracklen 2013).

> The superclubs had become about as corporate as you can get and clubbing had lost any kind of early acid house direction and politics. But these times turn out to be great times for clubs as they go back underground, left to the people who actually love electronic music, who set about creating something of substance again. (Lawson 2016)

The house party boom

The student house party scene grew quickly again, particularly in the suburbs of Hyde Park and Burley where the sounds that were being banished from the city centre were now reverberating from house basements. Some house parties became regular events with club style names, including 'Ketaloco', a portmanteau of drug ketamine and long running house music event night 'Casa Loco', which was based in the city centre. Hyde Park and Burley both shared borders with Headingley, but a clear divide was emerging musically. Promoter of dubstep night 'The Bash Out', Aidan Brain England explained that Headingley became synonymous with house and electro parties, while Hyde Park and Burley were more associated with dubstep, D&B and grime. One of the Hyde Park house parties 'Bangerang', a night which specialized in dubstep and D&B later became so popular that it moved to venue Stinky's Peephouse just outside of the city centre.

The divide in EDM choice between the predominantly student suburbs of Headingley, Hyde Park and Burley was perhaps dictated by class. Headingley, which has a distinct 'village' feel, consists of mixed housing types, many of which are large and semi-detached with gardens. Hyde Park and Burley lack the services that can be found in Headingley and in housing terms consists mainly of streets of dark red-bricked back-to-back terraced houses with very small or no garden space at all. Student housing in Headingley is overall more expensive than student housing in Hyde Park and Burley. Headingley, therefore, attracts students from more affluent backgrounds than Hyde Park and Burley. Many of the students in Headingley want to portray an upper-middle-class image of themselves, which is reflected in their appearance and lifestyle choices, one of which being the music that they listen to. Electro and house music of the early 2000s was minimalist, crisp and clean, and it suited an elitist image and was therefore popular in Headingley. The narrow, dark and heavily graffitied streets of Hyde Park and Burley are more suited to bass heavy more experimental sounds, which suits the more alternative lifestyles of those who live in these suburbs.

The free spirit of the rave scene has re-emerged in all of these suburbs in the house party scene. Electronic music, drugs and a desire to 'do what we wanna do' has thrived and is still thriving in student houses, echoing the subversive origins of 1970s disco and 1980s rave culture. Harrison (2017) highlights the growing trend for 'club' event style house parties in the student suburbs of Leeds. Party culture has become firmly entrenched in particularly the Hyde Park area of Leeds (Amin 2017).

These events often include full sound systems, lighting and DJs as entertainers. To meet the growing demand for this market, entrepreneurs have established organizations to provide technical equipment and even security. In Leeds, companies such as Complete Event Solutions, Leeds Party Rig, Crispy Aromatic, Reload Sound System and Elation DJs all specialize in this area. 'These operations are legitimate nightlife alternatives; as considered in execution as any illegal rave – perhaps more so' (Harrison 2017). Owner of Leeds Party Rig, Matty Rush noted that student parties in the LS6 area of Leeds are plentiful, with 'enough to go around, so competition is friendly' between party companies.

Student house parties are not subject to price barriers including entry and drinks prices within, there is also no CCTV and the risk of arrest for taking recreational drugs is lesser than what it is in a more traditional 'club' space, where concerns over law breaking and the impact this could have on venue licensing mean that security staff actively are often tasked with anti-drug enforcement measures. It was said of one house party, which was reviewed for the web site 'Vice', 'the DJs were excited to be there, the drugs were limitless but never overdone, the bouncer was interested in people having a good time, and the curfew was non-existent' (Harrison 2017). One of the most popular drugs at student house parties is nitrous oxide (known as noz), which in 2018 was the second most popular recreational drug after cannabis in England and Wales – this is despite it being outlawed in 2016 in the Psychoactive Substances Act (O'Donohue 2018). The drug is known to cause feelings of dizziness and euphoria, and often makes users laugh, earning it the nickname 'laughing gas'. The effects are short-lived, but being a drug that has connotations and associations with 'fun' makes it a popular 'party drug' choice. Nitrous oxide is traditionally consumed via balloons, something which is extremely conspicuous, and therefore not easily done in clubs without being seen, which may attract the attentions of security. Nitrous oxide is therefore popular in 'unofficial' settings such as raves and house parties, where the likelihood of conflict with security/police is often negligible. Spent nitrous oxide canisters are evident and visible as litter on the streets around Hyde Park (see Figure 9.4).

Figure 9.4 Discarded nitrous oxide canisters on a Hyde Park doorstep, Leeds.

The coronavirus pandemic and subsequent lockdown of 2020 have demonstrated that people who want to party will continue to do so, even if it means risking the wrath of the law and their own health. With bars, pubs, nightclubs and gig venues closed due to the threat of Covid-19 the unofficial house party scene has continued unabated in Leeds, helped by DJs live-streaming sets directly into the homes of partygoers, albeit with lower attendances as many students left the city early into lockdown for the sanctity of their parental residences.

Festivalization

The physicality of large-scale raves in industrial settings has re-emerged in officially licensed rave-style events in Leeds. These events are held periodically rather than weekly or monthly and often have festival-style DJ line-ups. Such events are typically held in venues outside of the city centre, within suburbs that are largely industrial rather than residential. In Leeds, such venues include(d): Beaver Works (Hunslet); Blueberry Hill Studios (Kirkstall); Canal Mills (Armley); Eiger Studios (Hunslet); Freedom Mills (LS3); Lake Victoria (Harehills); Mint Warehouse (Holbeck); the Musiquarium (Kirkstall); and Untold Sound (Hunslet). Such venues were not created as nightclubs or clubs and in the parlance of stakeholders are referred to as venues, with 'club nights' now being referred to as 'events'. This professionalization of language to use industry jargon rather than popular terms reflects a disassociation between attendees at such venues and high street/city centre clubs.

These suburban venues have followed a trend highlighted by Spracklen, Richter and Spracklen (2013) whereby alternative and niche subcultures have been displaced away from the places that they used to consider their leisure spaces. Alternative scenes and groups are on the margin of the city centre, due to the corporatization and 'eventization' of public leisure spaces. Promoter and DJ Ben Brown noted that in the mid-2000s when Mint Warehouse was called Kerbcrawler that it could be a difficult venue to sell out events at, due to it being a destination venue and many clubbers not wanting to leave the confines of the city centre. The venue is also within the city's recognized 'red light district'. Today, many of those attending events at Mint Warehouse go straight from their home to the venue, completely circumventing the city centre, the fact that the venue is in the red-light district gives it an 'edgy' appeal to attendees.

Downsizing in the city

With an overall decline in attendance, credible EDM venues that are located within in the city centre are now smaller in capacity than their 1990s contemporaries, with a quality rather than quantity approach to events, which are typically themed by music genre and promoted by third-party promoters. Notable and very different venues in Leeds city centre in 2020 include Distrikt, a stylish underground venue, which also functions as a tapas and cocktail bar, and the Old Red Bus Station, which is quite literally located in an old bus station building, with stripped back bare brick walls, giving an industrial aesthetic. House music is still popular, as is techno and more bass-heavy genres including D&B, dubstep and jungle. Events that take place in these venues are typically periodical (weekly or monthly) and each with its own neotribe of attendees.

The rave renaissance

Nationally in the UK, the illegal rave scene is on the rise, with 133 plans for illegal raves being uncovered by police in 2017, compared with just seventy in 2016 (Crisp 2018). In a throwback to the rave era, Wolfson (2018) noted that according to the Metropolitan Police, the number of free parties and raves in London doubled in 2017 with events getting larger and more elaborate. Ryan Keeling, editor of club-culture website Resident Advisor, is quoted in the same article as stating 'free parties are partly stemming from a desire to have people play by their own rules, trying to create a more liberated atmosphere'. What is happening in London is echoed across the UK, particularly in larger cities, where dedicated alternative dance music scenes are unfolding.

Larger scale events have and continue to take place with organizers and attendees playing a cat- and-mouse game with the police. Johnson (2020) reported on an illegal rave which took place in woodland on a nature reserve on the border of Kirkstall and Burley in May 2020, during the coronavirus lockdown, which attracted 200 attendees, some of whom had dangerously waded across the River Aire at night to reach the event. This perhaps enforces that as with taking drugs or attending venues outside of the perceived sanctity of the city centre, the attraction of the event is as much about the thrills and the rush as it is about the music. This spirit is perhaps epitomized in the opening monologue of Primal Scream's 1992 track 'Loaded', which began with a quote from the 1966 film *The Wild Angels*:

Just what is it that you want to do?

We wanna be free
We wanna be free to do what we wanna do
And we wanna get loaded
And we wanna have a good time
That's what we're gonna do
(No way baby let's go)
We're gonna have a good time
We're gonna have a party.

(*The Wild Angles*, 1966 quoted in Primal Scream, 1990)

The evolution of EDM venues in Leeds will continue, as people will always find a place to have a good time and dance, wherever that may be. In the words of Dave Beer, 'you can't spell Leeds without LSD and a couple of Es.'

Works cited

88to98 (2010). '1996', 88to98, https://88to98.co.uk/2010/11/05/1996/, accessed 17 June 2020.

88to98 (2014). 'The History of the Gallery Leeds', 88to98, https://88to98.co.uk/2014/09/02/teh-history-of-the-gallery-leeds/, accessed 17 June 2020.

88to98 (2015). 'SpeedQueen', 88to98. Leeds https://88to98.co.uk/2015/11/23/speedqueen-leeds/, accessed 8 June 2020.

AllMusic. (2020). 'Dubstep.' *AllMusic*. https://www.allmusic.com/style/dubstep-ma0000004465, accessed 22 June, 2020.

Amin, Tayyab (2017). 'DIY in 2017, How Leeds, Bristol and London Scenes Are Striving to Survive', *Fact*, http://www.factmag.com/2017/06/15/uk-diy-venues/, accessed 18 July 2017.

Anderson, Tammy (2009). *Rave Culture: The Alteration and Decline of a Music Scene*. Philadelphia: Temple University Press.

Austin, Larry and Denis Smalley (2000). 'Sound Diffusion in Composition and Performance: An Interview with Denis Smalley', *Computer Music Journal*, (Summer), pp. 10–21.

Barnes, Marcus (2018). 'Illegal Raves: How the Underground Scene Has Never Really Gone Away', BBC, https://www.bbc.co.uk/bbcthree/article/66df895b-af1c-416f-b32a-bb3576dbcb82, accessed 8 June 2018.

BBC (2010). 'Mephedrone Ban Comes into Force in UK', BBC, http://news.bbc.co.uk/1/hi/uk/8623958.stm, accessed 23 April 2020.

BBC (2011a). 'Leeds Gatecrasher Club Licence Revoked after Violence', BBC, http://www.bbc.co.uk/news/uk-england-leeds-12477935, accessed 20 February 2015.

BBC (2011b). 'Leeds Gatecrasher Club to Re-open with Metal Detectors', BBC, http://www.bbc.co.uk/news/uk-england-leeds-13858926, accessed 20 February 2015.

Bogdanov, Vladimir (2001). 'All Music Guide to Electronica: The Definitive Guide to Electronic Music', 4th edn. Guilford, CT: Backbeat Books.

Bourdieu, Pierre. (1984). *Distinction: A Social Critique of Judgement of Taste*. Cambridge, MA: Harvard University Press.

Bragin, Naomi and SanSan Kwan (2012). 'Contemporary Dance as Subversive Pedagogies', Center for Race & Gender, University of California, Berkeley, https://www.crg.berkeley.edu/podcasts/contemporary-dance-as-subversive-pedagogies/, accessed 25 January 2019.

Brewster, Bill (2017). 'Leeds – Warehouse', https://billbrewster.co.uk/2017/12/21/leeds-warehouse/, accessed 3 July 2020.

Cetin, Marissa (2018). 'Leeds' Mint Club Is Closing after 20 Years', *Resident Advisor*, https://www.residentadvisor.net/news/42535, accessed 22 June 2020.

Champion, Sarah (1997). *Disco Biscuits*. London: Sceptre.

Christodoulou, Chris (2011). 'Rumble in the Jungle', *Dancecult: Journal of Electronic Dance Music Culture*, 3(1), pp. 44–63.

Collard, James (1994). 'United Kingdom of Dance: If the Capital's Clubs Are too Cool for Comfort, the Rest of the Country Is Steaming on a Saturday Night, Says James Collard', *The Independent*, https://www.independent.co.uk/arts-entertainment/united-kingdom-of-dance-if-the-capitals-clubs-are-too-cool-for-comfort-the-rest-of-the-country-is-1443970.html, accessed 8 June 2020.

Collins, Hattie (2007). 'Deep Down and Dirty', *The Guardian*, https://www.theguardian.com/music/2007/nov/29/urban, accessed 22 June 2020.

Crisp, Wil (2018). 'Illegal Raves Are on the Rise as Traditional Nightclubs Close Their Doors, New Figures Reveal', *The Telegraph*, https://www.telegraph.co.uk/news/2018/03/04/illegal-raves-rise-traditional-nightclubs-close-doors-new-figures/, accessed 8 June 2018.

Critcher, Chas (2003). *Moral Panics and the Media*. New York: McGraw-Hill Education.

Dance Britannia (2008). 'Dangerous Dancing', Box of Broadcasts, https://learningonscreen.ac.uk/ondemand/index.php/prog/00796D11, accessed 20 November 2018.

'Dubstep', *AllMusic*, https://www.allmusic.com/style/dubstep-ma0000004465, accessed 22 June 2020.

Evelyn, George (2018). 'Chinwag Session with George Evelyn', One Foot in the Rave. Leeds, 29 April 2018.

FRANK (2020). 'Mephedrone', FRANK, https://www.talktofrank.com/drug/mephedrone#how-it-feels, accessed 23 June 2020.

Gadir, Tami (2016). 'Resistance or Reiteration? Rethinking Gender in DJ Cultures', *Contemporary Music Review*, 1, pp. 115–29.

Gall, Caroline (2009). *Service Crew*. Wrea Green: Milo Books.

Harrison, Angus (2017). 'House Party Review: Leeds', *Vice*, https://www.vice.com/en_uk/article/nzg3xb/house-party-review-leeds, accessed 27 March 2017.

Haslam, Dave (2001). *Adventures on the Wheels of Steel: The Rise of the Superstar DJs*. London: Fourth Estate.

Hook, Peter (2009). *The Hacienda: How Not to Run a Club*. London: Pocket Books.

Hutson, Scott (2000). 'The Rave: Spiritual Healing in Modern Western Subcultures', *Anthropological Quarterly*, 73(1), pp. 35–49.

ITN (1990). 'ITN ITV News Report on Leeds Rave Summer 1990', https://www.youtube.com/watch?v=u21d5fWWTZI, accessed 23 June 2020.

Izundu, Chi Chi, and Furst, Jessica (2017). 'Form 696: Concern over "Racist" Police Form to Be Raised', BBC, http://www.bbc.co.uk/news/entertainment-arts-39181672, accessed 27 March 2017.

James, Martin (2002). *Prodigy*. London: Sanctuary Publishing Ltd.

Johnson, Kristian (2020). 'Illegal Woodland Rave in Leeds Sparks Anger as 200 People Break Lockdown Rules to Party', Leeds Live, https://www.leeds-live.co.uk/news/leeds-news/illegal-woodland-rave-leeds-sparks-18310399, accessed 6 July 2020.

Lawson, Ralph (2007). 'History of Back to Basics Leeds', https://88to98.co.uk/2019/03/06/history-of-back-to-basics-leeds/, accessed 8 June 2020.

Lawson, Ralph (2016). 'Stinky's Peephouse 2006 – 2011', http://www.ralphlawson.co.uk/basic-vision/2016/11/23/stinkys-peephouse-2006-2011, accessed 29 June 2020.

Leeds City Council (2020). 'About Leeds', Leeds City Council, https://www.leeds.gov.uk/your-council/about-leeds, accessed 6 July 2020.

Lopez, Bernard (2009). 'Dan Pucciarelli', Disco Music, https://www.discomusic.com/28-dan-pucciarelli, accessed 3 July 2020.

Mason, Suzy (2018). 'Chinwag Session with Suzy Mason', One Foot in the Rave. Leeds, 1 May 2018.

O'Donohue, Liam (2018). 'Laughing Gas Laws Not Working, Says Ex-chief Crown Prosecutor', BBC, https://www.bbc.co.uk/news/uk-england-manchester-46591871, accessed 19 December 2018.

O'Grady, Alice (2012). 'Spaces of Play: The Spatial Dimensions of Underground Club Culture and Locating the Subjunctive', *Dancecult: Journal of Electronic Dance Music Culture*, 4(1): 86–106

Phillips, Dom (2009). *Super Star DJs Here We Go!* London: Ebury Press.

Primal Scream (1990). *Loaded*. London: Creation Records.

Rief, Silvia (2009). *Club Cultures: Boundaries, Identities and Otherness*. Abingdon: Routledge.

Schumpeter, Joseph (1934). *Fundamentals of Economic Development*. Cambridge, MA: Harvard University Press.

Spracklen, Karl, Anna Richter and Beverley Spracklen (2013). 'The Eventization of Leisure and the Strange Death of Alternative Leeds', *City*, 17(2), pp. 164–78.

Stebbins, Robert (2007). *Serious Leisure: A Perspective for Our Time*. New Brunswick: Transaction Publishers.

Swinney, Paul and Andrew Carter (2018). 'The UK's Rapid Return to City Centre Living', BBC. https://www.bbc.co.uk/news/uk-44482291, accessed 9 July 2018.

'The Agony and the Ecstasy: A Perfect Storm' (2017). Sky Arts. 11 August 2017.

'The City Talking: Music in Leeds – Volume I' (2015). Directed by L. Hicken and S. Hicken Leeds: Hebe Productions, https://www.bbc.co.uk/programmes/p03bv0xv, accessed 8 November 2018.

'The City Talking: Music in Leeds – Volume II' (2016). Directed by L. Hicken and S. Hicken. Leeds: Hebe Productions, http://www.bbc.co.uk/music/audiovideo/featured?sorting=justadded#p04d6nfp, accessed 8 November 2018.

The Gryphon (2015). 'Sound System Culture in Leeds: Sixty Years of Subculture', The Gryphon, https://www.thegryphon.co.uk/2015/10/17/sound-system-culture-in-leeds-sixty-years-of-a-subculture/, accessed 26 June 2020.

'The Summer of Rave, 1989' (2006), https://www.youtube.com/watch?v=A-XrlMpwEuM, accessed 3 March 2016.

The Wild Angels (1966). Directed by Roger Corman. American International Pictures: Los Angeles. [film: 35mm].

THUMP (2013). 'Silver Apples Made EDM in the 1960s – Supersonic – Ep. 6', https://www.youtube.com/watch?v=xReSZczxSsU, accessed 25 January 2019.

Towning, Kane and Rob Tissera (2020). 'Party Starters Podcast. Episode #15 – Rob Tissera – Life Story' (Podcast), https://open.spotify.com/episode/6qDgk8DRgmXjPGrNhRHHuy, accessed 29 June 2020.

Trailblazers of Acid House (2016). Sky Arts. 13 April 2018.

Turner, D. (2018). 'Live the Dream: How Blackburn Dominated Warehouse Raves in the Summer of Love'. Mixmag, https://mixmag.net/feature/blackburn-raves, accessed 4 July 2020.

Vine, Richard (2011). 'We Call It Acieed Banned on R1', *The Guardian*, http://www.theguardian.com/music/2011/jun/15/we-call-it-acieed-banned, accessed 2 March 2016.

Wilson, Greg (2013). 'From Garrard to Technics – How British DJs Began to Mix', https://blog.gregwilson.co.uk/2013/08/from-garrard-to-technics-how-british-djs-began-to-mix/?fbclid=IwAR3r7Fcg3AyuFHAkcqdz8pcrUHJXR3LrF3GPAZNXdODxinNiE-b1x9jBo1w, accessed 3 July 2020.

Wolfson, Sam (2018). 'The New Rules of Clubbing: From Illegal Raves to Spacehopper Hedonism', *The Guardian*, https://www.theguardian.com/music/2018/mar/14/the-new-rules-of-clubbing-from-illegal-raves-to-spacehopper-hedonism, accessed 16 March 2018.

Woodward, Grant (2008). 'Has the Clock Stopped for 24-Hour Leeds?' *Yorkshire Evening Post*, http://www.yorkshireeveningpost.co.uk/news/latest-news/top-stories/has-the-clocked-stopped-for-24-hour-leeds-1-2198519, accessed 21 June 2014.

Yorkshire Evening Post (2009a). 'Kerbcrawler: Leeds Nightclub Shutdown', *Yorkshire Evening Post*, http://www.yorkshireeveningpost.co.uk/news/latest-news/top-stories/kerbcrawler-leeds-nightclub-shutdown-1-2235564, accessed 26 February 2016.

Yorkshire Evening Post (2009b). 'Leeds Nightclub Closed over Drug Fatality Fears', *Yorkshire Evening Post*, http://www.yorkshireeveningpost.co.uk/news/latest-news/top-stories/leeds-nightclub-closed-over-drug-fatality-fears-1-2234071, accessed 26 February 2016.

10

Ageism and sexism in Manchester's club culture

Kamila Rymajdo

Pete Tong, Carl Cox, David Guetta, Giles Peterson, Patrick Forge, Norman Jay. No one says they're over the hill. In fact, it's respected for men to go over that threshold of fifty. As soon as a woman hits forty, they're too old. We don't even get that extra ten years.

–DJ Paulette

While there has been an increasing amount of research on women's role in electronic dance music (EDM) (Rodgers 2010; Farrugia 2012; Abtan 2016; Gadir 2017) and pockets of research on ageing clubbers (Bennett and Taylor 2012; Armour 2019; O'Grady and Madill 2019; Peter and Williams 2019) and ageing women within club culture (O'Grady and Madill 2019), not much research has been dedicated to ageing female DJs and, in turn, their experiences of sexism and ageism or the intersection of both. As such, this chapter aims to address this absence in scholarship by focusing on the experiences of seven older (aged between thirty-nine and fifty-seven) women DJs in Manchester. I begin by asking why women DJs are still under-represented in nightclubs and at festivals, especially given that many women DJs claim we live in a post-feminism world. Drawing on Katie Milestone's research on the impact of a male-focused Manchester music legacy on the city's current creative industries (Milestone 2016), I posit that in Manchester, this could be owing to the fact the city has a long history of underrepresentation of women within the city's club culture. Citing the examples of retrospectives such as the 2017 film *Manchester Keeps on Dancing* (dir. Javi Senz) and Boiler Room's 2018 *Queer Raving in Manchester's Twilight Zone*, it highlights the continued underrepresentation of BAME women and older women in particular. Furthermore, describing Manchester's position as a city focused on urban regeneration, historically driven by close networks of men, I also argue that women in Manchester have long been excluded from positions of power. The chapter thus suggests that their ongoing exclusion has created a 'boys' club' environment in the city's club culture, increasing prohibitive working conditions and diminishing opportunities for women and older women in particular. To do so, I first establish a theoretical context of sexism and gender inequality in electronic music, ageism in society and especially in the workplace, as well as ageism in club culture more generally.

Gender and age in electronic dance music

Towards the end of the 2010s, gender parity became a buzzword in music media, as newspapers and magazines reported on club scenes around the world fostering inclusive booking policies across festivals, at nightclubs and on radio, with big-name brands following suit. Some festivals, such as Barcelona's Primavera, made gender parity their guiding principle as they announced in 2019 that their line-up would be split 50/50 down gender lines, adopting #TheNewNormal as their campaign slogan. But despite such high-profile efforts, recent studies have shown that the music industry is still plagued by inequality. 'A 2016 *Vice* survey of 24 festivals that took place during the first half of 2016 found that the number of female-identifying DJs and producers at these events ranged from 3.2% to 28.9%' (Farrugia and Olszanowski 2017: 2). In 2017, a BBC England data unit study which analysed more than 600 separate headline performances across 14 UK festivals found that eight out of 10 top slots were occupied by all-male acts (Sherlock and Bradshaw 2017). Meanwhile, an October 2019 published report titled *Counting the Music Industry: The Gender Pay Gap* by former CEO of the British Academy of Songwriters, Composers and Authors (BASCA) Vick Bain revealed that 'just over 14% of those currently signed to 106 music publishers and just under 20% of those signed to 219 record labels are female' (2019: 2). These statistics were reflected in the upper echelons of the music industry too. Almost 82 per cent of CEOs of UK music publishing companies were found to be male (Bain 2019: 3). When line-ups do seem to be tackling equality, it is often in an underhand way. As pointed out by Australian producer/DJ HAAi in a 2019 interview, 'people say they have an equal line-up but all the women are at the bottom of the bill and therefore the worst paid' (Hughes 2019).

One explanation for this low representation of women is that music fans simply do not like women DJs. The DJ Mag readers' Top 100 DJs annual poll has historically featured very few women, with the list's female representation improving only marginally in the 2010s. Only four women reached the Top 100 in 2017, six in 2018 and eight in 2019. Indeed, as DJ Mag itself admitted, in 2019, over 90 per cent of the people in the list were male and white. Another, perhaps more likely reason is the fact that within various facets of the music industry legal protections against gender discrimination in the workplace do not apply. As argued by Tami Gadir in 'Forty-Seven DJs, Four Women: Meritocracy, Talent and Postfeminist Politics', 'nightclub managers, promoters, booking agents and DJs – as entrepreneurs in the private sector – are often self-employed and contracted to jobs on an ad hoc basis' (2017: 53). As Gadir argues, operating in informal networks means exemption 'from accountability on implementing equality policies' (2017: 53). This is especially troubling given the precariousness of work within the creative industries, which Angela McRobbie describes as 'Requiring risk-taking activity' (McRobbie quoted in McGuigan 2009: 187) and the fact that club culture is shrinking (Rymajdo 2019b). In effect, what this suggests is that women DJs are not only working in precarious conditions, but also they are not protected by gender discrimination laws as women might be in other industries. Furthermore, as Gadir underlines, concerns about equality are sidelined by a 'neoliberal narrative of individualism comprised of postfeminism, meritocracy and talent' (2017: 51). It is a view echoed when ageism is under discussion as well. As Sally Rodgers from British electronic music band A Man Called Adam asserted in a 2019 DJ Mag feature about ageism, 'Talent and hard work are ageless, genderless' (Heath 2019).

Such a stance makes sense, given that some female musicians prefer not to discuss or emphasize gender issues, seeing it as standing in their way of simply being recognized as an artist rather than a marginalized 'female artist' (Rodgers 2010: 17; Rymajdo 2016). However, it is dangerous because when people fail to acknowledge the inequalities at play and the lack of women on line-ups as a result, barriers to entry persist, which in turn creates a perpetual cycle of ever more barriers. As Gadir argues, 'it is less easy for a group that has been historically and systematically excluded from a community to compete for the first time with those who make up the vast majority of that community' (2017: 60). Abtan concurs, writing that 'The necessary skills are passed around closed communities and friendship networks, which are often predominantly male; as a result, solo female artists have more difficulty acquiring them' (2016: 55).

Some writers and DJs do point to the barriers that exist for women and older women in particular within electronic music, however, and discuss the male-centric industry and, in turn, male-focused study of the genre. For example, in *Pink Noises* Tara Rodgers points to scholars such as Simon Reynolds, who defined DJ cultures as 'distinctly masculine', Douglas Kahn, who she says positioned women as outside the scope of study in his 1999 *Noise Water Meat: A History of Sound in the Arts* (Rodgers 2010: 11) and Kai Fikentscher, who 'used observational statistics, such as that fewer than one in ten DJs is female' (Rodgers 2010: 11) to explain women's absence from his 2000 *"You Better Work!" Underground Dance Music in New York City*. And, as Rodgers argues, 'The question of who is counted in electronic music historiography is inevitably informed by the politics of social and professional networks, and by limited definitions and standards of achievement' (2010: 15). Moreover, 'the public face of electronic music – on cd releases, magazine covers, international festivals, scholarly publications – is typically male and does a certain kind of symbolic work' (Rodgers 2010: 15). To summarize: when women are under-represented in the history books of electronic music, the myth prevails that there simply are not that many women within this industry, which perpetuates the belief that underrepresentation is justified.

These barriers intensify as women get older. As I reported in a 2019 journalistic article for *Vice* titled 'The Rave Gap: How UK Nightlife Still Struggles with Ageism', festivals, nightclubs and radio stations book ever younger DJs, but the same rules do not seem to apply to men, as they do to women (Rymajdo 2019). Gadir suggests ageism is built into gender disciplining, which she describes as 'the "expiry date" imposed on women' (2017: 59), asserting that 'despite the presence of high profile women in dance music in their forties and beyond making inroads in the industry, older women who DJ are still not the idealised norm' (Gadir 2017: 59). Like Gadir, Rebekah Farrugia ascribes this to EDM becoming increasingly aligned with the profit-driven philosophy of neoliberalism and thus 'Unlike the 1990s and early 2000s . . . today corporations and dance clubs are increasingly hiring young (under age 25) celebrities and models (both male and female) as DJs, despite their limited experience or skills and without regard to their musical interests' (2012: 43). Such a state of affairs is not singular to EDM, however. High-profile artists such as Madonna have been vocal about ageism within pop music (Grigoriadis 2019), and there has been much discussion on ageism in hip-hop (Forman 2014; Little 2018). But, owing to the fact scholars such as Sarah Thornton theorize older people's investment in club cultures as a resistance towards ageing (Thornton, quoted in Bennett and Taylor 2012: 233) and older women clubbers report increasing harassment (O'Grady and Madill 2019), it is not a far-fetched assumption to presume that, thanks to the intersection of sexism in the workplace and ageism within club culture, older women DJs might face the highest discrimination of all. This is especially worrying given that in his DJ Mag feature on ageism Harold Heath wrote that within club culture 'ageism doesn't seem to be taken as seriously as other protected characteristics' (2019). He posited that 'Although the dance music community is generally quick to respond when a well-known DJ or producer makes a racist or homophobic "joke", jokes about age aren't given the same attention or considered as harmful' (Heath 2919).

These summations fall in line with studies on ageism. 'Stereotyping people based on their age, unlike these other groupings, goes largely unchallenged and even unnoticed', argued Amy J. C. Cuddy and Susan T. Fiske in 'Doddering but Dear: Process, Content, and Function in Stereotyping of Older Persons' (2004: 3). A 2019 Centre for Ageing Better report similarly titled *Doddery but Dear? Examining Age-related Stereotypes* also revealed that older people in the UK are mocked, patronized and demonized by the rest of society. And, when it comes to the workplace, 'Despite efforts to constrain discriminatory behaviour via law-making and employment policies in Europe and elsewhere, ageism is still prevalent in organizations and companies and affects the careers of older workers in terms of job opportunities, promotions and performance evaluations' (L. Naegele et al. 2018: 74). This is the case despite the fact that researchers have failed to find a relationship between age and job performance: 'Older people's alleged incompetence lies solely in the eye of the beholder,' assert Cuddy and Fiske (2004: 11–12). Such a summation accounts for the fact that in certain audience-facing industries like acting, looks matter too: female actors historically get fewer opportunities as they age. According to Cuddy and Fiske, ageism is also especially present among younger people: '[I]nasmuch as older people threaten younger people by reminding them of the transience of youth, young people will be motivated to protect themselves against this threat' (Cuddy and Fiske 2004: 16). For older women DJs operating within youth focused and youth ran places, such as nightclubs, this is especially worrying. Indeed, 'the bigger the difference between the individual's age and what is considered "normal" for a certain function, the higher the risk for discrimination' (L. Naegele et al. 2018: 77). Moreover, young people stick with young people: 'in line with the similarity-attraction theory, individuals tend to form informal networks in an organization with other individuals who are similar to them' (L. Naegele et al. 2018: 76). In other words, in workplaces predominated by younger people and operated by younger people, older workers are likely to come up against barriers to entry

Figure 10.1 DJ Paulette. Photo courtesy of Lee Baxter.

and/or discrimination. And, given that 'Age combines with other identities resulting in a "double jeopardy" whereby members of already marginalised groups are further stigmatised as they age' (Centre for Ageing Better 2019: 4), it is likely that older women will experience much greater ageism than older men and BAME older women even more so.

Manchester and its male-centric musical legacy

In her '"Northernness", Gender and Manchester's Creative Industries' paper, Katie Milestone quotes *NME* journalist Penny Anderson, who detailed how she was 'edited out' of *24 Hour Party People*, a 2002 Michael Winterbottom film about Factory Records and 'Madchester'. She is quoted as saying, 'Madchester was a time of corrosive, putrid, knuckle-dragging misogyny, and the fact that some music journalists around at the time were women is important. I would have enjoyed the opportunity to interrupt with: "I was there, too"' (Milestone 2016: 56). It is a sentiment shared by the eight women I interviewed for a 2018 journalistic article for *Dazed*, titled 'The Women Who've Been Written Out of Manchester Clubbing History', many of whom were similarly incensed about their roles being omitted from or diminished in such texts as Peter Hook's 2009 *The Hacienda: How Not to Run a Club* and the 2017 feature-length documentary *Manchester Keeps on Dancing*, directed by Javi Senz. DJ Paulette said of Hook's book:

> He [Peter Hook] listed what was on the Thursday, the Friday, the Saturday, and then when Flesh [LGBT club night where DJ Paulette was a resident] had a party he mentions DJs Tim Lennox and Luke Howard. When you look at the flyers, you can see the parties where Luke's played – but my name is on every single one of them! So it's like, how can you look through and actually make a point of itemising what these nights were and listing who the DJs were and miss a name that is on every fucking flyer? (Rymajdo 2018)

Manchester Keeps on Dancing is a similar example where women are under-represented. It features Haçienda DJs Greg Wilson, Mike Pickering, Dave Haslam and Laurent Garnier, among other era-defining names like Marshall Jefferson and Andrew Weatherall while chronicling what purports to be an 'exceptionally detailed' documentation of thirty years of Manchester music. And yet, it only features two women throughout. To add insult to injury, neither of them are associated with Manchester scenes. Alison Surtees, co-founder of Manchester Digital Music Archive (MDMA), told me at the time that the film's producers approached the organization about using their photos in February 2016. When MDMA pointed out the imbalance and suggested Flesh DJ Kath McDermott be interviewed, they were told three months later that the producers had run out of time and would not be able to speak to McDermott or any other women (Rymajdo 2018). Even texts that claim to be inclusive, such as the Boiler Room's 2018 *Queer Raving in Manchester's Twilight Zone*, fail to include the histories of BAME queer club events such as club night Black Angel.

The effects of such omissions do not affect just the people who played important roles in the various stages of Manchester's musical history. According to Milestone, the male-focused legacy of Manchester's music scenes and celebration of male figures such as Tony Wilson (Factory Records), Noel and Liam Gallagher (Oasis), Sean Ryder (the Happy Mondays), Morrisey (The Smiths) and Ian Curtis (Joy Division), whose images are used to market souvenirs from the city, have impacted women's opportunities in Manchester's contemporary creative industries. Stating that 'recent national sector specific research highlighted that the number of women working in the creative industries in the north of England is noticeably lower than the national average', she noted that 'the strength of linkages between the social constructs of northernness, masculinity and creativity appear to inhibit women's full participation in the creative industries' (Milestone 2016: 46). Indeed, Milestone writes that the city's contemporary creative industries are fashioned after the late 1980s and 1990s music scene and its male-dominated networks which she describes as centring on 'lads' that in turn have been informed by '[t]he cultural construct of the "angry young man" which emerged in literature and then film in the 1950s and early 1960s' (2016: 51). She also argues that being 'northern' has been constructed as a masculine subject position, which has inhibited women's access to high-status jobs in Manchester's creative industries. To illustrate her point, Milestone lists the top positions held by men in this sector in Manchester:

> The pop property developer Tom Bloxham (who began his working life selling posters in Affleck's Palace) was Chancellor of Manchester University and was awarded an MBE. Colin Sinclair (former musician and club promoter) became Chief Executive of MIDAS (Manchester's Inward Investment Agency), Peter Saville, one of the cutting edge graphic designers of Factory Records, was appointed the 'Creative Director' of Manchester in 2004 and was responsible for branding and marketing the city (2016: 52).

To this list can be added such figures as Sacha Lord, co-founder and director of the Warehouse Project and Parklife festival, who also now acts as Night-Time Economy Adviser for Greater Manchester, and Jon Drape, who is a director of Broadwick Entertainment and Parklife, as well as many other music-related businesses.

Milestone underlines that concurrently to the male-dominated music scenes which were to be celebrated for decades to come, 'Manchester also became a site for new forms of urban entrepreneurialism – particularly in the 1980s and 1990s when the Labour controlled City Council engaged with neoliberal strategies for urban renewal' (2016: 51). In their 'The Return of the Manchester Men' paper,

Adam Tickell and Jamie Peck characterized these 'newly influential business organizations' (1996: 612), driving the urban development as 'almost exclusively male-led and masculine in outlook' (1996: 612), charting their make-up back to the nineteenth century's 'Manchester Men', a group of powerful businessmen whose discourses of free trade were 'to become central to the liberal trading regime within which Britain was to assume the role of hegemon' (Tickell and Peck 1996: 605). Now, this male dominance of Manchester's regeneration continues. Featured in *Manctopia: Billion Pound Property Boom*, an August 2020 BBC documentary series on Manchester's recent property boom, Tim Heatley is the face of a new generation of Manchester's ambitious male developers. Tellingly described by the *Manchester Evening News* as a 'local lad' (Scullard 2020), his ascension signals the characterization of male northernness Milestone identified as a symbol of success within the city, continues. Importantly, the documentary confirms that the male-dominated networks of power persist. Heatley is shown being chosen by Manchester mayor Andy Burnham as the chairman of his charity A Bed Every Night, to which charity worker Judith Vickers responds to camera, 'I think it's a bit ironic really that a property developer is actually running the mayor's charity ... you can't help but laugh at the irony.' Later in the programme, Heatley is shown organizing a charity concert to raise funds for A Bed Every Night. Predictably, the line-up is dominated by local male groups such as the Courteeners and Blossoms, and features other male acts from Manchester such as the rapper Bugzy Malone and performance poet John Cooper Clarke. The only female artist on the line-up is singer-songwriter Lisa Stansfield.

Manchester's female DJs

The following section is based on interviews with seven female-identifying DJs who live and work within the Greater Manchester area, conducted between July 2018 and October 2020. Respondents ranged from women who DJed in the past and have now stopped and DJs who perform on a part-time basis and full-time DJs, for whom DJing was their only form of employment at the time of interview or was in the past. All the DJs interviewed played or play music that can broadly be described as EDM, including genres like house, techno and disco, as well as additional genres like R&B, soul and hip-hop. All DJs interviewed had experience of playing in both bars and nightclubs and three of the respondents played regularly on local radio station Reform at the time of interview. Aged between thirty-nine and fifty-seven at the time of writing in 2020, four of the DJs identified as white, one identified as mixed race, one identified as Black and one identified as Asian.

Five out of the seven respondents began their careers on the Manchester queer scene and cited a love for music as the reason they began or continued to DJ throughout their lives. Two of the respondents, Kath McDermott and Paulette Constable (aka DJ Paulette), made their names at the LGBT Flesh club night at the nightclub Haçienda in the early 1990s. Julie Wills from the collective Disco Mums began DJing in the late 1990s, playing her first gig at Velvet Bar in the Gay Village, while Ruth Allan began DJing in the early 2000s, playing queer at Club Brenda and afterparties at Salford venue Islington Mill. Rina Dabhi aka

Figure 10.2 Mix-Stress. Photo courtesy of Lauren Jo Kelly.

Ladybeige started DJing in the early 2000s before starting her club night The Social Service in 2012, named after her full-time career as a social worker. Carol Bushell aka BB and Rebecca Swarray aka Mix-Stress were two respondents who started DJing having already established careers in other fields. BB, who had previously played in punk bands, began DJing by setting up a 'friends only' vinyl night at Manchester venue Deaf Institute alongside husband and frequent DJ partner Richard Ward, which evolved into their club night Supernature Disco and collective Supernature. She began DJing in other nightclubs in 2015. Mix-Stress set up collective RnB (RebeccaNeverBecky) in 2018 and began DJing for the club night in 2019, after completing a professional DJing course.

Full-time dreams, part-time careers

All but one of the respondents, DJ Paulette, were not full-time DJs at the time of interview. Aside from those DJs who already had established careers in other fields, respondents usually never considered DJing as a full-time career because they did not feel it would sustain them financially. Indeed, Julie Wills noted the small number of full-time female DJs on Manchester's club scene as testament to lack of opportunities. 'Even amongst the biggest name DJs in Manchester, there's only a handful that probably do it as a career', she said. Some, such as Ruth Allan and Ladybeige, expressed a lack of role models and thus lack of guidance on how to pursue DJing full-time and/or professionally. 'I can't even think of a single female DJ that I even knew of until I kind of met Jayne [Compton, promoter of Club Brenda, where Allan played], so it just didn't strike me as a potential career path', Allan noted. Ladybeige said, 'It didn't even cross my mind that it was something that I could do, and now looking back I wonder if it was because there were so few female DJs. It kind of limits your possibilities when you don't see anyone that looks like you or behaves like you.' Kath McDermott, who did effectively work full-time during her time at Flesh, also taking on promoting duties, noted that 'even when it was my main source of income I never saw it as a career really because I had quite a lot of imposter syndrome'. She also commented on not fitting the mould of what a female DJ is supposed to look like: 'There's very few women who did well in the 90s that weren't wearing very little ... I don't think there was any way that a little dyke in a white t-shirt was going to go places at that point.' An exception to the rule among the DJs interviewed, DJ Paulette pursued a full-time DJ career from the outset, but she said:

There was no precedent for me. There really weren't any female DJs in the 90s. At the lower level parties that I was playing, there was a handful of women. Me, Kath McDermott, Paula and Tabs, Abs Ward, Philippa Jarman. I would say there were a couple more on the indie scene but you could count them probably on two hands in Manchester, Manchester and the north, then in Liverpool there was Girls On Top, but did we see those names on the line-ups? No.

In turn, Julie Wills said that having moved away from Manchester for seven years, she found few opportunities upon her return in 2010. She said that as a response she put on her own nights at the Manchester Roadhouse and the Carlton Club. 'It was the only real way to play the events that we wanted and when we wanted, as often as we'd like.' Ladybeige too said that putting on her own event created more opportunities for her and The Social Service's other residents. Meanwhile, for DJ Paulette, a lack of opportunities in Manchester following launching her career at Flesh meant that she left the city for good, not to return for decades. She said, 'I always move when I'm not getting any work or if I've got so far, or if I've hit the ceiling.'

These experiences are reflective of those discussed elsewhere. Donna Bentley writes in 'Onwards and Upwards: Playing My Way Through the Gender Division', her first-hand account of trying to forge a DJ career, that she settled on becoming a DJ hobbyist rather than trying to become a big-name DJ, because, she states, 'no matter how good I was or what potential I had, I wasn't quite good enough to be in there. I didn't even feel considered at times', while also describing that she was often mistaken for 'the DJ's girlfriend' (Bentley 2017).

Five of the respondents cited motherhood as a reason to pause DJing, DJ on a part-time basis or stop DJing for good. Ruth Allan found that the demands of being a mother impaired her ability to 'keep up with' new music and childcare was a cost which diminished her earnings, thus rendering DJing a less lucrative career choice than her other options. In addition, Allan described feeling shamed in nightclubs for being a mother who was either out clubbing or DJing, with it being perceived by other clubbers as not respectable conduct. BB remarked too that she started clubbing regularly and DJing when her daughter left home for university. Meanwhile, Julie Wills remarked on comments her collective received from clubbers on account of being a mother: 'We've had some good heckles. Loose Women, Tesco Mums.' She also described the collective being asked to change their name when they were booked to play in Ibiza: 'We played [Ibiza venue] Pikes, but they didn't like [the name] Disco Mums.' In turn, Ladybeige described her children as a motivation to start DJing again regularly. She said, 'as a mum for me it's really important that my kids see that my life is about them but also other stuff'. However, she cited motherhood also as part of the reason she chose to DJ part-time: 'I don't want to just be DJing all the time. I want to be able to turn things down because I want to spend time with the kids at the weekend.'

Sexism and ageism

All of the respondents interviewed expressed experiencing some form of sexism during their career. Kath McDermott described how on many occasions during the beginning of her career, clubbers would not believe that she was the DJ. She described this sexism as one of the reasons she decided not to pursue DJing full-time. 'People didn't really take me that seriously and so I think in turn I didn't take myself very seriously. I was like, right, I better get a job, I'll work in a record shop, even though I was a competent DJ even at that point.' Julie Wills described an incident where her collective Disco Mums was booked to play a well-known UK festival, where they were told just hours before they were due to take the stage that their slot was cancelled. 'If it was a bloke that had been written out of that line-up, there would have been an explanation and an apology, but he [the promoter] just said, "Oh don't worry about it, have a nice night, you've got a free ticket for the weekend, didn't you."' Ladybeige described, 'feeling you're getting bumped and getting the shit slot because you know, the girl can warm up or whatever'. In turn, BB described being mistaken for a cleaner at a Pride event at Manchester venue, The Refuge. Meanwhile, DJ Paulette asserted that sexism affects all female DJs at every level and at any age. She said, 'I can see it for all of the women who are working, who are DJs and producers, and how hard it is for all of us to get on line-ups, to get gigs, to get music signed.'

All of the respondents described at least one occasion when their technical ability was questioned by men and scepticism about their knowledge about the music that they were playing. Mix-Stress said, 'Sometimes if I've been behind the decks, I've had somebody trying to tell me how to do something, or I've had punters come up to me and go like, "how do you know these tunes?"' Julie Wills said, 'We've had comments along the way like "are these all your boyfriends' records?"' Two of the respondents, Kath McDermott and Mix-Stress, ascribed this lack of respect or belief in their ability and knowledge to their perceived young age at the time. In contrast, BB described clubbers being astonished at the music she was playing, because of her perceived old age. She reported that a male clubber said to her, 'I was really surprised when you came out because you're dressed like a granny, and you played this really dirty, sexy music, which shocked me.'

Three respondents described the age forty as the hallmark of being often perceived too old to be a DJ, playing EDM. DJ Paulette noted that 'for all the female DJs I know, when you hit forty, it's like you start going backwards. It's like no matter what you do, you can't latch onto what you need to latch onto to bring you forwards through this change.' She described her age as being a barrier to being 'seen' by younger promoters and bookers. She recounted consecutively not being booked for Manchester-based Parklife festival and the Warehouse Project superclub, despite high-profile bookings elsewhere and countless magazine features, simply because of what she believed to be the bookers' narrow criteria for desirable DJs. She also ascribed this to the bookers' belief that social media follower numbers and producers' Beatport chart positions are more important than experience, skill and exposure in music media. Julie Wills shared a similar view, commenting that 'I think after forty there's an image then, you're a mum, you're past it', and described the Disco Mums being initially perceived as a novelty act and sometimes being asked to play children's parties. Ruth Allan reported feeling similarly 'past it' as she neared forty, saying that men within the Manchester underground club scene made her feel like she was too old to be there. 'It wasn't explicitly like that, but it was definitely an issue, and I just thought, do I want to do this, or do I want to leave it to them?', she said.

DJ Paulette described experiencing more of what she perceived to be ageism as a radio presenter than she did as a DJ playing in bars and nightclubs:

I think Manchester is definitely ageist in terms of radio. I just know because I get a lot more traction as a DJ than I do as a radio presenter and it's interesting that the radio that listened to me and gave me a show was Worldwide FM, where the demographic of listeners is older, whereas I had no interest from Unity and NTS, where their demographic is younger.

Kath McDermott, Julie Wills and Mix-Stress also concurred in believing that nightclubs were less hostile spaces for women DJs, and older women DJs in particular, than bars. They ascribed this to nightclubs being spaces where there is usually more of a physical barrier between the DJ and her audience, thus less opportunity for direct interaction, but also a specific bar culture where punters feel entitled to hassle DJs, such as by asking them to play what they want rather than their own selections. However, respondents commented that they were frequently asked how old they are when they were playing regardless of whether they played in bars or nightclubs, and relayed that they felt that male counterparts would never be asked about their age. Despite this frequent focus on their age, respondents did not feel that they were marketed differently to their male counterparts on account of their age. Notably, they ascribed this partly to a lack of precedent, on account of there being so few older women DJs within club culture more generally. Kath McDermott and Julie Wills also pointed to the negative comments that DJs that do not fit traditional notions of female beauty, such as the Blessed Madonna, receive, as examples of the sexism and ageism that still pervade club culture more widely.

Paradoxically, respondents also reported gaining more respect, thanks to being close to or past forty. Kath McDermott reported becoming somewhat of a cult figure on the queer scene, while Julie Wills said that 'I think there is something that comes with age. I'm 43 now, and when I'm dealing with promoters, with blokes that are younger than me sometimes, I guess I get that little bit of respect that I wouldn't if I was ten years younger than them.' Meanwhile, BB reported younger clubbers respecting her as a mother figure, saying, 'I have a lot of young gay men who really look up to me and really value me.' Respondents also reported not being as affected by sexist and ageist comments as they might have been when they were younger, feeling that their confidence had grown. Typical of these comments was Julie Wills, who said, 'If somebody said a sexist or ageist comment to me now, I'd have a conversation with them.' DJ Paulette asserted, too, that Manchester was unique in its club scene being predominated by 'older' DJs. She described that most of her peers were aged thirty or older, but singled out Parklife festival and the Warehouse Project as employing much younger DJs than other venues and spaces. All of the respondents named the Unabombers (Luke Cowdrey and Justin Crawford) connected venues such as The Refuge, Freight Island, Electrik Bar and club nights like Homoelectric and Homobloc as being inclusive of both women and older women in particular. They signalled that they believed that because the Unabombers were older DJs themselves, they were more inclusive of other older DJs. Six of the responders also said they found queer nightclubs in general to be more inclusive of women and more specifically older women than mainstream nightclubs. 'The clubbing community that I'm a part of is actually really respectful and positive and sees these older women as a good thing', claimed Kath McDermott.

Despite the sexism and ageism they have experienced, most respondents signalled that they did not believe that sexism and ageism were more extreme within Manchester's music scene and club culture more widely than within mainstream society. Julie Wills said that 'when you're talking about the DJs and the opportunities that DJs get then that's the same in any hierarchy, in any industry. There's always a lack of opportunity for women at the top.' However, all of the respondents interviewed ascribed the lack of opportunities within Manchester's club scene for women and older women especially to a lack of women in the upper echelons of the night-time economy in the city. They described that while there were increasingly more women bookers in the city and male bookers who were pursuing more inclusive booking policies, venue owners were still predominantly male, and this had an adverse effect on how many women were booked. Typical of these comments was Ladybeige, who said, 'The top is still very much a lad's club.'

Figure 10.3 Kath McDermott at the Haçienda. Photo courtesy of Philippa Jarman.

Towards inclusivity?

All respondents reported finding that sexism and ageism within the Manchester club scene had diminished since they started DJing. Kath McDermott ascribed the change to the recent rewriting of Manchester music history, where events such as the 2017 exhibition *Queer Noise: The History of LGBT+ Music and Club Culture in Manchester* and documentaries spotlighting Flesh and Homoelectric have foregrounded female DJs' role in shaping the city's music scenes. Several of the respondents mentioned DJ Paulette's role in bringing attention to the role women played in Manchester's acid house history (via her 2018 *Homebird* exhibition at the Lowry gallery and interviews with media) and the positive effect this has had on how women and women from the acid house era specifically are perceived. They also noted her success as a DJ since returning to Manchester as inspiring more inclusive attitudes among bookers, which aligns with arguments by scholars such as Maren Hancock, who, when writing about the positive effect of Vancouver female, non-binary and trans DJ focusing nightclub Lick, asserted that 'the success of parties featuring female DJs caused local nightclubs to take notice for financial and creative reasons' (Hancock 2017: 82). Six of the seven women interviewed also cited the annual Suffragette City event, featuring a line-up of all female-identifying DJs (which initially launched in 2018 as a photography exhibition celebrating women from Manchester's music industry), as a response to the under appreciation of women on the Manchester music scene. 'There has been this narrative of Manchester which is a straight white male narrative which of course is just hogwash and I think people have made an effort to disrupt that narrative', Kath McDermott remarked, while Julie Wills said, 'it really put it out there and said, look at the talent that we've got, look at thirty female DJs over a weekend, and everybody had something to bring.' Ladybeige concurred, commenting on the camaraderie the women felt: 'All the DJs were dancing and getting into it rather than looking over their shoulder and seeing whether you're mixing it in right and what you were playing.' McDermott also relayed that she believed 'a lot of promoters have started realising that they need to just get back down to basics, and have the right DJs, and the right mix of DJs, and representation is really important' for changing attitudes. BB, who I had interviewed in 2019 for *Vice*, reported that since the publication of that article, her experience of ageism had also diminished. BB said, 'I had older women DJs contact me, so maybe it's generated that self belief and confidence which then, you know, everyone else feels, and so everyone feels empowered', a view which confirms the important role networks play in furthering the careers of women DJs (Hancock 2017: 74). Wills too said she believed a spotlight on age was an opportunity to change people's perceptions. 'If we can change somebody's view about us being middle aged women that's great', she commented. Respondents tended to feel that changing attitudes among clubbers would drive change on the issues of sexism and ageism rather than policy. As such, there was little faith among respondents in there being any imminent change within the upper echelons of the city's club culture and the music industry more widely. They viewed themselves individually and their collective visibility as DJs, as the drivers of that change. Ladybeige said, 'I still get women coming up to me when I DJ saying, "Oh my God you're so good, but thank you so much because just you being up there makes me feel like I might have a go."'

However, some of the respondents, such as BB, described perceiving some of their gigs as being offered because they were women, in a tokenistic gesture. BB commented that 'certainly sometimes I know some people think it'd be nice to have a female DJ, so they ask me'. It was a view shared by DJ Paulette, who expressed having seen tokenism throughout her career: 'It's that thing where if they've booked Amelie Lens or if they've booked Nicole Moudaber, they've got their woman, and if they've booked Honey Dijon, then they've got their Black woman, and they don't want any more than that.' Mix-Stress concurred, with specific reference to Manchester, saying that '[Bookers] always put certain people on the line-up and it never really steers away from that, unless it's time to be representational or equal opportunities or whatever. But then it goes back to, right, we're playing music of Black origin but all the DJs are white men.' For relative newcomer Mix-Stress, setting up her collective RebeccaNeverBecky was thus a response to what she described as 'a need for more female, QTIPOC, LGBT+, BAME and POC representation'. She said, 'for me as a queer woman, it's interesting being in LGBT spaces and not always seeing that representation. There's club nights that have been created by straight white men that are for a majority LGBT audience, so for me, where's the representation there?'

Moreover, four of the respondents described instances of receiving lower wages than their male counterparts or, at times, no wages at all. BB said, 'I'm just glad to get any money at all sometimes.' Describing her residency at Club Brenda, Ruth Allan said, 'I always felt like I couldn't ask for any money. Because I was just the DJ in "room two", I just always felt like she [the promoter] thought I was an amateur.' Meanwhile, Mix-Stress described writing grant applications, where she did not ask for the full amount of funds available. Julie Wills too

Figure 10.4 BB. Photo courtesy of Claire Angel.

described an incident where she was only paid half of what had been previously agreed with a popular Manchester club venue. However, Ladybeige relayed that being the boss of her club night she was paid equal if not more than her fellow residents, who are men. All of the respondents also described bars as being fairer spaces fees-wise, where they claimed wages were set for duration of time played, rather than negotiated with individual DJs.

Conclusion

Sexism continues to be pervasive across the music industry, with recent studies showing women to be under-represented across line-ups and to hold few positions of power. Coupled with an unchecked ageism within club culture, older women identifying DJs face perhaps the biggest discrimination of all, with their situation under-researched by scholars. In Manchester, this prejudice is arguably more pronounced, as the city continues to celebrate its male musicians of the past, which has had an effect on the number of women within its creative industries, including positions of power within its night-time economy and club culture. It is also a city which is focused on urban development, where historically and currently, men dominate across business and local government. At the same time, Manchester has a strong LGBT club scene, and, owing to its long-established club culture, pockets of ageing DJs and promoters, who offer opportunities to women and older women across bars and nightclubs. A pushback against the male-dominated narrative of Manchester music, by practitioners and scholars alike, has also resulted in increasing opportunities for older women DJs, as well as fostered networks and camaraderie between them. However, it should be mentioned that women's equal representation with men, and older women with older men, is not only a question of what nightclubs decide to offer their punters but also these punters' tastes, which might not change in step with specific policies. Given the challenges nightclubs experience, following Covid-19 restrictions, one might expect that nightclubs will be inclined to 'play safe', booking popular acts, thus disadvantaging female DJs, who tend to be less known. On the other hand, with more limited resources than in the past, nightclubs might be more willing to book local acts and thus give more women a chance. Time will only tell which of these strategies will prevail in Manchester and elsewhere.

Works Cited

Abtan, Freida (2016). 'Where Is She? Finding the Women in Electronic Music Culture', *Contemporary Music Review*, 35(1), pp. 53–60.

Armour, Zoe (2019). 'Baby Raves: Youth, Adulthood and Ageing in Contemporary British EDM Culture', *Dancecult: Journal of Electronic Dance Music Culture*, 11(1), pp. 53–71.

Bain, Vick (2019). 'Counting the Music Industry. The Gender Gap', *Counting Music*, October 2019, https://countingmusic.co.uk/, accessed 2 August 2020.

Bennett, Andy and Jodie Taylor (2012). 'Popular Music and the Aesthetics of Ageing', *Popular Music*, 31(2): pp. 231–43.

Bentley, Donna (2017). 'Onwards and Upwards: Playing My Way Through the Gender Division', *Dancecult: Journal of Electronic Dance Music Culture*, 9(1). DOI: 10.12801/1947-5403.2017.09.01.14.

Centre for Ageing Better (2019). *Doddery but Dear? Examining Age-related Stereotypes*. ageing-better.org.uk, accessed 10 September 2020.

Cuddy, Amy J. C. and Susan T. Fiske (2004). 'Doddering but Dear: Process, Content, and Function in Stereotyping of Older Persons', in Todd D. Nelson (ed.), *Ageism: Stereotyping and Prejudice Against Older Persons*. Cambridge, MA: MIT Press, pp. 3–26.

Farrugia, Rebekah (2012). *Beyond the Dance Floor: Female DJs, Technology and Electronic Dance Music Culture*. Bristol and Chicago: Intellect.

Farrugia, Rebekah and Magdalena Olszanowski (2017). 'Introduction to Women and Electronic Dance Music Culture', *Dancecult: Journal of Electronic Dance Music Culture*, 9(1), pp. 1–8.

Forman, Murray (2014). 'Visualizing Place, Representing Age in Hip-hop: Converging Themes in Scarface's "My Block"', *Continuum*, 28(3), pp. 300–13.

Gadir, Tami (2017). 'Forty-Seven DJs, Four Women: Meritocracy, Talent, and Postfeminist Politics', *Dancecult: Journal of Electronic Dance Music Culture*, 9(1), pp. 50–72.

Grigoriadis, Vanessa (2019). 'Madonna at Sixty', *New York Times*, 5 June, https://www.nytimes.com/2019/06/05/magazine/madonna-madame-x.html, accessed 1 September 2020.

Hancock, Maren (2017). 'Lick My Legacy: Are Women-Identified Spaces Still Needed to Nurture Women-Identified DJs?', *Dancecult: Journal of Electronic Dance Music Culture*, 9(1), pp. 73–89.

Heath, Harold (2019). 'Raving Is for Everyone: The Problem with Ageism in Dance Music', *DJ Mag*, 3 July 2019, https://djmag.com/longreads/raving-everyone-problem-ageism-dance-music, accessed 1 August 2020.

Hughes, Chelsea (2019). 'Meet the Kickass Female DJs Pushing for Gender Equality in the Industry', *Glamour*, 1 April 2019, https://www.glamourmagazine.co.uk/article/female-djs-gender-equality, accessed 3 August 2020.

Little, Sarah (2018). 'Women, Ageing, and Hip Hop: Discourses and Imageries of Ageing Femininity', *Feminist Media Studies*, 18(1), pp. 34–46.

McGuigan, Jim (2009). *Cool Capitalism*. London: Pluto Press.

Milestone, Katie (2016). '"Northernness", Gender and Manchester's Creative Industries', *Journal for Cultural Research*, 20(1), pp. 45–59.

Naegele, Laura and Wouter De Tavernier and Moritz Hess (2018). 'Work Environment and the Origin of Ageism', in LiatAyalon and ClemensTesch-Römer (eds), *International Perspectives on Aging*, vol. 19. Cham: Springer, pp. 73–90.

O'Grady, Alice and Anna Madill (2019). 'Being and Performing "Older" Woman in Electronic Dance Movement Culture', *Dancecult: Journal of Electronic Dance Music Culture*, 11(1), pp. 7–29.

Peter, Beate and Lisa Williams (2019). 'One Foot in the Rave: Aging Ravers' Transitions to Adulthood and Their Participation in Rave Culture', *Leisure Sciences*, pp. 1–19. DOI: 10.1080/01490400.2019.1675560.

Rodgers, Tara (2010). *Pink Noises*. Durham and London: Duke University Press.

Rymajdo, Kamila (2016). 'Do We Actually Need to Talk About "Female DJs" in 2016?', *Vice*, 8 March 2016, https://www.vice.com/en/article/gvn5y7/do-we-actually-need-to-talk-about-female-djs-in-2016, accessed 15 August 2020.

Rymajdo, Kamila (2018). 'The Women Who've Been Written Out of Manchester Clubbing History', *Dazed*, 25 September 2018, https://www.dazeddigital.com/music/article/41536/1/women-hacienda-manchester-clubbing-lgbt-history, accessed 14 September 2020.

Rymajdo, Kamila (2019a). 'The Rave Gap: How UK Nightlife Still Struggles with Ageism', *Vice*, 6 February 2019, https://www.vice.com/en/article/9kpa7e/the-rave-gap-how-uk-nightlife-still-struggles-with-ageism, accessed 1 August 2020.

Rymajdo, Kamila (2019b). 'The Hidden Worker Bees: Advanced Neoliberalism and Manchester's Underground Club Scene', in Ewa Mazierska, Les Gillon and Tony Rigg (eds), *Politics, Economy, Culture and Technology*. London: Bloomsbury, pp. 111–32.

Scullard, Vickie (2020). 'Is Manchester Becoming Unaffordable? Meet the Millionaire Property Developer Who Says It's Time for Change', *Manchester Evening News*, 18 August 2020, https://www.manchestereveningnews.co.uk/news/tv/manctopia-billion-pound-property-boom-18771110, accessed 3 September 2020.

Sherlock, Pete and Paul Bradshaw (2017). 'Festivals Dominated by Male Acts, Study Shows, as Glastonbury Begins', *BBC News*, 22 June 2017, https://www.bbc.co.uk/news/uk-england-40273193, accessed 2 August 2020.

Tickell, Adam and Jamie Peck (1996). 'The Return of the Manchester Men: Men's Words and Men's Deeds in the Remaking of the Local State', *Transactions of the Institute of British Geographers*, 21(4), pp. 595–616.

11

Transformation of dance culture in Poland as a battle over taste in music

Ewa Mazierska

This chapter looks at the specificity of dance culture in Poland, from the time Poland regained statehood in 1918 till the early 2000s. My argument is that it was always class-bound, but up to the 1970s its hierarchies were implicit and there was no open antagonism between different types of dance scenes. In due course, however, a culture war broke in Poland around dancing, which intensified after the fall of state socialism in the end of the 1990s. My task is to establish to what extent this antagonism reflects political and cultural circumstances specific to Poland. In order to do so, I will draw on the political and cultural history of Poland and research about dance culture in Western and Eastern Europe. My investigation is also based on the idea, articulated by Pierre Bourdieu, that taste in music reflects and asserts class position. As Bourdieu put it, 'nothing more clearly affirms one's "class", nothing more infallibly classifies, than tastes in music' (2010: 10; see also Born 2011). By the same token, criticism of specific music style might in reality reflect a sense of superiority over the class which indulges in this music and anxiety about one's own social position. What concerns music also refers to dancing, as there is no more direct way of expressing oneself as through dancing. Bourdieu and his followers focused on the capitalist West, but my argument is that his observations are equally valid to the socialist East, because in a situation when distinctions pertaining to wealth were reduced, those referring to other aspects of class position were magnified, for the benefit of the part of the population which perceived itself as an elite.

Dancing Poland of the interbellum

Poland regained sovereignty in 1918 after almost 120 years of partitions, when Poles were discouraged to enjoy themselves, both by the colonizing forces which thwarted any manifestations of Polish culture and by Polish own cultural elites, who regarded uninhibited expression of joy, characteristic of dance, as unsuitable to the despicable condition of subjugated Poles, which required permanent mourning. The euphoria of gaining statehood was expressed by numerous balls for different types of audience: upper-class people, bohemians and workers. Popular were balls for different categories of professionals, such as officers, diplomats and the media. Participants in such events competed for the title of the best dressed man and woman: King and Queen of Fashion.[1]

The working classes were typically dancing in summer in the open air on so-called boards (*na dechach*). In Warsaw, it happened in the Sielecki and Praski parks and on the beaches on both sides of the Vistula River. In summer the dance fans of the lower classes in Warsaw moved to indoor spaces, such as the Club of the Friends of Czerniaków (Towarzystwo Przyjaciół Czerniakowa). According to Stanisław Grzesiuk, famous urban folk musician and chronicler of this period, there was no entrance fee for these events, but the patrons had to pay separately for each dance. Moreover, due to the prevalence of men, it was expected that women will agree to change dance partners when requested, and men accompanying them would not object to that, so that every man would have a chance to dance (Zakrzewski 2016).

With the passage of time, more purpose-built sites were erected to house the amateurs of dancing. The most famous of them was Adria in Warsaw, opened in 1929. In its basement it had a dancing hall with a rotating stage for 1,500 people. The guests enjoyed themselves to the accompaniment of three different orchestras, playing respectively jazz, Argentinian rhythms and salon-type of music. Adria also had a Winter Gardens and two bars. What was characteristic of the dancing culture of this period was that there were no separate rooms for eating and dancing; the dancing stage was surrounded by tables at which the patrons were eating traditional Polish dishes of pork chops with potatoes.

How popular was dancing in Poland between the two wars, we can appreciate watching Polish films of this period, especially after cinema gained sound. Virtually every Polish film from the 1930s includes a scene showing people dancing (Mazierska 2021) (Figure 11.1).

We can gather that practically every restaurant had at least a small stage where couples could display their dancing skills. There were also large charity balls

Figure 11.1 Dancing in *Dorożkarz Nr 13* (*Cabman Nr 13*), directed by Marian Czauski.

where upper-class people danced, as well as open-air celebrations for working-class people and dances around fire, practised by Gypsies and people living in the mountains. The sign of importance of dancing for both pleasure and status was the profession of *fordanser(ka)*: somebody who danced for money with single men and women; such *fordanserzy* is at the centre of the film *Książątko* (*Little Prince*, 1937), directed by Konrad Tom and Władysław Szebego.

Although the dancing sites in the interwar Poland were segregated according to class divisions, there is nothing to suggest that there was a hostility on the part of one class towards the style of dancing of another class. Moreover, judging on the interwar films, the boundaries between these different sites and dancing styles were porous; the working-class boy or girl could easily find himself or herself in an upper-class establishment and enchant visitors with his or her dance; this was the case in the previously mentioned *Little Prince*.

Polish discotheques of the 1970s and 1980s

After the Second World War, Poland, in common with many other Eastern European countries, adopted a system of state socialism, which proclaimed the hegemony of the working class. In practice, this meant flattening the wages, which were decided by the central authorities and privileging working-class culture, at the expense of the culture of higher classes, which were regarded merely as the remnants of the prewar hierarchical system. In practice, however, such egalitarianism was contested after the end of Stalinism in Poland by new cultural elites, who wanted to distance themselves from the culture of the working classes. Such a desire was strengthened by the lack of economic distinctions, which under capitalism signify better access to cultural capital. Moreover, the state itself became averse to pure entertainment, regarding it as demoralizing. Entertainment under state socialism needed to be educational to assist in creation of a 'new man'. As a result, as Gregory Kveberg argues in relation to the Soviet Union, a certain hierarchy of music was established, with classical music being at the top of this grading, followed by folk music, with music produced solely for enjoyment, such as estrada songs and songs for dancing, being at the bottom of this ladder (2015: 213–15). Until the end of the 1960s this hierarchy was not contested and did not lead to a conflict. The situation changed in the 1970s due to a number of factors. One of them was a change in the political regime in Poland. In 1970, following some serious political unrest, Poland got a new political leader, Edward Gierek, who introduced a more conciliatory style of governing. Among its changes was extending the right of citizens to leisure, through phased introduction of free Saturdays. Another factor was a boom in discotheques and disco music, marked by 4/4 beat and the use of instruments more common in classical music than in rock (Straw 2001: 166).

In Poland, the 1970s also belonged to the discotheques and this term normally had two meanings: a venue where a party took place to the accompaniment of music played from records and the said party. It is difficult to establish the number of Polish discotheque venues in this decade, but most likely there were about 3,000 discotheques. Such a number was provided in the 'Report About the State of Discotheques in Poland' (Raport o Stanie Dyskotek w Polsce), commissioned by the Ministry of Culture and published in 1981. This report also stated that on average a Polish discotheque was visited each day by fifty people. Franciszek Walicki, who commented on these figures, noted that this meant that in a year 46,000,000 Poles visited discotheques, hence more than all Polish theatres put together (1984: 7).

The region in Poland where discotheque culture was born was the Baltic coast, which is also regarded as the birthplace of Polish rock music. The first Polish (proper) discotheque, Musicorama, was opened in 1970 by the 'father of Polish big beat', Franciszek Walicki, in the 'Tourist Hall' of the Grand Hotel, located in the most popular Polish coastal resort of Sopot, hence a couple of years later than in Yugoslavia, which was more advanced and culturally closer to the West (Zubak 2016: 199). However, it was not the first time when Poles gathered in public places to listen to music played from records. Marcin Jacobson, one of the first Polish DJs, recounted to me that in the 1960s and 1970s it was not uncommon to give a talk about a specific record or artist in a club, then play his or her record, which was followed by a proper concert. In this sense, the early Polish discotheques are not very different from the early discotheques, whose function was mostly educational. One can also notice a similarity between these early Polish discotheques and those functioning in Czechoslovakia from the mid-1960s, which, as Jan Blüml informs, involved a famous radio personality, usually coming from Prague, travelling with his records (as it was always he) to play them in youth clubs and other venues, such as restaurants and wine bars (Blüml 2019: 99–103). It is worth noting that discotheques working on these terms were 'quasi-colonial' institutions, in which the centre provided entertainment and enlightenment to the province.

Musicorama was a different kettle of fish from these early Polish and Czech discotheques, because there records were used for dancing. Moreover, it had a proper disco ambience, with equipment imported from Holland, whose clubs which Walicki visited in 1969 constituted for him the main source of inspiration (Walicki 1995: 205–6). This equipment included strobe lights, pulsating to the rhythm of the music. Many people came to Musicorama especially to see these lights being switched on (Jacobson, quoted in Puchalski 2016). The first discos Walicki ran with Piotr Kaczkowski, a well-known radio journalist, renowned for his programmes on the Polish radio Third Programme. In due course he involved a number of other journalists, working on radio, such as Marek Gaszyński, Witold Pograniczny and Dariusz Michalski, as well as future television personality and film director Jacek Bromski. According to Walicki, this exclusive group deserves the honour of being regarded as the first Polish disc jockeys (1995: 205–7). There were also several high-class discotheques in Warsaw, most importantly in the hotel Bristol, which was frequently visited by foreigners. According to the previously mentioned 'Report', different institutions were in charge of Polish discotheques. The largest proportion of them (over 1,500) belonged to culture houses (*domy kultury*), students and youth organizations. About 680 belonged to catering facilities, such as restaurants, 200 were run by Estrada. Over 600 were run by private people (Walicki 1984: 7). This high number points to the liberalizing tendencies of Gierek's regime on one hand and on the other, in its trust in discotheques as places which – if properly run and monitored – would have a 'civilizing' influence on the Polish youth. This was an important reason why discotheques as institutions and disco music had a bad press in Poland (Figures 11.2 and 11.3).

According to Walicki, a typical Polish discotheque (party) at the beginning of the 1980s was organized in a café or a youth club, six times a week, from 7 p.m. till midnight, had about 100 people capacity, used low-quality equipment and played music largely from tapes and more rarely from vinyl records, of which only 5 per cent was Polish music (Walicki 1984: 7). As in the West, for the

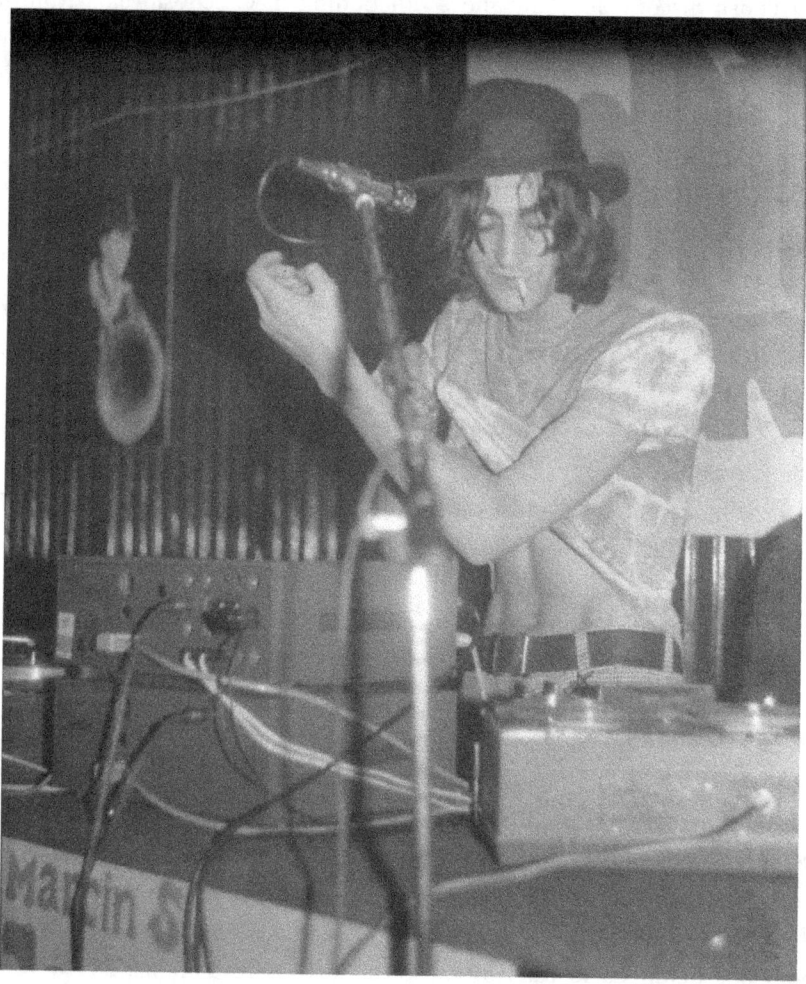

Figure 11.2 Early Polish DJ, Marcin Jacobson, in Musicorama (photo courtesy Marcin Jacobson).

Figure 11.3 First Polish DJ, Jana Kras (photo courtesy Marcin Jacobson).

Polish audience discotheques were an important source of knowledge about new trends in music. This function was heightened by the lack of Western records in the local record shops and the relative scarcity of Western popular music on the radio and television. In such circumstances, early disc jockeys acted as principal trendsetters.

Five years after opening Musicorama, Walicki became the head of the state commission which gave licenses to DJs, as well as awarding them special categories, reflecting their professional status (Walicki 1984: 7).[2] In order to become an official DJ, the candidate had to have at least college education and pass a state exam (Walicki 1984: 7). A similar requirement can be found in the Soviet Union. Gregory Kveberg, who analyses at length the Soviet political debates about Soviet *diskoteki*, explains the insistence on them having a professional cadre to two overlapping factors. One was the Stalinist (as well as 'real socialist') concept of culture as *kul'turnost*, which was a learned system of values, knowledge and appropriate responses. Culture, in this system, was certainly not a birthright but instead was, and *could only legitimately be*, earned through study and toil (Kveberg 2015: 213–14). The Soviet authorities could not afford the amateurs to usurp the place which was owed to those in possession of *kul'turnost*. The second was a view that trained DJs and managers would ensure the reintegration of discotheques into 'larger Soviet cultural hierarchies' (Kveberg 2015: 220). Although Walicki does not say explicitly that such approach was also behind the Polish policy of professionalization of the discotheques' cadres, it is not difficult to guess that this was indeed the case.

By the middle of the decade there were about 100 professional DJs in Poland (Zakrzewski 2016). In the socialist, heavily regulated economy, this meant that the earnings of the DJs depended on the category awarded them by the said commission. Such a system favoured metropolitan cultural elites, as the highest ranks were awarded to DJs who worked in the radio, as those previously mentioned. They were thus privileged twice: by having much greater exposure than their colleagues who lacked access to the state media and being paid better when they worked on live events.

From the Polish press and books publishing interviews with the veterans of the discos (Walicki 1984, 1995; Zakrzewski 2016; Boćkowska 2018), we learn that, thanks to the high price of records, the most prominent Polish DJs favoured 'high rock' and what had a chance to become 'classic', rather than typical disco hits. Jacobson mentions that in the 1970s he was able to buy one Western LP for his earnings from three nights as a DJ in a Polish disco (Danielewicz and Jacobson 2017: 77).

For the same reason, it made more sense to buy LPs rather than singles, because the relatively small difference in price between them and the ephemeral character of singles didn't justify the investment. For subsequent decades Jacobson played LPs almost exclusively. Inevitably, some records were played repeatedly and became imprinted on the audience's psyche. Other early DJs, operating on the Baltic coast, also favoured 'high rock'. They mention bands such as the Rolling Stones, Led Zeppelin, Deep Purple, the Moody Blues, Cream and Aretha Franklin (Danielewicz and Jacobson 2017: 78). However, when these DJs moved to the province, they experienced pressure to play more danceable music, such as Boney M. For the DJs of the highest category, such a request was an insult. Again, we can notice a similarity between the way Polish and Czechoslovak DJ operated, as both favoured rock over disco music. According to Blüml, the most played in Czech discotheques were records of bands such as Deep Purple, Black Sabbath, Led Zeppelin and Uriah Heep (Blüml 2019: 100). In Yugoslavia the situation was somewhat different. As Marko Zubak claims, 'rock dominated at first, but it was soon enriched by soul and rhythm and blues. Later on came funk and disco as a younger generation of disc jockeys diversified their repertoire' (2016: 205).

It is worth mentioning here the characteristics of disco culture offered by Carolyn Krasnow, echoed in several chapters in this collection:

> Rock had put great emphasis on its stars, but because disco circulated almost entirely through records, stars were less dominant; instead, the focus was on the dancers themselves and on the social milieu of the club. In this way discos recalled earlier times, when dance clubs, from the smallest neighbourhood gathering places to the most elite nightclubs, were focal points of entertainment. (2000)

In its focus on rock, stars and LPs, Polish discotheques of the highest prestige went against the international trend. By contrast, provincial discos were more in tune with the mainstream culture of disco and, especially, Eurodisco.

Contact with the West was essential for performing well the job of a DJ. For this reason DJs based on the Baltic coast occupied a privileged position as they could buy records from the sailors. Those who had family in the West, especially in the UK, fared even better.

Another specificity of Polish discotheques was their entanglement with the regulated politics of consumption, pertaining to the state socialist economy. This was to do with the fact (also not uncommon in the West) that the owners and managers of the music clubs got no direct profit from DJs playing music and people dancing to it. Profit was only created when the guests consumed something on the premises, such as food or alcohol. To ensure that such consumption took place, many Polish establishments which hosted discos asked the patrons to buy at the entrance 'consumption tokens', which allowed them to consume a specific amount of food and alcohol (Błażejewski 2011). The downside of this policy was the presence of drunken guests and, on occasions, conflict on the dancefloor. The larger the 'consumption tokens' were, the older the audience attending a specific event. This affected the disco's repertoire, as older audiences preferred Polish over Western music, which was not to the taste of the ambitious DJs, who were disparaging of the Polish musical fare (Danielewicz and Jacobson 2017: 82). The drive towards mixing dancing with consumption increased in the late 1970s, resulting in their decline as spaces of (high) culture. According to Walicki, they became a symbol of a nouveau riche lifestyle. Famous poet and lyricist Jonasz Kofta described them as places 'where pseudo-culture stifles culture, where the barman chooses a DJ and a prostitute chooses music' (quoted by Walicki 1995: 73).

It is worth mentioning that one of the first Polish DJs was female – Jana Kras, whom Jacobson describes as the 'queen of Polish discos'. Before she started to DJ, she worked as a model and performed with the band Perpetuum Mobile, set up by Jerzy Kossela (whom she later married), the founding member of the most popular Polish pop-rock band Czerwone Gitary and subsequently a DJ himself. Kras's first stint in DJ-ing was during a 'mixed event', when music played from a record player or a tape recorder was mixed with live music. On this occasion she replaced a missing (male) DJ. After her debut she became a DJ in the students' clubs in Tricity. Then she encountered a problem pertaining to all DJs from Eastern Europe and female DJs across the world: the meagreness of her record collection. At some point she decided to give up her job as it was not financially sustainable, but she was prevented from doing so by receiving the highest category of DJ, which brought both a larger financial reward and higher prestige. At this point she was the only woman who got this distinction and the only DJ who was not working in radio (Danielewicz and Jacobson 2017: 78–9). Despite being a woman, Kras followed the same principles concerning record collections and hence betrayed the same high-art/snobbish outlook as her male colleagues.

In the Polish discourse on popular music the culture of discotheques tends to be ignored or relegated to a (literal or figural) footnote in the studies of Polish rock. These footnotes typically show discotheques in a negative light, as institutions promoted by the state socialist regime as a way to pacify rebellious youngsters and driving them away from more dangerous Western music. For example, Remigiusz Kasprzycki claims that the music played in discotheques was much safer than the anarchic music of the likes of the Rolling Stones or Jimi Hendrix; it was a means to render young people conformist and passive (2013: 96–7). Similarly, in the celebrated documentary *Beats of Freedom – Zew wolności* (2010), directed by Wojciech Gnoiński and Leszek Słota, about Polish rock under the communist rule the narrator, one of the people interviewed, says that people like Edward Gierek (the Party General Secretary in the 1970s) did not like rock and favoured Boney M.

Disparaging attitudes to disco music and the culture of discotheques were also characteristic of Western scholarship. From the 1990s, however, Western scholars began to re-evaluate it, recognizing disc jockeys as knowledgeable collectors who acquire specific records and relate them to the community of dancers (Thornton 1995: 60-6; Straw 2001: 167-9). In the Polish and Eastern European context, this happened largely in the late 1990s to 2000s, when Poland started to have first DJ stars.

The birth of disco polo

When some Poles were dancing in discotheques, others were dancing under an open sky, including in the villages and small towns, at weddings and village festivals. During the first decades after the war, music of this type was played by bands using instruments such as violins, accordions, as well as drums and guitars. It was often folk music slightly 'spiced up'. By the end of the 1980s, it started to modernize itself in two ways. First, traditional instruments gave way to electronic instruments. This was in part to give the sounds more modern feel and in part to save on the personnel, with electric drum machines allowing to save on a drummer. Second, the lyrics changed, to account on new tastes of the listeners. In due course, this provincial music gave birth to an electronic dance music (EDM) known as 'disco polo'. Apart from Polish folk music and what can be regarded as 'illegitimate' Polish pop, its root was music disseminated among the Polish diaspora in the United States, known as Polonia. Bands such as Polskie Orły (Polish Eagles) and Biało Czerwoni (White-Reds), whose names conveyed their patriotic leaning, gained significant popularity across all the foreign countries where Poles lived (Muzyka Polskiej Polonii 2014). It was marked by simple melodies and mechanical rhythm, produced by drum machines, electronic keyboards and early synthesizers and patriotic lyrics, emphasizing that the best things come from Poland – the women are the most beautiful, men the bravest and the landscape most picturesque. Such claims reflected well Polish culture in which love of patria features prominently, but the more educated sections of society regarded such outpouring of patriotism as vulgar.

This music plugged gaps in the repertoire of Polish bands performing at weddings and provincial discos and encouraged local musicians to try their hand in producing similar tunes. Another source of inspiration for disco polo producers was Euro disco of the concurrent period, exemplified by German duo Modern Talking and Italo disco. Their productions characterized the prevalence of electric keyboards, drum machines and synthesizers, and optimistic lyrics. The fact that the singers of Euro disco used English facilitated its crossing national borders.

Initially disco polo was known as *muzyka chodnikowa* (pavement music or sidewalk music). This name most likely reflected the fact that the cassettes with this music were sold from folded deckchairs, put up on the pavements of the Polish cities, as well as from bazaar stalls. However, it also awakened connotation of *literatura brukowa* (cobblestone literature), a term used in Poland to describe commercial literature of the lowest standard, suggesting that pavement music was as bad as cobblestone literature.

The term 'disco polo' was coined by music producer Sławomir Skręta, who set up Blue Star, the first recording studio and label, specializing in releasing disco polo music. The term 'disco polo' was clever, being based on the same formula as 'italo disco'. Italo disco, as its inventors emphasized, is not the same as 'Italian disco' – it stands for a style, not the nationality of its performers or the language of the lyrics. It conveys only a vague allegiance to Italian culture. Similarly, 'disco polo' is not the same as 'Polish disco' – it suggests a loose connection with Polish (folk) culture and promises to rework and update it, without being over-respectful, as is indeed the case.

Probably the oldest disco polo band is Bayer Full, set up in 1984. Its leader is Sławomir Świerzyński (b. 1961), till now one of the most successful representatives of this genre. Świerzyński was born in Gostynin in Kujawy (the region in the central Poland, which I also come from), where disco polo has been very popular, among both its creators and the audience. Another stronghold of disco polo has been the Podlasie region (around the city of Białystok) in the east of Poland. Both regions are agricultural and relatively poor, and they belonged to the Russian Empire during the period of partition, where their patriotic feelings were probably at the strongest (due to hatred of the Russian colonizer, perceived as not only ruthless but uncivilized), although people living in Kujawy are on average less religious than those from Podlasie. Disco polo gave millions of Poles living in these province culture of their own, something which they can enjoy without the 'permission' of cultural elites.

In the 1990s disco polo became the most successful genre of Polish popular music. It also became an object of a heated cultural debate. Its subject was its cultural legitimacy within a wider world of Polish dance music and popular music at large. To understand it, it is worth consider the changes in politics and music which happened in the 1990s.

EDM in 1990s Poland

In 1989 state socialism officially fell in Poland, leading to the introduction of a new political system: that of market economy and parliament democracy. The first decade can be described as that of 'wild capitalism', when fortunes could be made quickly due to the hasty privatization of state assets, but also when it was easy to bankrupt due to high interest rates. The new system had an indirect influence on Polish popular music by depriving Polish rock music of its most important fuel – the hated political regime. In the 1990s it made little sense to sing about the (lack of) freedom, because freedom returned to Poland, in the form of freedom to vote in political elections, travel and buy consumer goods. Polish rock had to adjust to the new circumstances and it did, but in the 1990s it was in a state of crisis. For many Polish listeners, in the 1990s rock music with its macho posture started to look regressive. Electronic and especially techno music, with its shunning of Polish language and cosmopolitan outlook, appeared to capture the new decade better than rock. Hence, the 1990s belonged largely to techno and disco polo. During this decade Polish electronic artists were still working on primitive equipment and had to travel to Berlin to buy the dreamt-off electronic gadgets, often costing a large part of their savings. From the perspective of technology, there was thus no level-playing field for Polish electronic musicians.

Polish music media recognized that this music was new. One could encounter numerous articles describing meanings of such terms as 'techno', 'ambient', 'electro' and the genealogy of the respective styles. Techno and industrial were used most often, testifying to the specificity of the Polish electronic scene in this period. The prevalence of 'techno' points to close connections between Polish electronic musicians emerging in this period, such as Jacek Sienkiewicz and Wojciech Kucharczyk, with German and to a smaller extent Austrian centres of electronic music, where this term was used to capture a meta-genre, covering all forms of music played in clubs and all forms of electronic music based on rhythm. In the decades to come, the commemorative practices, including exhibitions (Dubrowska 2017) and documentary films, would reinforce the perception that from the 1990s the Polish electronic music scene was dominated by techno.

The proliferation of 'industrial music' can also be linked to the proximity of Berlin, where music engaging with the rhythm of heavy machines was seen in the 1990s as a monument to the fast disappearing heavy industry in East Germany, following the unification of Germany. Poland also went through a similar process, on even a larger scale, especially in the South, where the Polish coalmining industry was located. Not surprisingly, one of the first techno clubs in Poland was 'Kanty' in Jaworzno in Silesia, which was once an important centre of mining and metallurgic industries.

Techno in Poland was played in three types of places: clubs, raves and parades. Rather than go to purpose-built clubs, the 1990s saw a mushrooming of impromptu spaces, most importantly abandoned factories, warehouses and bankrupt state farms. It was played first in clubs which were previously associated with rock music, such as Hybrydy in Warsaw, but from the mid-1990s this genre was offered in specialized clubs. Apart from Warsaw, which had an advantage over other cities and towns, thanks to being the capital, club culture flourished most in those places which were closest to Berlin, such as Poznań and Szczecin or, like Łódź, had historic connections with Germany. I appreciated how important Berlin was for 'electronic' Poland when I once looked at the 'electronic map of Poland', published in an issue of *Laif*. This map demonstrated that the closer a given Polish town was to Germany, the more likely it had some electronic music festival and a network of clubs, while the East of Poland was largely immune from such influences.

In Szczecin, which was called 'little Berlin', the beginnings of clubbing started in the early to mid-1990s. The precursors of this phenomenon was the agency New Music Art, which organized events named Techno Dance Mission. They did not have a stable location but were set up in different places, often abandoned warehouses and attracted crowds of several thousand people. Among DJs performing there were Tresor regulars and guests from Detroit. At this time the electronic scene in Szczecin was not specialized; the best-known genres were techno and house, but it was not infrequent that a gig included hip-hop artists alongside representatives of techno. Many of the parties, as in Berlin, were illegal and had poor infrastructure; the sound systems did not work well; on occasion there were no toilets. There was also no continuity; after several events the organizers had to move elsewhere when their place was discovered by the police. These events were probably the first Polish raves, although this term was not used at the time.

Łódź, like Szczecin and Poznań, was also at the forefront of club music. At the beginning of the 1990s, techno parties were organized in the student clubs '77' and 'Szafa'. DJs working there, Amnesia Crew and Rebus played hip-hop, jungle and hardcore. The year 1994 saw the opening of the club New Alcatraz, managed by Sławomir Żak and Robert Jakubowski, in the old factory hall of a textile mill. The club, as its very name suggests, was styled to a prison and specialized in drum'n'bass, the genre with which Łódź became associated. Its unique atmosphere attracted visitors from all over Poland and abroad. In the second half of the 1990s, the main place for the fans of electronic music became Forum Fabricum, opened in 1999 in, as its very name suggests, an old factory. It closed down in 2003, partly due to a rise in rent and partly because of the exhaustion of its formula (Kowalewicz 2003).

The 1990s was the time of Love Parade in Berlin, which was attended by many young Poles. Its charm was the greater, as the sexual culture in Poland of state socialism was prudish and the country was riven with prejudice against alternative sexualities. Poles decided to emulate the Berlin event and from 1997 it has its own techno parade – 'Parada Wolności' (Freedom Parade) in Łódź, marching through Piotrkowska Street, the longest high street in Europe. It was a child of the previously mentioned Żak and Jakubowski. Freedom Parade was meant to be merely an addition to the large techno event, organized regularly in the sports' hall, but its success encouraged the organizers to repeat it (Kaazetka 2001: 44). The first Freedom Parade had five tracks with equipment and attracted 8,000 visitors; three years later the number of visitors was between 28,000 and 30,000. The parade included a competition for DJs and a Mega Party in two sports halls (Kaazetka 2001: 47). In total, it had fifty people involved in its organization and employed two hundred bouncers (Kaazetka 2001: 46). Judging by its coverage, this was the most important event in the calendar of Polish techno fans from its beginnings throughout the 2000s. However, apart from the Łódź's Parade, Polish electronic scene of the 1990s lacked larger events, such as raves and techno festivals. This was explained by the fact that techno music in Poland during this decade was regarded as a risky business, hence had problems attracting sponsors and promotors (Ostap 2002: 63).

Articles about clubbing, published in the Polish press, pointed to its elitist character, in part resulting from a relative scarcity of clubs and the limited channels of communication (there was no internet or mobile phones in Poland for most of the 1990s). Clubs did not advertise themselves and to be allowed entrance, one had to know somebody who knew a given place. The bouncers selected the visitors on the basis of appearance, making sure that 'dresiarze' (the Polish equivalent of 'chavs') did not enter such exclusive places. The clubs typically presented an eclectic programme, often offering instrumental electronic music along with hip-hop and rock music. That said, the closer we come to the year 2000, the more 'club music' or 'techno' became separated from other types of music. As in other places, people living in close proximity to clubs complained about noise, which often led to signing petitions and counter-petitions. In some cases, it was an important factor in closing of clubs, as in the case of New Alcatraz in Łódź.

The development of techno culture in Poland was more often met with criticism than enthusiasm. The majority of articles devoted to this phenomenon, published by magazines such as *Techno Party* or *Plastik*, are negative in tone, listing problems preventing cities like Warsaw or Łódź from rising to the level of not only Berlin or Vienna but even Budapest, Prague or Bratislava. For example, in a discussion with leading Polish DJs and promoters of techno music, published by *Techno Party*, the participants complained about the scarcity of clubs and the low spending power of Poles which means that the ticket prices had to be kept low, which precluded employing DJ stars from the West. Furthermore, they pointed to a tension between keeping techno as a niche and elitist pursuit and a demand to open it up, make it more mainstream, in order to make it profitable, and the difficulty to support oneself from techno music, experienced by even the most acclaimed DJs (rik 1998; Winczewski and Borzym 2000). These problems were not exclusive to the Polish context. What was, however, characteristic of Poland was the heightened anxiety to keep techno underground, avoiding its transformation into urban version of 'disco polo' (Sesin, quoted in rik 1998: 14). As in an earlier period, when DJs were reluctant to play disco music in discotheques, because they wanted them to be 'temples of elite taste', this anxiety reflected nervousness of the Polish intelligentsia about losing its privileged status, on this occasion resulting from the country becoming like any other capitalist country, where the most important capital is monetary capital, unlike cultural capital, as was the case under state socialism.

Disco polo in the 1990s

As with techno, for disco polo the 1990s was a time of building up an infrastructure and scene, namely channels through which producers and consumers of music can communicate. The most important of those were setting up record labels, channels of distribution and clubs (Borys 2019). Probably the first disco polo label was Blue Star, set up in 1990 by Sławomir Skręta in Reguły near Warsaw. Here the first stars of this genre such as Bayer Full, Shazza and Fanatic made their records. Blue Star also acted as a recording studio and a booking agency for its stars.

The next crop of labels appeared in the Białystok region in the East of Poland, where disco music was particularly popular. It started with the firm JNW owned by Jarosław Woźniewski, who produced the first two cassettes of the band Akcent ('Z chodnika do Panderozy' 95: 14). However, subsequently the label which dominated the market in this region was Green Star, set up in 1994 and owned by Jerzy Suszycki (Borys 2019: 58–9). Suszycki started his career in the music business as an owner of a record shop, which he opened in Białystok in 1986. There he was selling music from all over the world, including hard rock. However, the fact that its customers were seeking disco polo music (which did not even have this name then) gave him the idea to produce and distribute such records. First, he did so in collaboration with Blue Star and in due course independently. Subsequently, some of the most successful artists also set up their own labels.

Distribution of disco polo records in 1990s was facilitated by the type of unregulated capitalism, which flourished after the fall of the Berlin Wall all over Eastern Europe. It was epitomized by folded chairs on the edges of pavements, from which small entrepreneurs sold legal or illegal cassettes; hundreds of thousands of cassettes with disco polo were sold at the disused Stadion Dziesięciolecia (The Ten-Years Stadium), in Poland labelled the largest bazaar in Europe. A large proportion of the cassettes were pirated, but given the number of those which were sold, the remainder allowed their producers and artists to flourish. Their sales were also boosted by production of videos, whose natural home became the privately owned satellite channel Polsat (Borys 2019: 66–73).

At the same time as investing in recording, the creators worked on improving the infrastructure for live music. The previously mentioned Suszycki opened the first disco polo club (which he describes as a 'country discotheque'), 'Panderoza', in his home town Janów. Throughout the 1990s, fifty more such clubs were open, usually in rural areas, either in already existing buildings, such as barns and fire station, or later in specially constructed buildings ('Z chodnika do Panderozy' 95). Such buildings could host between 400 to over 1,000 people and typically offered its guests food and alcohol. The existence of such places was very important in the light of the fact that initially mainstream media shunned disco polo. The popularity of specific artists was thus achieved by live performance. Only after a specific band of performer gained 'street credibility' were they offered a record deal. However, even then the main source of income of the artists was playing at large events, such as weddings and country festivals.

Disco polo and techno in the eyes of Polish cultural elites

As I previously mentioned, after the Second World War there was a certain uneasiness in Poland about music used simply for entertainment, as it was expected that music should be educational and ideologically sound. This was reflected in class-coloured criticism of discotheques. However, this criticism was moderate when compared with the attacks of the cultural elites on disco polo, and it was limited to the field of music. By contrast, disco polo was seen as not only a musical but also a wider social and political phenomenon. In 1996 an eminent Polish film critic, Tadeusz Sobolewski, wrote an article, entitled 'Empty Beach', in which he presented disco polo as a symbol of the malaise of Polish culture post-1989. For Sobolewski, disco polo contaminated and displaced the dissident culture of artists such as Andrzej Wajda and Krzysztof Kieślowski, who during state socialism offered both an utopian moment and a deeper engagement with reality (Sobolewski 1996: 5). Sobolewski's fear of contamination of high culture by disco polo 'trash', which evokes Adorno's critique of mass culture, appears even stronger than that of emptiness. This is due to the fact that contamination of the 'popular high culture' with disco polo also brings a risk of displacing and rendering obsolete the old-style cultural critic (like Sobolewski) as a gatekeeper to the arcane knowledge of 'true and great' art. Predictably, although this article is ostensibly devoted to disco polo, the author writes almost nothing about this music as a specific genre. For Sobolewski the songs and stars of disco polo are interchangeable, in the same way that jazz compositions and jazz musicians were interchangeable for Adorno. In the same year, one of the most acclaimed Polish documentarists, Maria Zmarz-Koczanowicz made a documentary *Bara bara* (*Hanky Panky*, 1996) about disco polo, consisting of interviews with leading representatives of this genre, fragments of their performances, as well as presenting spaces where this genre is produced and consumed. Among the interviewees are Sławomir Skręta, who set up the recording studio and label Blue Star, Sławomir Świerzyński, leader of the band Bayer Full and Shazza, the main female star of disco polo. Throughout the film disco polo is presented as a lucrative business. Skręta explains the rationale for setting up Blue Star in terms of filling a gap in the market, rather than promoting music which he particularly enjoys and neither of the performers mentions their attachment to this music. Its importance is explained by its value to their fans rather than the artists themselves. We see a secretary working in Blue Star, negotiating a deal with a customer, wanting to book a band for a wedding. The discussion can be compared to that of negotiating the sale of any other commodity. Shazza and Świerzyński reveal how making disco polo music saved them from performing more mundane jobs, such as in the case of Shazza entering data onto a computer and Świerzyński, cutting the grass in the houses of rich Americans. A disco polo musician thus comes across not as an autonomous artist or a professional with high capital but as an amateur, who makes up for deficiencies in his or her talent and education with entrepreneurial spirit. This happens by following well-established recipes for success, such as projecting an image of success irrespective of one's actual situation, rather than creating one's own unique path to attainment. This point is reinforced by the film's mise-en-scene. The camera focuses on images of success achieved by the people linked to disco polo. On numerous occasions we see a villa where the Blue Star studio is located and the background of one of the interviews is most likely a car showroom, with several expensive cars behind the back of the interviewee. Zmarz-Koczanowicz also suggests that money generated by disco polo is of a nouveau riche type. This point is most conspicuously made by showing in close-up clay garden gnomes in front of Blue Star studio, associated with bad taste and large clay dogs which can be seen as bad taste multiplied.

Producing disco polo music comes across in *Hanky Panky* as a Fordist production: it consists of following the same formula, which, as Świerzyński explains, is based on the scheme of polka. The simplicity of disco polo in Zmarz-Koczanowicz's film is explained by crude exploitation of naive fans by its producers. This connection is shown by images from a bazaar where we see many traders from the East, playing disco polo songs on a keyboard which reduces the music to a few badly performed cords. Those who trade in disco polo, not unlike the musicians themselves, lack emotional attachment to their fare and are ignorant about what it contains, as shown in an episode where a woman selling cassettes on a stall reads in a monotonous voice the titles from the cover, without making any suggestions as to which ones are most suitable for her customer.

Disco polo is presented as music which helps to achieve extra-musical objectives, such as celebrating a family gathering or presenting a politician in a positive light, rather than existing for and by itself, as is the case with music created by romantic artists. Zmarz-Koczanowicz also draws attention to the sexual nature of disco polo performances, especially by female singers, where the camera lingers on the legs and bottoms of the singers. This aspect is also underscored by the title of the film, taken from a song by the band Milano, which is also a colloquial and semi-vulgar description of a sexual act. Eroticism, as Richard Dyer argues, is a crucial characteristic of disco and the author claims that the advantage of disco is that its eroticism focuses on the whole body, rather than being disembodied and cock-oriented, as is the case with rock (Dyer 1992: 152–4). However, the way Zmarz-Koczanowicz draws attention to the eroticism of disco polo spectacles renders them sleazy.

Six years after *Hanky Panky* Zmarz-Koczanowicz directed *Miłość do płyty winylowej* (*Love for a Vinyl Record*, 2002) about Polish techno culture, in this way covering the two most important genres of Polish EDM music. The time gap between these two films can be explained by the fact that techno entered Polish dance scene later than disco polo. A different attitude to this genre is signalled by the title of Zmarz-Koczanowicz's film. While 'bara bara' points to disco polo being a low, 'body genre', not unlike disco at large, *Love for a Vinyl Record* points to a much nobler attitude to music on the part of techno producers and consumers. This difference is confirmed in interviews with three leading Polish DJs, specializing in techno: Angelo Mike, Insane and Edee Dee. Unlike the stars of disco polo, they hardly talk about their involvement in techno as a form of business but ponder on it as a quasi-religious experience, claiming that techno allowed them to escape mundane life and access the core of their existence. Thus, paradoxically, although techno uses complex technology, it is a means of regaining lost innocence. The fusion of technology and nature is underscored in an episode where Angelo Mike says that we decide ourselves what is music and illustrate this fact by mentioning that a bird singing against the background of a moving train creates a perfect sound. Techno is like the bird singing combined with the noise emitted by a train: it has a purity of nature and the intoxicating rhythm of industry.

While production of disco polo was framed by Zmarz-Koczanowicz as a conveyor belt industry, leaving little scope for individualism and virtuosity, the director suggests that success in techno is based on combining hard work with a desire for personal expression. This aspect is highlighted by Edee Dee, who mentions that every day he spends long hours practising DJing and other skills required to be a successful techno artist. The virtuosity is accentuated by close-ups of DJs' hands touching the records, especially Edee Dee's. This contrasts with the way the performance of disco polo artists was presented by Zmarz-Koczanowicz, where the camera, in a highly objectifying way, focused on legs and bottoms of female performers. The interviewed DJs also evoke the concept of research, of making music as a form of learning about music, which brings association with Brian Eno's take on a 'studio musician' as a new type of musician as a researcher (Eno 2004). The idea that a DJ is not an artist in the old sense, namely somebody producing artefacts from scratch, is presented as an advantage as it allows him to remain mysterious and at some distance from the audience. DJs cast by Zmarz-Koczanowicz reject the idea of a pop star, regarding stardom as vulgar and an obstacle to cultivating one's love of music.

The importance of money is played down by the Polish DJs. While disco polo songs, as presented by Zmarz-Koczanowicz in *Hanky Panky*, were written with the intention of affording their producers and promotors a comfortable life, in the case of techno, profit appears to be merely a by-product of its development. Similarly as having little to do with money, techno artists are presented as being apolitical. Angelo Mike mentions that he knows nothing about politics and only recently learnt that there was a recession in Poland. He describes fans of techno as new hippies who escape a bourgeois existence marked by the pursuit of family and money. At the same time, however, he states with pride that their audience consists mostly of 'serious people employed in serious firms'. He also mentions that techno events have elitist characters; the guests are selected on the spot and so-called tracksuit trouser man (*dresiarz*) is not allowed to enter. The term *dresiarz* connotes an unruly working-class man and a provincial, the Polish equivalent of the British 'chav'. The DJ adds with regret that in some cases selection of the audience is not possible. The implicit assumption is that techno events are for representatives of higher classes. The concept of class is also evoked obliquely by mentioning Europe. The clubs where techno is played are described as 'European'. This term is implicitly contrasted with 'Polish', which means provincial and 'chav'. In this way there is a fit between techno artists and their fans. They are also connected by their individualism. Although techno raves gather thousands of people, Angelo Mike claims that the music does not connect the dancers with each other but with their inner selves. They dance and experience music solo.

The film finishes with an image of Polish techno fans attending Love Parade in Berlin. This image can be read as a symbol of Poland's road towards the

European Union. The ending to *Love for a Vinyl Record* can be compared to the beginning of *Hanky Panky*, where we saw people dancing to the disco hit 'Macarena', as both point to the international connections of the respective phenomena. However, the connotations of these two episodes cannot be more different. In *Hanky Panky* foreign music is brought to Poland for Poles to engage in some kind of mimicry. In *Love for a Vinyl Record* Polish techno fans are part of a colourful crowd, engaged in a cosmopolitan event, where there are no 'natives' and 'guests'; everybody is European and equal.

Almost twenty years has passed since *Love to a Vinyl Record* was made. Since then techno in Poland fragmented into different styles and disco polo hybridized with genres such as hip-hop. However, the prejudice against disco polo remained, although it mellowed. This music no longer symbolizes the wrong turn which Poland took after the end of state socialism, but just music for the masses living in the province over which the elites feel superior, but whose right to enjoy music of their choice they grudgingly accept. This acceptance reflects a wider cultural shift, marked by democratization of culture and a loss of cultural leaders, following the spread of the internet and the social media.

Conclusions

In this chapter I presented a brief history of dancing cultures in Poland from the perspective of social class. I argued that during the interbellum dancing was relatively apolitical activity. Under state socialism 'simple dancing' was frowned upon, as leisure was expected to be a form of education. In due course the most popular form of dance music, disco polo, was criticized by cultural elites for lacking in educational value and corrupting Polish society by its simple lyrics, melodies and its message to have fun. This criticism resulted from an anxiety of these elites about losing their status as trendsetters, in a situation when monetary capital gained in value and cultural capital was degraded. This anxiety has been justified, as proved by the fact that the position of cultural elites in postcommunist Poland has been weaker than under state socialism. The public condemnation of disco polo and its banning from most media outlets did not prevent it from becoming commercially the most successful genre of popular music in Poland – due to its adaptability, optimism and bottom-up approach – giving the listeners what they want, rather than demanding that they choose 'what is good for them'.

Works cited

Boćkowska, Aleksandra (2018). 'DJ z PRL-u: W ZSRR grałem dla 3 tys. ludzi. W Polsce dla ambasady amerykańskiej', Gazeta Wyborcza, http://weekend.gazeta.pl/weekend/1,152121,22224061,dj-z-prl-u-w-zsrr-gralem-dla-3-tys-ludzi-na-imprezie-dla.html, accessed 30 June 2018.

Błażejewski, Krzysztof (2011). 'Dancingowe mordownie PRL', *Express Bydgoski*, 29 July, http://www.expressbydgoski.pl/archiwum/a/dancingowe-mordownie-prl,11007133/, accessed 30 June 2018.

Blüml, Jan (2019). 'Czech Popular Music before 1989 and the Institution of the "Discotheque"', in Jan Blüml, Yvetta Kajanova and Rüdiger Ritter (eds), *Popular Music in Communist and Post-Communist Europe*. Oxford: Peter Lang, pp. 99–112.

Born, Georgina (2011). 'Music and the Materialization of Identities', *Journal of Material Culture*, 4, pp. 376–88.

Borys, Monika (2019). *Polski Bajer: Disco Polo i Lata 90*. Warszawa: WAB.

Bourdieu, Pierre (2010) [1984]. *Distinction: A Social Critique of the Judgement of Taste*. London: Routledge.

Danielewicz, Stanisław and Marcin Jacobson (2017). *Rockowisko Trójmiasta: Lata 70*. Pelplin: Bernardinum.

Dubrowska, Magdalena (2017). 'Techno, Wisła i odpicowany golf. Wystawa o kulturze rave i latach 90. w Muzeum Sztuki Nowoczesnej', *Gazeta Wyborcza*, 24 July, http://cojestgrane24.wyborcza.pl/cjg24/1,13,22123281,146950,Techno--Wisla-i-odpicowany-golf--Wystawa-o-kulturz.html, accessed 4 December 2018.

Dyer, Richard (1992). 'In Defence of Disco', in his *Only Entertainment*. London: Routledge, pp. 149–58.

Eno, Brian (2004). 'The Studio as Compositional Tool', in Christoph Cox and Daniel Warner (eds), *Audio Culture: Readings in Modern Music*. London: Continuum, pp. 127–30.

rik (1998). 'Kultura, która się tworzy: Debata didżejska', *Techno Party*, 7, pp. 13–5.

Kaazetka (2001). 'Łódź techniczna tańczy', *Laif*, 2, pp. 40–7.

Kasprzycki, Remigiusz (2013). *Dekada buntu. Punk w Polsce i krajach sąsiednich w latach 1977–1989*. Kraków: Libron.

Kowalewicz, Krzysztof (2003). 'Koniec klubu Forum Fabricum', *Gazeta Wyborcza*, 19 May, http://lodz.wyborcza.pl/lodz/1,35135,1485996.html, accessed 28 November 2018.

Krasnow, Carolyn H. (2000). 'Two Popular Dance Forms', in *Garland Encyclopedia of World Music*, Volume 3: The United States and Canada. London: Routledge.

Kveberg, Gregory (2015). 'Shostakovich versus Boney M.: Culture, Status, and History in the Debate over Soviet Diskoteki', in William Jay Risch (ed.), *Youth and Rock in the Soviet Bloc: Youth Cultures, Music, and the State in Russia and Eastern Europe*. Lanham: Lexington Books, pp. 211–27.

Łozińscy, Maja i Jan (2011). *W przedwojennej Polsce: Życie codzienne i niecodzienne.* Warszawa: Wydawnictwo Naukowe PWN.

Mazierska, Ewa (2021). *Polish Popular Music on Screen.* London: Palgrave.

'Muzyka Polskiej Polonii' (2014). *Prawicowy Internet*, 5 November, https://prawicowyinternet.pl/muzyka-polskiej-polonii/, accessed 16 October 2017.

Ostap, Mic (2002). 'Polska techniczna', *Laif*, 9, pp. 62–3.

Puchalski, Piotr (2016). 'Pierwsza polska dyskoteka? To było coś niesamowitego. Ludzie czekali na odpalenie stroboskopu', *Radio Gdańsk*, 29 April, https://radiogdansk.pl/component/k2/item/41388/41388, accessed 27 June 2018.

Sobolewski, Tadeusz (1996). 'Pusta plaża', *Tygodnik Powszechny*, 31, pp. 1 and 5.

Straw, Will (2001). 'Dance Music', in Simon Frith, Will Straw and John Street (eds), *The Cambridge Companion to Pop and Rock*. Cambridge: Cambridge University Press, pp. 158–75.

Thornton, Sarah (1995). *Club Cultures: Music, Media and Subcultural Capital.* London: Polity.

Walicki, Franciszek (1984). 'Wprowadzenie', in Marek Gaszynski and Adam Halber (eds), *ABC Prezentera dyskoteki*. Warszawa: Centralny Osrodek Metodyki Upowszechniania Kultury, pp. 3–11.

Walicki, Franciszek (1995). *Szukaj, burz, buduj.* Warszawa: TRZ.

Winczewski, Bartek and Robert Borzym (2000). 'Taniec jest dla elit?', *Machina*, 5, pp. 64–5.

Zakrzewski, Patryk (2016). 'Na dancingach i na dechach, czyli polskie parkiety XX wieku', *Culture.pl*, 31 December, https://culture.pl/pl/artykul/na-dancingach-i-na-dechach-czyli-polskie-parkiety-xx-wieku, accessed 23 June 2018.

'Z chodnika do Panderozy' (1995). *Disco Polo*, 1, 2, 3, pp. 14, 15, 14.

Zubak, Marko (2016). 'The Birth of Socialist Disc Jockey: Between Music Guru, DIY Ethos and Market Socialism', in Ewa Mazierska (ed.), *Popular Music in Eastern Europe: Breaking the Cold War Paradigm*. London: Palgrave, pp. 195–214.

Notes

Chapter 1

1 'The discourse community of electronic dance music is a multi-layered entity: it includes all people that are interested in electronic dance music and willing to communicate on such topics' (Jóri 2016).
2 The biggest advantage of the archive is that the scanned magazines have been processed by optical character recognition (OCR), which makes it possible to search for terms and text passages (full-text search).
3 An obstacle when performing full-text searches in a PDF is that the term is interrupted by a line or page break, it is possible that it cannot be identified by the search algorithm. Therefore, maybe my findings do not show the exact numbers.
4 I maintain these language samples without names in order to keep the anonymity of the forum participants. However, one can trace their sources back from the public forum thread (Ableton Forums 2006).
5 I added the German terms in square brackets in order to keep the original terminology.
6 The German '*Elektro*' with 'k' is often used as a shortened version of electronic music (*elektronische Musik*), mostly in mainstream discourses. See more about the same issue in French-speaking context in the next chapter.

Chapter 2

1 A recent illustration can be found in Gérôme Guibert, Catherine Rudent (eds), *Made in France: Studies in Popular Music* (New York: Routledge, 2018). The third part of the book, which focuses on 'French specificity', only deals with vocal genres such as *chanson française*, punk rock and rap.
2 We will consider the first house and techno records to be Jesse Saunders, *On & On* (Chicago: Jes Say Records, JS9999, 1984) and X-Ray, *Let's Go* (Detroit: Transmat, MS001, 1986), respectively.
3 *Saturday Night Fever* was based upon Nik Cohn's report of 7 June, 1976, for *New York* magazine, titled 'Tribal Rites of the New Saturday Night'. In 1997, *New York* magazine published an article in which Cohn confessed the complete fabrication

of said report. Nik Cohn, 'Saturday Night's Big Bang', *New York*, 8 December 1997, p. 34.

4   British readers will be well aware of the role played by Ibiza's club culture in sparking the British Second Summer of Love (1988–89), through clubs and parties such as Future (Paul Oakenfold, London), Shoom (Danny Rampling, London), Trip (Nicky Holloway, London) and the Haçienda and its Nude Nights (Mike Pickering and Graeme Park, Manchester).

5   While other closing times have been reported, the issue at hand is that clubs had to close before the partygoers wanted them to.

6   Major EBM bands include Nitzer Ebb, Portion Control and Throbbing Gristle (UK), Cabaret Voltaire, D.A.F., Front 242, Die Krupps and Liaisons Dangereuses (Germany), A Split-Second, à;GRUMH and the Neon Judgement (Belgium).

7   Bara notes that these figures, provided by the SNEP (*Syndicat national de l'édition phonographique*, National Union of Phonographic Publishing), exclude most of the production and distribution of independent labels and are therefore 'far from the mark'. It is also important to remember that vinyl sales, while driven by underground electronic dance music, were also supported by rap.

8   *Les victoires de la musique* are the French equivalent to the Grammy Awards and the Brit Awards.

9   Using the chartsinfrance.net database, we calculated that during the year 1993, an average of only fourteen out of the fifty bestselling music singles in France were French songs.

10 Etienne de Crécy, *Super Discount*, Disques Solid, SLD 007 CD, 1996.

11 Created in 1993, Le Bureau Export describes itself as 'a non-profit professional organisation with the aim of developing music made in France all around the world'.

12 Electronic exchanges with Martin James quoted here took place on 13 December 2009.

13 As of 10 June 2020 these quotes are available on the following media's websites: Arte, *Le Courier Picard*, *Les Échos*, Europe 1, *L'Express*, France 24, *Le Monde*, *Le Parisien*, *Le Point*, RTL, TV5 Monde, *La Voix du Nord*.

14 https://www.ouest-france.fr/culture/musiques/deces-du-compositeur-pierre-henry-grand-inspirateur-de-la-musique-techno-5116857, accessed 10 June 2020.

15 http://www.lci.fr/musique/video-mort-de-pierre-henry-maitre-de-la-musique-electro-et-inspirateur-des-daft-punk-2057718.html, accessed 10 June 2020.

16 http://www.francesoir.fr/actualites-france/deces-du-compositeur-francais-pierre-henry-maitre-de-la-musique-electroacoustique, accessed 10 June 2020.

17 In 2018, *Le Monde* published an online section titled 'The French Touch Conquering the World', cataloguing various French international successes in 'gastronomy, fashion, oenology, perfumery, luxury, mathematics and robotics'.

https://www.lemonde.fr/campus/article/2018/06/05/la-french-touch-a-la-conquete-du-monde_5309790_4401467.html, accessed 10 June 2020.
18 The very title of this EP is another stimulating fact, as Martin James told us that by writing 'French touch [he] was trying to allude to French film making where a generic style wasn't clearly defined but the use of mood, colour and style was'.
19 Farley 'Jackmaster' Funk & Jessie Saunders, *Love Can't Turn Around*, Chicago: House Records, FU-10, 1986. Garnier 2003: 9.
20 Laurent Garnier's first EP, *As French Connection*, logically contained acid house reminiscing of his early *Mancunian Nights*, but even on *Planet House EP* or the single-sided *Wake Up!*, subtitled *One Year of Music for House Music Lovers*, Garnier would not deviate from a techno aesthetic, heavily influenced by Detroit's style.
21 The Parisian house identified as the French Touch was naturally only part of the French electronic scene, rich of various electro or techno local scenes, for instance in Dijon (L'An-Fer club, Vitalic) or Grenoble (Kiko, Miss Kittin & The Hacker, Oxia). While based in Paris, let us also note that Laurent Garnier's F-Communications label was known for its eclecticism, with only a minor part of its catalogue devoted to house.
22 Such as Yellow Productions' *Funky Flute* (1994), Cutee B's *Fonky First* (1994), The Micronauts' *Get Funky Get Down* (1995), Arnaud Rebotini's *Funkhipa* (1995), DJ Gilb-R's *Espèce Funk* (1995), Paris Angeles's *Retour Funk* (1998), Pépé Bradock's *Atom Funk* (1998), Superfunk's *La Guerre du Funk* (1998), Didier Sinclair's *Funky Taste* (1999), Etienne de Crécy's *Disco Down Town* (2000) and Bob Sinclar's *A Space Funk Project* (1996), *Space Funk Project 2* (1997), *Ultimate Funk* (1998), *Super Funky Brake's* (1998) and *Disco 2000 Selector* (1998), to name a few.
23 The Black Eyed Peas, Lil' Wayne, Madonna, Nicki Minaj, Rihanna, Kelly Rowland, Snoop Dogg, Will.I.Am and so on.
24 The breakdown of these statistics (average tempo, average duration per album) is as follows: *Just a Little More Love* (2002): 121 bpm, 3:32. *Guetta Blaster* (2004): 127 bpm, 4:05. *Pop Life* (2007): 129 bpm, 3:57. *One Love* (2009): 124 bpm, 3:52. *One More Love* (2010): 127 bpm, 4:00. *Nothing But the Beat* (2011): 127 bpm, 3:32 (vocal CD)/128 bpm, 4:53 (instrumental CD). *Nothing But the Beat 2.0* (2012): 128 bpm, 3:32 (vocal CD)/127 bpm, 4:05 (instrumental CD). *Listen* (2014): 124 bpm, 3:42. The instrumental CD of *7* (2018) observes similar values: 124 bpm and 3:35.
25 The five singles extracted from this album are *Give Life Back to Music* (4:35, 119 bpm), *Get Lucky* (6:10, 116 bpm), *Lose Yourself to Dance* (5:54, 100 bpm), *Instant Crush* (5:38, 110 bpm), *Doin' It Right* (4:11, 89 bpm).
26 In French, *musique contemporaine* ('contemporary music') refers to contemporary classical music. The Ensemble Intercontemporain is an ensemble founded in 1976 by Pierre Boulez to perform and promote said music. The IRCAM was managed by Boulez until 1992.

27 This pattern, enclosed in a 4/4 time signature, consists of two rhythmic elements. A bass drum sound obeys the following pattern: dotted eight note, dotted eight note, quarter note, dotted quarter note. Simultaneously, the second and fourth beats will be accentuated, usually by a hi-hat sound.

28 Atkins remembers that his track '*Cosmic Cars* came out at the same time *Planet Rock* came out. The only thing was that *Planet Rock* was made in New York. They had the advantage of having the media behind them'. https://www.laweekly.com/an-interview-with-techno-kingpin-juan-atkins-l-a-is-still-behind-the-curve-three-or-four-years/, accessed 10 June 2020. We would like to mention that contrary to *Planet Rock* which sampled Kraftwerk's *Trans-Europe Express*, Atkins never used samples.

29 Eddie 'Flashin' Fowlkes, *Goodbye Kiss* (Detroit: Metroplex, M-006). Derrick May as X-Ray, *Let's Go* (Detroit: Transmat, MS001). Kevin Saunderson as Kreem, *Triangle of Love* (Detroit: Metroplex, M-007).

30 A simple analytical tool to distinguish between electro and techno or house is that the former does not adopt the four-to-the-floor rhythm pattern. An additional specification is that at this point in time, Atkins had already produced four-to-the-floor tracks but those were only instrumental versions of originally sung tunes, contrary to May's composition which did not derive from a song. It may be significant to note that Atkins did not want this track to be released or be mentioned on the records' labels, hence its lack of title.

31 Mike Banks as Underground Resistance, *The Final Frontier*, Detroit: Underground Resistance, UR 003, 1991. Mike Banks founded Underground Resistance with Jeff Mills in 1989, but his career as an electronic musician started with Members of the House, an house and garage house collective. Atkins eventually produced proper techno at least from 1987 onwards (Juan Atkins as Triple XXX, *The Bedroom Scene*, Detroit: Express Records, EXP011, 1987).

32 Numerous Detroit labels releasing electro can be listed, such as 430 West, Dataphysix Engineering, Direct Beat, Electrofunk, Metroplex, Motor City Electro Company, Puzzlebox, Underground Resistance, Somewhere in Detroit, Submerge, Twilight 76.

33 On 21 October 2006, 'Roots of Techno: Black DJs and the Detroit Scene', an academic conference on techno music and its African American origins, was already taking place in Indiana University Bloomington.

34 The breakdown of this statistics is as follows: on the week of 26 January 2013, inception of Billboard's Hot Dance/Electronic songs chart, ten entries out of the top forty were produced by American musicians (three of which due to Skrillex), one was Euro-American and four came from other parts of the world (Korea, Canada and two from Australia). Of the twenty-five European entries, eight originated from the UK (three by Calvin Harris), six from Sweden (including one featuring a white

American singer), six from France (five by David Guetta, of which three featured a black American singer), one from Estonia, one from Germany, one from the Netherlands and two were produced by German-Russian musician Zedd. Of these forty entries, thirty-four were produced by white musicians (of which five featured a black singer), three by black musicians, one was Korean and two were racially mixed.

As of 28 December 2019, the top forty of this same chart consists of twelve North American entries, eight of them due to Haitian-Canadian Kaytranada. Four entries are Euro-American productions, two are Canadian, two are Australian and twelve are European (of which four originate from the UK, three from the Netherlands and two from Sweden). Of these forty entries, twenty-six are produced by white musicians (of which four feature a black singer), ten by black musicians (including the eight due to the sole Kaytranada, who produces one white singer), two are racially mixed, one is produced by a musician of Asian descent and one by a musician of Middle Eastern descent.

35 In 'Formal Functions and Rotations in Top-40 EDM', Brad Osborn offers a detailed analysis, demonstrating that 'music charting on the Billboard Top-40 has now absorbed the influence of electronic dance music (EDM) in a way that has fundamentally changed its formal structure. These songs still have verses, but they forgo prechorus and chorus in favor of "riser" and "drop" functions' (Peres 2016), https://guide.societymusictheory.org/sessions/thu/afternoon/form-motive-pop-film-music, accessed 10 June 2020.

36 Data gathered from the discogs.com database on 3 December 2019.

37 https://abcnews.go.com/Nightline/video/david-guetta-latest-album-rise-top-5 8666371, accessed 10 June 2020.

Chapter 3

1 Richard Barratt (DJ Parrot Sweet Exorcist, Add N to X, All Seeing I); Bob Bhamra (WNCL); Andy Carthy (Mr Scruff); Denney (artist and DJ); Paul Hammond (Ultramarine); Aston Harvey (Freestylers, Sol Brothers); Dean Honer (All Seeing I, I Monster, Eccentronic Research Council); Alex Paterson (The Orb); Martin Reeves (Krafty Kuts); Jez Willis (Utah Saints). Semi-structured interviews, in some cases followed up with additional questions and discussion, were conducted between 2011 and 2018.

2 Matt Black and Jonathan Moore who are also the founders of the record label Ninja Tune, to which Andy Carthy is signed under his artist and DJ name Mr Scruff.

3 Steinski has acknowledged the influence of Buchanan and Goodman's break-in records, and *Lesson 3* includes a sample from *The Flying Saucer*.

4 Particularly notable examples in terms of their mainstream success are 'Pump Up the Volume' by M/A/R/R/S, UK# 1, US Dance Chart# 1, 'Theme From S'Express' by S'Express, UK# 1, US Dance Chart# 1, and 'Beat Dis' by Bomb the Bass, UK# 2, US Dance Chart# 1.

5 An informal request to subscribers to the International Association to the Study of Popular Music (IASPM) mailing list about their recollections of the availability of FE or HE music technology and music production courses in the UK between 1985 and 1995 indicated that there was limited availability before 1992 and a steady proliferation of courses thereafter. While this remains anecdotal evidence, it is relatively authoritative because respondents were either academics responsible for initiating such provision or current incumbents at FE or HE providers with an awareness of the history of their courses.

6 It has been argued that a similar lack of user knowledge informed the tempo of grime; many early producers used the DAW Fruity Loops (later FL Studio), which had a default tempo of 140 bpm (the standard tempo of grime), and Wiley, a pioneer of the genre notes in his autobiography that he made his early tracks at 140 bpm for that reason.

7 Other tracks besides *Charly* by the Prodigy released in 1991 included *Summers Magic* by Mark Summers, featuring a sample of the theme tune to the cartoon *Magic Roundabout* and a bassline sampled from *Expansions* by Lonnie Liston Smith, and *Roobarb and Custard* by Shaft, which featured the theme tune to the cartoon of the same name, which also happened to be the name of a popular make of Ecstasy tablet at the time.

8 Other key sociocultural developments besides the availability of affordable digital sampling technology – the final years of Thatcherism, the wide-scale introduction of Ecstasy to the UK and the rave culture that this helped to create, for example – were also important in the development of UK sampling practice but are beyond the scope of discussion of this chapter.

Chapter 5

1 For a history of the DJ, see Brewster and Broughton (2006) and Poschard (2015).
2 Hall and Zukic also point to female DJs such as Mia Moretti, KaFemme, Mis Kittin and Smoking Jo but confirm a dominance of male DJs within the DJ culture. For detailed discussions on gender and DJing, see Reitsamer (2011), Gavanas and Reitsamer (2013, 2016), Farrugia (2012) and Farrugia and Swiss (2008).
3 Translation: MP.
4 These statements are taken from the artist's homepage aviciitruestories.com (accessed 12 August 2020).

5 After his death, Avicii's family shared in their farewell letter that he was a seeker, a 'fragile artistic soul searching for answering to existential questions'.
6 This becomes especially apparent in the context of the Tomorrowland Festival: it is part of the marketing of the festival that visitors, when entering the festival grounds, are supposed to find themselves in a different world, which is supposed to enable them to forget their problems and worries and fully devote themselves to Tomorrowland (Wernke-Schmiesing 2015; see also Holt 2016).
7 This post (the last before Bergling's death) was published on Avicii's Facebook account on 1 April 2018.
8 See https://aviciiexperience.com (accessed 14 August 2020).

Chapter 6

1 During that Grammy Awards, Grohl delivered an acceptance speech that some saw as a jab at electronic music. The frontman later walked back the speech in a lengthy Facebook post where he praised all kinds of music, electronic or otherwise. Read the post at https://www.facebook.com/foofighters/posts/10151306962865545.

Chapter 7

1 For more on the standard formal structure of EDM tracks, see Butler (2006: chap. 6), Snoman (2019: chap. 26), and Solberg (2014).
2 Another part of deadmau5's masterclass that expresses his strong desire for originality is his lesson on 'Experimenting with Modular Synths'. Modular synthesizers are not very commonly used in contemporary music production, and deadmau5 is known as an artist that uses them. They are associated with originality, because their sounds are notoriously hard to reproduce or regenerate on command.
3 'Big room' (sometimes called 'big room house') is an EDM genre associated with large events such as concerts in arenas and festivals in outdoor spaces. It is associated with popularity, the mainstream, and musically, with clear melodies and drops. Deadmau5 is speaking in broad terms here, saying that many of his popular tracks could fall within the umbrella of 'big room house' but that other tracks on *While(1<2)* do not fit under that umbrella at all.
4 Tracks on *While(1<2)* that have a typical dance structure and/or style include 'Infra Turbo Pigcart Racer', 'Mercedes', 'Pets' and 'Phantoms Can't Hang'. Those that do not have a typical dance structure and/or style include 'Invidia', 'Ira', 'Monday', 'Silent Picture', 'Somewhere Up Here' and 'Superbia' (which are predominantly calm

and acoustic), as well as 'A Moment to Myself', 'Bleed', 'Creep' and 'Errors in My Bread' (which are predominantly electronic but not EDM).

5   He also expresses similar thoughts about entire albums in a podcast from 2018, saying that his album *where's the drop?* (2018) is 'more of a side project' and that his upcoming album will be more appreciated by his fans because it is 'more akin to what people usually hear from me', that is, 'dance music' (H3 Podcast 2018).

6   He expresses a similar thought in the 2014 interview discussed earlier, when he says 'if I wanted to I could make one dance hit, and then I'd go into real estate' (Canadian Music Week 2014: 49:28).

7   This is one of his most famous and beloved tracks despite him not originally liking it very much and almost scrapping it before putting it out, as explained in Amazon Live (2020).

8   He even released an album of orchestral arrangements of his pieces titled *where's the drop?* (2018), followed by an album of remixes (by other artists) of those orchestral arrangements (*here's the drop*, 2019).

9   For a list of many of deadmau5's collaborators, see (Rishty 2019).

10 He says, 'I can get along with just about anyone', but that 'do I even like you as a human being?' is 'the first thing on the checklist' (Canadian Music Week 2014).

11 Also, deadmau5 has occasionally collaborated with Steve Duda to form a duo called BSOD, which 'according to a press release "could be short for Blue Screen of Death or Better Sounding on Drugs"' (Bain 2020).

12 He often makes this distinction and does not want to be called a DJ (Horgen 2010).

13 For a list of his concert performances, see 'Deadmau5's Concert & Tour History | Concert Archives, n.d..

14 Deadmau5 talks about this in an interview, saying that big festivals should be focused more on promoting the artists than promoting the brand of the festival (Canadian Music Week 2014: 35:15).

15 For a list of deadmau5's concert performances, including those at festivals, see 'Deadmau5's Concert & Tour History | Concert Archives, n.d..

16 Another instance of him calling out performers for doing this is discussed in C. Smith (2015).

17 An example of this can be seen at the beginning of this video for the first show on the tour, in Dallas, Texas (Vizsla 2020).

18 In multiple interviews, he recognizes that 'Ghosts 'n' Stuff' is his most popular track. It has remained popular despite being initially released in 2008. In one interview he says he knows that his style has evolved, but he still performs earlier tracks because he does not want to 'alienate his fans' (Canadian Music Week 2014: 40:17). Specifically about 'Ghosts 'n' Stuff', he said 'it means a lot to a lot of kids and people who like that kind of music so I'll embrace that because it's like "hey if makes you happy"'. (Canadian Music Week 2014: 41:47).

19 As of this writing, deadmau5 has accounts on Facebook, Twitter, Instagram, YouTube and Reddit but not other sites such as Tumblr.
20 https://twitter.com/deadmau5/status/1265990309659492356, accessed 22 June 2020 (deadmau5 2020).
21 One notable example of this is an interview for Hot Topic, in which he talks about his hobbies and clearly expresses a preference for playing video games that are innovative and original, before they become very popular (Hot Topic 2015). Two other examples of this are his Q&A for Amazon Live (2020) and his apartment tour video for Coca-Cola and RED in support of an 'AIDS free generation' (Omaze 2014).

Chapter 11

1 The part about dance culture in Poland is in a large part based on a book by Maja i Jan Łozińscy, *W przedwojennej Polsce* (2011: 108–48).
2 The same approach was also taken in relation to Polish popular music performers, whose earnings depended on the category awarded to them by a committee.

Index

1st EP (1993)   50
3,4-Methylenedioxymethamphetamine (MDMA). *See* Ecstasy
4×4=12 (2010)   124
4ware (2016)   148
7 (2018)   55
15 Again (2006)   55
24 Hour Party People (2002)   217
30 (1997)   45
77   247
100% Pure (Amsterdam)   10

ABC   61
A Bed Every Night   219
Ableton   126
Ableton Forums   32
Above & Beyond   137
Absolut Vodka   128
Abs Ward   222
acid house   7, 50, 65, 67, 73, 184, 186, 187, 227
Acid House Bill. *See* Entertainments (Increased Penalties) Act (1990)
Acid Tracks (1987)   67
Activated   29
Act of Creation, The (Koestler)   92
Adagio for Strings (2005)   137
Adelt, Ulric   5
Adria, Warsaw   234
Afrika Bambaataa   59
Afterhours (2007)   151
'Against Interpretation' (Sontag)   15
Agence France Press   49
Age of Chance   186
A Guy Called Gerald   186
Air   49, 50, 51, 52
Air Mail Special (1957)   171
Aiva   86, 90
Akcent   249
Åkerlund, Jonas   124, 137, 138

Alive (1994)   50
Allan, Ruth   220-2, 224
Alleys of Your Mind (1981)   59
allosonic sampling   171
Almond, Marc   183
AlphaZero   89
Amadeus Code   84
A Man Called Adam   213
Amazon Live   156
American Music Awards   34
Amnesia Crew   247
Amper Music   85, 90
Anderson, Penny   216
Anderson, Tammy   30
Anz, Philipp   34
Aoki, Steve   106
Apple Music   85
Arcadia   192
Archies   66
Ark   190
Armstrong, Louis   164
AronChupa   171
Arrest the President (1990)   72
Arte   45
artificial general intelligence (AGI)   83
    artificial intelligence (AI)   16, 17, 81-2
    and EDM artists   83-8, 96-7
    new forms of creativity   88-95
'Artificial Intelligence' (1992)   9-10
artificial narrow intelligence (ANI)   82-3
artificial superintelligence (ASI)   83, 85
Association for Electronic Music (AFEM)   105
Atkins, Juan   58, 59, 67, 260 nn.28, 30
Au Rêve (2002)   55
authenticity   134-9, 145, 146, 148-60, 156
authorship   94
Autopilot   85
autosonic sampling   170-1

Avicii   12, 13, 17, 34, 105–8, 165
   death   105, 115–18
   role as star, lifestyle and health   109–17, 120
Avicii: True Stories (2018)   105, 109–15

Back2Basics   192, 196
Badham, John   8
Bain, Vick   212
Bains Douches   54
Baker, Arthur   183
Bambaataa, Afrika   183
Bandcamp   134
'Bangerang' parties   201
Banks, Mike   59, 260 n.31
Bara, Guillaume   45, 50–2
Bara bara (*Hanky Panky,* 1996)   250–4
Barber, Samuel   137
Barcelona's Primavera   212
Bar-Kays   53
Barker, Hugh   130, 134, 135
Barqué-Duran, Albert   89
Barratt, Richard   76
Bart & Baker   173
Barthes, Roland   87, 92
'The Bash Out' event   200, 201
bassline music   197–8, 200
Bassnectar   132
Bataclan   54
Baudrillard, Jean   88, 93
Baxter, Blake   10
Bayer Full   244, 249, 250
Bayle, Laurent   49, 50, 61
BB. *See* Bushell, Carol
BBDO   130
bEAN, Rush   29
Beatles   66
Beatport   124
Beats of Freedom - Zew wolności (2010)   242
Beaver Works   204
Beckett, Steve   9
Beer, Dave   190, 192, 196, 206
Bellotte, Pete   6
Benjamin, Walter   97
Bennett, Andy   30
Bennett, Joe   73
Bentley, Donna   222

Benton, Brook   169, 171
Bergling, Tim. *See* Avicii
Berlin   8–10, 31, 246, 247, 253
Berlin, Techno und der Easyjetset (Rapp)   35
Bertrand   52
Bhagwan Shree Rajneesh   184
Bhamra, Bob   69, 72
Biało Czerwoni (White-Reds)   243
big beat   65, 72, 78
'Bigger than Barry' event   200
Billboard's Hot Dance/Electronic songs chart   60, 260–1 n.34
Bionic Santa (1976)   66
Björk   53
Black, Matt   68
Black Sabbath   241
Blade   133
Blanc-Francard, Hubert 'Boom Bass'   52
Blaze   29
The Blessed Madonna   117
Blossoms   219
Blueberry Hill Studios   204
blues clubs (shebeens)   187, 188
Blue Star   244, 249, 250, 251
Blüml, Jan   237, 241
Boiler Room   211, 217
Bomb the Bass   186
Bond, Danny   198
Bondi Beach Bar   195
Boney M.   241, 243
Boomtown festival (2015)   174
Borgstedt, Silke   108
Bostrom, Nick   85, 88, 90, 91, 94
Boulez, Pierre   56, 57, 259 n.26
Bourdieu, Pierre   63, 64, 75, 198, 233
Bowie, David   82
breakbeats   65, 182
break-in records   66–9
Brend, Mark   125
Brewster, Bill   25, 30
Britain's Got Talent (TV show)   173
British Academy of Songwriters, Composers and Authors (BASCA)   212
Broad   54
broadcast quotas   47
Broadwick Entertainment   218

Bromski, Jacek 237
Broughton, Frank 25, 30
Brown, Ben 197, 204
Brown, James 71
Brown, Kevin 159
BSOD 159
BT 137
B.Traits 117
Buchanan and Goodman 66
Bucher, Taina 86
Burial 127
Burke, Jim. *See* Mr B the Gentleman Rhymer
Burley 185, 193, 195, 201, 202
Burnard, Pamela 64, 65
Burnham, Andy 219
Burnin' (1997) 53
Bush, Kate 66
Bushell, Carol 221–3, 225, 227, 228
Butler, Mark J. 5, 26, 31, 61, 152, 155
Byrd, Bobby 67
Byrne, David 89

Cabbage 194
Cage, John 85, 92
Can 5–6
Canal Mills 204
Carlton Club 222
Carré, Benoit 85
Carter, Andrew 201
Carter, Derrick 196
Carthy, Andy 66, 67, 69, 74
'Casa Loco' event 201
Cassius 52, 55
CBC 135
celebrity 164, 176. *See also* stardom
  changing face of 165–8
  status 165
Centre for Ageing Better 215
Cerboneschi, Philippe 'Zdar' 49, 52
Chainsmokers 34
Chalmers, David J. 94
chanson 45
Chapeltown 187, 188
Chapman, Tracy 158
Charly (1991) 76
Chase the Devil (1976) 72
Che, Deborah 7

Cheap Records 7
Chic 53
Chicago house 7, 51, 53, 70, 75, 184
Chislenko, Alexander 92
Ciel mon mardi 44
Circulaire Pasqua 44
Cité de la Musique 49
City Talking: Music in Leeds, The - Volume I (2015) 193
Clarke, John Cooper 219
Clinton, George 58, 59
closed-circuit synthesizers 125
Club Brenda 220, 228
Club Cultures: Music, Media, and Subcultural Capital (Thornton) 30, 129
Club Des Belugas 171, 173
Club of the Friends of Czerniaków (Towarzystwo Przyjaciół Czerniakowa) 234
Cobain, Kurt 116
Cohen, Lorna 193
Coldcut 67–9, 76, 186
collective superintelligence 91–2
Collier, Ken 58
Collin, Matthew 13
Collins, Nick 4, 27
Columbia Records 55
Communic8r 29
Complete Event Solutions 202
Computer and the Brain, The (von Neumann) 88
Concrete 56
Constable, Paulette 211, 217, 220, 221, 223–5, 227, 228
'Contemporary Dance Music and Club Cultures' (Bennett) 30
Cooke, Alistair 190, 192
copyright 74, 76, 78, 94
Correspondents 173
Cotgrove, Mark 166
Counting the Music Industry: The Gender Pay Gap 212
Courteeners 219
Cowdrey, Luke 225
Cox, Carl 117, 191
Craig, Jon 137
Crawford, Justin 225

Cream   240
creativity   82, 84, 86–95, 97, 148, 153
Crécy, Etienne de   52, 53
Criminal Justice and Public Order Act (1994)   43, 44
Crispy Aromatic   202
Csikszentmihalyi, Mihalyi   63–5, 77
Cthulhu Sleeps (2010)   150
Cubase   73
Cube   133
Cube V3 (2019)   153, 155
Cuddy, Amy J. C.   215
culture   2, 4
  disco   8, 42, 202, 241
  festivalization of   15
  gay   6
  Polish dance   12, 18, 233–5
  pop   1, 2, 12, 106
  rave   29, 30, 71, 186, 190, 202
  techno   8, 248
Cultures of Popular Music (Bennett)   30
Culverwell, Tony   172
Curtis, Ian   218
cutting-edge technology   67, 183
Cybotron   58, 59, 183
Cypress Hill   151
Czerwone Gitary   242

Dabhi, Rina   220–3, 227–9
Daftendirekt (1997)   53
Daft Punk   45, 49, 50, 53, 55, 56, 135, 137
Da Funk (1997)   53
Dahl, Steve   129
Dakeyne   67, 68
Dammone, Gip   192
Dancecult   2, 14, 26, 31
Das ist Elektro (2005)   60
Dataism   88
Dazed   217
Deadmau5   13, 17, 124, 125, 132, 159, 160, 165, 263 n.2, 264 n.11
  EDM producers and   129
  electronic music and its software   126–7
  involvement with video games   128
  live performances   138, 146, 152–5
  meeting with Zimmer   136–7

online communications   124, 137, 146, 147, 150, 155–8
  performance at Grammy Awards   131
  scoring feature film   124, 137
  shows   133
  stardom   145
  strategies   135
  techniques in recorded music   146–52
Deaf Institute   221
Deep Artificial Composer (Colombo, Seeholzerm and Gerstner)   86
Deep Purple   240, 241
Deluze, Dominique   45
Denk, Felix   35
Dennett, Daniel C.   94
De Pompidou   52
Der Klang der Familie: Berlin, Techno und die Wende (Denk)   35
Detroit techno   58, 67, 70, 75, 106
Die Wirtschaft der Techno-Szene. Die Wirtschaft der Techno-Szene (Kühn)   35
digital audio workstations (DAWs)   76, 77, 125, 126, 138
Dijon, Honey   228
Dimitri from Paris   49–51, 53, 54
Dirty Larry (1996)   53
Disco D   52
Disco Demolition Night (1979)   129
Disco Mix Club (DMC)   67, 74, 192
Disco Mums   220, 223, 224
disco music   5, 6, 13, 42, 52, 53, 58, 68, 129–31, 134, 166, 181, 184, 187, 192
disco polo   18, 243–5, 248–54
'Disco Sucks' campaign   129
discotheques   5, 18, 129, 181, 182, 192. *See also* Polish discotheques
Discovery (2001)   55
Distrikt   196, 205
DJ Mag   212–13, 215
DJs   2, 12–14, 17, 44, 75, 78, 106, 175, 176, 182, 183, 191, 198
  behaviours and lifestyle of   117, 119, 131
  black   185
  live performances   65
  mental health of   105, 106, 116, 117, 120

Polish   237, 239–42
'push-button   25, 34
stardom, image and 'self'
   construction   106–8, 111, 115,
   116, 120
'superstar'   34, 105, 107, 117
technical mixes   63, 66–9, 74
women   18, 211–15, 219–21, 227–8,
   230, 242
D Mob   184
'Doddering but Dear: Process, Content,
   and Function in Stereotyping
   of Older Persons' (Cuddy and
   Fiske)   215
*Doddery but Dear? Examining Age-related
   Stereotypes*   215
Don't Mean a Thing (2015)   173
Double Dee and Steinski   66, 68, 69
Drape, Jon   218
'drop'   147, 148, 150, 151
drug trafficking and consumption   44
drum & bass (D&B)   78, 194, 205
dubstep   200, 201, 205
Duchamp, Marcel   85
Duda, Steve   126, 159, 264 n.11
Duke Ellington Reader, The (Tucker)   164
Dupuy, Jean-Jérome   52
Dutty Moonshine   167, 174
Dyer, Richard   6, 107, 108, 252

Earth, Wind & Fire   53
E.A.S.E. *See* Evelyn, George
Ebeneezer Goode (1992)   186
Ecstasy   8, 11, 184–5, 188, 194, 262 n.8
Ed Banger   55
Edee Dee   252–3
'EDM Pop. A Soft Shell Formulation in a
   New Festival Economy' (Holt)   33
Eells, Josh   132, 151
Eggermont, Jaap   66
Eiger Studios   204
Elation   202
Electric Daisy Carnival   33, 106, 175
Electric Entourage (1987)   67
Electric Zoo   33, 106
Electrik Bar   225
electrofunk   58, 59
electro-hop   183

electrology   55–7
electronica   31, 33, 181, 183–6
electronic dance music (EDM)   25,
   35, 36, 60, 146, 159, 181. *See also
   individual entries*
   in 1990s Poland   245–8
   definition   4
   etymology   26–8
   festivals   12, 14, 33–4, 106
   in France   44, 56
   historical overview   28–31
   as mainstream   31–4
   research about   12–16
   US   60
Electronic Dance Music Awards   25, 29
electronic dance music culture
   (EDMC)   26, 31
'Electronic Dance Music Culture and
   Religion: An Overview' (St.
   John)   31
electronic music   16, 25, 27–8, 30, 36,
   43, 56, 58, 59, 72, 75, 77, 134, 135,
   138, 181, 183, 196, 202. *See also*
   popular music
   criticisms   129–33
   French   49, 50, 52, 55
   in Germany   5, 9–11, 25–8, 31, 43,
   58, 60
   instrumental   248
   styles   51, 58, 61, 184
   and technological
   development   124–9
   UK   65
'Electronic Music and Instruments'
   (Miessner)   27
electropop   51, 58, 59
electro swing   10, 17, 164, 165, 167–
   9, 171–7
Electro Swing IV (2011)   173
*Elektronische Klangerzeugung:
   Elektronische Musik und
   Synthetische Sprache* (Meyer-
   Eppler)   27
Elektronische Musik   16, 25, 27, 28
elektronische Tanzmusik. See electronic
   dance music (EDM)
*Ella Fitzgerald - "Air Mail Special (Club
   Des Belugas Remix)"*   171

Elle and the Pocket Belles   173
Ellington, Duke   164, 165, 168, 173
Emerald, Caro   169, 171, 175
'Empty Beach' (Sobolewski)   250
EMU SP-12   74
Encore Un Terlude (1996)   53
Endel   94
Energy Flash: A Journey through Rave Music and Dance Culture (Reynolds)   31, 166
England, Aidan Brain   201
Eno, Brian   85, 253
Entertainments (Increased Penalties) Act (1990)   189, 190
Eric B & Rakim   67
Estrada   237
Eternity   29
Eurodisco   18, 241, 244
Eurovision (2001)   53
Evelyn, George   185
Evening Standard   131
Evolution   193, 198
experimental music   5, 147, 150, 158
Ezio (1996)   53

Fabbri, Franco   36
Facebook   135
Fairlight CMI   70
Fanatic   249
fanzines   29, 36
Farrugia, Rebekah   214
Fatboy Slim   106
Faze Magazine   105
F-Communications   55
Feser, Kim   35
Fiat Lux   52
Fikentscher, Kai   214
Filter De Luxe (1997)   52
first person authenticity   145, 146
Fiske, Susan T.   215
Fitzgerald, Ella   171
Flex-Foot Cheetah prosthetic   84
Flow Machines   85
Flux   29
Flying Fingers (1996)   53
Flying Saucer, The (1956)   66
Fnac Music Dance Division   48
Fn Pig (2012)   150

Folies Pigalle   54
Foo Fighters   131
fordanserzy   235
For Lack of a Better Name (2009)   148
Fortnite (video game)   128
'Forty-Seven DJs, Four Women: Meritocracy, Talent and Postfeminist Politics' (Gadir)   213
Forum Fabricum   247
Fowlkes, Eddie   58
France   5, 43, 44
  academic discourse   56, 57
  culture   41, 43, 46, 47, 49
  house music   52–5
francophone songs   47
Franklin, Aretha   240
Freedom Mills   204
Free ton Style (1996)   53
Freight Island   225
French Communist Party   44
French Music Bureau   49
French New Wave   5
French school Musique Concrète   27
French Touch   41, 43, 45, 47–55, 259 n.21
Fresh (1997)   53
Frontpage   29
Fry, Andrew   13
Fryer, Paul   192
Fuckin' Filter (1998)   52
funk   52, 53, 58, 184
The Future Sound of London   29

Gabriel   118, 119
Gadir, Tami   196, 213, 214
Gallagher, Liam   218
Gallagher, Noel   218
The Gallery nightclub   191
Gamson, Joshua   164, 167, 168, 174, 176
Garnier, Laurent   44, 45, 50, 51, 55, 106, 217, 259 n.20
Garrix, Martin   12, 107
Gaszyński, Marek   237
Gatecrasher   198–9
gay clubs   43, 44
General Franco   184
Generation Ecstasy (Reynolds)   13
gentrification   18

Germany   8, 9, 43, 60, 246
Gershwin, George   66
Ghosts 'n' Stuff (2008)   124, 154, 158, 264 n.18
Gibson, Peter   73
Gierek, Edward   236, 237, 243
Giles, David C.   168, 176
Glass, Philip   93, 96
Glazer, Joshua   28, 119
Glitch Mob   133
Gnoiński, Wojciech   242
Godard, Jean-Luc   5
Golden Earring   66
Golem XIV (Lem)   93
Goodman, Benny   164, 173
Goodman, Dickie   66
Goodwin, Andrew   13
Gopher, Alex   52
GQ Magazine   111
Grandmaster Flash (1982)   43
Great Curve, The (1980)   89
Greater Manchester   188
Greens Keepers   173
Green Star   249
Grohl, Dave   132
Groove   29, 105
Grzesiuk, Stanisław   234
Guardian, The   10
Guetta, David   12, 13, 25, 32, 34, 54–5, 61, 106, 132
Gunders, John   146, 150, 152
Guthrie, Gwen   53

HAAi   212
Haçienda   217, 220
Hacienda: How Not to Run a Club, The (Hook)   217
Hale, Richard   174
Hampton, Lionel   173
Hancock, Herbie   53, 59
Hancock, Maren   227
The Happy Mondays   186
Harari, Yuval Noah   92
hardcore   43, 65, 75, 76, 78, 194
Harris, Calvin   34, 106
Harris, Simon   186
Harrison, Angus   202
Harvey, Aston   71, 73, 75

Haslam, Dave   217
Hawtin, Richie   125
Hayes, Isaac   53
Headingley   195, 201–2
Heap, Imogen   151
Heath, Harold   215
Heatley, Tim   219
Hegemann, Dimitri   9
Hello World (2018)   85
Hendrix, Jimi   116, 242
Henry, Pierre   49–50, 61
Herc, Kool   70
here's the drop (2019)   138, 264 n.8
Herndon, Holly   81, 86, 96
Hesmondhalgh, David   14, 70
Hey Baby (2006)   151
Hi-Fi Club   200
Hi-Flyers Club   192
high culture   242, 250
High-R   29
Hill, Chris   66
Hills, Daniel   198
hip hop   4, 41–3, 45, 54, 56, 63, 67, 68, 70–2, 74, 75, 89, 166, 182, 183, 185, 197, 214, 248
'hippies'   184, 186
'Historia Electronica: The Case for Electronic Dance Music Culture' (Reynolds)   1
Hitzler, Ronald   35
Holmes, Su   168
Holmes, Thom   27
Holt, Fabian   33, 106
Homebird (exhibition, 2018)   227
Homework (1997)   45, 50, 53, 56, 57
Homobloc   225
Homoelectric   225, 227
Honey Drippers   53
Hood, Robert   7
Hook, Peter   217
Hornby, Nick   107
House Masterboyz   67
house music   6–8, 10, 35, 41–4, 47–54, 57, 58, 60, 61, 67, 74, 89, 129, 130, 166, 183–5, 187, 191–3, 195, 196, 202, 205
'House Nation' (House Masterboyz)   67
house parties   181, 188, 195, 200–4

Huggy 190
Hurley, Steve 'Silk' 67
hybrid bar 197
Hybrydy 246
Hyden, Steven 134
Hyde Park 187, 197, 201–3

I AM AI (2017) 85
Ibiza 8, 115, 184, 222, 258 n.4
IBM 92
I Feel Love (1977) 6, 15
If I Ever Feel Better (2000) 54
Imaginary Friends (2016) 148
imposter syndrome 135, 136
In Crowd 72
Indeep 53
'In Defence of Disco' (Dyer) 6
'indie-dance' music 12, 185–6
Indo Silver Club (1997) 53
industrial music 246
Ingrosso, Sebastian 132
Insane 252
intellectual property rights 94
Intelligent Hoodlum 72
intelligent techno 10
In-Ter-Dance 29
The International Association of Athletics Federations 84
International Federation of the Phonographic Industry (IFPI) 1
International Music Summit 129
Ishkur's Guide 33
Islington Mill 220
Isobel (1995) 53
I-Spy 193
Italo disco 244

Jacke, Christoph 107
Jackson, Chad 67
'Jack Your Body' (Hurley) 67
Jacobson, Marcin 237, 240, 242
Jaehn, Felix 107, 117
Jakubowski, Robert 247
Jamaica 187
James, Chris 129
James, Greg 183
James, Martin 48–9, 52, 53
James, Robin 106

Jarman, Philippa 222
Jayne 221
jazz 5, 10, 57, 164, 167, 168, 250
J Dilla 66
Jefferson, Marshall 217
Jesus Jones 186
JNW 249
Johnson, Charles 'The Electrifying Mojo' 58
Johnson, Kristian 205
Joker 127
Jóri, Anita 4
Jouvenet, Morgan 56
Joy (1989) 190–1
jungle 3, 35, 72, 194, 205
Junkie XL 137
Justice 51, 55, 56
The Justified Ancients of Mu Mu (JAMM) 186

Kaczkowski, Piotr 237
Kahn, Douglas 214
Kantine am Berghain 31
Kanty 246
Kasprzycki, Remigiusz 242
Keeling, Ryan 205
Kelly, Kevin 82
Keoki 29
Kerrigan, Susan 65
'Ketaloco' event 201
Kieślowski, Krzysztof 250
Kit Kat Club 192
Kitten and the Hip 173, 174
KLF. See The Justified Ancients of Mu Mu (JAMM)
Knuckles, Frankie 58, 129
Kode9 86
Koestler, Arthur 92
Kofta, Jonasz 242
Kool & the Gang 53
Koosha, Ash 86
Kossela, Jerzy 242
Kraftwerk 2, 5–6, 9, 10, 58, 59, 130
Kras, Jana 242
Krasnow, Carolyn 13, 241
Krautrock 5
Kruder and Dorfmeister 106
Kryder 12

Książątko (*Little Prince*, 1937)   235
Kucharczyk, Wojciech   245
Kühn, Jan-Michael   35
kul'turnost   240
Kuti, Fela   89
Kut N' Paste   52
Kveberg, Gregory   236, 239
Kyrou, Ariel   56

La Boucle (the loop, 1997)   52
Lacasse, Serge   170, 171
Lack of a Better Name (2009)   148, 150
La Coste   192
'La Déferlante techno' (the techno landslide, 1998)   45
Ladybeige. *See* Dabhi, Rina
La Funk Mob   52
Lagrèze, Jean-Claude   48
Laif   246
Lake Victoria   204
La Luna   44
La Machine du Moulin Rouge   56
Lancashire   188
LANDR   90
Lang, Jack   45
Last Girl Scout, The   29
Last Night a DJ Saved My Life. The Story of the Disc Jockey (Brewster and Broughton)   30
Latin Rascals   66
Lawson, Ralph   192
Le Boy   44
Led Zeppelin   240, 241
Leeds, UK   181–2
   1980s electronic music development   183–4
   'alternative' music   185–6
   city centre venues   190–3, 200
   credibility and competition   196–7
   downsizing EDM venues   205
   drugs and bass   193–5
   early 1980s   182–3
   Ecstasy   184–5
   festivalization   204
   house party boom   201–4
   the Millennium effect   195–6
   musical forms and problems   197–201
   rave   186–90, 205–6

Leeds City Council   193, 201
Leeds Club History Project   182
Leeds Corn Exchange   190
Leeds Party Rig   202
Leeds Polytechnic Students' Union (LPSU)   190
Leeds Service Crew (LSC)   185, 188
Leeds Town and Country Club   190
Leeds University   193
Leeds University Student's Union (LUSU)   190, 191, 198, 200
Leeds West Indian Centre   194
Le Gai Pied   44
Lem   93
Lens, Amelie   228
Le Palace   48
Le Patron Est Devenu Fou (1996)   53
Lesson 3 (1985)   68
Lessons (1983, 1984, 1985)   68, 69
Lestrade, Didier   44
Let Go (2016)   148
Let's Go (1986)   59
Levan, Larry   53, 58
Levels (2011)   110
LGBT Flesh club   217, 220–2, 227
L'Humanité   44
Libération   44
The Licensing Act (2003)   196, 197
Lick club   227
Lights   151, 154
Lil' Fuck (1999)   53
Lindop, Robin   36
Lipps Inc.   53
live music performance   12, 14, 15, 50, 127, 133, 137, 159, 249, 250
Live Nation   34
live streaming   17, 145, 146, 155, 157, 204
Loaded (1992)   206
Łódź, Poland   247, 248
Loft   58
L'Olympia   50
Long Play (LP)   67, 240, 241
Lord, Sacha   218
'Lost in Space' (1989)   188
Louis Vuitton   192
'Love Can't Turn Around' (1986)   51
'Love Decade' (1990)   188–9

Lovelock, James   83, 90, 91
'Love Parade' Festival   9, 247, 253
Lowry gallery   227
Luciano   117
Lucker, Katja   31, 32
'Lucky Star' (1999)   54
Luigi, Steve   191
Luke, Laidback   109
Lynch, Will   117

McDermott, Kath   217, 220–7
Maceo and the Macks   67
Mach   53
McIntyre, Philip   64
McLeod, Kembrew   3, 26, 28, 36, 146
McLuhan   87
McRobbie, Angela   213
Madonna   159, 214
Maestro   157
Major, John   192
Malone, Bugzy   219
Manchester Digital Music Archive (MDMA)   217
Manchester Evening News   219
Manchester Keeps on Dancing (2017)   211, 217
'Manchester Men'   219
Manchester Roadhouse   222
Manchester's club   211, 227, 229. *See also* women in EDM
  female DJs   219–21, 227, 228, 230
  and its male-centric musical legacy   216–19
Manchester's Picadilly Radio   74
Manctopia: Billion Pound Property Boom (2020)   219
Mantronix   183
Marcus, Barnes   194
Mark B. Sandler   85
Markie, Biz   67
Marshall, David P.   108
Marshmallow (Marshmello)   34, 127, 135
Mason, Suzy   192
Mason, Vaughan   53
Massive Attack   71
Massive Magazine   29
MasterClass   124, 136, 137
Matos, Michaelangelo   135

Matson, Andrew   134
mau5trap   156, 157
Maurel, Henri   44, 55
May, Derrick   58, 59, 67
Mayring, Philipp   32
Mazierska, Ewa   12, 14
medleys   66–9
Melechi, Antonio   14
Melleefresh   151
Melodrive   90
Melville, Casper   70
mental prosthesis   84
mephedrone (MCAT)   200
Merck   184
Metalheadz   70
Meyer-Eppler, Werner   27
MFSB   53
Miami Music Week   33
Michalski, Dariusz   237
Midnight Funk Association   58
Miessner, Benjamin F.   27
Mike, Angelo   252, 253
Milano   252
Milestone, Katie   211, 216, 218, 219
Millennium New Year's Eve event   195
Mille Plateaux   10
Mills, Jeff   10, 137
Miłość do płyty winylowej (*Love for a Vinyl Record*, 2002)   252, 254
Ministry of Culture   6, 236
Ministry of Sound   10, 12
Mint Club   196, 200
Mint Warehouse   204
Mista Trick   174
Misuse of Drugs Act (1971)   200
Mixcloud   157
Mixer   157
Mixmag   105, 191
Mixmag Award for Best Club   192
Mix-Stress. *See* Swarray, Rebecca
Moby   29, 134, 146
Model 500   67
Modern Talking   244
modular systems   125, 126
Moffat, David   85
Monstercat   127
Moody Blues   240
Moog, Robert   125

Mooney, James 73
Moon Safari (1997) 51
Moonshine Records 29
Moore, Allan 145, 152, 228
More, Jonathan 68
Morillo, Erick 117
Moroder, Giorgio 2, 6, 127
Morrisey 218
Mortal Kombat 11 (video game) 127
Motorbass 50, 53, 55
Moudaber, Nicole 228
'Movement' (2006) 198
Mr B the Gentleman Rhymer 174
Mr JAWS (1979) 66
Mr. Oizo 55
Mr Switch. *See* Culverwell, Tony
MTV 106
Munich Machine 53
Musical Instrument Digital Interface (MIDI) 125, 132
Musicboard Berlin 31
Music Factory 192
music industry 18, 25, 31, 33, 34, 74, 82, 93, 94, 96, 105, 118, 212, 213
musicology 41, 57, 60
Musicorama 236, 237, 239
Music Revenues Report 131
'Music Sounds Better with You' (1998) 54
the Musiquarium 204
musique contemporaine (contemporary music) 259 n.26
muzyka chodnikowa. *See* disco polo
'My Only Love' (1998) 54

Napster 134
Nation Rap (1990) 54
Nato 193
Navarre, Ludovic 53–4
Naylor, Tom 10
Negus, Keith 36
Nervous Records 29
Netflix 109, 124, 137
New Age of EDM and Club Culture, The (2017) 31
New Alcatraz 247, 248
Newcleus 183
New Music Art 246
New Wave, The (1994) 50

New York
  block party culture 70
  disco 193
  style sound system 183
Nicolay, Franz 134
Nicolson, Adam 88
nightclubs 5, 13–15, 17, 18, 28, 181, 182, 187, 188, 190, 192, 195–7, 224, 230
Nine Inch Nails 137
nitrous oxide (noz) 203
N-Joy 117
NME 216
Noise Water Meat: A History of Sound in the Arts (Rodgers) 214
No Problem (2016) 148
Norman, Donald 73
'"Northernness," Gender and Manchester's Creative Industries' (Milestone) 216
Northside 186
Nothing But the Beat (2011) 54
Nothing But the Beat 2.0 (2012) 54
Novacene (Lovelock and Appleyard) 83
Nude Photo (1987) 67
Nu-Sound Express, Ltd. 53

Oakenfold, Paul 106
Old Red Bus Station 205
On & On
  1980 53
  1984 53
'Onwards and Upwards: Playing My Way Through the Gender Division' (Bentley) 222
Oral B 96
Orb 8
Original Dixieland Jass Band 61
Oswald, John 171
Out of My Hands (2000) 53
Out of Space (1992) 72
Oz rave (1993) 44

Palace 54
Panderoza 249
Pansoul (1996) 50, 53
'Parada Wolności' (Freedom Parade) 247
Paradise Garage 42, 58, 183
Paris Angeles 52
Parisian house producers 52

Parisian Nights 48
Parklife festival 218, 224, 225
Parlophone 54
Parrot. *See* Barratt, Richard
Pasdzierny, Matthias 35
Pasqua, Charles 44
Patreon 134
Paula and Tabs 222
Paulette. *See* Constable, Paulette
pavement/sidewalk music. *See* disco polo
Pearce, Ben 117
Peck, Jamie 219
Pendergrass, Teddy 53
Penguin Encyclopedia of Popular Music 130
Perpetuum Mobile 242
Perry, Lee 'Scratch' 2
Pettibone, Shep 66
Pfadenhauer, Michaela 35
Philharmonie de Paris 49
Phillips, Dom 185
Phoenix Club 54, 190
phonographic sampling 74, 77, 78
Phuture 67
Piccadilly Radio 67
Pickering, Mike 217
Pink Floyd 9, 10
Pink Noises (Rodgers) 214
Pink Paradise 54
Pistorius, Oscar 84
Planet Rock (1982) 59
Play (1999) 134
Playback 53
plug-ins 17, 76, 85, 125
Pograniczny, Witold 237
Polar (2019) 124, 137, 147
Polish discotheques 6, 235–43
Polonia 243
Polsat 249
Polskie Orły (Polish Eagles) 243
Pompidou 57
Popgun 85
pop life 54–5
pop music 1, 13, 31, 36, 106, 146, 214
popular music 1, 2, 5, 12, 15, 16, 36, 41, 43, 50, 56, 58–61, 145, 159, 239, 242, 245, 254. *See also* electronic music

Pop Will Eat Itself (PWEI) 186
post-punk 182, 186
Poumtchak 52
'Precious' club night 192
Premiers Symptômes (1997) 51
Prendergast 166
Pressler, Jessica 115, 116
press-play approach 25, 34
Pride event 223
Primal Scream 186, 205–6
Prix Choc (1996) 53
Prodigy 72, 76, 106
production quotas 47
progressive house 147–9
Project CARS (videogame) 128
Project X Magazine 25, 29, 30
ProleteR 173
Pro-Zak Trax 52
Psychoactive Substances Act (2016) 203
Psyonix 127
psytrance 2, 194
Public Enemy 67
Pucciarelli, Dan 183
punk 3, 8, 182, 186, 187
Puppini Sisters 173
'Pushing Buttons or Pushing Boundaries' (Ashton) 132
'pyramid effect' 169, 176

Queen 54
Queer Noise: The History of LGBT+ Music and Club Culture in Manchester (exhibition, 2017) 227
Queer Raving in Manchester's Twilight Zone (2018) 211, 217

R-9 (1985) 59
Rack, Michael 167, 174
Radio 1 184
Radio FG 55
Radio Fréquence Gaie (FG) 44
Radio Maxximum 44
Radio Nova 44
ragga-rave breakbeats 76
Ragga Twins 72
Random Access Memories (2013) 55
Rapp, Tobias 35
Rapper's Delight (1979) 70

Rave Archive   29
'rave-club culture continuum'   30
'The Rave Gap: How UK Nightlife Still Struggles with Ageism'   214
Raveline   29
rave(s)   9, 15, 28, 30, 31, 43, 44, 50, 55, 65, 72, 73, 76, 78, 186–90
 illegal   181, 190, 202, 205
 style events   204
 zines   29
R&B   54
RebeccaNeverBecky (RnB)   221, 228
Rebus   247
'Reclaim the Streets' movement   192–3
'record selectors'   187
Redmond, Sean   168, 172
Reeves, Martin   71, 72
Reform   219
The Refuge   223, 225
reggae   71, 72, 187, 194
Reich, Steve   8
Reload Sound System   202
'Report About the State of Discotheques in Poland' (Raport o Stanie Dyskotek w Polsce)   6, 236
Resident Advisor   105, 117
'The Return of the Manchester Men' (Tickell and Peck)   218–19
Rex Club   44, 54
Reynolds, Simon   1, 9–11, 13, 15, 25, 30, 31, 72, 75, 146, 155, 166, 214
Reznor, Trent   137
RIAA   131
Richter, Anna   200, 204
Riehl, Damien   94
'Rocker Vs. DJ' (video)   130–1
Rocket League (video game)   127
rock music   1, 5, 6, 13, 36, 41, 45, 57, 146, 236, 242, 245, 246, 248
Rodgers, Sally   213
Rodgers, Tara   214
Rogers, Rosita   196
Roland TB-303 synthesizer   184
Roland TR-808   183
Rolling Stone   44, 151, 153
Rolling Stone Italia   130–2
Rolling Stones   240, 242
Romeo, Max   72

Rope (2011)   131
Ross, Diana   53
Rother, Anthony   60
R&S Records   10
Rubin, Noah   94
'Ruffage' event   200
Rufus & Chaka Khan   53
Rush, Matty   202
Ruyer, Raymond   47
Ryder, Sean   218
Rythim Is Rythim   67
Ryuichi Sakamoto   59

Sacrebleu (1996)   51, 53
St. John, Graham   26, 31
Sander Van Doorn   12
Sasha   106
Saturday Night Fever (1977)   8, 42
Saunders, Jesse   53
Saunderson, Kevin   58
Say Kids, What Time Is It? (1987)   68
Scene, The   29
Schaeffer, Pierre   50, 95
Schedel, Margaret   4, 27
Schloss, Joseph   70
scholarship system   31
Schuegraf, Martina   107
Schumpeter, Joseph   192
Schwartz, Barry   77
Scott, Travis   128
Seaman, Dave   106
second-hand stardom   165, 177
Second Summer of Love (1988–9)   258 n.4
Secretlab   128
Seek Romance (2010)   109
Senz, Javi   211, 217
Serial Records   52
Serum   126, 127
Sex Slave (2007)   151
Shall We Take a Trip? (1991)   186
The Shamen   186
Shazz   54
Shazza   249–51
Sheffield   76
Sherwood, Adrian   186
Shocking Blue   66
Showcase   56
Shut Up & Dance   71–2, 76

Sicko, Dan   34, 58
'Side A (*House*)'   67
'Side B, Hip-Hop' (Jackson)   67
Sienkiewicz, Jacek   245
Silver Apples   181
Simmons, Alex   198
Simone, Nina   67
Simpson, Ken   66
Sinclar, Bob   54
Sing, Sing, Sing (*With a Swing*) (2016)   173
Skręta, Sławomir   244, 249, 250, 251
Skrillex   126, 127, 132
SKYGGE   85
Slater, Ashley   173, 174
Słota, Leszek   242
Sly & the Family Stone   53
Smith, Delano   58
Snoman, Rick   117, 118
Snowcone (2016)   149
Sobolewski, Tadeusz   250
social class   18, 233–6, 253, 254
Social Club   56
social media   115, 116, 135, 145, 146, 155–7, 224
The Social Service   221, 222
Sodatone   93
Soft Cell   183
Solms, Mark   94
Something Good (1992)   66
Sonique   106
Sontag, Susan   15
Sony   12
soul music   67, 71, 74, 182, 187, 188, 219
SoundCloud   94
sound system   70, 71, 75, 187, 188, 194
Southern, Taryn   85
Spawn   86, 96
Spinning   12
Splash Pro   85
Splice   76
Spliffhead (1991)   72
sponsorship   31, 152, 156, 158
Spotify   94
Spracklen, Beverley   201
Spracklen, Karl   200, 204
Springsteen, Bruce   158, 173

Stadion Dziesięciolecia (The Ten-Years Stadium)   249
Stadium   195
Stansfield, Lisa   219
stardom   106–8, 111, 115, 116, 120, 145, 146, 159, 164, 165, 176. *See also* celebrity; second-hand stardom
  electro swing   171–5
  model of   168–71
Stardust   54
Stars on 45   66
Stars on 45 (1981)   66, 70
state socialism   235, 236, 245, 247, 248, 250, 254
Stelar, Parov   17, 165, 171, 173, 175, 176
Stellar Awareness   29
Sterling, Amy Robinson   86
Stinky's Peephouse   201
Stockhausen, Karlheinz   5
Stories (2015)   114
'The Strange, Lingering Death of Minimal Techno' (Naylor)   10
Strauss, Richard   12
Straw, Will   5
Strobe (2009)   150, 158
student nights   193, 195, 196, 201–3
Studio for Electronic Music of the West German Radio (WDR Studio)   27
Studlar, Gaylyn   164
Sturm, Bob L.T.   94
Subdub event   194, 200
Suffragette City event   227
Sugar Hill Gang   70
Sugar Sugar (1969)   66
Summer, Donna   6, 53
Sunrise   194
Super Discount (1996)   48, 52, 53
Super Disco (1996)   53
Superfunk   54
superintelligence   88–91, 93
Supernature Disco   221
'Surface *versus* Depth' (Sontag)   15
Surtees, Alison   217
Suszycki, Jerzy   249
Svenska Dagbladet   85
Swarray, Rebecca   221, 223, 224, 228
Swedish House Mafia   132
Świerzyński, Sławomir   244, 250, 251

Index

Swingamajig festival (2015)   173
Swinney, Paul   201
synthesizers   6, 12, 125, 126
synthpop   184
System and Asylum   196
systems model of creativity   64
Szafa   247
Szczecin, Poland   246
Szebego, Władysław   235

Tangerine Dream   137
Tape Music   27
tape splicing and editing   68
Tasca   46
Taylor, Yuval   130, 134, 135
T-Coy   186
Teachers (1997)   53
Techno (Anz and Walder)   34
Techno Dance Mission   246
techno music   4–5, 7–10, 26, 31, 34–6, 41–5, 50, 51, 53, 56–8, 60, 61, 130, 159, 184, 191, 205, 246, 247, 250–4
Techno Parade   45, 56, 57
Techno Party   248
Technopilot. *See* Deadmau5
Technopol   45
Techno Rebelle (Kyrou)   56
Techno Rebels. The Renegades of Electronic Funk (Sicko)   34
Techno- Soziologie: Erkundungen einer Jugendkultur (Pfadenhauer)   35
Techno Studies. Ästhetik und Geschichte elektronischer Tanzmusik (Feser and Pasdzierny)   35
'Techno: The Dance Sound of Detroit'   6
Technotronic   186
Telemiscommunications (2012)   151
Télérama   45
Telharmonium   125
Tenaglia, Danny   29
Terje, Todd   106
Tesla   85, 96
Têtu   44
TF1   44
Thema (1996)   45
Theremin   125
Third Programme   237
Thornton, Sarah   6, 7, 30, 75, 129, 214

Three Pound Chicken Wing (2016)   148
Tickell, Adam   219
Tiësto   13, 106, 137, 165
Tissera, Rob   189, 190
Tofu, Chris   172
Tom, Konrad   235
Tomorrowland   106, 175
Tong, Pete   106, 117, 191
Toubon, Jacques   47
Tout Doit Disparaître (1996)   53
Towning, Kane   198
trance   3, 32, 33, 147, 193, 194
Trance 5000   29
'Tresor II: Berlin & Detroit - A Techno Alliance' (1993)   10
Tresor Records   9, 10
TRIBAL America Records   29
trompe l'oeil   94
Tron Run/r (video game)   127
Tsikurishvili, Levan   109
Tsugi   56
Tucker, Mark   164
Tumblr   132
Twitch   128, 129, 134, 156, 157
Twitter   135, 156

UEFA Euro   25
UK sampling practice   262 n.8
    affordances and constraints   73–4
    distinctiveness of   70–2
    early influences   66–9
    future   77–8
    scarcity and tyranny of choice   74–7
    theoretical perspective and methodological approach   63–6
Ultra Miami   114
Ultra Music Festival   33, 106
Unabombers. *See* Cowdrey, Luke; Crawford, Justin
Underworld   29
United States   5, 30, 34, 42, 46, 60, 71, 72, 74, 75, 94, 165
Universal Techno   45
Unlocking the Groove. Rhythm, Meter, and Musical Design in Electronic Dance Music (Butler)   5, 31
Un Terlude (1996)   53
Untold Sound   204

Up & Away (1994)   54
Uriah Heep   241
Uropa   193
Ustream   128
Utah Saints   66, 191

'Vagabondz' event   200
Vague club night   192
Van Doorn, Sander   12
van Dyk, Paul   106
Vangelis   137
van Helden, Armand   106
Van Krieken, Robert   169, 176
Vasquez, Junior   29
Väth, Sven   106, 196
The Veldt (2012)   128–9
Velvet Bar, Gay Village   220
Venus (1969)   66
Vertigo   191
Vice   212, 214, 227
Vickers, Judith   219
Victoire de la Musique   45
Victoria Works   198
video games   127, 128, 137, 157
Villalobos, Ricardo   119, 196
Virgin Records   6, 45, 54, 55
virtual reality (VR)   128
virtual studio technology (VST)   125
Vivienne Westwood   192
Vivre sa vie (1962)   5
von Neumann, John   88

W:/2016ALBUM/ (2016)   148
Wajda, Andrzej   250
Walder, Patrick   34
Walicki, Franciszek   6, 236–40, 242
Ward, Richard   221
Warehouse   183, 192, 218, 224, 225
Warner Music Group   12, 54, 56, 93, 94, 96
Warp Records   9, 76
Watson   92
'Wax: On' event   200
WDPK 83.7 FM (1997)   53
Weatherall, Andrew   217
We Call It Acieed (1988)   184
We Play Reggae (1977)   72
'We Play Vinyl' events   198–9

Western music   242
where's the drop? (2018)   138, 264 nn.5, 8
While (1<2) (2014)   147, 149
White, Barry   53
White Mink: Black Cotton, Volume 3 (2013)   173
Why do you hate EDM? 'House, Techno, Trance' (2006)   32
Why We DJ - Slaves to the Rhythm (2017)   117
Wiand, Mike   183
Wild Angels, The (1966)   206
Wild Bunch, The (1983–9)   71
Williams, Justin   170
Williams, Pharrell   55
Willis, Jez   66
Wills, Julie   220–9
Wills, Viola   53
Wilsmore, Robert   171
Wilson, Greg   67, 217
Wilson, Scott   4, 27
Wilson, Tony   218
Winehouse, Amy   116
Winter, Pierre 'Pedro'   55
Winterbottom, Michael   217
Winx   29
Wire   200
women in EDM   211. *See also* DJs, women
    full-time dreams, part-time careers   221–3
    gender and age   212–16, 223–6, 230
'The Women Who've Been Written Out of Manchester Clubbing History' (Rymajdo)   217
World Trade Organization   46
Worldwide FM   224
Woźniewski, Jarosław   249
Wright, Bernard   53

X Factor, The (TV show)   173
X-Ray   59

Yellow Productions   52
Yona   86
"You Better Work!" Underground Dance Music in New York (Fikentscher)   214

Young, Karen 53
Young & Company 53
Young-Holt Unlimited 53
YoungPaint 86
You're All I Want For Christmas (2011) 169
YouTube 11, 75, 137

Żak, Sławomir 247
Zimmer, Hans 136, 137
Zimmerman, Joel. *See* Deadmau5
Zmarz-Koczanowicz, Maria 250–3
Zubak, Marko 241

www.ingramcontent.com/pod-product-compliance
Lightning Source LLC
Chambersburg PA
CBHW052213300426
44115CB00011B/1672